SAVING THE JEWS

SAVING THE JEWS

Amazing Stories of Men and Women
Who Defied the "Final Solution"

MORDECAI PALDIEL

Schreiber Publishing
Rockville, Maryland

Saving the Jews

by Mordecai Paldiel

Published by:

Schreiber Publishing
Post Office Box 4193
Rockville, MD 20849 USA
spbooks@aol.com   www.schreibernet.com

First Printing

All photographs are courtesy of Yad Vashem, Jerusalem, unless otherwise indicated.

Library of Congress Cataloging-in-Publication Data

Paldiel, Mordecai.
  Saving the Jews : amazing stories of men and women who defied the "final solution" / Mordecai Paldiel.
    p. cm.
  Includes bibliographical references (p.) and index.
  ISBN 1-887563-55-5
  1. Righteous Gentiles in the Holocaust. 2. World War, 1939-1945--Jews--Rescue. 3. Holocaust, Jewish (1939-1945) I. Title.

D804.65 .P35 2000
940.53'18--dc21

                                                                00-056350

Printed in the United States of America

To the Unknown Righteous of the Holocaust Period

The world exists even for one Righteous, as it is stated: 'The Righteous one is the world's foundation' (Proverbs 10:25)

Talmud Yoma 38b

Acknowledgements

This study of the world of the Righteous of the Holocaust period is made possible thanks to the generous contribution of Dr. Felix Zandman, whose moving rescue story appears in this book. I am especially indebted to Felix and his lovely wife Ruta for their inspiration and long friendship.

Special thanks are also in order to Yad Vashem, the institution to which I owe the privilege of heading the Department for the Righteous these past 18 years, and to the devoted staff of this department. Also, to the Commission for the Designation of the Righteous, whose members dedicate themselves to the sometimes arduous task of deciding on whom to bestow the prestigious title of "Righteous Among the Nations."

To all these persons — my sincerest thanks and deepest appreciation.

CONTENTS

Preface

In 1941, when I was barely two years old, most of my relatives were murdered in Poland by the invading Germans with the help of antisemitic elements among the local Ukrainians and Poles. As a child growing up in my native Israel, I had no grandparents, uncles, aunts, or cousins. My extended family had perished in what would become known as the "Holocaust."

Even though I personally had never gone through the horrors of the Holocaust, it has been the most defining event of my life. In time, it would become the most defining event of Western civilization. Jean-Paul Sartre wrote: "The blood which the Nazis shed falls on all of our heads." It is not only the Germans who bear the burden of guilt. It is all those people, governments, and regimes in Europe and around the world who stood by the blood of the innocent millions and did nothing to help.

In the summer of 1998 I went on a cruise of the Greek Isles. On the island of Rhodes I visited the local synagogue. In a back room, behind the sanctuary, there was a small Holocaust museum. It took me by surprise, since the Holocaust is not usually associated with this part of the world. I saw photographs of the deportation of the Jews of Rhodes to Auschwitz. Rhodes is very far from Poland, where some three million Polish Jews were systematically done unto death from 1939 to 1945. The Jews on Rhodes had been part of the Sephardic Jewish world, spread over the Mediterranean and Arab countries. Most of them had mercifully escaped the Holocaust. The fact that my family's fate in Poland was tied to the fate of this small Sephardic Jewish community in the middle of the Mediterranean shocked me in a whole new way. It made me realize how far-reaching human evil was. It made me wonder if the human race was redeemable.

A year later I had the privilege of reading the manuscript of *Saving the Jews* by Mordecai Paldiel. I came across the tale of the Turkish consul on Rhodes, who saved 50 Jews during the deportation which I had seen documented in that little museum. I was amazed. A Turk? A Muslim? Saving Jews? There was another side to the human condition after all, where you least expected it — even in the lowest reaches of hell.

After going over the entire manuscript I learned that in every corner of Europe, from 1933 — the year of Hitler's rise to power, to 1945 — the year Hitlerism was finally crushed, during the dreariest events in human history, there was always a kind soul who, at a risk to his or her own life, defied the forces of evil and saved lives. Such kind souls ranged from a gypsy in Bosnia to a courier of the Polish underground, from a peasant in Lithuania to a woman physician in France, and from a young Albanian store clerk to a German woman in Berlin.

The author, who has been heading the Department for the Righteous Among the Nations at Yad Vashem (Israel's national Jewish Holocaust museum in Jerusalem), has selected the stories of those individuals from among hundreds of files compiled by his office. The task of this office is to find men and women who qualify for the designation of "Righteous Among the Nations," one who saved lives during the Nazi era. To qualify, those individuals must undergo careful scrutiny, based on very strict criteria, as the author explains in the first chapter.

It is important to note (as can be seen in the last chapter of this book), that the line between good and evil is not always clear, and in some instances the decision to designate a certain person as "Righteous" was extremely difficult. Given the complex circumstances of the places and times where the Holocaust unfolded, people's motives and behavior were not always easy to determine, or fully revealed. Great good was accomplished by persons of questionable motives (as in the famous case of Oskar Schindler), while those who meant well at times became accessories to evil.

The term "Righteous" is taken from the Talmudic term *hasid umot ha'olam*, or "Righteous Among the Nations," referring to those who, though not direct recipients of the Ten Commandments and the Torah, have demonstrated by their actions that their sense of justice and mercy is indeed rooted in those teachings which, according to Jewish tradition, lead to the highest degree of human goodness. Because of the righteous, the world endures.

It is important to bear in mind that in every generation, from the time of Noah, Abraham, and Moses, a handful of righteous people have always made all the difference. Furthermore, those few individuals who were the righteous ones of their generation invariably acted alone, as individuals, defying the general will. Even if such an individual was in a position of power, as was the above-mentioned Turkish consul on Rhodes, or the papal nuncio in Hungary, even then the individual acted on his or her own, and not as an official representative. Ultimately, it is the individual who redeems the world, not governments or institutions.

And there lies the great lesson of Yad Vashem's "Righteous Among the Nations" program. It may well be one of the most noble programs ever conceived. After Auschwitz, we Jews have every right to persist in our sense of pain and outrage at what the world has done to us. We have reason to believe, as did André Schwartz-Bart, the author of *Le dernier des justes* (The Last of the Just), that the last righteous person in the world died at Auschwitz, and therefore human existence is irredeemable. And yet, Jews realized a few short years after the Holocaust that they must recognize and repay those who defied the death decree issued against them by the Third Reich, not only for their own sake, but for the sake of the entire human race. While Jews are commanded never to forget the evil perpetrated against them, and always to honor the memory of the martyrs, we are further commanded to "choose life," to celebrate life in every way possible, and to give the highest honor to those who preserved life.

The memory of the Holocaust will never fade or disappear. On the contrary, it will intensify with time. The atrocities are well documented and the documents well preserved. The evidence keeps growing from year to year. But alongside the litany of vast and unfathomable evil there grows another story — the emerging testimony regarding thousands of men and women of all faiths and nationalities and of all walks of life in Europe during the long night who, unlike the Nazis, whose race doctrine denied certain portions of humankind the right to exist, did not forget that every human being, whether Jew, Gentile, gypsy, handicapped, gay, black or white, is the reflection of the Creator of all life, and therefore every single human life is sacred.

It seems to me that, like the Good Samaritan in the New Testament, the Righteous Gentiles in this book will go down in history as those who made a difference in the human condition. Their countries, their faiths, their cultures will embrace them with pride and gratitude, for they do honor to their own people and to all people. Human goodness exists everywhere. It knows no political or religious boundaries. I am grateful to the author for teaching me this valuable lesson.

I said before that the Holocaust left me without any immediate relatives. However, some second and third cousins did survive. Among them, the author himself, who is my second cousin. I am proud of him for having devoted his life to the search for the righteous. I am also proud of a third cousin, Ronnie Brauman, whose family survived the Holocaust in France. He also dedicated his life to mankind. His organization, *Médecins sans Frontières* (Doctors without Borders), won the Nobel Peace Prize in 1999. The lives of both cousins is living proof that the good works of the righteous in this book have already begun to redeem the world.

Rabbi Mordecai Schreiber
Rockville, Maryland

Entrance to the Avenue of the Righteous at the Yad Vashem Memorial in Jerusalem.

Chapter 1

Setting the Stage

The Holocaust is a term signifying the planned and state-organized persecution and murder of the Jewish people by the Nazi German government during the years 1933-1945.[1] From the moment Hitler, who headed the Nazi party, took power on January 30, 1933, he made it clear that one of his principal goals was first to disenfranchise then physically remove, in one way or another, the Jewish population in the country. There were, at the time, some 550,000 Jews in Germany, a country numbering over 70 million inhabitants — in other words, less than 1% of the population. But to Hitler, the Jews in Germany, and elsewhere, represented a threat to the German people since, in his demented mind, they competed with the Germanic races for world domination.

The Nazis viewed the world as divided into superior and inferior races, with each struggling, through war and competition, for dominance or, at least, for a more privileged status. The Jews were the spoilers in the sporting event (termed by the Nazis "the aristocratic principle in nature"), since their ideas — rooted in the biblical teachings of universal principles of morality and justice, and applied to various secular ideologies such as democracy, communism, and, at least in Hitler's mind, even to Christianity — were contrary to those espoused by the Nazis. Thus, the Jews threatened the Nazi goal of restructuring mankind based on principles of superior and inferior races. For Hitler and his close aides, the Jewish-inspired teachings of the brotherhood and unity of mankind threatened to undermine the supremacy of the Aryan races and, hence, would doom civilization.

In Hitler's mind, the conclusion to be drawn from this was clear — the Jews, as the bastion and pillars of these "false" philosophies had to be removed — not through assimilation or some form of cultural genocide, but by physical elimination. This, according to the Nazi mind, would free the world of a poisonous infection, and allow the races of the world to continue the "natural" free interplay and the struggle of the survival of the fittest.

Historians still debate whether Hitler had already decided on the murder of the Jewish people when he assumed power in 1933, or whether this idea became crystallized in his mind at a later period. What is clear from his writings and pronouncements is that from the start, he was captive to a psychotic and mythic notion of what the Jews really represented. In his book *Mein Kampf*, the Nazi bible, written by Hitler while he sat in prison in 1924 for his unsuccessful attempt to grab power in Munich, he portrays the Jews in terms of infectious diseases; such as maggots in a rotting corpse, germ carriers, vampires sucking the blood of others, and spreaders of syphilis. In the midst of World War Two, he prided himself on having discovered the "Jewish virus," "one of the greatest revolutions that have taken place in the world," which he likened to Pasteur's discovery of microbes.

To Hitler, the Jew was not really a human being, but a grimacing and leering devil, infested with infernal powers—the very incarnation of evil. This, he often stated, encompassed all Jews, "no matter whether he is high or low, speculator or rabbi, baptized or circumcised." Therefore, Hitler told an audience as early as 1924, "It does not matter whether the individual Jew is good or evil; he cannot but behave according to the laws of his race, [namely] to attempt to destroy. He cannot otherwise, whether he wills it or not. . . His sole concern remains: how to propel my people to dominance." As the ferment of the decomposition of all peoples, he is "the inexorable mortal enemy of all light, a hater of all true culture." To leave the Jews untouched, Hitler warned, would inevitably result "in the collapse of human civilization and the consequent devastation of the world." Consequently, as the self-appointed liberator of mankind, he wrote in *Mein Kampf*, that "by defending myself against the Jew, I am fighting for the work of the Lord." This, from a man who, as a young boy, once thought of joining the priesthood.[2]

True to his word, already in 1924, he advocated "the most stringent measures" against Jews, and in January 1939, he foretold the extermination of the Jewish people in the event of another war. This he repeated on several occasions during the war, such as in January 1942: "We fully realize that this war can end only either in the extermination of the Aryan peoples or in the disappearance of Jewry in Europe." Finally, before committing suicide, on April 30, 1945, in his underground Berlin bunker, in the final words of his Political Testament, he admonished the future leaders of Germany "to mercilessly oppose the universal poisoner of all peoples, International Jewry."[3]

Obeyed by the masses of Germany as the undisputed dictator of a whole nation, and revered by his followers as semi-divine figure, as soon as he assumed power Hitler immediately set in motion a gradual and accelerating process of anti-Jewish measures, which led to murder on a grand scale across the European continent. Hardly three months after the Nazi assumption of power in Germany, in April 1933, Jews were barred from holding public office (code-worded: "Law for the Reestablishment of the Professional Civil Service"). That same month, Jews were no longer permitted to attend public schools and universities (code-worded: "Law Against Overcrowding of German Schools and Universities"). This was followed with the torching of books written by Jewish authors, on whatever subject, in nightly massive torch-lit ceremonies, recalling the religious *auto-da-fe* of the Spanish Inquisition. Two years later, in September 1935, in the infamous Nuremberg Laws (so called, for the city where it was proclaimed, during the Nazi party's annual rally), the government prohibited the intermarriage of Jews and non-Jews, and declared sexual intercourse between the parties to be a serious offense. In January 1937, for easy identification, all Jews were forced to add compulsory Jewish names on their ID cards: "Israel" for men and "Sarah" for women. A year later, for yet easier identification, the letter "J" (for *Jude*) in red color, was added on all ID cards held by Jews. That same year, non-Jews were no longer permitted to patronize Jewish doctors, and Jews were barred from the streets during Nazi holidays. Towards the end of 1938, a decree ordered all Jewish-held real estate to be liquidated and sold to the State, mostly at a fraction of their value. Non-Jews were also prohibited to live in homes inhabited by Jews. That same year, in November 1938, all synagogues and Jewish-held properties were burned, in a state-organized pogrom throughout Germany — which by then included Austria, annexed to the Reich in March of that year. In September 1941, all Jews were ordered to mark their outer garments with the Yellow Star badge, and later on their homes as well. That same month, Jews were restricted to their homes.[4] By then, the deportation of Jews was already in full swing.

Before the first deportations of Jews were carried out, several hundred thousand Jews had managed to leave Germany to various destinations. The remaining, close to two hundred thousand Jews, had, in the meantime, been reduced to a pariah status and placed outside the pale of the law. In late 1940, the first batch of several thousand Jewish deportees were unceremoniously dumped in French-held detention camps (France was by then a defeated nation). The following September 1941, trains loaded with exiled Jews intermittently left for various locations in German-occupied Poland. Most were dumped in already overcrowded Jewish ghettos, to await their fate. In May 1943, Nazi Propaganda Minister Josef Goebbels proclaimed Berlin "clean" of Jews. In fact, untold numbers were in hiding in the Nazi capital and other locations in Germany.[5]

German policy during the war in the occupied countries, which included most of Europe, followed the four-stage model outlined by Holocaust historian Raul Hilberg: Definition (who is to be considered a

Jew?), Expropriation (the forced liquidation of Jewish assets), Concentration (isolating the Jews from the rest of the population), and Annihilation (deportation and murder at prearranged killing sites).[6] In Poland, with its over three million Jews, they were first herded into enclosed ghettos, their assets frozen, and they were forced to wear the identifying Yellow Star badge. In addition, practically all able-bodied men were conscripted for various manual and hard labor assignments. Food was reduced to a minimum, which caused thousands to die from starvation and malnutrition. Others were randomly shot for the slightest infraction or for no reason at all. In most other occupied countries, the Germans followed a similar pattern, although with less severity than in Poland. Jews in the Netherlands were ordered to register, then relocate to "Jewish" homes or streets, with many drafted to perform various tasks of hard labor for the German army in the country, or in nearby Belgium and France. The Germans considered the Dutch a lost Germanic tribe, to be reintegrated into the German Reich; hence, the accelerated "cleansing" pace of all non-Aryan elements — namely, the Jews. Nazi officials were appointed to administer the conquered nation.

Belgium and northern France fared slightly better, since they experienced only a military occupation. Local matters were left in the hands of native authorities. Still, the Jews saw themselves gradually restricted and removed from their social milieu and their privileges annulled. Similarly, the semi-independent French state, centered in Vichy, was headed by the aged marshal Pétain. Not waiting for a cue by their German overlords, the French authorities hurried to legislate anti-Jews laws, which forced them out of important positions in various branches of the economy and social life, and practically reduced them to second-class citizenship. All Jews were also ordered to register with the police. Here, as elsewhere in German-occupied Europe, all Jews had their identifications stamped with a large "J" in red, for better identification and easier harassment. Similar restrictions were imposed on Jews in Greece and Yugoslavia. In all these impositions, the Germans were aided by local collaborators who, for a mixture of motivations — political and a dose of antisemitism — allied themselves to the Nazi cause, such as the NSB movement in the Netherlands, the Rexists in Belgium, and the Vichy regime in France. In Yugoslavia, the Germans gave their blessing to the dissection of the country. The pro-Nazi Ustasha movement in Croatia declared the country's independence. To cement its alliance with Germany, Croatia began an intensive persecution of Jews, including random killings. Similarly for the pro-Nazi Slovak state, which rose in 1939, after the German occupation of the Czech part of former Czechoslovakia. There too, under the leadership of a Catholic priest, Josef Tiso, the Fascist Hlinka movement instituted anti-Jewish measures, to please its German overlords and give vent to their own antisemitic sentiments. It was bad for Jews in all countries, whether directly occupied or under German influence—and it was getting worse.

The United States, though not yet at war, restricted to a bare minimum the intake of Jewish refugees from war-torn Europe. The refusal to allow some 900 fleeing Jews from Germany to land on its shores, who arrived there aboard the *St. Louis* boat, sent a chilling message that not even the barest minimum of Jewish refugees would be permitted to land. The *St. Louis* with its human cargo steamed back to Europe. Luckily, at the last moment, England, France, Belgium, and the Netherlands declared their willingness to absorb these refugees. Most eventually perished in the Holocaust, when three of these countries fell under German occupation.

With the German invasion of the Soviet Union, in June 1941, the Nazi leadership decided to pass to the killing stage. Special mobile units, known as *Einsatzgruppen*, followed the German army across a wide front, from the Baltic Sea in the north to the Black Sea in the south, and began to mercilessly shoot all Jews whom they accosted. Over a million persons died at the hands of these execution units, shot in the back over open ditches. The most infamous of these killings took place outside Kiev, Ukraine, over ravines in the Babi Yar forest, where some 30,000 Jews were murdered in September 1941. The Nazi leadership was, however, not satisfied with the pace of these killings. Moreover, these mass shootings drained too much manpower, and began to bear down on the military discipline of the soldiers. In addition, these open-air killings attracted onlookers, and the Germans feared that these terrible events would soon become an open secret.

What was needed was a more secretive and more economically efficient killing policy. The Nazi leadership gathered in a posh Berlin suburb villa, overlooking a charming lake, and decided on the next steps. At this Wannsee conference, in January 1942, all government agencies were told by SS chief Heydrich to streamline and coordinate their operations with the SS, for the next stage of the murder of the Jewish people, which would henceforth be mostly done through suffocation in specially constructed gas chambers. This would consume less manpower, was more economical and could be kept secret from the rest of the world. The conference approved the setting up of these killing centers in occupied-Poland, to which all of European Jewry were to be transported by train. Upon arrival, the victims would be hurried through a quick selection. Old men and women and young children, as well as others not qualified for hard labor (such as pregnant women) would immediately be committed to the gas chambers, and their bodies burned in specially-installed large ovens. However, not before their teeth would be inspected for gold fillings, which would be extracted with pliers and sent to the German central bank in Berlin. Special teams of prisoners would also set apart valuables left behind by the victims, shorn women's hair, crutches, shoes and clothing in relatively good conditions — to be recycled for the war economy and the German population back home. The fortunate ones selected for hard labor would, according to the Wannsee plan, be reduced through brutal treatment, physically hard labor and undernourishment, so that they too would eventually perish — but not before contributing to the German war effort.

Such was the heinous plan, conceived and carried out by heads of ministries and security agencies, many of them university graduates and sporting PhD degrees. This government-orchestrated murder actually continued operating unabated until the last day of the war, on May 8, 1945. All told, the Wannsee conferees were responsible for more than 4 million Jewish deaths. This, together with the mass executions by the *Einsatz-gruppen*, and the other forms of brutal treatment, accounted for the 6 million Jewish victims of the Holocaust. To this number must be added the tens of thousands of Gypsies exterminated because they were considered racially unfit to live, as well as the numerous other victims of Nazism, killed in various concentration camps.

Following the Wannsee conference — with the coming of summer 1942, trains began rolling from all parts of German-dominated Europe to the killing centers in Poland: 105,000 from the Netherlands; close to 30,000 from Belgium; some 80,000 from France; almost all of the remaining close to 200,000 German and Austrian Jews, as well as tens of thousands from Slovakia, Greece and Macedonia. In Poland, Ukraine, Belarus, and the Baltic countries, the large Jewish cities and ghettos were quickly emptied of their Jewish inhabitants and dispatched to nearby killing centers, such as Chelmno, Belzec, Treblinka, Sobibor, and Auschwitz, where most were immediately gassed. The remainder of the Jewish population in Eastern Europe continued to be liquidated in front of open pits.[7] Fascist Italy was the sole Nazi-allied country which stood back from killing its Jewish inhabit-ants; hence, many Jews sought succor in Italian-administered countries — in southeastern France and the Balkans. When Italy fell under direct German sway in September 1943, the Nazis enlarged their hunt for Jews in these newly acquired areas, going so far, in August 1944, as to round up the 1,500 Jews on the island of Rhodes, which lies offshore the Turkish mainland. When Hungary came under direct German control in March 1944, the death knoll began ringing for its over 750,000 Jews. The gas chambers in Ausch-witz were consequently enlarged to receive the new victims, of whom over 400,000 were committed to the gas chambers upon arrival.

As the fortunes of war turned against Germany, and its armies grad-ually withdrew from conquered lands, the surviving Jewish concentration camp inmates were forced to accompany the retreating armies, in forced Death Marches, in inclement weather (in many instances, such as the

Auschwitz evacuation, in sub-zero temperature). Tens of thousands fell, either from the cold, exhaustion, or were simply shot by their SS captors, and their bodies straddled the frozen roads leading out from many concentration camps. These Death Marches and other forms of killings continued until literally the last days of the war. In the mind of Hitler and his devoted cronies, it was indeed a "War Against the Jews,"[8] as reconfirmed by the last entry in his Political Testament, hours before he put an end to his life. The Nazis lost the war, but they had decimated the best and bravest of the Jewish communities that stood in their murderous path. The six million murdered Jews accounted for approximately 75% of the Jewish population under direct or indirect Nazi rule. Had the war lasted another year — perhaps even less — that rate would undoubtedly have been even higher. In order to have a minimum chance to survive the Nazi onslaught on their lives, unprecedented in scope and with the use of modern technology, Jews desperately needed the help of their non-Jewish neighbors.[9]

To view this from a different perspective: Any Jewish person, in a Nazi-occupied country in late 1943, who was still at liberty — that is, he was not in a ghetto or consigned to a Nazi-supervised residence, neither in any of the labor and concentration camps, nor with a partisan and underground network operating from mountain and forest lairs, but was circulating freely — had to be someone enjoying the hospitality of a non-Jewish person, in whose home or farm he had been admitted for hiding, or was circulating under an assumed name, again with the help of non-Jews. These constituted active forms of aid. There were also passive forms of assistance — such as not betraying to the authorities a Jew known to be residing in one's neighborhood or village. Estimates vary on the number of Jews aided in each country through charitable help by non-Jewish persons. In West Europe, the numbers rise well into the thousands, in each country. In the Netherlands, for instance, some 22,000 Jews are estimated to have gone into hiding, out of a total Jewish population of 140,000, or close to 16%. One may easily assume that at least a similar number of non-Jews actively participated in these rescue endeavors. In Belgium, close to 30,000 Jews lived in hiding, or passed as non-Jews. In France, the figure is even higher; over two-thirds of the 300,000 Jews who resided in the country at the start of the German occupation, survived. Similarly in Italy, where three-quarters of the 35,000 Jews who lived there at the start of the German occupation, in September 1943, survived the Holocaust. In Eastern Europe, the figures are much less encouraging. In Poland, with its prewar Jewish population of 3,250,000 Jews, it is estimated that some 40,000 survived either in hiding or by passing as non-Jews. Another 300,000 were saved by fleeing to the Soviet zone of the dismembered nation. In the Baltic countries, only a small fraction of Jews survived, whereas in Hungary, close to a fourth of the 750,000 Jews survived—most of them thanks to the intervention of foreign diplomats stationed in Budapest. Several thousands survived in Slovakia and in each of the Balkan countries. In Bulgaria proper (that is, less the annexed territories) the Jewish population of close to 60,000 remained intact, thanks to the intervention of civil and church figures who stayed the government's hand in planning the deportation of the Jews to German death camps. In Ukraine, Belarus and Russia, thousands of Jews (it is still hard to ascertain a more precise figure) survived through the active help of the native population, while hundreds of thousands of others were murdered by the Germans and collaborating militias of the native populations. In summary, well over 250,000 Jews survived the Holocaust throughout Europe, through the active help of non-Jews. Viewed statistically, this figure is a small consolation when compared with the awesome number of six million murdered Jews. At the same time, to truly appreciate the significance of these rescue acts, a rather qualitative appraisal is needed, for the simple reason that during the Holocaust it was much easier to kill than to save. To ward off the Nazi onslaught on their existence, Jews desperately needed immediate assistance from their non-Jewish neighbors. While such assistance was forthcoming, it was not in sufficient numbers to save the bulk of Europe's disarrayed and disoriented Jewish populations who faced a well-oiled and efficient government-orchestrated murder machine.

Types of Help

When discussing assistance available to Jews by non-Jews during the Holocaust, one may group them under four principal headings. These are: sheltering, dissimulating, moving, and help to children.

1) *Sheltering*: This involved finding a safe and secure hiding place for the fleeing Jew, in the rescuer's household; of a secluded space, unobservable from the outside, and safe from suspecting eyes of persons wishing to harm Jews. Hiding places varied in size and personal discomfort. It could be a dark corner in the attic, a shaft under the rescuer's home, with only mice and insects as close companions, or worse, a hole under the barn or pigsty, and having to bear the terrible stench. In less unpalatable circumstances, it could be a dark corner in the rescuer's home, hidden from outside view by a piece of furniture; an unused section of a business storage room or inside a large double wall or ceiling. All this, for as long as it may take; from a temporary arrangement lasting only days or weeks, to perhaps several months, and in some cases, for as long as two and a half years—that is, until

the Germans and other paramilitary antisemitic elements had been evicted from that particular area. In all these instances, the hidden Jew was dependent on his rescuer for the fulfillment of one's basic existential needs – such as food, washing, and the removal of biological wastes. All these burdens (on top of the difficulties already posed by the war situation) now fell on the shoulders of the rescuer and his family.

For a few examples: in the Netherlands, Victor Kugler and Miep Gies, former business associates of Otto Frank, cared for his and another family, and saw to its daily needs, including Otto's daughter Anne Frank, who remained hidden for two years, in an annex of their former business house. In Warsaw, Poland, the Wolski family hid several dozen Jews, including the famed Polish-Jewish historian Emmanuel Ringelblum, in an underground vegetable hothouse near their home. In the same city, zoologist Jan Zabinski hid a group of Jews in emptied animal cages of the Warsaw zoo. Outside Kaunas, Lithuania, Jonas Paulavicius hid a dozen Jews in several bunkers near his home, so that in the event that one shelter were uncovered, the captured persons would not be able, even under torture, to reveal the presence of other hidden persons. In several isolated cases, people even hid in tombs, after the coffins had been removed, such as in Buczacz, Poland, where three people huddled in a tomb for over one and a half years, and were cared for by the cemetery janitor, Manko Szwierczszak.

These are but a few of many examples of hiding in the most uncommon places, in the hope of surviving the Nazi hell, with the help of others.[10]

2) **Dissimulating**:   Another major form of aid was helping a fleeing Jew dissimulate his or her real identity by assuming a new and less Jewish-sounding name, coupled with a new personal history. This included fetching new credentials for the rescued person, including birth or baptismal certificates, and a new place of residence. Passing as a non-Jew was easier said than done, for one had first to carefully ascertain whether one had what was considered a Jewish appearance. This is not something one could take lightly, for the slightest error could be fatal. Not having pronounced Jewish features was not in itself sufficient. One also had to be familiar with the local customs, proper language inflection, folk mannerism, jokes, and religious beliefs; in short, everything needed to dissimulate one's otherness from the people with whom one mingled. Anyone wishing to pass as a non-Jew – and there were thousands of such persons all over Europe – needed other persons to assist him, first with obtaining proper credentials, then with moving the fleeing Jew to a new location, arranging for him living quarters and a place of work and be on hand to help during emergencies.

Another form of dissimulation was to be registered as a vital worker in a war-related industry, under German supervision. Berthold Beitz employed over 1,000 mostly unskilled Jews through the ruse that they were needed to operate the oil refinery installations in Drohobycz, Poland. Julius Madritsch and Alfred Rossner did likewise for their many Jewish workers in the military uniform firms in Cracow and Bendin, and Hermann Graebe—for his Jewish workers in railroad installations in Zdolbunov, Ukraine. The most celebrated case in this category is that of Oskar Schindler who claimed that his 1,200 Jewish workers were indispensable for the war effort in his factory in Brunnlitz, Moravia, when in fact, they did not produce a single shell during the whole eight months of the firm's operation.[11]

A third form of deception was by claiming that certain groups of people were nationals of a country with which Germany entertained friendly relations, and should therefore not be harmed. Numerous such "protective letters" were issued by the ambassadors of neutral countries in Budapest in 1944, who were thus able to prevent the deportation of thousands of Jews. Included in this group one may mention the legendary Raoul Wallenberg, of Sweden; Giorgio Perlasca, an Italian who masqueraded as the Spanish chargé d'affaires; Carl Lutz, on behalf of Switzerland, and Monsignor Angelo Rotta, the papal nuncio. All these diplomats utilized the "protective pass" ruse to try to save in combination tens of thousands of Jews in the Hungarian capital during the most critical phase of the Holocaust in that country.[12]

3. *Moving*: Another major form of assistance was to help Jews flee from one place to another; either within German-dominated regions, or across frontiers to countries not embroiled in the war, such as Switzerland, Sweden, Spain and Turkey. Even in areas under German spheres of influence, conditions for Jews varied. In France, for instance, it was somewhat easier to survive in the so-called "free" zone of the Vichy government, where anti-Jewish measures were not applied with the same severity as in the German-occupied north (including Paris). Conditions were even more favorable in regions of France under Italian administration, where Jews were not mistreated. Similar lenient conditions prevailed in other regions under Italian rule, up to September 1943—in western Yugoslavia, Albania, and the Italian zone in Greece, which included Athens. In Ukraine, persons close to the Romanian zone of occupation wished to flee there; again, because of the less severe conditions prevailing for Jews after the initial period of widespread killings by the Romanian military. In Ukraine and Belarus, many able-bodied people wished to flee into the deep forests, to join up with friendly partisans fighting the Nazis. In Greece, Jews sought to escape into the hills, where the partisans prevailed, or by boat to neutral Turkey, where they were permitted to land. Similarly, in Norway

and Denmark, thousands of Jews escaped either by boat or by negotiating tortuous passes through the hills, to Sweden, where they were welcomed. In France, after the whole country, including the Italian zone, came under direct Nazi control after September 1943, Jews sought to flee either to Switzerland or to Spain. In all these endeavors, to travel over long distances and tortuous trails and negotiate well-guarded border crossings, without being apprehended, help was needed by non-Jews, for the simple reason that the use of public transportation and public accommodations were denied to Jews by law.

Of the many examples in this category, only a few may be mentioned here. Tadeusz Soroka helped a group of nine Jews flee from the Grodno Ghetto, in Poland, which was about to be liquidated in March 1944, to Vilnius, where conditions for Jews were at that particular moment somewhat more bearable. The flight was accomplished aboard a German military train on its way to the front. Himself a railroad worker, Soroka accompanied them for a long night ride, as they lay huddled on the roof of the military convoy. In Italy, Father Arrigo Beccari arranged the flight of over 100 Jewish children from the mountainous village of Nonantola to the Swiss border, which they safely crossed. In Italy as well, Father Beniamino Schivo constantly moved a Jewish family from one location to another, and past German lines; in one instance he hid them in a monastery, dressed as nuns, until he had seen them to safety with the arrival of the Allied army. In the Netherlands, Joop Westerweel arranged and led groups of Jewish youth on long treks, past occupied Belgium and France, and up to the Spanish border, high on the Pyrenean mountains. Several diplomats also facilitated the flight of many Jews out of German hands. Aristides de Sousa Mendes, the Portuguese Consul-General in Bordeaux, France, freely issued thousands of Portuguese transit visas to Jewish refugees in the city, on the eve of its surrender to the Germans; Jan Zwartendijk and Sempo Sugihara, the Dutch and Japanese consuls in Kaunas, Lithuania, respectively, likewise issued transit visas to thousands of Jews stranded in that country; finally, Paul Grüninger, the Swiss police border officer in St. Gallen, Switzerland, who issued false entry permits to several thousand fleeing Jews who appeared on his border outpost after the *Kristallnacht* pogrom, of November 1938, and desperately sought a safe haven in Switzerland.[13]

4. *Children*: The fourth and final category pertains to the rescue of children, a particularly sensitive subject. Obviously, where adult Jewish persons had to fend for themselves, in some instances in hiding places where silence and strict discipline were the order of the day, or circulating freely under an assumed identity, children could hardly be part of this conspiracy of shelter and subterfuge. If both parents and their children were to have a chance to

survive, the two sides had to separate—perhaps never to see each other again. This meant turning over one's child for an indefinite period for safekeeping and adoption in either a children's home, or with a private family. Children old enough to distinguish between their natural and adopted parents had to be "reprogrammed;" that is, to erase from their minds the remembrance of their erstwhile true parents and their own earlier names, forget their Jewish affiliation and religious customs—all this for reasons not fully, if at all, comprehended by these tender minds—and readapt to totally new filial and group relationships, and new cultural and religious environments. Persons involved in this rescue operation included those who traveled long distances to make the proper arrangements, escorted the children to their new homes, and made routine inspection visits to make sure the children were well cared. Not to overlook the host families who took the frightened children into their homes and showered them with affection, love and patience, while fabricating stories to neighbors to explain the sudden appearance of a strange child in their household.

Of the many examples, one may mention Yvonne Nevejean, who as head of Belgian's national child care agency, opened the agency's doors for hundreds of Jewish children on their way to host families. In the Netherlands, the NV group is the most noteworthy of the several clandestine cells which dedicated themselves to rescuing Jewish children by dispersing them with various host families, in distant locations. In France, Dr. Rita Breton dispersed several hundred children in the Normandy countryside, while Denise Bergon sheltered Jewish children in Catholic institutions. Rolande Birgy, who worked on behalf of a Catholic youth organization, and the Quaker-affiliated Helga Holbek and Alice Synnestvedt spirited many children across the Swiss border. In Poland, Irena Sendler spirited children from the Warsaw Ghetto, and with the help of trustworthy aides, helped to disperse them in private homes and religious institutions. Still in Poland, Sister Matylda Getter is one of several nuns awarded the Righteous title for sheltering many Jewish girls in her religious orphanage.[14]

Risks to the Rescuer

The Nazis prided themselves on their anti-Jewish measures and boasted that they would solve what they termed the Jewish Question once-and-for-all, through the use of the most drastic steps. However, when it came to wholesale murder, they decided to conceal from the world-at-large this heinous intention with code-worded language—words understood only by those directly involved in the sordid act, but fooling many others (even those privy to classified information) on the exact nature of the Final Solution. Most—even suspecting persons—refused to believe that a nation, until recently considered one of most civilized in the world, would embark on such an unprecedented mass-scale murder operation, especially as the Germans stood nothing to gain from butchering defenseless Jews. Hard as it was to conceive of such an idea, the tone of the Nazi language and the choice of words, when addressing the Jewish issue, made it clear that they were determined to consign the Jews to a bitter fate. For everyone with eyes to see and ears to hear, it was no secret that the Nazis meant to rid the European continent of the Jewish population, in one way or another. To the populations under Nazi dominance (and allied regimes), it was also made crystal-clear that the Nazis intended to deal harshly with anyone placing obstacles by offering aid to fleeing Jews. To remove any doubts, the Nazis publicly warned the local population of the dire consequences, including the death penalty, awaiting non-Jews who aided Jews to avoid falling into the Nazi dragnet. In Poland, for instance, large posters appeared on bulletin boards in the major cities, warning of the death penalty for various forms of aid to Jews on the run, including sheltering them in one's home, selling them provisions, and moving them from one place to another.

Some rescuers indeed paid with their lives for helping Jews. Such was the fate of the rescuers of the noted Polish-Jewish historian Emmanual Ringelblum, who was hidden together with a large group of Jews in an underground shelter on the Aryan side of Warsaw. When the place was discovered, the Germans shot all the bunker's residents, including their rescuers—the Wolski family. Yad Vashem archives contain additional documents of Poles sentenced to death for the above mentioned offenses. Jan and Stanislaw Kurdziel were likewise executed for helping two Jewish women leave the ghetto in Zarki. Jakob and Zofia Gargasz were sentenced to death for sheltering an old Jewish women in their home in Brzezow. Rescuers in other countries fared no better. In Germany, the farmer Heinrich List was sent to Dachau camp in 1942, where he died the same year, after being apprehended for sheltering a Jewish acquaintance on his farm. Still in Germany, Ilse Totzke was deported to Ravensbrück camp, for trying to help a Jewish woman flee to Switzerland. In Fiume, Italy, police chief Giovanni Palatucci was also sent to Dachau, where he perished, for aiding Jews and other persons sought by the Nazis. In Denmark, Henry Thomsen was arrested and sent to Neuengamme camp, where he died, for his involvement in ferrying Jews across to Sweden. In Avon, France, Father Jacques (Lucien Bunel), was arrested in his Catholic seminary, after he was betrayed for hiding three Jewish boys. He was sent to a concentration camp, where he died. Suzanne Spaak, deeply immersed in the rescue of Jewish children in the Paris region, was executed by the Nazis on the eve of the liberation of the city, in August 1944. In the Netherlands, Joop Westerweel, Jaap Musch, Joop Woortman, and Albertus Zefat, were executed on Dutch soil for their involvement in the rescue of Jews. Sometimes, not directly aiding but merely showing sympathy with Jews could land a person in a concentration camp. Adelaide Hautval, who complained about the harsh treatment of Jews in a French prison, was dubbed a "Friend of the Jews," and deported to Auschwitz, which she luckily survived. These are but a few of many examples of rescuers who suffered martyrdom, or severe sufferings, for their attempt to help Jews to stay alive.[15]

Much as the rescuers feared the Germans, the danger did not only stem from them but also from other quarters, such as: (a) local collaborators with the Nazis who, for political and ideological reasons, dealt with the Jews sometimes more cruelly than the Nazis; (b) anti-German partisans units, especially in Eastern Europe, who persecuted and even killed Jews with the same dedication as shown in their courageous struggle against the Germans; (c) various antisemitic elements (pro- or anti-Nazi) who did not want to miss out on the opportunity to help the occupiers rid their country of Jews; finally, (d) blackmailers, holding to no ideological or political conviction, who simply wanted to cash in on the opportunity to fleece Jews and their rescuers in return for not turning them in to the authorities; or betray them in return for a reward promised anyone fetching a Jew on the run.

Would-be rescuers had to take into account the danger that could emanate from any of these quarters, on top of the obvious danger from the Germans. Consequently, while not belittling aid afforded to Jews from persons not facing such threats to their person (such as benefactors in countries not under German domination) — those who faced such dangers and did not waver in their commitment toward their wards are considered by Yad Vashem, Israel's national Holocaust memorial, to be worthy of the title of "Righteous Among the Nations." This is an honor which Jewish tradition has reserved for non-Jews who act according to universal standards of justice, and, whenever necessary, above and beyond the prevailing norms in their society.

Yad Vashem's Program of "Righteous Among the Nations"

In 1953, the Knesset (Israeli parliament) legislated the country's national memorial for Holocaust victims, known as Yad Vashem. In the law's preamble, the Righteous Among the Nations are mentioned as one of the memorial's principal functions; persons who, in the lawmaker's words, "risked their lives to save Jews." The term "Righteous Among the Nations" has its origin in Jewish lore, and has known various interpretations, including the popular one of non-Jews who showed favor to Jews during periods of distress and persecution. The Israeli legislator, therefore, chose this ancient Jewish title to designate non-Jewish rescuers of Jews during the Holocaust.

Nine years after the law's passage, in 1962, Yad Vashem acted by creating a public commission to assist it in the implementation of the Righteous Among the Nations provision of the 1953 law. Headed by a Supreme Court judge, the "Commission for the Designation of the Righteous" defined the principal criteria for according the Righteous title to non-Jewish rescuers of Jews. The commission's first chairman was Justice Moshe Landau, who a year earlier presided over the trial of Nazi war criminal Adolf Eichmann, and was later appointed President of the Israeli Supreme Court. He was succeeded by Supreme Court judge Moshe Bejski (who survived the Holocaust through the help of the German Oskar Schindler), then by Supreme Court Judge Yaakov Maltz (formerly the State Comptroller). The Righteous title may be bestowed on non-Jewish rescuers of Jews, when the following conditions are met:

— The very attempt by a non-Jewish rescuer, including his, or her, personal participation in a serious attempt to help at least one Jewish person to survive, irrespective of whether the rescue operation proved successful or not;
— At a time when the Jewish person was helpless and, in order to survive, had to rely on help by others;
— And in that undertaking, the rescuer placed his own life and well-being in jeopardy;
— The rescue act not having been preconditioned on the receipt of a substantial monetary or other tangible reward and compensation;
— The humanitarian motivation proved to be the rescuer's principal incentive;
— The rescuer not having, before and during the rescue operation, been in a position to directly or indirectly cause physical harm to Jews and/or other nationalities;
— Verification of the story exists through elaborate and convincing testimonies by the rescued party and/or incontestable documentary material.

The "risk to life" clause remains the principle criterion for the bestowing of the Righteous title—the Jewish people's highest honor to non-Jews who were prepared to stake their lives—the highest price one can be asked to forego—in return for helping Jews survive the Nazi onslaught on their physical existence.[16]

Over the three decades of the commission's existence, the aforementioned guidelines have guided it in its deliberations on the attribution of the Righteous title which, since 1962, has been awarded to over 17,000 men and women, representing roughly some 8,000 accredited rescue stories.

This, however, is but a small fraction of the actual number of persons involved in the rescue of Jews, but who for a variety of reasons have not been identified. In many cases, both rescuers and rescued have died and cannot, therefore, testify on the rescue operation. There is, moreover, an important psychological factor which militates against revealing one's rescue many years past at the hands of others. Reopening old wounds, and recalling past traumas, are understandably excruciatingly painful experiences to many survivors. Evoking a period when they underwent the most horrible inhumane treatment, which resulted in the loss of loved ones, is something that many prefer to keep to themselves, or repress in their subconscious, to the end of their lives, including their rescue at the hands of non-Jews. Who are we—from a position of undisturbed and comfortable lives—to judge?

Through this brief introduction we hope to have enlightened the reader on the circumstances of rescue operations against the setting of the darkened world of the Holocaust (sometimes referred to by its Hebrew term *Shoah,* or Catastrophe). Having delimited the scope of the Righteous program, one sometimes wonders how these magnificent stories of human behavior at its best, soon to be illustrated, have come to the attention of the Jerusalem-based institution; of deeds that occurred in distant places and many decades ago? In general, most rescue stories originate with the rescued party — that is, the survivors, who take the first step by informing Yad Vashem of their travails during the Holocaust, including their rescue at the hands of one or several non-Jewish rescuers, coupled with a request to have them recognized and honored. Upon the receipt of such a detailed testimony by the rescued person, a statement is also solicited from the side of the rescuer party. The story is then carefully examined in light of the historical data of the period, as well as the criteria governing the attribution of the Righteous title. It is then submitted to the Commission for the Designation of the Righteous for its verdict on the case. In other instances, the discovery of a potential Righteous occurs as the result of scholarly research or due to information received from sources other than the rescued or their rescuers.

To highlight the stories of these knights of the spirit, Yad Vashem is currently engaged in a vast enterprise, the publishing of a multi-volume alphabetical *Lexicon of the Righteous,* with a summary of the deeds of each of the honorees. In this book, more space is devoted to a select few of these uncommon humanitarian stories, which have been chosen for their special interest and unique dramatic character. As a starter, we mention the stories of a few who either protested against the antisemitic measures of the Nazi

Righteous Commission chairman, Judge Yaakov Maltz (left),
is making a point. Next to him is Yad Vashem's Vice Chairman Johanan Bein, and Commission member Yitzhak Artzi.
Photo by Author

regime or tried to alert the world of what was happening in the Nazi
kingdom of hell—alarms which, alas, went unheeded. We then continue
with select stories outlining the various facets of rescue, such as sheltering
and hiding in the rescuer's home, covering-up one's Jewish identity and
other subterfuge methods, in order to avoid detection by the Nazis; and help
through escape from Nazi-held territory. We then illustrate cases where the
rescuers were apprehended and suffered punishment, including the death
penalty. A special chapter is dedicated to the world of hidden children, and
the post-traumatic effects this had on their lives. We also illustrate rescue
stories spearheaded by the clergy. An additional chapter examines the
vexing cases of persons who saved, but for various reasons were declined
the righteous title. Following the Concluding Thoughts chapter, appendix
A discusses the vital role played by some Jewish rescuers, and the need to
find a proper honorary framework for them; Appendix B highlights the
uniqueness of a Belgian rescuer of many children; Appendix C deals with
the unknown righteous of the Holocaust period; and Appendix D provides
a statistical country-by-country breakdown of the righteous on Yad
Vashem's Roll of Honor.

I believe that the world is sustained through the good deeds of the
few—perhaps too few. Whatever the numbers, their role is still sufficient to

free the world (if only momentarily, during periodic moments) from the suffocating stranglehold of the forces of evil. This book is dedicated to the Righteous — those known to us, and the anonymous — known only to God.

Chapter 2

Protest and Alarm Sounding

S ociety can thwart the actions of criminal regimes, such as Hitler's Nazi Germany, when responsible civic and religious leaders rise to the challenge, protest and sound the alarm, and openly call their supporters to open and passive resistance, coupled with public demonstrations and manifestations. Such behavior, however, was sorely lacking in the Germany of 1933. Quite to the contrary; all political movements, save the Nazi party, as well as labor unions and other civic and religious organizations, shut their offices and disbanded, and joined the chorus of those hailing the advent of a new messiah in Germany. Only a few lone voices were heard; too few to make a dent—especially on the Jewish issue. So we begin with several stories of persons who, although they did not actually save—they tried to save, by sounding the alarm, which sadly was not believed by others. But first, a unique case of a German scientist who preferred exile from his country to taking advantage of a situation arising from the Nazi government's initial anti-Jewish measures.

Otto Krayer

The German Scientist Who Refused a Vacant Post on Moral Grounds

In the spring of 1933, Professor Otto Krayer, the acting head of the Department of Pharmacology and Toxicology at Berlin University, was invited by the head of the regional education department to fill the Chair of Pharmacology at the Medical Academy of Düsseldorf, due to the vacancy created by the dismissal of the Jewish incumbent, Professor Philip Ellinger. Declining this offer, Krayer outlined his reason, in a letter dated May 16, 1933, to Stuckart, the Prussian Minister of Science, Art, and National Education, in the new Hitler regime:

> *The primary reason for my reluctance is that I feel the exclusion of Jewish scientists to be an injustice, the necessity of which I cannot understand, since it has been justified by reasons that lie outside the domain of science. This feeling of injustice is an ethical phenomenon. It is innate to the structure of my personality, and not something imposed from the outside. Under these circumstances, assuming such a position as the one in Düsseldorf would impose a great mental burden on me – a burden that would make it difficult to take up my duties as a teacher with joy and a sense of dedication, without which I cannot teach properly. I place a high value on the role of university teacher, and I myself would want the privilege of engaging in this activity to be given only to men who, apart from their research capabilities, also have special human qualities. Had I not expressed to you the misgivings that made me hesitate to accept your offer immediately, I would have compromised one of these essential human qualities, that of honesty. . . I therefore prefer to forego this appointment, though it is suited to my inclinations and capabilities, rather than having to betray my convictions; or that by remaining silent I would encourage an opinion about me that does not correspond with the facts.*

Krayer's unwillingness to take advantage of a vacated position, due to the dismissal of a Jewish scientist, as a result of the Nazi government's firing of all Jewish academicians, is perhaps unique in the annals of German academia.[1] Had many others followed in his footsteps, one cannot withhold speculating what effect this may have produced on the Nazi leadership, at this initial period of their rule. As Krayer's lone challenge to the regime's new antisemitic policy proved to be the exception to the rule, it was not to go unanswered, and Stuckart in his reply to the ethically stalwart professor informed him that he would henceforth be barred from teaching in a German university. Furthermore, "pending final decision on the basis of section 4 of the Law on the Restoration of the Professional Civil Service [a law meant to bar employment in the civil service to non-Aryans; i.e., Jews], I herewith forbid you, effective immediately, from entering any government academic institution, and from using any State libraries or scientific facilities."

For a time, Krayer made use of private libraries, to pursue his scientific work. Later that same year, Krayer's academic privileges at the University of Berlin were restored. However, the winds of change in Germany were not to Krayer's liking, and he accepted an invitation to join a position at University College, London, with the support of the Rockefeller Foundation. He then taught pharmacology at the American University of Beirut and Harvard Medical School. Through the following years, Krayer contributed extensively to research on cardiovascular pharmacology, and wrote some 120 research articles. He died in 1982.

Since Krayer was not involved in the rescue of Jews, nor voiced publicly his opposition to the antisemitic measures, the case of this morally-upright person was not consistent with the criteria for the Righteous title. At the same time, the Yad Vashem's Commission for the Righteous noted the man's meritorious behavior, in stark contrast to the passivity of his colleagues, and urged that Krayer's action be given publicity. Hopefully, the few lines here will serve as a modest contribution to a person who preferred exile from his native country, rather than take advantage of a vacant position caused by the dismissal of a Jewish academician, in the first year of Nazi rule in Germany.[2]

Dr. Otto Krayer
From the Harvard Medical Library in the Francis A. Countway Library of Medicine. Photo by Albert R. Frederick, Jr.

Armin T. Wegner

The German Activist Who addressed a Protest to Hitler

There was, however, one man who decided not to restrict himself to a silent protest but to try to galvanize the German public against the antisemitic measures of the new regime with an open letter (in the style of Emile Zola's *J'accuse,* during the Dreyfus affair in France),[3] to appear in one of Germany's leading newspapers. As all newspapers declined to print a denunciation of the government's antisemitism, Armin T. Wegner decided to take his case directly to the head of the new regime — to Adolf Hitler himself. As he mailed his long-worded letter on April 11, 1933 to Hitler, Wegner had a premonition that dire things were in store for him. But as he did over a decade ago, when the Turkish massacre of the Armenians prompted him to voice his protest, he felt that the virulent antisemitic measures of the new regime were a challenge to the moral fiber of his country, and as such, in contrast to other Germans, he could not remain silent.

In the letter, which he entitled "For Germany," but which today is better known as "The Warning," Wegner blasted, in no unclear terms, the government's dismissal of Jews from all positions of influence in the life of the country. He warned of the shameful stain which such a policy, if allowed to continue, would leave on the good name of Germany and, therefore, called to reverse directions and annul the anti-Jewish laws just recently promulgated. The Jews, Wegner reminded Hitler, through their scientific discoveries, had contributed greatly to Germany's fame:

> We should say in all candor that Jews contributed to Germany's becoming famous and held in esteem by the world. . . Remember Albert Einstein, a German Jew, who made the universe tremble; who, like Copernicus, penetrated space to give mankind a new vision of the universe. Remember Albert Ballin, a German Jew, creator of the big transatlantic line to the West, where the mightiest ship in the world sailed in the direction of the country of freedom. . . It was Haber, a Jew, who like a magician, drew nitrogen out of air in his flask. It was Ehrlich, the wise doctor, who introduced a remedy to overcome syphilis among our people. . . I could fill many, many pages, if I only wanted to enumerate the names of those, whose diligence and intelligence are registered once and for all in our history. I ask you, whether all these men and women have done all that as Jews or Germans?. . . We accepted the blood sacrifice of 12,000 Jewish men during the war. Are we permitted. . . to deny their parents, sons, brothers, grandchildren, wives and sisters the right, gained through the

generations, to have a country, to be at home?

Before continuing further to examine Wegner's long and carefully-crafted letter to Hitler, let us briefly sketch the man's background up to this moment. Born in 1886, in Wuppertal, Armin Theophil Wegner studied law and political science in Zurich, Paris, Berlin and Breslau, earning him, in 1914, a doctorate in jurisprudence. During World War One, he was a military medic, on duty with the German army in Turkey, then an ally of Germany. While in Iraq and Syria (both under Turkish rule), he witnessed the massacre of the Armenians, which he reported in letters and photographs to friends in Germany. Because of these censorship violations, he was recalled to Berlin. There he tried in vain to raise public opinion on the plight of the Armenians. In 1919, on the eve of the Versailles Conference, he drafted an open letter to U.S. President Woodrow Wilson (which also appeared in several German journals), to enlist his intervention in the cause of Armenia at the conference, but to no avail. After the war, he wrote widely on travels to many countries, as well as various germane topics (including pacifism and nonviolence, causes greatly favored by him). With the rise of the Nazis to power, his books and articles were banned. This did not deter him from appealing directly to Hitler on an issue of great moral import.

Ridiculing the idea of a pure Germanic race, in his letter Wegner underlined the disparate origins of the German people: Franks, Frisians; even a blood infusion from a Slav tribe. "Didn't you come yourself from a neighboring country," Wegner taunted the Führer. As for patriotism, the Jews "are more attached to their home country than those who never left it." Witness the unwillingness of many Jews, at this early stage of Nazi rule, to leave the country. "I think such emotional feeling is to be admired," Wegner pointed out. He then warned of the consequences of the regime's antisemitism on Germany's name:

> *Herr Reichkanzler, not only the fate of our Jewish brothers is at stake –*
> *the fate of Germany is here at stake!. . . I address my words to you: 'Put*
> *an end to these events!' The Jews survived the Babylonian Exile, the years*
> *of slavery in Egypt, the Spanish Inquisition, the persecution of the*
> *Crusaders and sixteen hundred pogroms in Russia. With the same*
> *toughness that helped this people survive every hardship, the Jews will*
> *overcome this danger, too. The insult and misfortune that Germany is*
> *burdening on itself, will, however, not be forgotten for a long time!. . . The*
> *day will come when the first of April* [the day the Nazis proclaimed a
> general boycott of Jewish businesses] *will arouse a hideous shame in*
> *the memory of all Germans, when they have to judge their deeds.*

Why then, Wegner argued, were Jews hated and persecuted? The answer was simple: "Because this people places law and justice above everything else." However, it was also by divine design (a term which, Wegner reminded Hitler, he used in his speeches) that the Jews have been inserted among the Germans, for they serve "like salt into the leaven of bread." In fact, the Jews are "a social and ethical necessity" by their power of judgment and their understanding of the strengths and weaknesses of human behavior.

In the concluding part of his letter, Wegner pleaded with Hitler to cease the persecution of the Jews:

> *A tormented heart speaks to you. The words are not only my words, they are the voice of fate admonishing you: 'Protect Germany by protecting the Jews.' . . . It has always been the privilege of a great soul to admit mistakes made. . . Restore to their position those cast out, the doctors to their hospitals, the judges to their courts. Don't exclude any longer the children from their schools. Heal the afflicted hearts of the mothers, and the whole nation will be thankful to you. Think of it — Germany may be able to live without the Jews, but it cannot live without its honor and values. . . I say this not as a friend of the Jews, but as a friend of the Germans, being myself rooted in a family whose origins I can trace back to the days of the Crusaders. Out of love for my own people, I direct my words to you.*

While everyone remained silent, he could not do so. "I ask you fervently," Wegner concluded his long letter, "preserve the generosity, the pride, the conscience, which are essential for our existence—preserve the honor of the German people!"

Wegner was not left to wonder too long how his letter would be received. At first, an innocent letter of acknowledgment was sent to him by Martin Bormann, Hitler's personal aide. Then, suddenly, on August 19, 1933, Wegner was arrested by the Gestapo, and taken for interrogation. He was brutally beaten, until he lost consciousness, then transferred to several concentration camps, including Oranienburg. The British Quakers interceded on his behalf, and he was released the following year. He subsequently knew no peace, moving from one place to another, and finally settling in Italy, where he was again arrested for five weeks in 1940, at the request of the Gestapo. In September 1943, when the Germans occupied Rome and northern Italy, Wegner fled, with his common-law wife Irene Kowaliska to southern Italy. After the war, he eked out an income from articles and radio plays in Geman and Swiss newspapers. On a visit to his homeland Germany in 1952, he found it difficult to readjust and returned to Italy, where he lived until his death in 1978, in his 92nd year. Ten years earlier, the Armenian Soviet Republic, in recognition of his service on behalf of the Armenian cause, awarded him the Order of St. Gregory. In April 1996, his remains were interred in the Armenian capital Yerevan, at the invitation of the government, in the now fully independent Armenia.

His case was first brought to Yad Vashem's attention in January 1967. Most Commission members followed the lead of Justice Moshe Landau, the Commission chairman (who several years earlier presided over the trial of Adolf Eichmann), in praise of the man's courageous conduct. Landau reminded Commission members that in 1933 people were already being arrested and sent to the camps. "Nazi rule was ruthless from the start." Hence, Wegner was perfectly aware of the risks to his person by his open defiance addressed to the Nazi head of state. Moreover, Wegner seemingly was the only German who suffered greatly for daring to write directly to Hitler on the Jewish issue, in no uncertain terms. If he did not directly save anyone, his action was aimed at preventing the persecution of Jews on a greater scale. Just as we do not differentiate between war criminals with blood on their hands from those who give the order, Justice Landau remarked [*probably having in mind Adolf Eichmann, over whose judgment he presided*], likewise when considering rescuers of Jews one ought not to differentiate between the various forms of rescue attempts, especially when such action placed its author in dire jeopardy of life. The uniqueness of Wegner's stand and open defiance of Nazi antisemitism placed him in a special category — that of a Righteous person. In 1967, Armin Wegner was, indeed awarded this high distinction. The following year, on a visit to Israel, he planted a tree in his name in the Avenue of the Righteous, at Yad Vashem.[4]

Armin T. Wegner

Jan Karski

The Polish Underground Courier Whose Alarm Went Unheeded

The phone call at his London hotel room, in the fall of 1942, left Jan Karski devastated. He had just been informed that Szmul Zygelbojm, a leader of the Jewish Bund organization, had committed suicide by turning on the gas in his apartment. Several weeks earlier, Karski had given him an eyewitness account of the horrendous situation of Polish Jewry, which was being decimated by the Germans.

It had all begun a few months earlier. Jan Karski, a courier for the Polish underground, was instructed by his superiors that, before leaving on another secret errand to England, he was to meet two Jewish underground leaders in Warsaw, from whom he was to accept a message to be delivered to the Polish Government-in-exile in London. Before the war, Karski had studied Law and Diplomatic Sciences at a Lwow university. Taken prisoner by the Russians, in September 1939, he fled to the German-occupied area of Poland and immediately enlisted in the Polish underground. In June 1940, he underwent severe torture at the hands of the Gestapo, after being apprehended trying to cross into Slovakia, on his way to England via Hungary. In his cell, he attempted suicide by cutting his veins, and was rushed to a hospital, whence he made his escape, by leaping through a window. He was now about to undertake another similar dangerous mission.

Meeting the two Jewish leaders in a Warsaw suburb apartment, in late summer of 1942, at the height of the German extermination of the largest Jewish ghetto in Poland, Karski was struck by the complete hopelessness of their predicament. For Leon Feiner and Menachem Kirschenbaum, the killing of Polish Jewry meant the end of their world. Added to their despondency was the depressing feeling that this war, which they hoped would be won by the Allies, would however end with the Jewish people gone. As they put it to the startled Karski:

> *You other Poles are fortunate. You are suffering too. Many of you will die, but at least your nation goes on living. After the war Poland will be resurrected. Your cities will be rebuilt and your wounds will slowly heal. From this ocean of tears, pain, rage and humiliation your country will emerge again but the Polish Jews will no longer exist. We will be dead. Hitler will lose his war against the human, the just, and the good, but he*

will win his war against the Polish Jews. No — it will not be a victory; the Jewish people will be murdered.[5]

In order to save the remnants of Polish Jewry, the two leaders appealed to Karski to call upon Jewish leaders in England and America to stage sit-down hunger strikes in front of governmental chancelleries in their countries. "Let them accept no food or drink, let them die a slow death while the world is looking on. Let them die. This may shake the conscience of the world." Profoundly shaken, Karski sank in his armchair. "I was shivering and I felt the pulses in my temples pounding. I rose to go." The two leaders stopped him, for they had another message to deliver — an uprising in the Warsaw Ghetto which was being planned and would take place. "We are not going to die in slow torment, but fighting," but this would be "the most hopeless declaration of war that has ever been made."

Afraid that he would not be believed in London and Washington, Karski asked to be smuggled inside the Warsaw Ghetto, to witness the liquidation taking place at the time, as well as in a forward post of a concentration camp (dressed as a pro-German Latvian guard), to see with his own eyes the brutal treatment of Jews arriving in cattle wagons. After these eyesight encounters in the Nazi Kingdom of Hell, he had seen more than he could stomach.

In London, several weeks later, he was in a state of numbness. He had lost interest in the original purpose of his mission — to report on matters dealing with the Polish underground. The tragedy affecting the Jewish people in Poland had taken hold of him, and he became obsessed with it. When he met Zygelbojm, he described to him the terrible state of the dwindling Jewish population in the Warsaw Ghetto. "Conditions are horrible. The people in the ghetto live in constant agony, a lingering, tormenting death." He then repeated the appeal for world Jewish leaders to stage hunger strikes. Zygelbojm snapped back: "It is impossible. . . You know what would happen. They would simply bring in two policemen and have me dragged away to an institution." Then came the news of Zygelbojm's suicide, which coincided with the news of the start of the Warsaw Ghetto Uprising on April 19, 1943. Karski felt deeply remorseful at having triggered Zygelbojm's suicide by revealing to him the desperate situation of his people in Poland. "I had personally handed Zygelbojm his death warrant, even though I had been only the instrument." This man's death symbolized to Karski the world's indifference to the plight of other people. "For days afterwards," he confided in his 1944-published memoirs, "I felt all my confidence in myself and in my work vanishing." Unbeknownst to him, at this low point in his mental state, his mission had been born!

Quickly regaining his composure, he began a series of meetings with Jewish leaders and British officials. He then left for the United States where he continued to raise the alarm on the tragic fate of Polish Jewry, personally reporting to President Roosevelt, Secretary of State Cordell Hull, and War Secretary Henry Stimson. He related all this in a special chapter, *Story of a Secret State*, which was published in 1944, while the war was still on, and which became a Book-of-the-Month-Club selection. He remembers his emotional state as he was about to be ushered into the presence of Roosevelt. "I was overwhelmed. I was going to see the lord of the world in the White House." The meeting lasted one hour and 20 minutes, and most of it was taken up with the state of affairs in occupied Poland. Finally, allowed to speak on the Jewish question, Karski stated bluntly: "The Jewish leaders are totally helpless. The Poles can save only individuals; they cannot stop extermination. Only the powerful Allied leaders can do that." Brushing aside the Jewish issue, Roosevelt assured his host that the Poles "have a friend in the White House," and that they would be vindicated for the crimes committed against them. "Justice and freedom shall prevail," the President raised his arm as he waived goodbye to the subdued Karski. When he related a similar message to Supreme Court Justice Felix Frankfurter, the latter expressed doubt: "I am unable to believe you," he responded. Karski was uncertain what he meant by this: did he have doubts on the veracity of the facts, or did he find them so shocking as to make them unacceptable to the human mind? Probably both.

Disappointed and disillusioned at the failure to evoke a proper response, while the Holocaust continued to deliver its victims to the Nazi Moloch, Karski decided to withdraw from the limelight and fade into anonymity. He felt he had failed in his mission. With his underground connection glaringly exposed, he could no longer return to his native country. Instead, he settled in the United States and resumed his studies, which earned him a PhD in political science. He taught Eastern European Affairs and comparative government at Georgetown University in Washington, DC, toured various countries on lecture tours on behalf of the State Department and, in 1965, married former dancer, Pola Nirenska, whose family perished in the Holocaust.[6] His wartime role in alarming the world to the Holocaust seemed to have been completely forgotten, and he did not feel sorry for it. "I wanted to run away after the war," Karski stated in 1989. "I saw too much misery, hatred, ruthlessness, human losses. I saw horrible things. What I learned from the war made me silent for 30 years." He was especially shaken by the insincere responses of "all those great individuals, presidents, ambassadors, cardinals, who said they were shocked. They lied. They knew or didn't want to know. This shocked me.

I didn't want to have anything to do with it. I said to myself, 'Karski, you are helpless. Give up the subject.'"

In 1981, he was persuaded by Holocaust author and later Nobel prize laureate Elie Wiesel to break his silence, by agreeing to address an audience of Holocaust survivors, meeting in Washington, DC. There were tears when he described the Warsaw Ghetto in its misery, and he received an ovation when he vowed never to forget what his eyes had seen there. Wiesel's impression of Karski was that of a "wounded person; that he carried secret, invisible wounds in him. . . I saw the tears in his eyes. . . I think he feels that he failed. He tried to speak and people didn't want to hear." Since this first public appearance, he spoke before many audiences. "At the beginning," he admits, "going over it all affected me badly, showing up in terrifying dreams. But I got over it."

At times, in retrospect, he felt that the task imposed on him was too big for a man of his low stature at the time. "I was too small for the enormity of my mission; I was too insignificant. This was the tragedy. I was too little. . . I have a feeling that the Jews had bad luck with me. They charged me with this terrible mission. . . I was on hand." However, "I was too insignificant to make an impression." He also minced no words on his denunciation of antisemitism, which he characterized as people suffering from inferiority complex, insecurity or plain jealousy. During a ceremony in his honor at Yad Vashem, in 1996, he described the antisemite as a person who realizes "he is inferior to Jews," or at best an ignoramus. However people may disagree with this definition, Karski continues to make no secret of his contempt and scorn of all hues and shades of anti-semitism.

In 1994, when he was awarded an Israeli Honorary Citizenship, he responded as follows:

> This is the proudest and the most meaningful day in my life. Through the honorary citizenship of the State of Israel, I have reached the spiritual source of my Christian faith. In a way, I also became a part of the Jewish community. . . Since the early years of my school in Lodz, I have been getting understanding, friendship or help from the Jews; and now, they took me in; and now, I, Jan Karski, a Pole, an American, a Catholic, have also become an Israelite! Gloria, Gloria in excelsis Deo. Our Lord revealed Himself to many nations in His own ways, but always with the same Commandment — Love thy neighbor. . . He endowed us with a free will. We have infinite capacity to do good, and an infinite capacity to be evil. We are all schizophrenic.

When Karski's name was first mentioned in Israel, in the 1970's, during the period of his self-imposed silence, Yad Vashem was not fully cognizant of his role in trying to alarm the world on the Holocaust, by appealing to leaders in the Allied countries. Finally, in 1981, after Karski's renewed first public appearance, and especially in 1982, during his first visit to Israel, and his lecture before a select group of Yad Vashem researchers and members of the Commission of the Righteous — there could be no doubt in the minds of his listeners that he deserved serious consideration to the Righteous title. The Commission took note of the personal risks undertaken by him, both in visiting the sealed-off Warsaw Ghetto at the height of the extermination process, and a concentration camp affiliate — visits done on a voluntary basis, over and above what his underground superiors had asked of him and which would have cost him his life if apprehended. In the words of Commission chairman, Justice Moshe Bejski: "The very fact that a person takes the trouble to enter the ghetto twice, and to the vicinity of a concentration camp, so as to be able to say: 'I saw it with my own eyes' — here I see the 'risk' element." Gideon Hausner (who during 1960-61 served as prosecutor in the Eichmann trial) added: "The Germans described him as an emissary for the Jews. He not only volunteered, not only made the Jews the central issue, but in all his activities, he alarmed the world on the Jewish fate." He had jeopardized his life in the attempt to stop the Holocaust by sounding a cry of alarm in countries at war with Nazi Germany. Tragically, his appeal went unheard. This, however, in no way impinged on the man's courage and stature, and Yad Vashem acted quickly to award Jan Karski the title of "Righteous Among the Nations." A tree in the Avenue of the Righteous proudly bears his name, astride an imposing monument honoring those who fought against the Nazis.[7]

Jan Karski

Kurt Gerstein

The German SS Who Attempted to Expose the Horrors

As the express night train sped off from Warsaw for Berlin, on a hot August 1942 summer night, Baron Göran von Otter, Secretary in the Swedish Legation in Berlin, scurried to find a sleeper. Looking behind his back, he noticed a man in an SS uniform, with intense eyes, following him closely. "I could feel that he was very agitated and depressed," von Otter related many years later. "There was a queer look in his eyes. . . a look that was not ordinary." Finally the SS officer approached the Swedish diplomat, introduced himself and said he had an important secret message to divulge. The two chose an isolated spot in the corridor and sat on the floor. Then, SS Lieutenant (*Obersturmführer*) Kurt Gerstein, in a voice cracking with emotion and occasional sobs, told the startled diplomat of the terrible experience he had just undergone—he had witnessed the gassing of several thousand Jews in a death camp named Belzec. Gerstein asked von Otter to relay the message to his government with a request to pass it on to the Allies. If the Allies were to inform the German populace of the extermination of Jews by their government, through leaflets dropped by planes, Gerstein was sure that the German people would rise to take action to stop this criminal act.

Who was this SS officer who wished to alert the world of the Nazi-orchestrated Final Solution of the Jewish people?

Born in 1905 to a nationalist-minded father who served as a judge, Kurt Gerstein received a university degree in 1931 in mining engineering. He had, however, taken a keen interest in religious matters, and for a time considered entering the ministry as a pastor in the Protestant church. He, therefore, surprised his friends when in May 1933, only three months after Hitler's rise to power, Gerstein joined the Nazi party, and five months later enlisted in the SA (the party's brown-shirt private militia).[8] However, the attempt of the Nazis to infiltrate the Protestant churches caused a disenchantment in Gerstein's heart, and in 1935 he found himself expelled from the Nazi party.

A year later, he was imprisoned, after a search of his home revealed thousands of pamphlets of the Confessing Church, critical of Nazi anti-Church policies, and ready for mailing. He was released after a six-week stay in jail, thanks to the intercession of his father, but he lost his job with the State mines. Pleading for a redress, he appealed to the party's Supreme Court in Munich in 1937, but to no avail. In 1939, with the help of his family and friends, the expulsion was changed to a "dismissal." Before then, however, in 1938, he was again arrested for criticism leveled against the regime's policy against the churches; this time, he was sent to the Welzheim concentration camp, where he spent six weeks, before his release—again, thanks to the intercession of his family. In August 1940, he petitioned for readmission into the Nazi Party. Failing that, to the shock and consternation of his friends, in late 1940, he sought admission in the SS. To explain this bizarre move, he stated to Pastor Kurt Rehling, in 1941, that he was certain that the Nazi regime would collapse, and there will be a Day of Judgment. "When that moment comes," Gerstein told Rehling, "these ruthless desperados will do all they can to get rid of anyone left whom they regard as their enemy." He wanted to know who gave the orders to send people to concentration camps, and the mentally handicapped to be gassed. "When the end comes, I want to be one of those who will testify against them."[9] On March 10, 1941, Kurt Gerstein was admitted into the Waffen SS.

The SS leadership was of course only too happy to recruit into their ranks a person considered an intellectual and a "repentant sinner." In light of his professional credentials, he was assigned to the SS Hygiene Department, in Berlin, where he headed a project dealing with constructing and improving decontamination facilities in prisoner-of-war and concentration camps. He visited many such camps, and his dedication and efficient work soon merited him the rank of lieutenant. While on the job, he heard of several killing methods, and to prove his credentials, Gerstein suggested some improvements of the killing techniques.[10] His trip to Belzec camp, however, had a decisive effect on his state of mind, leading to a near mental breakdown.

The Belzec incident took place in mid-August 1942, when he was ordered by an SS higher officer to leave for a secret mission to a potash plant, near Prague, where he was to pick up 260 kilos of prussic acid and take them to a place, to be further revealed. Asked by a French officer, after his capture at the end of the war, why he was chosen for this assignment, Gerstein replied: "I was considered a specialist in cyanide disinfectants."[11] It was by then no secret that death by asphyxiation through gas was the favored method. However, when he arrived at his destination, at Belzec camp, he learned that the method used there was still the inefficient one of pumping motor gas through an exhaust pipe. Arriving first in Lublin, he was greeted by the top SS area commander, Odilo Globocnik, who was in charge of the mass murder of most of Polish Jewry (known as *Operation Reinhard*), in four notorious camps: Belzec, Sobibor, Treblinka and Maidanek.[12] In each of these camps, Globocnik happily informed his guests, over 10,000 persons were being killed on a daily basis.

Gerstein was asked to devise plans to efficiently disinfect the large quantities of clothes and belongings left behind by the victims, as well as improve the functioning of the gas chambers, by introducing the more toxic prussic acid. To demonstrate the inefficient engine exhaust method, Gerstein and his party of SS officers were led to Belzec camp to witness the killing of several thousand Jews, but not before being warned by Globocnik that this was a top secret operation, and the death penalty would be imposed on persons disclosing any of the details. In Belzec, Gerstein and his party watched as a transport of newly-arrived Jews, including men, women and children, were forced by guards to enter the gas chambers — seven to eight hundred in each chamber. Many were murmuring their last prayer as they were whip-lashed into the dark chamber. This was a moment of crisis for Gerstein, as he admitted in his post-war testimony:

I prayed with them. . . and cried out to my God and theirs. How glad I should have been to go into the gas chambers with them! How gladly I should have died the same death as theirs! Then an SS officer in uniform would have been found in the gas chambers. People would have believed it was an accident and the story would have been buried and forgotten. But I could not do this yet. I felt I must not succumb to the temptation to die with these people. I now knew a great deal about these murders.

What especially affected Gerstein was the suffering exacted on the people inside the gas chambers, due to the failure of the diesel engine which caused the several thousand panic-struck and stark naked people to wait for two hours and forty-nine minutes until the SS guards succeeded in activating the engine. After 32 minutes, all inside were dead by suffocation. Gerstein had witnessed it all, including the opening the doors, and the sight of the dead glued to each other like marble statues. After which, the SS party continued to Treblinka camp, where they were treated to a sumptuous dinner by the local commander. The following day, a visibly shaken Gerstein boarded the Warsaw-Berlin night express train and confronted the Swedish diplomat von Otter.

As he related what he saw in Belzec, Gerstein constantly sobbed and buried his head in his hands, repeating, "yesterday, I saw something frightening." He begged von Otter to report everything he heard to his government, and further to the Allies. He was convinced that if the German people would learn of their government's extermination policy, it would immediately take action to remove the Nazi regime. A few months later, Gerstein waited outside the Swedish legation in Berlin (dressed in mufti) for von Otter to appear. When they met, Gerstein asked him if he had relayed the message to Stockholm. "He seemed utterly desperate," von Otter recalls, "and could scarcely articulate a sentence. He looked as though his nerves were absolutely spent." The Swedish government did nothing with von Otter's message, perhaps out of concern not to harm its relations with Germany. Only in August 1945, three months after Germany's surrender, was the report communicated to the British government. Gerstein also told of his harrowing experience to a select group of trustworthy friends. Bishop Otto Dibelius related that he received him in a state of terrible agitation. Gerstein pleaded with him: "Help us! Help us! The outside world must know! These things must become the talk of the world." Dibelius was shaken, but took no action. "After all, we ourselves were prisoners," Dibelius excused his passivity. Gerstein then tried to alarm the Vatican through its representative in Berlin, the Nuncio Orsenigo. According to Horst Dickten, to whom Gerstein confided the story, Gerstein had introduced himself to the Nuncio as a member of the Confessional Church as well as an SS officer. The Nuncio asked: "What can I do for you?" Gerstein then related what he had seen at Belzec. Suddenly the Nuncio screamed: "Go away! Get out!" In his postwar account, Gerstein bitterly complained:

> *What could be required from an average citizen to do against the Nazis when the very representative on earth of Jesus refused even to hear me although tens of thousands of people were being murdered every day.*[13]

He was never to recover from the shattering effect of this visit. When Helmut Franz saw Gerstein in September 1942, "he was completely shattered." He looked like a ghost—totally disoriented. He was filled with a horrifying premonition as to the future, and the same time he was utterly convinced of the historic importance of his mission. He was also worried about the danger which his resolve to document the Nazi atrocities would place on his wife and children, and at times contemplated suicide. To Alexandra Bälz, to whom he poured out his heart in September 1942, he wept and sobbed bitterly and uncontrollably, all the time repeating: "I can't go on! I can't go on." He then blurted out: "My God, we've got to do something to stop it! But what?" The only possible recourse was to destroy some of the prussic acid he was ordered to deliver to the camps. "But how many times will I get away with it?" He then wept endlessly, "in a way I've never known a man to do in the presence of a woman. We sat there till four in the morning." He was convinced that Nazi Germany, a regime to which he was now violently opposed, deserved to lose the war. He reportedly told a Dutch confidante: "I'd rather we had Versailles [when Germany was forced to sign a humiliating peace treaty] a hundred times than have this gang of criminals remain." The Church in Germany, he felt, had forfeited the right to represent the Christian religion. Until the rise of a new church, it was best to take comfort in the Bible, a book into which Gerstein now delved more deeply, so as to flee even for brief moments from the despicable work he was forced to do at SS headquarters, and find solace for his troubled soul.

One would be led to believe that Gerstein's awakening from his earlier mistaken beliefs that in a twisted way, some good would come out of the Nazi experience, would after his Belzec visit have led him to try distancing himself from a type of work which involved delivering the poisonous gas to the concentration camp. However, quite on the contrary; he stayed on his job at the SS Hygiene Department, and personally handled deliveries of Zyklon B gas pellets to their fatal destinations. Invoices to the Degesch firm, which produced the poisoned substance, including deliveries of Zyklon B to Auschwitz camp, which by 1943-44 had replaced the other camps as the main killing site, continued to bear Gerstein's signature.[14] In fact, in February 1943, he was promoted to full Lieutenant (*Obersturmführer*), and praised for building up his section "far beyond the tasks originally assigned to it."

On April 22, 1945, Gerstein surrendered to the French army in the Reutlingen area. At his confinement place, he borrowed a typewriter and wrote his testimony—first in French, then in German—hoping to bear witness against Nazi war criminals. He attached to the report twelve invoices from the Degesch company, addressed to him, on deliveries of the toxic gas Zyklon B to Oranienburg and Auschwitz camps. To two U.S. and British army officers, he told he was anxious to bear witness, since he was probably the only one capable of doing so, in light of his involvement in the deliveries of the poisonous gas and his many visits to the concentration camps. To French officer Raymond Cartier, Gerstein admitted his mistake in joining the SS; that now life meant little to him, but before dying he wanted to know whether if any action was taken following his reports to the Swedish and Vatican diplomats. Gerstein was eventually moved to Paris, where charges were drawn against him for complicity in the extermination process by the Nazi regime, and he was placed in solitary confinement. The shock of being consigned to jail as a Nazi criminal, side-by-side with other imprisoned Nazis, was the last straw, and on July 25, 1945, Gerstein was found hanging in his cell.

In 1950, a German Denazification Court refrained from exonerating Gerstein, but held back from classifying him a criminal; only of being "tainted." The court agreed that by passing the news of the killings in the camps by gas to foreign sources, at great risk to himself, he committed acts of resistance. At the same time, the court felt that after the harrowing Belzec experience, he ought not to have allowed himself to become a tool of an organized mass murder. "It is incomprehensible and inexcusable," the court opined, "that, as a convinced Christian who in earlier years had repeatedly shown such an upright and courageous bearing in the face of National Socialist actions, he allowed himself to be used, in a decisive manner a year later, as an agent passing orders to the Degesch Company." It should, moreover, have been clear to him that as an individual, he was in no position, by destroying or rendering useless small quantities of the poisonous gas, to prevent or diminish the scope of the exterminations. "What happened at Auschwitz was so monstrous that it may reasonably have been expected of the subject that he would do everything humanly possible not to blacken his own conscience, even though he could not thereby prevent what was happening." Ten years later, in 1965, the Baden-Württenburg provincial government rehabilitated Gerstein, but the debate over the man's actions and motivations is far from over.

Since 1964, when Hochhuth's *The Deputy* played in many theaters throughout the world, a play based on Gerstein's confrontation with Vatican Nuncio Orsenigo in Berlin, Yad Vashem was petitioned to consider Gerstein's nomination to the Righteous title. Foremost in this endeavor were Holocaust historian Léon Poliakov and the French author Pierre Joffroy. Poliakov felt that the extraordinary nature of this case made it imperative for Yad Vashem to disregard some of the criteria attached to this honor. In their opinion, Gerstein remained morally upright to his last moments, and had in the interest of his morality sacrificed his honor and life. Yad Vashem was therefore committing an injustice to this man's memory by withholding the Righteous title. According to Joffroy, "the man who at first seemed to me possessed of a crafty and doubtful character, was a Righteous in the strongest and truest sense of the term." His joining the Nazi party, as well as the SS was part of a grand strategy, to enter the Devil's kingdom in order to combat it from the inside. This explains his renewed efforts to be readmitted to the Nazi party after his expulsion. As to the claim that his efforts at diverting the acid gas was of meager and insignificant results, Joffroy countered that what's important is that Gerstein did destroy some of the consignment, and he should therefore be judged by his intention and effort, rather than the result.

Yad Vashem countered by pointing out the difficulty which this case presented to an institution dedicated to commemorate the Holocaust victims. Kurt Gerstein had of his free will entered the Nazi Party and the SA (Storm Troopers); when expelled, he repeatedly appealed to be reinstated;

then — again of his free will — he enlisted in the SS, fully conscious of what this organization stood for. In the SS, he contributed, willy-nilly in making the Holocaust possible. Disregarding these terrible facts, and solely judging the man's ulterior motives, as well as his effort in alerting the world on the nature of the Holocaust, but at the same time continuing his services in the SS (including deliveries of the poisonous Zyklon B to the gas chambers) right up to the end — this would be whitewashing the non-salacious data of the man's past, and in the minds of many Holocaust survivors who lost relatives to the poisonous gas, would constitute a mockery of the Righteous program.

Perhaps the best evaluation of this mysterious and inordinate person was best given by Pastor Mochalsky, the cleric to whom Gerstein admitted his predicament after listening to his sermon on the theme: 'Thou Shalt Not Kill."

> *Gerstein represented the type of man who. . . disavowed the Nazi regime, even hated it inwardly, but collaborated with it in order to combat it from within. . . Gerstein, however, was no more than. . . a cog of secondary importance. . . Despite his greatest efforts and the best of intentions, he was not sufficiently important or influential to stop this machine. . . The machine was stronger than he was.*[15]

Holocaust historian Saul Friedländer (who incidentally also felt that the Righteous title would not be proper in this case), in his summing up of the man, in a book, aptly subtitled *The Ambiguity of Good*, states that had there been in Germany thousands, even hundreds of Gersteins, that is, persons in the Nazi apparatus who were prepared to divert or damage the shipment of the gaseous poison to the camps, then surely hundreds of thousands of the intended victims would have been saved. But there were none, save Gerstein. The Righteous title, however, had to be denied him because of his role in the Nazi killing-machine, and his involvement (though perhaps involuntarily) in one of the most horrendous aspects of the Holo-caust — the ordering and shipping of the poisonous Zyklon B to the gas chambers. Such activities made it impossible for an institution consecrated to the memory of the Holocaust victims to bestow on him its highest and most morally-edifying honor.[16]

Chapter 3

Escape and Visas

To the misfortune of the Jews, the Nazi period also coincided with harsh immigration policies by the Western democracies who, for a variety of reasons, refused their country's haven but for a trickle of fleeing refugees. However, a few diplomats, public servants and official emissaries, who were stationed or found themselves at critical junctures on the refugees' flight paths, found ways to bend the rules and the mandates of their assignments, and grant life-saving visas to the refugees. These were times, when a brief-worded official seal on a piece of paper meant the difference between life and death for countless Jews, as in the following three stories.

Francis Foley

The British Official in Berlin Who Issued Visas to Many Places in the British Empire

In 1919, a nondescript British lieutenant by the name of Francis Foley arrived in Berlin, on an intelligence assignment—to report to his superiors on the activities of communist-led organizations who were aimed to obtain power by force, as occurred in Russia two years earlier.[1] As a cover for his spy work, his official capacity was Chief Passport Control Officer in the British embassy. As such, although officially a member of the British team of diplomats in Berlin, he was given wide latitude to judge and decide on the admission of foreigners into areas of the British empire in accordance with his interpretation of existing immigration rules and regulations. At the same time, in his real and more important assignment in the German capital, he was directly responsible to the MI6 branch of the British Intelligence. As told, his main duty was to keep close watch over the activities of the various communist movements in Germany, and in particular, the many Soviet spies in Berlin. The Comintern—the international communist movement, created in 1919 in Moscow to foment communist revolutions in other countries—had targeted Germany as the country most likely to succumb in the 1920's to a communist takeover, and had therefore infiltrated the country with its agents. A short-lived workers' uprising in Hamburg erupted at about the same time as Hitler's short-lived grab for power, known as the 1923 Munich Beer Hall Putsch. With the Nazi rise to power, in 1933, Foley's main focus shifted to the rearmament of Germany, which he, as did others in Britain, viewed with great alarm. In this, he was at odds with Foreign Office circles, including Neville Henderson, the British ambassador in Berlin, who favored a policy of rapprochement and appeasement vis-a-vis the Hitler regime. However, with the intensification of Jewish persecutions by the Nazi regime, Foley underwent a transformation, as he began to be more preoccupied with helping as many Jews as possible to emigrate from Germany. This need became urgent, especially during and after the Nazi mass-staged pogrom of November 8, 1938, known as *Kristallnacht* (Night of the Broken Glasses), during which Jewish businesses, synagogues and residences throughout the country (including Austria, which was annexed to Germany) were attacked and torched, and thousands of Jews hauled off to concentration camps. Thereafter, Foley saw himself even more consumed with a mission to help as many Jews leave the country, via legal means, whenever possible, or by bending British immigration rules at his discretion, when other means proved ineffective.

The situation facing Foley proved daunting to diplomats who wished to help. Most chose to abide by the black-and-white immigration rules of their governments. Only a few, like Foley, were willing to explore loopholes in these rules, so as to exploit them to maximum advantage by granting visas to numerous terror-stricken Jews on the run. The stiff quota system adopted by the United States and other countries effectively ruled out the admission of but a fraction of the tens, and later hundreds of thousands of Jews wanting to leave Germany. Insofar as Great Britain was concerned, regulations stated that visas were to be denied to persons with professions liable to compete with similar professionals in England, such as lawyers, medical doctors—even shopkeepers and certain categories of laborers. Also excluded were the very aged, the sick and handicapped, and persons associated with the communist party. As for entry to Palestine, then a British Mandate, a "capitalist" visa could be issued, within certain limitations, to persons with £1,000 on hand—a sizable sum at the time (equivalent to several dozens that sum today) for many Jews, whose bank and other assets had been frozen by the Nazi authorities. Whenever approached by Jews, seeking frantically to leave the country, Foley would seek loopholes in these restrictions to allow him to issue visas, and when that proved impossible—to simply disregard these regulations. Such as for Elisheva Lernau (nee Elsbeth Kahn), whose bank deposits were frozen by the Nazis, when she approached Foley through an intermediary, in August 1935, with only £10, after running the gauntlet at other embassies. On the strength of his impression that the balance of £990 would be available to her the minute she landed in Haifa, Foley issued her a visa for Palestine. "I am convinced that without the 'unlawful' help of Captain Foley, I would not have reached Palestine in time," she stated in her deposition.

Wolfgang Meyer-Michael faced a similar problem—not having the necessary £1,000 for entry to Palestine. Here, Foley came up with a different stratagem. Learning that Wolfgang had a cousin living in Holland, Foley suggested that Wolfgang's cousin send him a written commitment, vouchsafing that the money would be available on demand. "Just get a promise; you don't have to use it," Foley told the bewildered Wolfgang. Two letters were subsequently sent to him by his cousin; in one, the cousin promised to lend Wolfgang the required sum; in the second— Wolfgang declared the first letter to be invalid and promised not to make use of it. Foley thereupon issued the visa, and Wolfgang landed in Palestine in 1935. "This was truly a good man," Wolfgang wrote in his memoirs; "it is thanks to Mr. Foley that I am alive today." Not forgetting his benefactor, in 1946, right after the war, he sent Foley a tobacco jar he made in his pottery studio in Haifa as a gift to his benefactor. Similarly, Zeev Estreicher was issued a "capitalist" visa in 1935, when he showed Foley a document stating that the requisite money was in his account, although Foley knew well that Zeev's bank account was still frozen. "Foley almost certainly saved my life."

Foley was especially helpful to Jewish persons imprisoned by the Nazis on various charges, including those stemming from the 1935 Nuremberg racial laws forbidding intimate relations between Jews and non-Jews (so-called Aryans). In this he was sometimes co-opted by Hubert Pollack, a Jewish community worker, who counseled Jewish emigrant candidates. He was adept at bribing Gestapo officials in return for release permits of Jews threatened with arrest, and then went to Foley to ask for appropriate British entry visas. In one such case, Gunter Powitzer was jailed for a violation of the racial law. Upon his release, in December 1938, after a 21-month jail imprisonment, he was hauled by the SS and incarcerated in the Sachsenhausen concentration camp, outside Berlin. There he underwent constant beatings. One day he was told by a shouting SS man to get cleaned up, combed, and dressed. He was led to the camp office, where he was met by a man with eyeglasses, who introduced himself as Foley, from the British consulate, who told him: "tomorrow you are free, and there are papers for you at the consulate for travel to Palestine." "What about my son?"(the product of the intimate relationship with the Aryan woman for which he had been jailed), the anxious Gunter asked. "He too is included in the papers. Don't worry," Foley replied. "I am that boy," Israel radio worker Zeev Padan wrote to Yad Vashem. On February 1, 1939, a car was waiting for Gunter at the exit of the camp, and twelve days later, father and son left for Palestine, on a visa issued by Foley.

An additional example was the case of Dr. August Weber — a known anti-Nazi parliamentarian, before Hitler's advent to power. The Nazis had jailed him seven times when, in 1939, he was warned that he was again to be jailed; this time, for good. Foley had already arranged for August's Jewish wife to leave Germany after *Kristallnacht*. For her husband, Foley quickly arranged a one-week tourist visa, at the same time notifying his family that once in London, it would be converted into an immigration visa. After the outbreak of the war, in September 1939, Foley moved to Oslo, Norway. There he arranged for Weber's daughter, Paula, to be admitted to England, although she was officially an enemy alien. She wrote: "My Jewish mother, my anti-Nazi father and I owe our lives to Frank Foley."[2] A further example is that of Willi Preis, who was incarcerated following the *Kristallnacht* pogrom. When Foley learned that Preis already had an entry certificate to Palestine, he took a cab and went directly to the prison and had Preis released. "There was something exceptionally special in his behavior," Willi's son Eliyahu stated about Frank Foley, in his deposition to Yad Vashem. "Father always told that he did a lot to many people. I don't know whether he acted above and beyond; certainly above. . ." In another episode, Pollack brought to Foley's attention the case of a Jewish gynecologist, who had to be gotten out of the country immediately, after he had been sentenced to prison on the charge of having performed abortions. According to British regulations, such persons were to be denied visas. Foley, however, concurred with Pollack that the real and ulterior aim of the doctor's arrest was to be rid of competing Jewish medical doctors, so that in issuing a visa to Palestine for the threatened doctor, he was not really violating British immigration laws in this regard.

Yet another affirmative decision by Foley involved the urgent matter of a 20-year-old woman imprisoned because of her membership in the outlawed communist party. While in jail, she had given birth to a child, whose father had already managed to leave to Rhodesia (then, a British colony), and now wished her to join him. The Gestapo had released her from jail, on condition that she leave the country within a two-week period. "How old is the young lady today?" Foley asked Pollack, who had brought this case to his attention. "Twenty," Pollack replied. Foley: "She has been in jail for two years; in other words, she was 18 when arrested. Well, as we say in German, *Jugendeselei* (youthful fervor). This is, in any case, my impression. Or, do you believe that this young lady will be an active communist in Rhodesia?" "Hardly so," Pollack winked. Foley: "Then, send her over here. Is the child's paper included?" Pollack: "Yes." Foley: "Brilliant. *Auf Wiedersehen!*" Mother and daughter left on the last day of the Gestapo grace-period. These are a few of some of the methods used by Foley to help Jews leave Germany. There were more.

Heinz Romberg's need for a visa stemmed from different circumstances. He had left Germany for Spain, in 1934, leaving behind the woman he planned to marry. Since she had expressed her wish to emigrate to Palestine, the necessary papers had be issued by the Zionist office in Berlin. So, in 1935, he returned to Germany, where he and his future wife learned that a Palestine certificate would not come before his three-month stay expired. In the words of the 90-year old Heinz Romberg, who wrote to Yad Vashem:

We were desperate. What would happen when the Nazis caught us with the round-trip train ticket was no longer valid? From word of mouth, we heard that there is a certain Captain Foley in the British embassy who evidently was already helping Jews. We asked to be interviewed. The idea of receiving an entry visa as a craftsman proved unrealistic. He, therefore, armed us with a capitalist visa (for which the sum of £1,000 was required, which of course we did not have). We left Berlin on October 16, 1935, the last day of the validity of the Barcelona round-trip train ticket. . . I have not forgotten, and shall never forget that man. He enriched the country [Israel] with three children (mine and my wife), eight grandchildren, and five great-grandchildren (so far).

Adele Wertheimer was another Jewish person on the run who sought out Foley "as the last possible source of help," after all her efforts to leave Gemany in 1938 proved in vain. She was granted a visa to Palestine, in Foley's words, "for the sake of the child," today's Simon Wertheimer—as stated in his deposition. Ida Weisz similarly sought out Frank Foley on a tip from a friend. She traveled from Vienna to Berlin, in 1939, to see him. Learning from her that she had nowhere to stay in Berlin, he invited her to his house for a few days, until her travel documents were in order. Foley parted with her at the train station, as she left for Belgium. Her son notes wryly that upon arrival in England, she was treated as an enemy alien, which contrasted sharply with the treatment shown her by Foley. But, at least, she was saved.

Not restraining himself with simply issuing visas, on top of his burdensome espionage work, Foley also made known his opposition to his government's restrictive immigration policy. He urged that quotas for Palestine be enlarged in view of increased persecution of Jews in Germany, "which was as relentless as ever though perhaps more subtle in method." In one such report, Foley noted that "it is no exaggeration to say that Jews have been hunted like rats in their homes, and for fear of arrest many of them sleep at a different address overnight." In a strongly worded telegram to Eric Mills, the British immigration head in Palestine, Foley asked for a number of blank certificates to be sent to him for urgently needed cases. Mills obliged and added a personal note: "God bless you, Foley."

After Kristallnacht, in November 1938, Jews stampeded to foreign consulates and the still-operating Jewish emigration organizations, seeking desperately to leave the country, which had by then placed them outside the pale of the law, and had now resorted to open violence against them. Benno Cohn, head of the Zionist Federation in Germany, testified during the Eichmann trial in Jerusalem, in 1960, on the chaotic situation of those times.

I put a call through to Mr. Moshe Shertok, head of the Political Department of the Jewish Agency [in Jerusalem]. . . and I told him—I had to conduct this conversation with great caution, after it was obvious that

"Der Feind hört mit" (the enemy is listening). I said only a few words. .. 'Mr. Shertok, S.O.S.; Save our Souls;' 40,000 men are in concentration camps; send us certificates. Pikuach Nefesh *(Hebrew for 'Danger to Life'). I stressed the phrase* Pikuach Nefesh *several times. . . To our great sorrow, this produced only a negligible result. Nevertheless we succeeded in getting a sizable number of Jews to Palestine. That was thanks to a man who is to my mind to be counted among the Righteous Gentiles.* **Question by Presiding Judge:** *Who was that man?* **Answer:** *Captain Foley. The British Passport Control Officer. . . in the British Consulate in Berlin. He did all he could to enable Jews to immigrate to Palestine. He helped a lot, people of all the categories ("A" certificates were for "capitalists" who had 1,000 Pound Sterling, "C" were the "Labor Schedules," "D" were students, etc.). One may say that he saved thousands of Jews from death.*

It was in those days that Foley showed himself at his best, as a great humanitarian, and his help to Jews turned into a personal obsession, and assumed legendary proportions. Aharon Lindenstrauss, representing the still Nazi-government sanctioned Palestine immigration office in Berlin, recalled seeing hundreds of people queuing up for visas to Palestine in front of the British Passport Office. "It was not always possible to help," Lindenstrauss stated during the Eichmann trial, "although this man [Foley] tried to help as much as he could." Foley's wife Katharine (known affectionately as Kay) related in a 1961 interview how in that period, she and her husband gave shelter to Jews in their private residence.

It was after the infamous Kristallnacht of November 1938 that we began to hide Jews in our flat. They would ring up and ask for help and Frank would slip down to the door late at night and let them in. They knew that if they stayed in their own houses at night there was the risk of being dragged away by the Gestapo. There was one young Jew whom we sheltered many nights. He had always left the flat by the time I got up for breakfast. But he never failed to leave something on my plate as a token of his grati- tude. . . a little box of chocolates. . . sometimes a solitary rose. . . One night we were already hiding four men when a fifth arrived and pleaded to be let in. I told him that there was not so much as an armchair left, but he merely said: 'Please may I sit on the floor?' I do not know what the Nazis would have done if they had discovered we were hiding people. We had to remember that we had our young daughter, Ursula, with us.[3]

As England and Germany edged closer to war, in the spring and summer of 1939, Foley worked feverishly to hand out visas to as many Jewish persons as he could. On August 24, 1939, with tension between Great Britain and Germany reaching a pitch, Foley informed a Zionist operative to come over immediately and pick up the last batch of 80 entry permits to England, before the consulate closed its doors at 4 p.m. Slightly earlier, in a May 26, 1939 dispatch to London, Foley appealed again for a more liberal immigration policy to Palestine, adding: "Perhaps the Chancery will forgive me for stating my opinion that both on grounds of humanity and of wider British interests, it is an infinite pity these unfortunate people are not allowed to immigrate to Palestine. We in this office are the daily witnesses of the sufferings of old and broken people under orders to leave this country. They beseech us to allow them to join their children in Palestine. I have referred hundreds of cases to Palestine." Foley was undoubtedly aware that British policy in 1939 dictated appeasing the Arabs, with a consequent severe reduction of the quota of Jewish immigrants to Palestine to a mere pitiable fraction by contrast to preceding years — this, at a time when the need for safe refuge for Jews grew immensely larger by the day, as the Nazis embarked on the Final Solution.

Dr. David Arian, whose aged mother Foley had helped leave in May 1939, wrote to him words of thanks from Palestine. "Destiny has placed you in a position where you daily come in touch with sorrow and despair, and where a man like you always feels the restrictions of power to help those who suffer. However, I know that whenever you find a possibility to assist the oppressed you do all you can to help them. . . It may also please you to hear that wherever your name is mentioned 'from Dan to Beersheva' — you are talked of with the greatest respect and devotion." To which, Foley replied, in July 1939 (two months before the war) that conditions were getting worse for Jews remaining in Germany, and added: "I dread to think of the misery and suffering they — especially the older people — will have to face next winter. Their funds are running low, and they do not know where they will find accommodation." He blasted the quota system as a "calamity, especially in the days of rabid persecution and permanent cold pogrom." He had only words "beyond praise" for the courage and fortitude of the Jews — "they have our profound admiration."

With the start of World War Two, true to his profession, Foley was deeply immersed in various intelligence operations, including the interrogation of Rudolf Hess, Hitler's misguided adjutant who landed in Scotland in May 1941, hoping to strike a deal between Germany and Britain, on the eve of Hitler's attack on Russia. At the same time, the plight of the Jews was never removed from his mind. Immediately after the war, he wrote to Dr. Senator about the opening the concentration camps. "Now the people here really and finally believe that the stories of 1938-1939 [of which he had amply warned] were not exaggerated. They were understated in fact. Looking back, I feel grateful that our little office in Tiergartenstrasse was able to assist some — far too few — to escape in time." He retired after the war, and died in 1958, at the age of 73.[4] His wife Katharine (Kay) survived him for 21 years, dying in 1979, to be followed by their sole surviving childless daughter, Ursula, three years later.

There is no doubt that Foley made it possible for thousands of Jews to emigrate from Germany to Britain and its empire dominions and colonies, before the start of the war. In his deposition to Yad Vashem, Hubert Pollack emphasizes that:

> *People who did not, or only knew Foley superficially, may think that I am exaggerating or for some reason wish to excessively laud him. This is far beyond my intention. The number of Jews who were saved in Germany, would have been ten thousand times — yes, ten thousand — less, if a "competent official" had occupied that post instead of Captain Foley. No amount of thanks and appreciation by Jews to this person are exaggerated.[5]*

In 1959, Benno Cohn, who had known him from the Berlin days, explained Foley's motivations in the following terms: "The basic factor was — he was a *Mensch* (an upright human being). It was really a rare experience to meet a person like him behind a desk. . . He gave back to some of us the belief in mankind." Yad Vashem concurred, and with the welter of material on hand, his name was added among the rank of the Righteous and publicly honored, in October 1999, in a ceremony, in the presence of his nephew, Pastor John Kelley, survivors, and . . . Robin Cook, the British Minister of Foreign Affairs, who specifically asked to be allowed to attend the ceremony, during his official visit to Israel — as a token of appreciation by the British government to this exceptional kind-hearted public servant; a humanitarian, indeed — par excellence.[6]

Francis Foley

Varian Fry

The American Who Saved Thousands in France

Almost a year to the day after Foley's departure from Berlin, an American emissary arrived in Marseilles, France, on a rescue mission. This amazingly dramatic story began over a month earlier, during a hastily-called gathering in a New York hotel, a week after France had agreed to a humiliating armistice with Germany, in June 1940. At that meeting at the Commodore hotel, a group of East-board intellectuals, headed by Frank Kingdon, decided to create an Emergency Rescue Committee, for the purpose of spiriting out of recently-fallen France renowned persons in the field of humanities, as well as German and Austrian socialist leaders – mostly Jews – who because of their past activities and anti-Nazi pronouncements stood in danger of being turned over to the Germans. Time was of the essence, because under clause 19 of the Franco-German armistice, the French government was obliged "to surrender on demand all persons under German jurisdiction named by the German government." In 1940, France counted three million aliens, among them 54,000 from Germany, for whom their host country had now become a death trap. This included refugees from countries such as Austria, Czechoslovakia, Poland, the Netherlands, and Belgium, presently under German control.

To bypass State Department quota restrictions, the group made an impromptu appointment with the First Lady, Mrs. Eleanor Roosevelt, who was then staying in her Manhattan apartment. According to one of those present, after listening to the delegation's plea, Mrs. Roosevelt talked on the phone to her husband in the White House – in the group's presence. After a 20-minute-long conversation, in which she tried to counter her husband's unresponsiveness, Eleanor was heard saying: "If Washington refuses to authorize these visas immediately, German and American emigré leaders, with the help of American friends, will rent a ship and in this ship will bring as many of the endangered refugees as possible across the Atlantic. If necessary, the ship will cruise up and down the East Coast until the American people, out of shame and anger, force the President and the Congress to permit these victims of political persecution to land!" The President relented, and ordered the State Department to bypass the restrictive quota system and issue 200 emergency visitors' visas to a select group of people.[7]

As its emissary to Vichy France (the mostly southern part of the country, in which a pro-German government headed by World War One hero, Marshal Philippe Pétain, was installed and with which the U.S. maintained diplomatic relations), to get the 200 people out, the Committee chose Varian Fry, a Harvard graduate and editor of several liberal journals, with no previous practical experience in anything approaching clandestine work. He was always, even later in France, noted for his impeccable dress, and sported a pair of horn-rimmed glasses. Impressed by Fry's enthusiasm, and faced with the lack of other candidates for this dangerous mission, the Committee settled for this unpretentious man. The first problem was to choose the fortunate 200 names out of a master list of several thousand endangered persons.

When the list was finally drawn up, Fry was set to go. Later in France, Fry revealed to Mary Jayne Gold, an American heiress who served as one of his assistants, what prompted him to accept the assignment. In 1935, as editor of the journal *The Living Age,* he visited Germany. In Berlin, Fry witnessed a bloody pogrom against Jews, and a scene which was to remain etched in his memory. Several SA men (Stormtroopers) ran a knife through a Jewish man's hand in a coffee shop on posh Kurfürstendamm Boulevard. "I think the mental image of that hand nailed to the table beside the beer mug had something to do with his decision to go," Gold later wrote. Recalling that Berlin incident, Fry wrote in 1945: "I could not remain idle as long as I had any chances at all of saving even a few of its intended victims."[8]

His letter of assignment by the Emergency Rescue Committee mandated him "reasonable latitude" and his personal judgment to explore rescue possibilities for the individuals on his list, so as to get them either to Lisbon or Casablanca, via various land and sea routes (and in that capacity he was permitted even to negotiate with underworld figures). He was also to inform the American consul in Marseilles on the nature of his work. "How much you tell him, and what degree of cooperation can be established between you, is a matter left to your discretion." In addition, he was to coordinate his work with Dr. Frank Bohn, who was on a similar assignment, on behalf of the AFL (American Federation of Labor) — known as the Dubinsky list, and which was geared to rescue members of the former German Social Democratic party, now stranded in France and in danger of being turned over to the Gestapo. Fry was also to investigate conditions in French internment camps. A seat had been reserved for him on a Pan Am Clipper, for August 4, 1940, with a return date set for August 29. He had one month's leave of absence, with pay. An extension of stay was possible, but not later than October 31, 1940. All this was spelled out in his letter of assignment by the newly-created Emergency Rescue Committee.

"I had never done underground work before and I did not know a single person on the list, but I had traveled widely in Europe and I spoke French," Fry candidly admitted years later. "Armed with $3,000 in cash [which was taped to his leg] and the conviction that every Jew in France... was in danger of his life, I arrived in Marseilles on August 15, 1940." However, once there, "I was at a complete loss about how to begin, and where. My job was to save certain refugees. But how was I to do it? How was I to get in touch with them: What could I do for them when I found them?" He took a small back room in hotel Splendide, and began writing letters to all those on his 200-name list whose addresses were known. There was soon a stampede of people to his hotel room, and letters began arriving from many parts of Vichy France. By the end of his second week, the lines outside his door were so long that the hotel manager complained. Fry thereupon decided to open an office on Rue Grignan, and towards the end of August the *Centre Américain de Secours* was officially launched on French soil. Sadly, he discovered that some of the intellectuals on his rescue list, for fear of being turned over to the Germans, had committed suicide, as was the case with the German-Jewish philosopher Walter Benjamin.[9]

To understand the climate in which Fry operated, one should keep in mind the political changes in France under Marshal Pétain. It was an autocratic regime, which repudiated the republican and democratic ideals of the French revolution and replaced it with a Mussolini-type Fascist dictatorship, headed by an 84-year-old World War One hero, who now favored accommodation with Nazi Germany. In September 1940, came the first anti-Jewish laws, reducing the Jewish population to second-class citizenship and barring them from influential posts in the life of the country. Prefects (regional heads) were authorized to arrest all foreign non-naturalized Jews and intern them, or place them in "forced residence," without justification, nor the right of appeal.[10]

As told, Fry was stampeded with persons asking to be taken out of the country—"their nerves were shattered," Fry notes in his 1945-published book. On the day of his arrival, Fry met with the noted author of Jewish descent, Franz Werfel, who asked Fry to save him. The AFL-representative Frank Bohn, and the German political refugee Fritz Heine urged Fry to explore more circumspect and secret ways—such as escape routes over mountains, and the use of false passports and boats. Fry immediately realized that the job was beyond the capacity of one man, and he assembled a staff of trustworthy persons to help him in what would become a vast rescue operation—far beyond the 200 persons on his limited list. One of the first to join was Albert Hirschman, a young economist, who had fought in the Spanish Civil War, and was dubbed "Beamish" by Fry because of the broad grin on his face. Together with other staff members (they ranged from a dozen to twenty), they would interview between sixty to seventy refugees a day, from early morning until midnight or even later. Daniel Bénédite, a former police officer in Paris, was chosen as office manager. Willi Spira, known as Bill Freier, a Viennese cartoonist, was added to the team, to help with falsifying credentials.

With so many persons applying for help to flee the country, Fry was faced with the difficult task of separating the genuine applicants from Gestapo-planted agents. The rule adopted was to refuse assistance to persons without references — for fear of entrapment. In the frantic search for visas, even diplomats of distant countries, such as Siam (Thailand) and China were solicited. The Chinese obliged but not exactly as Fry had hoped. The Chinese visa read: "This person shall not, under any circumstances, be allowed to enter China." French border guards, however, hardly read Chinese, and it looked to them as a legally approved visa to China, and the holder of this document was allowed to leave the country. By Christmas 1940, Fry had given up on seeking United States or other overseas visas; the aim now was just to get the people out of the country by whatever way possible. By then, Fry had sent 350 people out of the France, most of them without exit visas, and not one with an exit visa which would stand up under careful scrutiny, "and I had come to think of illegal emigration as the normal, if not the only way to go."[11]

Concerned with the extent of Fry's unorthodox methods, the French lodged protests with the American consul in Marseilles, but Fry decided to stick to his unorthodox methods. "Our work was by no means finished. We had not succeeded in sending out everyone we had located. . . Somehow, we had to find a way to get them out of France." The police mounted its pressure and several times raided Fry's premises in search of incriminating documents. Fears of phone tapping led Fry to leave the water faucets on whenever he was in the midst of planning escape operations with his aides.[12] In this respect, Miriam Davenport-Ebel, one of Fry's chief aides, notes: "We each tried not to know who was doing precisely what, when, and where, but we all knew that Varian was exporting refugees on either temporary American visitors visas in lieu of passport, or on valid, false Czech passports, supplied by the Czech consul who hated Nazis, and was happy to put any name Varian suggested under whatever photos Varian brought for him to apply to a passport." Those not able to be helped by Fry's organization, were handed Salvation Army meal tickets and referred to other relief agencies in Marseilles.

The escape routes utilized by the Emergency Rescue Committee included the following: *Route A* — from Marseille to Lisbon, by hiking through the hills surrounding the Cerbere railroad station into Spain (Port Bou). On this route, refugees were guided by two of Fry's aides — Johannes (Hans) and Lisa Fittko, and secretly helped by the sympathetic mayor (named Azéma) from the nearby French town of Banyuls. *Route B* — for refugees in greatest danger, the crossing into Spain over the Pyrenees was negotiated in locations more to the interior of the country. *Route C* — for refugees with good quality and authentic-looking forged papers and exit visas, who journeyed by train from Pau (in France) to Saragossa (in Spain); then continued to Madrid and Lisbon. *Route D* — refugees with Cuban visas on questionable passports avoided Lisbon and went directly from Spain to Cuba. *Route E* — from Marseilles by boat to Oran (Algeria). *Route F* — alternative passage into Spain from the border town of Banyuls. *Route G* — for refugees with valid exit visas, who sailed from Marseilles directly to the French colony of Martinique.

The Franz Werfels and Golo Manns (he was the son of the German novelist Thomas Mann) were among those smuggled into Spain on foot over mountain routes. To avoid detection, Fry advised the party to make a long and weary climb over the foothills of the Pyrenees, and assigned them a guide. Fry himself traveled by train, taking with him the 17 pieces of luggage and documents, claiming them as his own, and meeting the party on arrival on the Spanish side. Lion Feuchtwanger was also helped to flee France in time. Included among the distinguished intellectuals and artists which were helped by Fry's organizations are the following: painter Marc Chagall; sculptor Jacques Lipchitz; pianist Erich Itor-Kahn; film critic Siegfried Kracauer; political scientist Hannah Arendt; journal editor Georg Bernhard; novelists Franz Werfel, Lion Feuchtwanger, Hertha Pauli and Hans Sahl; Hebraic scholar Oscar Goldberg; novelist Hans Habe; journalists Wilhelm Herzog and Berthold Jacob; publisher Jacques Schiffrin; statistician E.S. Gumbel; mathematician Jacques-Salomon Hadamard; physiologist Otto Meyerhof; psychiatrist Bruno Strauss, and lawyer Arthur Wolff. By Fry's account, by May 1941, the office had handled more than 15,000 cases, of which 1,800 fell within the scope of Fry's direct work, representing some 4,000 people. Altogether, 1,000 were sent out of the country, and support allowances were distributed to 560 others.[13]

With food scarce in wartime France, everyone felt hungry, and by spring 1941, Fry and his workers showed signs of malnutrition. "I lost twenty pounds and was hungry all the time," Fry wrote. As a result, Fry's workers needed more sleep and were always tired and sometimes irritable. Not the least dampened, Fry on June 6, 1941, wrote to his wife Eileen how happy he felt with what he was doing:

> *The truth is that I like this job better than any I have ever had in my life... I enjoy it so thoroughly... I have twelve employees (and volunteers), and over two hundred and fifty clients more or less, dependent on my continued presence here... It isn't that I think myself irreplaceable... The job is very complex, not to say delicate. [It is not] something which could*

be abandoned with a light conscience, or handed over to someone who
would have to begin again from the beginning. . . It is a question of all the
refugees here; and ours is the only office that is doing anything for them
as individual human beings with individual human problems. If I leave,
I abandon those human beings, many of whom I have come to know and
to like very much, and most of whom have come to depend on me.[14]

It is understandable that French officials of the new pro-German Vichy
regime were not too happy with Fry's rescue operation, and they wanted
him out of the country. As pressure on him mounted, the local prefect, in
a report to his superior, at the Ministry of Interior, complained of Fry's use
of illegal methods and, moreover, noted that the U.S. government, as well,
which kept an ambassador in Vichy, agreed that Fry's operation was hurting
the "good relations" the United States wished to entertain with France, and
had asked him to return to the United States forthwith. "Mr. Fullerton, the
U.S. consul-general in Marseille," the prefect added, "often came to see me
on the Fry matter. He told me among others. . . that the U.S. embassy has
ordered the U.S. press association not to assist Fry, and he asked me to do
whatever necessary in order to rid [the consul] of him (*de faire le nécessaire*
pour le débarrasser de lui). The prefect ended his report by recommending
Fry's expulsion.

In December 1940, on the eve of Pétain's official visit to Marseilles, the
French police arrested people on its subversive list, including Varian Fry.
The whole group, consisting of 600 persons, was taken aboard the SS Sinaia,
docked in the harbor, and kept incommunicado for three days. After his
release, Fry was trailed by French secret agents for two weeks, on orders of
the Sûreté (intelligence service). In June 1941, the police became bolder in
its harassment of Fry, and his premises were often raided. It was all, in Fry's
words, "part of a campaign to frighten me into leaving France of my own
free will." Fry was then summoned to the police head of Marseilles, who told
him straightforward: "You have caused my good friend the Consul-General
of the United States much embarrassment." Assuming a more threatening
tone, he warned Fry that unless he left the country willingly, he would be
placed in forced residence in some small town, "where you can do no harm."
Why all this? Fry asked. "Because you have defended Jews and anti-Nazis
too much" ("*Parce que vous avez trop protégé des juifs et des anti-Nazis*"), the
police chief blandly replied.[15] Finally, in August 1941, Fry was arrested and
given one hour to pack. Driven to the Spanish border, he was told that his
expulsion has been ordered by the Ministry of Interior, "with the approval
of the American embassy."[16] Fry's functions were taken over by his French
aide Bénédite, who continued the rescue operation for an additional nine
months, and succeeded in evacuating nearly 300 more people by the time

of the office's closure by the authorities on June 2, 1942.

It is perhaps not too surprising that Varian Fry's activity should have greatly irritated the French, considering their policy of collaboration with Nazi Germany. However, for the United States—Fry's home country, and the proud self-vaunted "Arsenal of Democracy"—to have been a partner in the hounding and harassment of Fry, not because of any pronounced anti-American activity on his part, but simply because of his commitment to a strictly humanitarian endeavor—this, even in hindsight, is hard to swallow; it is frankly shocking.

The campaign against Fry by U.S. diplomats began soon after his arrival in France. Fry's aide, Mary Jane Gold, wrote that "the State Department through the intermediary of the Consul [in Marseilles] put spokes in our wheels whenever they could, stating that they did not wish to give help or sympathy to agitators in a friendly country. . . Some times their resistance to granting visas was tinged with antisemitism." In his post-war memoirs, Fry complained of U.S. diplomats' collusion with the French police in exerting pressure on him to leave. In truth, U.S. consul-general Hugh S. Fullerton, in Marseille, described by a fellow diplomat as "fairly pro-German" and unsympathetic to the refugees, consistently urged Fry to leave immediately or face arrest or expulsion.[17]

To illustrate the hostility of U.S. diplomats in France toward refugees, Fry recounted two episodes in which visas were denied on absurd grounds. To a Jewish man, held in Gurs internment camp, the U.S. vice-consul asked whether he would back the United States even if it acted counter to the interests of Italy and Germany. Upon the man's positive response, the vice-consul snapped: "Visa refused. We don't want anyone in the United States who is going to mix up in politics." Recalling that story in 1942, Fry noted: "Bewildered and heartbroken, the man went back to Gurs. He is still there, wondering why his answer was wrong."[18] The U.S. State Department, in a dispatch to its Vichy embassy in September 1940 regretted Fry's rescue methods, and that it "can not, repeat not, countenance [Fry's] activities," however well meaning his motives, since it evades the laws of a country "with which the United States maintains friendly relations." The State Department turned its pressure on the Emergency Rescue Committee office in New York to recall Fry since "his usefulness has ceased and . . . his continued presence was an embarrassment to everybody."

To counter this harassment by his own country's diplomats, Fry appealed directly to Cordell Hull, the U.S. Secretary of State. In a letter, dated November 10, 1940, Fry called the Secretary's attention to the plight of the refugees. "Thousands find themselves in prisons and concentration camps of Europe without hope of release because they have no government to represent them. . . Cannot U.S. and other nations of Western Hemisphere take immediate steps, such as creation new Nansen Passports [formerly used to help stateless Russian refugees] and extension of at least limited diplomatic protection to holders of them?" A week later, on November 18, he wrote again to Hull: "I wish to take the occasion to direct your attention particularly to the tragic plight of the many thousands of human beings who have lost their nationality in recent years through the action of the German government. Deprived of all hope of diplomatic or consular intervention in their behalf, hundreds of these new stateless are confined in the concentration camps of France and Spain." Attaching a report on conditions at one of the French detention camps (Argeles), Fry asked: "Is this not an occasion for the United States and the other nations of the Western Hemisphere to take extraordinary measures? Cannot the Government of the United States intervene in behalf at least of those upon whom it has seen fit to confer its visas, so that they may be released from the concentration camps, be granted French sortie visas and Spanish and Portuguese transit visas, and then be able to proceed on their way to Liberty?" Fry's two letters remained unanswered.

In January 1941, when Fry's passport expired, the consul in Marseilles refused to renew it, and his passport was confiscated. Fullerton told Fry: "My instructions are to renew it only for immediate return to the United States, and then only for a period of two weeks. So I'm afraid I'll have to keep it here until you're ready to go." Fry tried again in May to recover his passport, but with the same result. Though bereft of a passport, he still refused to leave France. The consul then informed Fry that unless he left voluntarily, the French police would arrest or expel him, adding that the Gestapo had also demanded Fry's expulsion. Ambassador Leahy, in a message to the State Department, on June 15, 1941, strongly urged Fry's immediate recall by his New York office. Secretary of State Welles replied that the request had been passed on. Trying to avoid his expulsion, Fry appealed to Alvin Johnson, of the New York based New School for Social Research, who wrote to Adolf Berle, Assistant Secretary of State, at the State Department, not to force Fry out of France, if only because he had had effected the release to the School of two professors interned by the French. "His labors are a thorn in the side of the worst pro-Nazi element elements at Vichy," Johnson added. "He is, nevertheless, apparently getting less than he has a right to expect in the way of support or aid or even tolerance from some of our foreign service officials at Vichy." Berle's response was negative. "Varian Fry has got to get home as soon he can," he wrote. "The chance of his getting anything done there is now completely finished; and I should not be surprised to find that he has been, and is now, in considerable danger of arrest."

On September 1, 1941, Fullerton informed Leahy and some friends of his relief that Fry had finally been expelled, and attributed to himself much credit in having Fry "kicked out" of France. Fullerton added that the situation in French internment camps was deteriorating but there was nothing that could be done. Helping them with supplies purchased locally was no solution, as it simply represented 'robbing Peter to pay Paul.' So much for Fullerton's concern for the hapless refugees.

After his forcible return to the United States, understandably bitter at the treatment by his own government, Fry lashed out against the State Department's immigration policy. He was, subsequently, trailed by the FBI, on orders of J. Edgar Hoover, as a subversive agent. Ignored by former friends and colleagues, overlooked by the Jewish community right up to his premature death at the age of 59, he slowly slipped into anonymity. A few months before his death, in 1967, France – the country that had expelled him in 1941 – conferred upon him the *Chevalier de Légion* honor. Long before that, in one of several wartime articles, he addressed the issue of his country's off-handed attitude toward the Nazi extermination of the Jews in Europe. In an article, entitled "The Massacre of the Jews," in the December 21, 1942 issue of *The New Republic*, Fry expressed his horror at what was happening to the Jews:

> *There are some things so horrible that decent men and women find them impossible to believe, so monstrous that the civilized world recoils incredulous before them. The recent reports of the systematic extermination of the Jews in Nazi Europe are of this order. . . President Roosevelt could and should speak out against these monstrous events. . . A joint declaration, couched in the most solemn terms, by the Allied governments, of the retribution to come might be of some avail. Tribunals should be set up now to begin to amass the facts. . . The Christian churches might also help. . . the Pope by threatening with excommunication all Catholics who in any way participate in these frightful crimes, the Protestant leaders by exhorting their fellow communicants to resist to the utmost the Nazis' fiendish designs. . . If we do any or all of these things, we should broadcast the news of them day and night to every country of Europe, in every European language. . . We have nothing to gain by 'appeasing' the anti-Semites and the murderers. We have much to gain by using the facts to create resistance and eventually rebellion. The fact that the Nazis do not commit their massacres in western Europe, but transport their victims to the East before destroying them, is certain proof that they fear the effect on the local populations of the news of their crimes. . . Finally, and it is a little thing, but at the same time a big thing, we can offer asylum now, without delay or red tape, to those few fortunate enough to escape from the Aryan paradise. There have been bureaucratic delays in visa procedure which have literally condemned to death many stalwart democrats. . . This is a chal-*

lenge which we cannot, must not, ignore.

His plea, like the Polish emissary Jan Karski, went unheeded. Unable
to come to terms with this, he became restless, and drifted from one job to
another. His marriage to Eileen broke up; he remarried and fathered three
children. Nothing seeming to work for him, as his unbound energy found
no new outlet. The sculptor Lipchitz, whom Fry had saved, once described
him as race horse hitched to a wagon-load of stone. When he died in 1967,
he was teaching Latin at a private boys' high school.

Learning of his death, in 1967, many of his beneficiaries wrote to his
widow Annette in praise of the man. Jacques Lipchitz stated "in some way
I owe him my life. I did not want to go away from France. It was his severe
and clairvoyant letters which helped me finally to do so. . . I will cherish his
memory to the end of my life." Marc Chagall stated that he will never forget
all the good Fry did during the war. Hans Sahl wrote: "He had saved my
life and brought me to this country." Referring to Fry's tragic fate, Sahl
added: "The fact that a man like him, one of the kindest men I ever met,
sensitive, of high intelligence and great talents, a man of utmost integrity
and moral courage, born to become a leading figure in American public life,
did not receive the recognition he deserved was an indictment of the same
'American Way of Life' he had opened to us when he rescued us from the
'old world.'"

Writing to this author in 1994, Miriam Davenport-Ebel (one of Fry's close
aides) pondered on the mystery of Fry's successful rescue operation, which
had aroused the ire of his own government:

*What made Varian Fry so effective? He had never done any clandestine
work. . . He had grown up in a posh New Jersey suburb, had been sent to
an 'exclusive' preparatory school, was a graduate of Harvard in Classics,
and had a modest job as an editor in New York. Such an individual would
seem to be the last person on earth to set out for a war-torn, defeated
country, armed only with a down-filled sleeping bag, an air mattress, two
letters of lukewarm recommendation, an ordinary (not diplomatic) passport, $3,000 taped to his leg, the names of 200 individuals needing to be
rescued, and a month's leave of absence from his job. Needless to say he
soon had to choose between saving people's lives and saving that job! He
lost his job. It is all too easy to forget what the climate in the USA was like
when he decided to become a risk-taking, militant anti-Nazi on foreign,
unfriendly soil. Americans of his persuasion were rare. The USA was far
from taking sides in the war. Anti-war, anti-Allied sentiment was rife. In
truth, many influential men and women still considered Hitler our last
bastion against Communism. . . Not many cared what was happening to*

the Jews; America was, for he most part, quite openly and unpleasantly anti-Semitic. . . Certainly his work was dangerous! Vichy France did not like foreigners who had the gall to disapprove of their collaboration with Nazi Germany. They could not have been expected tolerantly to overlook someone running an office devoted to helping Jews, 'degenerate' artists and poets, political opponents, trade unionists, dissident lawyers. . . Dealing in false passports, false French identity cards, false demobilization papers, and funds obtained on the black market were all crimes.

Mary Jayne Gold, in a letter to this author, in 1994, also wrote in praise of the man. "Varian Fry felt very strongly about his country's indifference to the plight of the Jews and others in their darkest hour." She added: "I feel it MUST BE SAID, namely that when the Jewish refugees in France were being treated like cattle, the United States did virtually nothing. . . there was nothing then, when something could have been done; it was only later when almost nothing could be done that the War Refugee Board was created." She then quoted from the unpublished closing words by Varian Fry from his manuscript for the book *Surrender on Demand*, words that were deleted by the publisher:

If I have any regret at all about the work we did, it is that it was so slight. In all we saved some two thousand human beings. We ought to have saved many times that number. But we did what we could. And when we failed it was all too often because of the incomprehension of the government of the United States. . . As Danny [Bénédite] said in his last report, that in the great crisis of the refugees in France, 'Little Switzerland. . . contributed more. . . than the great and wealthy North American republic, its loud acclamations about the rights of peoples and the defense of liberty notwithstanding. As an American citizen, I hope I may never have to endure the shame of hearing such words said of my country again.'

On September 7, 1941, immediately after his expulsion from France, Varian Fry wrote from Hotel España, in Barcelona, to his wife Eileen a long letter in which he tried to describe the transformation which he underwent as a result of his experience in France, which turned him into an almost new person.

I have just reached the end of the most intense twelve months I have ever lived through. . . I still don't quite know what happened to me. . . What I do know is that I have lived far more intensely in these last years, far more objectively, actively, really, if you like, than I ever have before, and that experience has changed me profoundly. . . I do not think that I shall ever be quite the same person I was when I kissed you goodbye at the airport and went down the gangplank to the waiting Clipper. For the experiences of ten, fifteen and even twenty years have been pressed into one. Sometimes I feel as if I lived a whole life. . . I have developed, or discovered within me powers of resourcefulness, of imagination and courage which I never before knew I possessed, and I have fought a fight, against enormous odds, of which, in spite of the final defeat, I think I can always be proud. . . When I look back upon this year, the thing which impresses me most is the growth I have undergone. The roots of a plant in a pot too small will eventually burst the pot. Transplanted to a larger pot and it will soon fill it. But if you transplant it to a pot altogether too large, it will 'go to root,' as gardeners say, and may even die from the shock. I was transplanted, 13 months ago, to a pot which I more than once had occasion to fear was too large; but I didn't die; in the end, I think I very nearly filled it -- not entirely, but nearly. At least I didn't die from the shock or the sense of my own inadequacy. The knowledge of that fact has given me a new quality which I think I needed: self-confidence.

From right: **Varian Fry** with artists **André Breton, André Masson,** and **Jacqueline Lamba Breton.**

When the record of the man's rescue achievement was presented before the Commission for the Designation of the Righteous, there was no doubt in anybody's mind that this first American merited being added to the list of the thousands on the honor roll of "Righteous Among the Nations." In

February 1996, U.S. Secretary of State Warren Christopher, on his way to another negotiating round in the Middle East, asked that Yad Vashem's honoring of Varian Fry take place in his presence, and that a member of the Fry family be invited, on U.S. government pay, to join him in the ceremony. On that solemn occasion, Christopher apologized on behalf of the State Department for its earlier abusive treatment of Fry and underlined the pride that the United States felt that a man of such high moral caliber was now honored as a great humanitarian under the Yad Vashem-sponsored program of "Righteous Among the Nations." A great injustice had finally been corrected — too late, undoubtedly, for the man himself, but not so to assure that his name be added to the list of mankind's great humanitarians and the lesson of his deeds be imparted to future generations.[19]

Jan Zwartendijk

One-Way Ticket to Curaçao Via Japan

As Fry launched his rescue mission in Marseilles, France, in July-August
1940, two diplomats were acting frantically to save thousands of Jews in
another corner of Europe. Many readers may be familiar with the story of
the Japanese diplomat Chiune (Sempo) Sugihara who, as consul-general in
Kaunas, Lithuania, in August 1940, issued Japanese transit visas to several
thousand Jews, making it possible for them to leave the country in time and
be saved.[20] The persons who came to plead before Sugihara, headed by
Zerach Warhaftig (years later, a minister in the Israeli government), claimed
they were on their way to the distant Dutch-controlled Carribean island of
Curaçao, for which they were assured no entry visas were required. In light
of the war situation prevailing on the European continent, the only route
to that fabled distant island was by way of the Soviet Union and Japan. The
Soviets, however, fearing the refugees would remain stranded on its territory, would not allow passage through their vast country, unless the
voyagers produced visas for travel beyond its frontiers; hence, the need for
the Japanese visas. Sugihara, after some soul-searching issued these visas,
and several thousand Jews left Lithuania in time, and were saved from the
Holocaust. In 1984, the still-living Sugihara was awarded the Righteous title,
and properly hailed as a rescuer on a grand scale. However, another important hero in this drama was overlooked — the Dutch businessman, turned
diplomat, Jan Zwartendijk.

He had arrived from prewar Holland to Lithuania, to represent the
Dutch Philips concern, which dealt with electronics. Opening an office in
Kaunas, in mid-1939, he befriended some of the few Dutch residents in the
city, including several Dutch-Jewish seminarians studying in the world-
renowned Lithuanian Talmudic schools, known as Yeshivot. As the war
clouds gathered over Europe the fall of that year, Zwartendijk busied himself
with selling the products of his company. When Germany occupied Poland,
in September 1939, launching World War Two, thousands of refugees
flooded into still-independent Lithuania. With the disappearance of the
Polish state, these refugees had become stateless persons, and were at the
whim of Lithuanian authorities who were not too happy with the addition
of Jews in their tiny country. When Germany invaded the Netherlands, on
May 10, 1940, the Dutch ambassador for the Baltic region, L.P.J. de Dekker,
who worked out of neighboring Riga, Latvia, dismissed the pro-German
Dutch consul in Kaunas, and began to search for a replacement. Learning
of Jan Zwartendijk's anti-Nazi credentials, he turned to him to fill in the post

Jewish refugees waiting for visas outside the Japanese
Legation in Kaunas, Lithuania, in August 1940.

of Dutch honorary consul-general. Zwartendijk prevaricated for several
weeks, and finally on May 14, he consented. The following day, the Soviet
Union invaded Lithuania, and for all practical purposes, the country ceased
to be independent.

The Soviets moved immediately to officially incorporate Lithuania and
its two sister Baltic states into the Soviet Union, a process that was swiftly
accomplished in the summer of that year. A week after the Soviet invasion,
on June 21, Zwartendijk cabled his superiors in Holland on the virtual
stoppage of commercial activity in the country: "the banks are closed. . . the
general mood is rather nervous. . . The coming weeks look rather somber.
What is going to happen exactly is not entirely clear yet, but I'm convinced
that there will no longer be an independent Lithuania. . . Commercially we
are finished here, whatever the further developments may be. It can only
become bad or still worse." He then waited for instructions from his head
office, in now German-occupied Holland, when to wrap up his business. He
also waited for a word from his diplomatic senior, ambassador de Dekker
in Soviet-occupied Latvia, as to the future of the Dutch consulate in Kaunas,
which Zwartendijk operated out of his business office.

While Zwartendijk was pondering his future stay in Lithuania, events
on the Jewish refugee side were unfolding in the summer of that year, which
were to engulf him in a rescue operation of great magnitude. It all began
when Pessia Lewin wrote to ambassador De Dekker for a Dutch visa to the
Dutch East Indies on her Polish passport. Although originally a Dutch
citizen, she had assumed Polish nationality in 1935, when she married the
Polish-Jewish political leader Isaac Lewin. The Dutch ambassador politely

answered her that the issuance of such visas had been terminated. Not taking no for an answer, Mrs. Lewin wrote back to de Dekker, asking for his help in some way, especially to a person who was once a Dutch citizen. De Dekker again replied evasively that he did not know how he could be of assistance, since no visas were being issued at all to the Carribean possessions of the Dutch government. To enter these colonies, the ambassador added, one had to have a permit from the local governor in Curaçao. The ambassador did not mention that such a permission was unlikely due to the militarily-important oil refinery installations on the island. The island was under the control of the Dutch government-in-exile, based in London, which vowed to continue the war against Germany, side by side with England, in spite of the loss of its homeland. Attempting one more time, Mrs. Lewin asked whether the ambassador would agree to mention on her Polish passport the first part of his statement, namely that no visa was required for entrance to Curaçao, and leave out the second part on the need of a special permit by the island governor, as she had no intention, anyway, to visit that area, but was simply looking for a way to leave war-torn Europe, and for this purpose needed a final-destination visa. De Dekker instructed her to send him her passport, which was returned with the ambassador's handwritten statement: "The Dutch Royal Legation in Riga hereby declares that no visa is required for entrance by foreigners to Surinam, Curaçao and the other Dutch possessions in America. Riga, July 11, 1940." This later became known as the "Curaçao visa." When, on July 22, Mrs. Lewin showed this handwritten visa to Zwartendijk, he agreed to copy the same wording on her husband's passport. Four days later, both applied to Sugihara for a Japanese transit visit.

While Mrs. Lewin was prodding the Dutch ambassador in Riga for a visa to one of the Dutch colonies, another person, unbeknownst to her, had the same idea in mind. Nathan Gutwirth was a 23-year-old student at the Telshe Talmudic Yeshiva, and a Dutch citizen. As such, he was told by Zwartendijk that he needed no visa to travel to a Dutch-controlled territory. Gutwirth, nevertheless insisted that a final-destination, or "end-visa," be appended on his passport, to avoid bureaucratic red-tape by overzealous passport control officers while en route to these distant islands. When Zwartendijk was shown De Dekker's statement on Mrs. Lewin's passport, he saw no reason not to oblige Gutwirth with a similar one, and on July 23, a day after Zwartendijk had appended the "Curaçao visa" statement on Mr. Lewin's passport, he did likewise on Gutwirth's Dutch passport.

Gutwirth then spread the word of the Curaçao scheme among his fellow students, and word soon reached Dr. Zerach Warhaftig — a Polish refugee and Zionist leader, who was frantically searching for ways to spirit Polish-Jewish refugees out of the country and the European continent, for fear of either being engulfed in a war that many feared would break out between Nazi Germany and the Soviet Union, or alternatively be exiled by the Soviets for hard labor in Siberia. The "Curaçao visa" seemed an ideal scheme to avoid either of these two possibilities. Warhaftig then inquired with Gutwirth whether Zwartendijk would be willing to issue Curaçao visas to more people; to anyone, indeed, who requested it. Without asking permission from his superior in Riga, who had only issued a few such visas, Zwartendijk promptly told Gutwirth that he would issue Curaçao visas to anyone demanding it, no questions asked. He, moreover, urged Gutwirth to hurry, since the Soviets (who bore a special grudge against the Dutch government for never having granted diplomatic recognition to the Communist regime in Russia) had ordered Zwartendijk to close his dual-purpose office within days. To drive their message home, the new masters of Lithuania pinned a large portrait of Stalin on Zwartendijk's office display window.

Gutwirth returned with Zwartendijk's positive response to Warhaftig, who hurriedly spread the word among the refugee community, urging all to take advance of this unique opportunity to leave the country in time. Many turned a deaf ear, not believing that one could find succor by heading via the whole breadth of the Soviet Union, then pass Japan, a country on the brink of war, and continue across the Pacific to an unknown island. But there were enough persons who grabbed this chance—more than enough for Zwartendijk to handle, in the little time left to him before closing shop in Lithuania. During an intense four-day period, from July 24 through the 27th, the former Philips electronics salesman, turned temporary diplomat, issued over 1,300 such visas. He continued in the same tempo, in the following days, until he had issued a total of 2,200 Curaçao visas by the August 1, two days ahead of the August 3 deadline for winding up his operation. Two office aides helped him with the stamping of the visas.

In the meantime, the persons with the Curaçao visa, headed directly to the Japanese consulate. There, Sugihara who had already agreed to issue Japanese transit visas to everyone with a Curaçao end-visa, could not keep up with Zwartendijk's work. To begin with, because of the calligraphy, the Japanese visa took longer to append than the Dutch one. To overcome this hurdle, Sugihara was helped by several Yeshiva students who prepared a rubber seal with the Japanese inscription, and stamped the visas of the impatient persons waiting in line outside the Japanese consulate. The Russian deadline for Sugihara's closing of his office, as well as all other accredited diplomats in Kaunas, was August 31, which gave him a bit more latitude than that afforded to Zwartendijk.

On August 3, 1940, Zwartendijk shut his office and moved his family outside the city, to await permission from the Soviet authorities to allow his family (wife and three children) to return to German-occupied Netherlands.

Permission was finally received in mid-September 1940, and Zwartendijk returned to his homeland, and to a new assignment with the Philips company.[21] Throughout the German occupation of Holland, he was worried about the possible fallback of his action in Kaunas on his safety. The Curaçao visa scheme had become public knowledge in a city teeming with Gestapo agents (Sugihara's chief aide, Wolfgang Gudze, turned out to be a Gestapo spy). On one occasion, the threat of arrest seemed a frightening reality, when Gestapo agents showed up to question Zwartendijk. It turned out that their object was someone else, who had been shot trying to elude the Gestapo, and Zwartendijk's name was found in his coat. The Gestapo did not question Zwartendijk on his large-scale rescue operation of Jews in Lithuania.

After the war, Jan Zwartendijk declined any mention of this episode. In 1976, through the mediation of Ernest Heppner, a leader in the Jewish community in Indianapolis, contact was made with the Holocaust historian David Kranzler. Zwartendijk was then afflicted with terminal cancer, and he died that same year. Before dying, he was told by Kranzler that he had saved an entire Talmudic seminary, that among those saved was Zerach Warhaftig, at the time a minister in the Israeli government. In the 1990's an ever-increasing information on the crucial role of Zwartendijk in the Curaçao rescue scheme began to flow to Yad Vashem, and an intensive examination of all the available documentation was undertaken. From the U.S. side, Professor Kranzler kept pressing the point of doing justice to the memory of the late Zwartendijk. In Jerusalem, the children the Jan Zwartendijk were feted by the Mirer Yeshiva, whose hundreds of Talmudic students constituted the single largest group of seminarians saved by him. Finally, in 1998, Yad Vashem officially accepted Jan Zwartendijk into the ranks of the Righteous Among the Nations.

Zwartendijk's unique role also has to be measured in light of the behavior of the U.S. consulate in Lithuania. Its consuls in Kaunas, adhering to the hard-line State Department anti-refugee policy, repeatedly turned a deaf ear to pleas for American visas. On top of requiring from petitioners to produce sponsors in the USA, the consulate added an additional burdensome requirement: a "moral certificate" from the local police that the petitioner was of good character. The people who needed visas—mostly stranded refugees from German-conquered Poland—could only with the greatest difficulties, including bribes to the police, produce such certificates. On August 17, 1940, as the U.S. consulate was closing its doors, vice-consul Bernard Guffler satisfactorily cabled to Washington that U.S. visas "are useless to 99% of the applicants despite the demand for them since few can obtain proper travel documents and few can obtain exit visas or arrange transportation."[22] At the same time, when U.S. diplomats were seeking excuses to deny visas to refugee Jews in Lithuania, a lone diplomat of a de-

Left: Jan Zwartendijk. Right: Edith Jes-Zwartendijk, daughter of Jan Zwartendijk, on a visit to Yad Vashem in front of her father's name, with her son (left) and with Dr. Paldiel.

feated country, and facing an uncertain future, threw caution to the wind, and issued over 2,000 visas to needy Jewish persons, so as to rescue them from a terrible fate.

Writing about his father in 1996, Zwartendijk's son, also named Jan, who was with him during the Kaunas visa episode, explains that his father "appears to have launched into this eight-day flurry of action on his own, in spontaneous reaction to an overwhelming need. It required an immediate decision and immediate action." To the end of his life, he remained opposed to any honors. All he wanted to know was: "How many made it eventually along this 'Curaçao route'?" He was told that all succeeded in eluding the Holocaust, although none reached the island of Curaçao. But reaching this distant island had never been the original intention of the refugees, nor of Zwartendijk, who together with the Japanese diplomat Sugihara were instrumental in saving several thousand Jewish lives — in the nick of time! Zwartendijk's role in this rescue operation was finally recognized, a moral debt requited, and a lesson drawn on moral rectitude by public servants.[23]

Chapter 4

Sheltering and Hiding

I n 1942 and until the war's end three years later, throughout German-occupied Europe, Jews were the most endangered species on earth. For in January of that year, the Nazi leadership, in the infamous Wannsee conference, had decided to "comb" all of Europe for Jews, in order to murder them. Facing a well-oiled and efficient killing machine (men in uniform, bureaucrats, train operators and informers), to stay alive Jews desperately needed to get out of sight, in order to avoid being "combed" out. This meant going into hiding — that is, literally disappearing from the face of the earth, while still being there, and being cared by non-Jewish benefactors. Most of those fortunate to be admitted into a non-Jewish household (some were betrayed and killed), survived to tell of their ordeal during that terrible period, and of their rescue thanks to the beneficent help of non-Jews — as in the following few selected stories.

Jan and Anna Puchalski

Mathematical Schooling in an Underground Shelter

Friday, February 12, 1943, seemed another day of forced labor for the Germans, as 15-year-old Felix Zandman made his way from the Grodno Ghetto to his work assignment outside the ghetto's perimeter. Suddenly an order came for everyone to immediately return to the ghetto. It meant only one thing—another German violent "action" was under way. "As soon as I heard that, I started walking," Felix reminisces in his memoirs, but he at first had no idea where to head. His mind quickly turned to the Polish lady who a few hours earlier had sold him vodka. "My husband would kill me," she responded. Felix pleaded with her, but to no avail.[1] Felix knew that he must not return to the ghetto, but where to go? Instinctively, he removed the identifying Yellow Star patches from his jacket, and decided to head for the home of the former nanny of his uncle's family. She allowed him to hide in the stable, but just for that evening. "If anybody finds you, I didn't have anything to do with it," she added in a scared voice. That night, Felix couched closely to the lone cow in the barn to keep himself warm. In the morning, the nanny brought him some hot porridge. He then decided to head to Losossno. Carefully measuring his steps, and watchful not to be noticed by strangers, he suddenly recalled the summer months he spent in Losossno, where his family owned vacation cottages, and the caretaker couples—Jan and Anna Puchalski, but especially Anna. She was a strong-willed and determined woman, and displayed a special affectionate relationship toward Felix. "She would give me a kiss when she saw me and hold my hand when we went out." Somehow, she reminded him of his own grandmother, Tema, left behind in the Grodno Ghetto, who on this fateful day seemed to be doomed to oblivion.

The previous one and a half years since the German occupation of Grodno (previously in Poland, and today in Belarus) in June 1941 had seen one execution raid after the other on the city's 30,000 Jews. Confined in a narrow ghetto, the Germans gradually diminished what had once been a vibrant community, until its full extermination in March 1943. In one previous "action," thousands were led, accompanied with volleys of machine gun fire, and with whipping and clubbing, toward the nearby Kielbasin labor camp. Conditions there were below any acceptable standards: without heat, minimal nutrition and hygienic conditions. Many died of dysentery; others were shot, beaten to death or hanged. Felix had managed to escape and return to the ghetto, where he was momentarily reunited with his family.

In January 1943, another German action claimed 10,000 more victims — sent to die in the Treblinka and Auschwitz death camps. There were now only 7,000 Jews left. Felix watched helplessly as his father and mother, Aaron and Genia, and grandmother Tema succumbed to despondency and indifference to their ultimate fate. Grandmother Tema, once a tower of strength, had resigned herself for the worst. "She was waiting for death to come to take her."[2]

As he furtively made his way to Losossno, the memory of his loved ones hauntingly raced through his mind, but Felix was resolved to make a last-ditch effort to keep alive the memory of his lost family, by staying alive himself, through perhaps joining up with the partisans known to be operating in the vicinity. The problem was how to reach them in the forest depths and in below-zero temperature. The Losossno cottages seemed to him an ideal solution, as a relay station. Earlier, during the January "action," a relative of Felix had sought temporary shelter in one of the cottages there, and reported on the magnanimity of the Puchalskis who had cared for her. Would she be equally kind to him, Felix wondered and remembered the days when she showered him with motherly affection?

When Felix knocked on the Puchalski door, he was greeted by a broadly lit and surprised face of Anna. "Then she took me in her arms and kissed me." In a hesitating voice, Felix asked whether he could stay just for one night; for the next morning he would be on his way to the partisans. "You'll go nowhere," Anna peremptorily responded. She added that no one knew exactly where the partisans were to be found; besides, they could be violently antisemitic, and would kill a Jew on sight. "God sent you to me as a gift," she intoned in a prayerful voice. Later that evening, Anna elaborated on that point with a story of bygone years, when she was pregnant with her second daughter Sabina. One evening, her husband had come home drunk, and a row erupted which ended with Anna on the street. She had nowhere to go, so she went to Felix's grandmother, Tema, in Grodno, and was admitted. Tema also arranged for Anna to give birth in Grodno's Jewish hospital. "So you see," Anna concluded, staring into Felix's eyes, "I prayed that one day I could repay that, and here you are, God sent you. I will not let you perish, Felix. If you perish, we will all perish together. . . You do not go anyplace."[3] That evening, five more people showed up — escapees from that day's Nazi deadly raid on the Ghetto's remaining Jews; among them: uncle Sender Freydowicz, who had made his escape with bullets whizzing in his direction; Mottel and wife Goldie Bass, and two more Jewish fugitives. The Puchalski household now counted 13 persons: Jan & Anna and their five children, and the six fugitive Jews.

At first, the six were hidden in a cellar where potatoes were usually stored. Then, with the help of the Puchalski household, a shaft was dug under one of the two Puchalski bedrooms, with the three elder girls (Sabina, Irena, Krystyna) keeping watch outside. The hole was about 1.5 meters in width and length, and one meter in height. The entrance was through a narrow opening beneath the Puchalskis' bed, which would then be closed with a wooden trap. "To me it looked like a grave," Felix recalls. An air pipe was dug out leading to the garden with the opening covered with some bushes. For added security, Jan Puchalski moved the doghouse to that corner of the house, in the hope that the dog's barking would give sufficient advance warning of any approaching strangers. When the hole was finished, the six runaway fugitives climbed down but soon realized that the hole was too small to contain them all. With hardly any fresh air to breathe, the fear of death by suffocation prompted two of the hiders to leave and seek succor elsewhere. There were now four persons: Felix, uncle Sender, and the couple Bass.

In the hiding place, no outside light penetrated. "Like some nocturnal creature, I began to get used to living in dark," Felix recalls. In addition, one had to keep quiet during the hours of activity in the house, for fear that the two Puchalski smaller children (aged three and one) would discover their presence and unintentionally give them away. To reduce discomfort, it was decided to rotate positions every several hours, with three lying down, and one sitting on the toilet bucket. The Basses had some money, which helped the Puchalskis with their additional expenses, as their only earnings were derived from Jan's poorly-paid work in a tobacco factory. An additional rule, imposed by Sender, was for the recently married Basses to indulge in no sex, to avoid complications, with four bodies pressed to each other. There was to be total abstinence and almost total silence in that gravelike hole for as long as it may take—in fact, for the 17 months that the four stayed there. Anna would bring food once or twice a day, and remove the bucket. She would also occasionally come with news from the outside—sometimes sad ones, such as the talk of neighbors of rescuers murdering the Jewish people they were hiding, to lay their hands on the gold and fur coats which the Jewish fugitives had brought with them. Totally cut off from the outside world, the only companions were worms and fleas, which caused all to itch and scratch. Over time, Felix developed an expertise how to catch the fleas and kill them, by licking one's finger with saliva, which would then act as glue, and make it easier to catch a flea. When Anna tapped on the floor, it was a signal that Germans were approaching. On such occasions, no one moved a muscle. Outside, the dog could be heard barking.

Inside the dark hole, each of the hiders was enveloped in his private thoughts, shattered as the four were by the tragic events of the days. "We were absorbed in pain," Felix writes, of the losses among their loved ones. They naturally wondered whether they themselves would share the same fate or hopefully survive. "Each knock on the front door, each strange sound in the house, each bark from the yard could mean an informant, or the Germans."[4] Uncle Sender, who had suffered the loss of a wife and two children, presently assumed a paternal attitude toward the orphaned Felix. Since evoking recent events was too painful, it seemed best to choose a totally neutral subject; one that needed one's full mental concentration and was at the same time totally removed from any subjective feelings—such as mathematics. Crouching in the dark hole, Sender began by questioning Felix: "A triangle has three sides; do you know Felix what a right angle is?" This gave way to giving names to the three angles: alpha, beta and gamma. Sender continued: "the tangent is the ratio of the first side to the second side." This was followed with more difficult math questions, such as equations of the second degree. If AX squared plus BX plus C equals 0—find X1 and X2. The answers to this and other difficult theorems had to be worked out mentally—no textbooks, scrap paper and writing tools. With Mottel Bass, a lawyer by profession, Felix trained on remembering important historical dates and geography. These mental exercises, especially in math, developed in an underground hole and in almost total darkness (occasionally they were allowed the use of an oil lamp), were to prove handy to Felix after liberation.

In the meantime, with the Germans in constant retreat before the Russians, the front moved to the Puchalski household, with German soldiers putting up positions around the house, and actually settling in the house. The Puchalskis saw themselves evicted from the house. Left to themselves, the four hidden persons were able to slip out at night, and wander for several days, feeding on the tall corn stalks in the fields (it was July 1944), and occasionally running into Germans soldiers, before whom they presented themselves as refugees fleeing from the Russians; this, until they caught up with the advancing Russians, on July 24.

With everything around them constantly reminding them of the terrible losses of their loved ones, coupled with the antisemitic climate in post-war Poland, Felix and Sender decided to move westward, and settled in France. With his mathematical skills sharpened while in hiding, Felix had no trouble catching up with his schooling and was admitted into one of France's most prestigious engineering schools where he earned a diploma in engineering. He then enrolled in the University of Paris (Sorbonne), where he earned a doctorate in physics. During his research for the doctorate he developed a new optical method of stress measurements, very useful for airplane design and testing. After receiving his doctorate he worked in a French jet airplane factory and lectured at the French Academy of Aeronautics. This new stress analysis method developed by him earned him many patents and worldwide recognition. In 1956 he was brought to the United States to continue his work in that field. In 1961 Felix came up with an idea of making an electronic resistor that would be virtually insensitive to temperature changes.

The time had come to set up his own business, so as to manufacture the new product, and in 1962 the Vishay company was created, in Malvern, Pennsylvania, as a partnership. Felix chose this name from the town where his beloved grandmother Tema was born. "I had always heard Tema talk about Vishay," Felix later wrote, "what life had been like there, how she and her brothers and sisters had grown up there. . . It gave me the feeling of my family's origins.[5] Sales of the Vishay resistor took off, and in the following years, the company expanded its activities by acquiring and buying out other companies in the United States and overseas. A major purchase was Dale Electronics, in 1985, at the time the largest wire-wound resistor maker in the world, which was bought for the price of $94 million. After acquiring more companies, by 1987 Vishay had gone from $55 million to $400 million in annual sales, and it owned companies in England, Germany, France, Mexico, in addition to the USA and Israel. Then came further acquisitions, increasing the annual sales to one billion dollars. In 1993 Vishay became a Fortune 500 company. Recent acquisitions include Telefunken of Germany, and Siliconix in the Silicon Valley, increasing current annual revenues to 2 billion dollars. Through all this, taking on life with a vengeance, after surviving the Holocaust, Zandman "had become more aggressive, more eager to search out opportunities and grasp them."[6]

With each business success, it seemed that the memory of the Holocaust would recede into the background or would even be totally repressed in the unconscious mind. But this was not the case. The frightful memories of the Holocaust years kept haunting him, making it hard for Felix to come to terms with this harrowing past. "I am a person who should have been dead in 1943," he wrote in his autobiography. "Four or five times I escaped death by a hair's breath — why me rather than the twenty-nine thousand Grodno Jews who did not escape, I cannot begin to say" — words understandably written with much pain. "I just could not open up — not to a friend," nor anyone else. "When I tried, I felt tremors. I would begin to tremble inside."[7] With the help of his wife Ruta, he was nevertheless able to open up, but this did not come easily. "When I woke up screaming at night, she listened to my dreams." The pain didn't fade, but he could now try to slowly come to terms with what he terms his "demons." While still under the impress of these demonic images, visiting the Yad Vashem memorial, in Jerusalem, was out of the question. "The very thought of it made me shake." With Ruta's encouragement, he made one such effort, but as he approached the memorial entrance, he was suddenly gripped with terrible pains in his chest. "I had the old sensation of not being able to breathe." With his wife and eldest daughter on his side, he quickly made his way back to his car. At the same time, Felix was deeply conscious of the need to acquit himself of the moral

obligation toward his rescuers, Jan and Anna Puchalski, through their
honoring by Yad Vashem, and this fact is what perhaps eventually made
it possible for him to come to grips with his past and visit the Yad Vashem
premises.

In 1986, his testimony, as well as several of the other rescued
persons,was received at Yad Vashem, which made possible the awarding
of the Righteous title to the Puchalskis in June 1986. A year later, on June

The Puchalski children kneeling to recite a prayer in the Hall of Remembrance at Yad Vashem in front of the Eternal Flame.

14, 1987, in a ceremony attending by Felix and Ruta, the children of the
already departed Puchalski parents planted a tree in the Garden of the
Righteous at Yad Vashem. This was preceded with the rekindling of the
Eternal Flame in the Hall of Commemoration. There, the Puchalski children
sank to their knees in front of the slab covering the ashes of seven concentration camps, and silently recited the Lord's Prayer in Polish. Since then,
Zandman's linkage to Yad Vashem has grown: the sponsoring of a study
of four lost Jewish communities in the Grodno region,[8] as well as a major
contribution to create a site, astride a path visited by students and researchers, dedicated to the memory of the Jewish family of the Holocaust period.

Zandman's visit to Yad Vashem was preceded by a long-term interest in Israel, a country he once aspired to live in, and which he considers his second, or rather first, home. In many of the previously mentioned business purchases, one of the objectives was to transfer some of the production lines of the new acquisitions to Israel, to meet a double challenge: the idealistic one of helping Israel by creating jobs for new immigrants, and the practical one, of utilizing the higher profits from his Israel plants (due to special taxation breaks) to pay back debts incurred in these purchases elsewhere. His commitment to Israel's cause went so far as to help the military with devising a special thermal sleeve on the cannon of the new heavy tank, Merkava, to offset the heating effect caused by extensive firing and the accompanying decrease in the firing accuracy. This new invention allowed for the temperature differences to equalize and the heat to dissipate, and thereby cut down the inaccuracy from 3 meters to a mere 20 centimeters — for a firing distance of 1 km.

Felix Zandman with the author, while visiting Yad Vashem, next to the olive tree bearing the Puchalski name.

For Felix, Israel soon became a vicarious new home, replacing the intimate atmosphere of a lost home in Grodno. "Every time I went there I felt I was going home," he candidly admits. Finally, in March 1994, Felix cemented this special attachment by formally becoming an Israeli citizen. While deeply appreciative to France and the United States for the opportunity of a new life characterized by freedom, education and business opportunities, Felix considers himself an Israeli at heart. "I was Israeli before there was an Israel. Israel was in my heart's birth." While his business obligations make it necessary for him to spend most of his time in the United States, for him, only Israel gives him the feeling of being "at home. . . completely free, completely welcome." He likens his frequent visits to Israel (where two of his children live) to "going back to the womb of my mother."[9] This may be psychologically viewed as recurring attempts to recapture the intimate atmosphere of a closely-knit family in distant Grodno, shattered and forever lost during the earthquake which was the Holocaust. His commitment to the remembrance of the Holocaust has led him to insist that all his plant managers, mostly non-Jewish, visit Yad Vashem, in Jerusalem, in order to acquaint themselves with a terrible historical deed which one dared not to forget. While on this visit, the business executives are also led to the growing olive tree in the name of Jan & Anna Puchalski — an equal reminder of the strength of the human spirit, exemplified by this couple and their children, who braved risks to themselves and hid four persons in an underground shaft for 17 long months.

Jonas Paulavicius

A Lithuanian Carpenter's Determination to Save Many Lives

On July 5, 1984, a group of Jews gathered at Yad Vashem to pay respect to their rescuer's memory, after he, his wife and two children were declared "Righteous Among the Nations." At the tree planting, David Rubin bewailed his benefactor's tragic death:

> *Jonas, dearest of all men... You lived and grew up among the Lithuanian people, many of whose sons participated in the murder of our people, and most of whom remained indifferent to our fate... We promise to keep in our hearts forever your memory, and teach our children to cherish your memory with love and respect. You knew much suffering in your life. You lost your sole daughter whom you loved much. At the end, evil hands put an end to your life. I was not there when the murderous hand was lifted on you; my ears did not hear your pain's cries. My heart is broken from much pain... Allow us to recall the admiration of your rescued persons. May your soul be eternally alive.*

August 10, 1944 proved to be a fateful day for Miriam Krakinowski. She had until then survived the deprivations of the Kaunas (also known as "Kovno") Ghetto, in Lithuania, and several Nazi labor camps. As the Russians advanced closer to Lithuania, the Germans began evacuating remaining Jewish forced laborers toward the German border. In the Kaunas area, a bridge spanning the Niemen river, had to be crossed. As the column of Jews, including Miriam, made its way across the crowded bridge, with pedestrians and German troops moving in opposite directions, a man from the labor group decided to make a run for freedom, and jumped over the railing into the river. During the melee on the bridge, caused by the startled German guards who began shooting in the direction of the man in the water, Miriam suddenly felt herself jerked aside by an unknown Jewish laborer. Before she was noticed by a German guard, she had managed to quickly rid herself of the identifying Jewish star on her dress. A German sentry, mistaking her for a non-Jewish woman, pushed her aside and down toward the river embankment. Miriam stumbled, picked herself up and started to walk. She was free, alone, and not knowing where to go. What follows is best recounted in her 1983 testimony:

I kept walking along the river when I saw a man in a boat with a sack of flour. He called to me in Lithuanian, and I answered his greeting. He asked me if I saw what happened on the bridge, and I told him that I didn't know. I kept walking. A few minutes later, I heard the man's voice again behind me. I turned around and asked him why he was following me in his boat. He said that he felt I needed help. I firmly answered that I was in no need of any help and to please stop following me. The man told me. . . that the Germans were checking everyone's personal documents and I would be caught by them. I told him that I didn't have any money or jewelry to give him and asked him why he wanted to save me. The man asked me to trust him. I didn't really trust him, but I had no place to go.

At a loss what else to do, Miriam decided to follow this strange person to his home. Before entering, he told her that since he had a guest at home, she should tell him she had fled from Prenai, a city engulfed in the recent fighting. He led her down a cellar and told her to wait. "I was sure he went to bring the German police to arrest me. I considered running away, but I was too frightened and exhausted. I just sat and waited." The man returned and asked Miriam to join him with his family and guests at the dinner table. However, overwhelmed with tension and fear, she could not partake of the food and excused herself. The man led her upstairs and told her to lie down and rest. Returning later, he motioned her back to the cellar. Taking a broom, he swept the wood shavings on the floor and gave several knocks. As a small door was being pushed up from the inside, the man told her to step down into the dark hole. Gradually, a glimmer of light made visible the space below. It was a room filled with people. In her moving testimony, Miriam recalls how "I found myself in a very small, hot room filled with half-naked Jews. I began to cry as they asked questions about the fate of the [Kaunas] ghetto."

Miriam's, and the other Jews' rescuer was Jonas Paulavicius. In that dank hole, he was sheltering seven adult Jews, and a four-year-old Jewish child. Every morning, he would bring the group coffee and freshly baked bread. Occasionally, he would allow them to go upstairs to the house to wash themselves. Eventually, two more Jews, whom Jonas found wandering aimlessly, were added. When the Russians liberated that area in the latter part of August 1944, twelve Jews, two Russian POWs and two Lithuanians emerged from their separate hiding places. Who was that strange man who had committed himself to saving so many Jews?

Jonas Paulavicius was born in 1898, the third of six children of a poor farmer's family. After a few grades of elementary school, at age of 14, he began working in upholstery, in which he quickly gained expertise. Physically robust and strong, he was also known as a loner, and did not mix socially. After Lithuania gained its independence, at the end of the First World War, Jonas acquired a plot of land in Panemune, near Kaunas, on the Niemen river. He built a two-story frame house with his own hands. To sustain his family, which included his wife Antonina, daughter Danute and son Kestutis, Jonas worked as a carpenter with the Lithuanian railways. Before the current war, he had leaned toward communism, although he never formally joined the party. For the first three years of the German occupation of his country, which began in June 1941, Jonas kept to himself, when suddenly in 1944 he was catapulted into a large-scale rescue operation. It began when a friend approached him with a request to save a Jewish child from the nearby Kaunas Ghetto.

Yitzhak and his wife Lena Shames were desperate. Their four-year-old son had survived the Nazi raid of Jewish children inside the ghetto, infamously dubbed the "Children Action" of March 1944. Shames wished to save his son at any price, and turned to a non-Jewish friend, living outside the ghetto, with whom he had left some valuables for safekeeping. The man, however, fearing for his life if discovered sheltering a Jewish child, declined his help. At the same time, touched by Yitzhak's terrible plight, this man turned to his friend, Jonas Paulavicius, who after consulting with his wife agreed to admit the boy. During the first several months of the child's stay in his home, Jonas would steal up to Lena's workplace with news on the child's care. Soon, the boy's weeping, and his constant drawing near the window, where he could be observed from the outside, made it imperative that he be under constant watch and care. Since it was out of the question to return the child to the ghetto, a move which would certainly have doomed him, Jonas resolved that it was best to invite the mother and father to join their son. With Lena insisting that her aged mother also not be left behind, there were now a total of four people sheltered in the Paulavicius household. To accommodate them, Jonas decided to build a shelter under his home's cellar. Then, for some strange and unexplainable reason, the thought came to him that since he had committed himself to save four Jews—why not more? If more, why not include the educated and professionals; that is, persons such as doctors, engineers and intellectuals who would be required after the war to help restore a viable Jewish community? His mind made up, he told the surprised Yitzhak Shames to find for him suitable candidates.

Yitzhak immediately thought of his two physician friends, Drs. Chaim and Tania Ipp. When Chaim heard about a strange Lithuanian who wished to save Jews, not known to him, simply for reasons of principle, he suspected a trap. "My husband could not imagine that a Lithuanian would do it only for the sake of saving a Jew," Tania recalls; "but Jonas proved himself to be an outstanding man, a man that one seldom meets in life—an honest man, a man with integrity." Earlier, the two Ipps decided in desperation to commit suicide by cyanide injection. Discovered by a fellow doctor in the ghetto makeshift dispensary, who opened the door to the toilet, he had stopped them, right on time! The two now reasoned that their lives were spared for some reason — perhaps to be saved by this unknown Lithuanian. So the two physicians agreed to take up Jonas's charitable offer, and both escaped from the ghetto in April 1944.

In the meantime, Jonas had set himself to work on the underground bunker. Together with his son Kestutis, they removed large quantities of soil, which they collected at night in sacks, and either spread them out at some distance from their isolated home or, on the pretext of leaving for night fishing, took the soil with them in their boat, and dumped it the middle of the Niemen river. Inside the excavated hole, built in the form of a train wagon, Jonas fenced up the walls with boards from his carpentry, arranged double bunks, a table in the middle, a night pot behind a partition for the hiders' biological needs, a map with lines showing the approximate positions on the front, a radio with earphones, and a narrow opening, leading to the vegetable garden, to allow for fresh air to penetrate. The hiding place measured 8.5 square meters. When all was done and ready, the four Shameses and two Ipps moved in. At this point, Jonas decided there was room for additional persons in that narrow space. So he took up Shames' advice to add the latter's cousin, the engineer Gershenman, his wife Musia, and her mother. When Musia met Jonas for the first time outside the ghetto perimeter to be led to his home, a distance of 15 kilometers, she was afraid she would be stopped on the way, in light of her pronounced Jewish looks. Jonas told her that when crossing the city, she should follow him at a certain distance. In the event she should be stopped, he would continue, for there was no point for him also to be arrested, when he had to care for six persons who depended on him. Luckily for both, it all went without a hitch. There were now eight people in the Paulavicius hideout.

Jonas would spend as much time as possible with his wards at night. As a precautionary measure, he rented a room for his daughter Danute in Kaunas, so that in the event of the hideout's disclosure, at least one member of the rescuer family would be spared the dire penalty awaiting them at the hands of the Germans and their Lithuanian collaborators. To feed that many people — buying locally was out of the question, for the fear of arousing suspicion by curious shoppers as to the large quantities of food needed by a family of only three persons (with one daughter not on family premises). Instead, Jonas somehow acquired second-hand military coats, which he sold on the black market. The return he handed over to Antosia who purchased flour at several distant locations, with which she baked bread for the hidden people. Inside the bunker, the heat became unbearable, especially during the summer months of 1944. The persons even decided to forego using the electricity which Jonas had installed, in order not to consume the little oxygen in the hole. The suffocating heat forced the people to dress down to their underwear. In Musia's words: "We did not stop sweating, and we sat half-naked." Then in August 1944, Miriam Krakinowski was added to the group, for a total of nine persons. When Jonas joyfully announced that the Russians had liberated the area, the hiding people quietly slipped out of the hole, which had served as their home for five months, to be met by stupefied Russian soldiers. "When they saw us exiting through the narrow opening, dirty, half-naked, deathly pale, disheveled, and very thin, they withdrew and stood at a distance from us," Musia recalls. "They were shocked by the sight in front of them, and stood open-mouthed." But they were at last free, and they were happy. As they approached the Paulavicius house for a festive dinner celebration, they were surprised to meet three more Jews saved by Jonas, who were hidden elsewhere, inside and near his house, as well as two Russian POWs and two Lithuanians sought by the Germans — for a total of 16 persons saved, of whom 12 were Jews.

Johanan Fein was one of Jonas's additional wards. His story is of particular interest. Born in 1929, together with his parents, a grandmother, a brother and two sisters he was herded into the Kaunas Ghetto. His brother Zevi was killed during a Nazi raid, in October 1941, which decimated 10,000 of the ghetto's 30,000 inhabitants. More executions followed in the succeeding months, and in February 1942, after his parents were deported, Johanan

Jonas and Antonina Paulavicius in a prewar photograph.

was left with his sister Judith (another sister had managed to flee to the Soviet Union). With little to occupy his attention, he practiced his violin, an instrument he had become fond of before the war. His violin playing brought him to the attention of Jonas Paulavicius, not directly, but through his son, and this brings us to Kestutis.

Kestutis, who was a classmate of Johanan in the prewar period, remembered Johanan's violin performances, and asked his father to include the aspiring violinist among the professionals that he wished to save. Jonas agreed, and made arrangements for a person to contact Johanan in the ghetto, through his sister Judith, whose forced labor assignments took her outside the ghetto perimeter. When news of this reached his sister, at first she refused to believe it. It was a time when double-crossing and betraying fleeing Jews to the Nazis was a widespread sport. The idea that a man, unknown to the Feins, would want to save the youthful Johanan, simply because he was a violin *wunderkind*, with all the attendant risks to the rescuer, did not make sense. In Johanan's words: "It sounded so absurd, and a bit funny, that he begged to be able to save me, and without asking anything in return." But Jonas persisted, as an excuse, that he was also interested in the boy in order for him to teach his son the violin, and had for this purpose acquired a violin. Jonas continued to prod Johanan's sister, appearing at her place of work, and urging her to let her brother go. In the meantime, the bell kept tolling louder for the last Jews of the ghetto.

On March 27, 1944, the infamous "Children's Action" took place, claiming the lives of the ghetto's remaining children. Johanan witnessed children being tossed on buses as though they were lifeless objects. After this action, remaining Jewish children were outside the pale of the law, and every armed man was permitted to shoot them on sight. Judith decided that there was nothing to gain and everything to lose in waiting longer, and she accepted Jonas' bidding. On April 2, Johanan sneaked out of the ghetto, and met Kestutis at a prearranged place. Arriving at his home, he was treated to a hearty meal. Afterwards, Jonas asked Johanan to play a tune on the violin, in the presence of his family. "I played the tune 'Dear Lithuania, beautiful homeland,' a sad and sentimental song." All wept with emotion. Johanan was then ushered in an upper-floor room, where meals were brought to him and his bodily wastes removed. Kestutis, who was two years older, spent most of the time with Johanan, who taught him chess. In the isolation of the upstairs room, Johanan was unaware that eight people were hiding in a shaft under the building's cellar.

One day, a German soldier wishing to catch as many fish as possible with one shot, threw a grenade in the nearby river, but the grenade exploded in his hands. The man was rushed to the Paulavicius home, and a host of German army personnel sped in and out. After this and another incident, where the risk of Johanan's detection was miraculously overcome, Johanan was moved to a hiding place in the field adjacent to the house, in one of the underground niches used for storing tomatoes and potatoes. In one of these holes, Jonas added David Rubin, another fugitive Jew, as well as two Russian POW escapees. In the meantime, Jonas tried to induce Judith to join his brother, but she demurred. When the Russians liberated the area, Johanan was surprised to meet the nine Jewish persons hidden underneath the cellar.

After the war, the rescued Jews stayed in close touch with their benefactor, until they left Lithuania, in 1946. They later learned that Jonas was assassinated by a fellow Lithuanian who, goaded by others who resented Jonas' saving so many Jews (he was occasionally dubbed: *Zhido Tevas* – Father of the Jews), shot him through an open window, in 1952, as Jonas lay asleep. The assassin was arrested, sentenced to death and executed.

Jonas Paulavicius, who began by saving a four-year old boy, discovered that his heart was large enough to save fifteen more lives. Unknowingly, he fulfilled the rabbinic maxim: one good deed leads to another.[10]

Helena Pawlikowska

Detective Work to Rediscover a Rescuer

It was late afternoon, on a July 1997 day. I was about to leave work for home, when two unannounced persons knocked on my office door, at Yad Vashem, and politely asked whether I could spare them a few moments to clarify an important personal matter. They introduced themselves as Stephen and William Lindner, two attorney brothers from Australia, who had just returned from a visit to Poland, and were sure they had met and uncovered the woman who had saved their parents' lives. They wished to know the procedures for submitting that person's name for recognition as a Righteous person. After eliciting more information from them, to satisfy myself that their account had the marking of a rescue story, I explained to them the criteria and procedure for this title, including the need for a written testimony, by themselves as well as their mother – the principal rescued person. What follows is an extraordinary tale of how two second-generation survivors accidentally discovered the person who had saved their parents' lives by sheltering them in their home attic.

Earlier that same year, the two brothers decided to visit Poland in order to locate the places where their parents originally lived, including the Warsaw Ghetto, and also to find the attic where they had hidden for over a year. For decades, after the war, their parents kept silent on their Holocaust years' experience, but rather preferred to dwell on more pleasant memories from the prewar years, such as their father earning a law degree from Warsaw University in 1938, and the happy prewar family reunions with the Lindner's many relatives – all of whom tragically perished during the Holocaust. Before he died in 1982, however, Rafal Lindner revealed to his sons how he escaped from the burning Warsaw Ghetto, in May 1943, armed with false credentials, and boarded a train which left for Srodborow, a holiday resort town, hemmed in by a pine forest, southeast of Warsaw, where they owned a vacation home. He also told them how the Polish caretaker of that home had hidden them during the following 14 months – in fact, until they were liberated by the Russians. They especially praised the caretaker's wife, who each night brought them a bowl of hot soup. As to the identity of the rescuers, the elder Lindners could only recall "Alexander," but not whether it was a first or family name. They also remembered that the house was about a twenty-minute walk from the town's train station, that the resort home had two floors and four flats, and that the caretaker's house was located to the rear of the resort home. Armed with this information, the two brothers bid farewell to their 82-year-old mother and, arriving in Poland in June 1997, began retracing the places visited by their parents during the somber Holocaust years.

A day after arriving in Warsaw, the two brothers boarded a train for Srodborow. After an hour's ride, they arrived in the former resort town and noted its pine tree location, which fitted the description given by their parents. Aimlessly walking the streets, they realized that to make headway, they needed the assistance of wartime knowledgeable people. At Otwock, where the regional prewar home ownership archives were kept, which included the town of Srodborow, the two brothers unearthed a German list of confiscated Jewish property in Srodborow — which also mentioned a home owned by a Lindner on Alexandra Fredry Street, but without indicating the street number. Bearing in mind the Lindner parents' account that the resort home was about a 20-minute walk from the train station, the party set out on foot to check the homes within that approximate radius. A woman at house number 12 recalled a certain caretaker, named Alexander, who had lived across the street, house number 9. The two brothers, along with a local guide and interpreter, crossed over the street and approached a woman, who introduced herself as one of the daughters of the elderly Helena and Alexander Pawlikowski, who she confirmed had, indeed, been caretakers of the Lindner home before the war. She thereupon led the party inside her apartment, and introduced her to the 91-year-old Helena Pawlikowska. The conversation with this elderly woman was immediately taken down on video camera, so that the brothers' mother, Wanda Lindner in Australia, would be able to comment on the contents of the registered information.

Helena Pawlikowska indeed confirmed being the caretaker's wife that had sheltered and fed the Lindner parents for 14 months, during 1943-44. She told the two brothers that she had known their parents from before the war, and recalled that the Lindners had owned a musical instruments store in Warsaw — which the surprised Lindner sons suddenly remembered had been mentioned years earlier by their parents, and the store was also listed in a 1930 telephone directory found in the main Warsaw library. Helena described how she had cared for the Lindner parents in the attic of their previous cottage, which no longer exists, and produced a photo showing the cottage, adding that she was glad that her efforts in hiding the two Lindners had not been in vain. She also described the dangers to her and her family (which at the time included six children), in light of the fact that some Germans had billeted themselves in an adjacent home, and had required of her to do their laundry. In addition, she claimed that she kept the caring of the two Lindners a secret, not only from her children, but (probably unbeknownst to the hiding persons) from her husband Alexander, as well.

After this emotional meeting with Helena—in consideration of her advanced age, the two brothers decided to forego returning to Australia, and head directly to Yad Vashem, in Israel (their first visit ever to this country), and to their impromptu meeting with me. In addition to of Helena's video statement, I asked them to prepare their own written statements, as well as that of their mother, so that the case could be presented before the Commission for the Righteous without undue delays.

A short time thereafter, the mother's testimony was received as well. In her statement, Wanda (nee Ber) described how she met Rafal Lindner in Warsaw, and married him in May 1942, inside the Warsaw Ghetto. How, during the ghetto uprising, in April 1943, they luckily made their way outside the burning ghetto, taking nothing along save the clothes which they wore and a set of false credentials. On the train to Srodborow, she recalled Polish passengers expressing satisfaction at the flames and smoke rising from the burning ghetto in the distance. Arriving at their former resort home, they were met by the caretaker's wife, who hurriedly hid them in the small space between the ceiling and roof of their cottage home, which was near the resort home. "Although not comfortable," Wanda indicates, "it was enough for the two of us to lie down. It was too low to stand upright." There they hid for 14 months. The nightly bowl of soup left by the caretaker's wife was brought after her husband and daughters had gone to sleep, none of whom knew of the two persons hiding above the ceiling. She also gave them some blankets on which the two slept, as well as used clothes to keep them warm during the cold winter months. "Had her actions been discovered, she would surely have been killed along with her family," Wanda indicated. From time to time, Wanda sneaked out of the cottage, and with her false identities traveled to Warsaw to fetch additional nutrition from a man who was a former teacher of her husband at the university law school. With her blond hair and blue eyes, Wanda did not stand out among her fellow travelers.

In mid-1944, the Russians occupied Srodborow, and the two Lindners left the cottage with only Helena knowing of their departure. They eventually moved to Australia (one son was born in Poland, in 1946; the other in Australia), where her husband died in 1982. As for her lack of communication with Helena all these years, Wanda explained that she was concerned not to place her benefactress in any danger from antisemitic elements, through disclosure of her help to Jews which the sending of mail or parcels would have revealed. "We did not wish to compromise her. So we had no contact since the day we left." When she saw the videotape of the conversation between Helena and her two sons, she was able to identify that woman as the person who had sheltered her and her husband, who in the darkness of night left each day a bowl of soup and retrieved the bucket holding the excrement. "I commend Mrs. Helena Pawlikowska to your committee as a person appropriate to be honored as a Righteous Gentile," Wanda Lindner concluded her testimony, "for the extraordinary risks taken by her. . . of hiding my husband and I, of feeding and caring for us and of scrupulously avoiding telling anyone, including her closest family [including her husband, who died in 1949] of our presence. . . We owe our eventual survival to her, and our children and grandchildren are a living testament of her courage." The identity of the person who sheltered their parents, thus saving their lives, was the result of the resolve of two second-generation survivors — a venture miraculously crowned with success.[11]

Boguslaw Howil

A Chance Meeting in Warsaw Reunites Rescuer and Rescued

When Jerzy Lando decided, in 1992, to attend a reunion of former Jewish inhabitants of Lodz, Poland, he thought that perhaps this was a good occasion to make an effort to find the man who had saved him during the Holocaust by sheltering him in his leather goods store. Since arriving in England in 1946, he had avoided visiting Poland, where so many of his relatives perished, including his father. But when the Lodz Jewish Association decided to hold its 1992 reunion in Lodz, Lando felt that, as a former resident of that large metropolis, he had an obligation to show up. Flying into Warsaw, he checked the local phone directory, and found listed the name of a Mrs. Howil. Perhaps, he said to himself, she was a relative of Boguslaw Howil, the man who saved his life. Over the phone, she confirmed to him that she was the daughter of Boguslaw, who incidentally could be reached at his ladies clothing store in the heart of Warsaw — only a stone's throw from where the rescue operation took place — "almost exactly to a day," in Lando's words, fifty years earlier. On his way there, his mind took him back to the dramatic events half a century ago.

Jerzy Lando was born in Lodz in 1922, but found himself with his family in the Warsaw Ghetto during the German occupation. His father Jakub had known Boguslaw from prewar business contacts when, together with his brother Henryk, he operated a large retail store in the heart of Warsaw — on the corner of Marszalkowska Street and Aleje Jerozolimskie (Polish for Jerusalem Avenue). During the ghetto period, Jakub went into partnership with another Howil business associate, to manufacture leather goods and sell them to the two Howil brothers.

Jakub's Jewish associate, Joziek Plomnik, had a one-year old daughter whom he wished to save, and Boguslaw volunteered to take the child. Since he was a bachelor, he placed the child in the care of his mother, who lived in Cracow, where the infant would be presented as the orphaned child of distant relatives. Then, in September 1942, during a lull in the deportation of Jews from the ghetto (during the summer months several hundred thousands had already been dispatched to their death), Jerzy's father decided that the family should try to escape to the other, the non-Jewish (or Aryan) side, of the city. The choice fell on Jerzy, since in his words: "I did not look Jewish and had the greatest chance of surviving. I was to go first." He was provided with a false birth certificate and given the Polish-sounding name of Kazimierz Kowalski. Trying to leave the ghetto was fraught with great danger. In Jerzy's case, it had been arranged for him to join a group of 20 Polish non-Jewish workers, who were leaving the ghetto towards evening, after finishing their daily work assignment. Since he was passing as a laborer, Jerzy could carry no personal belongings with him, so he put on several pairs of pants, shirts and vests, two pullovers, a winter coat and a specially made pair of boots — clothing he would certainly need to keep him warm during the approaching winter season. The party of workers then made its way toward one of the ghetto gates. Jerzy recalls the tense thoughts that crossed his mind:

> As I saw in the distance the German and Polish policemen guarding the crossing point my heart began to beat loudly. I was praying fervently for help. Did any of my companions remember that I was not amongst them in the morning when they came in? Would they denounce me? What about the group leader? Could I trust him with my life? I knew my father paid him for his services but was he a man of honor? Assuming I could rely on them, would the sentries recognize me as a Jew?

Jerzy's worst fears seemed to materialize. After passing the gate, he was suddenly called back. One of the German guards then ordered him to unbutton his coat. Trembling with uncontrollable fear, Jerzy revealed all the heavy clothing on him, one by one. However, the guard took special notice of the medallion Jerzy wore around his neck, which, when he opened it, exposed the arsenic powder he, as many other Jews, carried with them, as a last resort — to end one's life to avoid submitting to Nazi tortures. But why would an ostensibly non-Jewish worker be carrying this poison on him? Sensing the danger for Jerzy and himself, the group guide quickly pointed a finger to his forehead and shook it. The guard got the message — that this particular worker was a plain idiot. Jerzy was free to move on.

Once on the Aryan side, Jerzy decided to look up a certain Pole, living on the other side of the city, who had promised to help him with new credentials. To get there, Jerzy boarded the tramway.

> I felt like a bird after escaping from a cage, free yet apprehensive of its next move. I knew that anyone knowingly harboring a Jew was liable to be executed and that my presence could be an embarrassment to anyone I would approach, and yet without immediate help I would be doomed. There were some German soldiers in the tram, I looked at everyone with fear lest they would recognize me as a Jew. For the first time for over two years I was not wearing the Magen David armband of shame.

Jerzy's contact was away from home for several days, but his wife, not knowing Jerzy's true identity, allowed him to spend the night there. After listening to her opinion that the Jews were only getting from the Germans what they well deserved and, furthermore, that at last, true justice was being done to the anti-Christs — Jerzy decided to move on. Walking aimlessly on the streets of downtown Warsaw, and not knowing where to turn for help, the idea suddenly struck him to drop in unannounced at Howil's leather goods store, which was located in Warsaw's busiest intersection, with shoppers and German soldiers milling around, and the main railway station only a few hundred yards away. Looking through the glass door, Jerzy observed Boguslaw for a while; then, he decided to make his move.

"As I walked in, he looked as if he saw a ghost, hardly able to trust his eyes." With customers inside, Howil led Lando to the store office and began to inquire on news of Jerzy's family inside the ghetto. Not wasting any time, Jerzy point-blankly asked whether Howil could help him, in whatever way. Boguslaw thought for a moment, then replied that he had to consult his brother, and in the meantime he asked one of his attendants to treat Jerzy to lunch at a nearby restaurant. "It was strange to be served by a waiter, everything seemed unreal," Jerzy Lando noted in his testimony. Not sure whether this was not a setup, he constantly glanced at the door for any Germans to walk in "and take me away." Returning to the store, Howil led him to a back room in the courtyard of the large building where he and other stores were located. "This is my pied-a-terre (spare room)," he said to the bewildered Jerzy, "and this is where you are going to live for the time being. You will work in the shop and apart from me, my brother and the manager, nobody will know who you really are. I shall sort out your salary some other time, but if you need some money I shall let you have some in advance." Jerzy could not find words to thank him.

For a while, Jerzy served customers in the store, and passed the nights in Boguslaw's secret back room. His fears, however, were not gone. "There were already too many people around who had reason to suspect me of being a fugitive; at any moment there might be a knock on the door." One afternoon, Howil showed him an unsigned letter, threatening to denounce Howil to the Gestapo for the sheltering of a Jewish child by his parents, unless a certain sum was left at a specified hour, in a waste paper bin, opposite the main post office. With the help of several friends, to whom Howil denied the Jew-sheltering accusation, the culprits were apprehended at the point of approaching the waste bin, hurriedly shoved into two waiting horse-drawn cabs, and taken to Howil's store basement. It turned out these were two youths, who together with a third friend had learned of Howil's parents hiding of a Jewish child in distant Cracow, and had decided to capitalize on the discovery, and exact a stiff ransom sum from Howil, so as to be able to buy — of all things in these difficult times — a pleasure river boat. After being given a sound beating, and threatened with additional reprisals if they ventured forth with their threats, they were released. That same evening, Howil arranged for Lando to take the night train to Cracow, and look up his mother.

Arriving in Cracow the next morning, he was welcomed by Mrs. Howil, "a gentle old lady with gray hair and a good natured smile," who, after treating him to a hearty meal, asked him to play the piano, and arranged a place for him with some friends. They were, of course, not told of his true identity; only that he was a distant relative. She also arranged for him work at a local laboratory.

After the war, with Warsaw in ruins, Boguslaw Howil moved in with Jerzy and his mother (her husband had perished in the Holocaust) in their Lodz home. Mother and son then moved to England in 1946, and contacts between both sides were lost.

And now, after a lapse of 50 years, he was about to meet the man who had saved his life. How would he receive him? Entering Howil's store, he was shown to an adjoining office, "where I saw a slight man of eighty with gray hair, rather stooped but unmistakably Bogus Howil." What happened then is best described in Jerzy's moving words. "He could not stop embracing me, saying this was one of the happiest moments of his life." The two reminisced on the war years, and brought each other up on postwar family news. Jerzy then turned to Boguslaw's daughter and said that her father was a hero, "and that I (and other Jews) owed our lives to him and his family." After returning to England, Jerzy Lando immediately applied for Howil's recognition as a Righteous, and the request was granted without any reservations. A chance one-night stopover in Warsaw had reunited rescuer and rescued after half-a-century interval, and eventually brought to light a story of rescue and shelter, taking place in the heart of Warsaw's wartime shopping center.[12]

Joseph Jaksy

The Slovak Surgeon Who Rescued His Patients

In April 1990, Dr. Amira Kohn-Trattner, a practicing psychoanalyst in New York, accidentally discovered that a neighbor of hers, "a humble, near-90-year-old physician from Bratislava, Slovakia," named Professor Dr. Joseph Jaksy, had sheltered and cared for many Jews during the Holocaust.

This startling revelation came about when Jaksy's wife asked Dr. Trattner, a neighbor in her Manhattan Upper West Side apartment building, for a favor. As Mrs. Jaksy was stepping out for an errand, would Dr. Trattner take the key to the Jaksy apartment and be on hand to look in on her ailing husband in case of a distress call? The retired physician had a beeper equipped to alarm a local Red Cross station for emergency assistance, when alone at home. Dr. Trattner readily agreed, and as she got to know him better in the following days, she realized they had something in common. As a practicing psychotherapist, she regularly worked with Holocaust survivors; he, too, was telling her of life in Slovakia during the war years and, to the Trattner's surprise, how he had saved Jews from the Nazis. (Amira's father, Dr. Eliyahu Kohn, escaped from Slovakia one day before the border was closed in August 1939.) "He would tell me stories, and I would write them down," Trattner later related to a journalist.

In her communication to Yad Vashem, Dr. Trattner elaborated on her findings regarding Jaksy's rescue activities. As a practicing professor of urology in Bratislava, capital of Slovakia, he had admitted over 20 Jewish men in his clinic, ostensibly for surgery, but in fact to hide them temporarily. He also hid in his clinic, where he also had a small apartment, a 60-year old Jewish woman—wife of a hospital doctor. One evening, while a Jewish friend, a certain Paul Suran and his wife, were visiting, the Gestapo raided the place. The couple slipped into a hiding place in the house, while Jaksy placed himself before the Gestapo and told them he had an important operation to perform the next morning, and would therefore appreciate to be allowed to rest. Disregarding Jaksy's plea, the agents searched the premises. Luckily for his friends, their hiding place was not uncovered. Early next morning, Jaksy drove them to the train station, and instructed them how to proceed further to a border point with the false credentials they had with them.

After the war, Jaksy moved to the United States and joined the staff of the New York University Medical Center. Never once, during his 35 years there, did he allow anyone to be privy to his wartime rescue record. He had since long retired, and was afflicted with Parkinson's Disease and quite frail.

Dr. Joseph Jaksy

"He deserves to be counted as a Righteous," Trattner emphasized, adding that "time is of the essence."

More on Jaksy's rescue activity was to be found in documentation culled in the Yad Vashem archives, such as in the file of Dr. Karl Koch, a man already honored as a Righteous, in 1971, whom Jaksy had admitted for work in his clinic. Furthermore, a 1959 medical statement, bearing Jaksy's signature, told of a certain Livia Klein (presently seeking redress in the form of compensation), whom Jaksy had treated during the war, in her hiding place. In Jaksy's words:

> *Because of her Jewish descent, the plaintiff had been hidden somewhere in Bratislava. Together with several other persecuted persons she was in a hiding place. . . I was brought there and treated her several times. . . However, one cannot really speak of regular treatment. Several times I gave her medical assistance. In this regard I want to declare the following: I am a Christian and was not persecuted by the Germans because of race. However, I belonged to the Underground movement and have treated many hidden Jews in Bratislava. . . I even hid Jews in the clinic. I can assert that I have saved the life of many Jews. Thus I also treated Livia Klein during these years as well as could be managed. . . The hiding place was wet, cold (naturally unheated), unhygienic in the highest degree and difficult to endure. A horse stable would be a palace by comparison. Due to these conditions the plaintiff suffered primarily from infections of the respiratory organs and canals. . . I brought her my own medications from the clinic . . . Naturally, it was impossible to render customary therapy. Merely the trip to the hiding place meant risking the life of all participants. Bratislava was headquarters for the German Gestapo for the entire Balkans. It was therefore naturally extremely dangerous to comply with a request to go there. One also had to be on guard for spies and agents. . . It is clear to me*

*that these infections and inflammations suffered by the patient for years
caused serious consequences during her entire life. . . It is my opinion that
permanent damage has resulted.*

An additional statement by the late Alex Ekstein told of how Jaksy made
an incision on the body of a Jewish man, moments before the Gestapo came
to arrest him. The Gestapo grudgingly demurred from fetching a person on
the operating table. After they had left, Jaksy quickly stitched up the slight
incision on the man's open belly, and arranged for his safe departure. In
addition, a signed statement by a Mrs. Kvetuse Feldmann told how Jaksy
arranged for her to be hidden, together with her daughter, in a village, after
her husband's arrest by the Germans. In her words: "I am grateful to
Professor Jaksy for saving my daughter's life and mine. My husband died
in 1950 of brain cancer, caused by the beatings on his head in the
concentration camp."

In March 1991, as Dr. Jaksy celebrated his 90th birthday, a special
citation was presented to him on behalf of New York State Governor Mario
Cuomo. That same month, Yad Vashem added its own recognition of Jaksy's
humanitarian deeds, by awarding him Israel's highest honor to non-Jews,
the title of "Righteous Among the Nations." The medal and Certificate of
Honor in Dr. Jaksy's name were hurriedly dispatched to New York, where
they were to be presented by Israel's Consul-General to Jaksy in an official
ceremony at the New York University Medical Center, on June 27. Sadly,
Jaksy died several days before the actual ceremony, but in full knowledge
that he had been elevated to the ranks of the Righteous, for sheltering many
persons in his clinic, and providing medical assistance to persons in
hiding—a story which came to light thanks to the initiative of a next-door
neighbor.

Governor Cuomo's citation reads as follows:

*A Jewish legend has it that the world is sustained in its existence on
account of 36 righteous persons, known neither to themselves nor to the
world. In a lifetime, each of us comes to know a few select individuals
whose own lives of service to others, of love, compassion and humility
outbalance our world's great weight of sin and evil, sustaining us and the
world. Dr. Joseph J. Jaksy is such a person. Medical students and patients
in our state came to know him as a skilled and caring physician, and sensed
a depth in him that went beyond his professional competence. They did not
know, because he did not tell them, of his earlier years in Bratislava,
Czechoslovakia. Himself a Christian, he put himself in harm's way, risking
his life to rescue Jews from the horrible, single-minded evil of the Nazis.*

His first wife and many others survived the Holocaust because he used his influence, his wits, his money, his talents to hide them and feed them, to treat them, to remove them from danger — all of it with the certain knowledge that at any moment the official terror of the state could turn on him and destroy him. Sometimes we look for heroes in the wrong places. They are among us — quietly, humbly, courageously sustaining our world. We are proud that Dr. Jaksy has been among us these many years. Now, Therefore, I, Mario M. Cuomo, Governor of the State of New York, do hereby confer this special citation upon Joseph J. Jaksy, M.D. with our profound gratitude for the singular example he has provided us of what the human spirit is at its best. [Mario M. Cuomo] Governor. March 4, 1991.[13]

Elisabeth Wust

The German Woman Who Loved a Jewish Woman

The following story is of a rescue act which had its origin in an amorous relationship between two women — one Jewish, the other, not. In November 1942, Elisabeth Wust was a married woman with four sons, and a husband in the German army. She had earned from the government a special distinction for having added four sons to the country's population. Her marriage, however, seemed to be floundering as her husband partook in extramarital affairs with other women. One day, her state-supported housemaid suggested that Elisabeth take time off from the loneliness and drudgery of home chores, for an afternoon relaxation in a posh Berlin coffee-shop. "Come, I want you to meet some of my friends," Ursula Schaaf, the housemaid urged her matron. What Elisabeth did not suspect, was that these women friends of Ursula belonged to an intimate group of lesbians who occasionally met in that coffee shop. "Meet my friend Felicie," Ursula told Elisabeth, or "Lili" as she was affectionally known. The lady introduced herself as Felicie Schrader. The shy and introverted Lili immediately felt a strong attraction to this strange person. She later confided in her diary that this was a day that changed her life.

Soon, the elegantly-dressed Felicie became a companion to Elisabeth, and often visited her at home. She comforted Lili when she learned of her husband's flirtations with other women. Then in spring 1943, Elisabeth was hospitalized for a jaw operation. Felicie visited her and brought her a large bouquet. She embraced her and showered her with kisses. "I desire nothing but to give you everything," Felicie told the recuperating Lili, adding: "I have only a single thought: you! I love you!" That day, the two decided to room together. Elizabeth later wrote: "With Felicie, I finally understood who I am and what I want. . . With her I feel like I am walking on clouds." The intimate relationship between the two women was, of course, kept a secret from others. However, Elisabeth decided to seek a divorce from her husband, feeling that with Felicie she had finally found her true love. Felicie, under the code-name of "Jaguar," gave free vent to her feelings to her lover in love letters to Elisabeth, addressed as Aimée ("beloved" in French; also the name of a popular play in the 1930's), which Elisabeth kept in a special album.

Soon thereafter, in a moment of intimate conversation, Felicie asked Elisabeth: "Will you love me if I reveal to you a dangerous secret?" Upon Elisabeth's positive response, Felicie said: "Lili, I am Jewish, and my name is Schragenheim, not Schrader." For a moment, Elisabeth stood still. "Suddenly, I realized in what danger Felicie was. . . The moment she revealed her identity, it was as though she had placed her fate in my hands. That whole evening, we wept together, and swore loyalty to each other."

Elisabeth then learned more of Felicie's past. She was born Rachel Schragenheim in 1922 to parents both of whom practiced dentistry. Her father had fought in the German army in World War One. In 1930, Felicie lost her mother in a traffic accident, and five years later, her father succumbed to a heart attack. Felicie was slated to leave Germany, to either Palestine or the United States, but bureaucratic entanglements prolonged the process, until the war broke out, and Jews no longer could leave the country. When in October 1942 she was summoned to report for deportation, she removed the telltale Yellow Star and began a clandestine existence. She soon found a secure haven in the home of Elisabeth housemaid's parents, and then met Elisabeth in a posh Berlin coffee shop. To support herself, she worked in a bookstore, under an assumed name.

Elisabeth and Felicie continued their idyllic romantic relationship until August 1944, when Felicie was arrested by the Gestapo in Elisabeth's home, after both returned from an outing in the park. "Today was the worst day imaginable," Elisabeth later confided in her diary. "They have taken away from me my most beloved. God Almighty, please return my love." Acting upon her strong feelings, Elisabeth visited Felicie in her Berlin jail and brought her fruits and vegetables. Before her deportation to Theresienstadt camp, in September 1944, Felicie was able to send a letter to Elisabeth: "My beloved Aimeé. . . Many thanks for everything. Keep your fingers crossed for me. . . See you again; from me, Jaguar; imprisoned in the zoo."

Two weeks later, Elisabeth appeared in the office of the Theresienstadt camp commandant to find out how Felicie was doing, as well as deliver her a package. Aghast that an Aryan woman should take the trouble to journey from Berlin to this camp, on Czech territory, so as to care for a Jewish woman, the SS camp commandant threatened her with arrest. "Where is your racial pride?" he shouted at her. She responded: "I met my friend before I knew she was Jewish." The SS officer had her thrown out, and reported the incident to Gestapo headquarters in Berlin. Upon her return, Elisabeth was summoned for questioning. However, due to the distinction earned for bearing four sons for the Reich, and her husband's military service (the marriage was dissolved that year, and he was reported missing in Hungary), she was released with a slap on the wrist, and an order that she report once a week to the police station.

Elisabeth and Felicie continued writing to each other until the letters stopping coming from the Gross Rosen camp, whence Felicie had been transferred. There was nothing further to be done until the end of the war. In the meantime, Elisabeth took three elderly Jewish women, who belonged to the lesbian community, into her home for hiding. In her well-guarded diary, she continue to express her innermost thoughts toward her departed lover, presently languishing in a Nazi concentration camp, as in the following words:

> *Twice each evening there is an air raid alarm, and each time there is considerable shooting. I love you so much, Felicie. I feel so lonesome, although now people surround me, who need my love and care. Through them, I love you all the more . . . But, nevertheless, I feel lonely. I miss you so ardently. . . and I long for you . . . you my only beloved.*

Immediately after the war she inquired with the Red Cross and was informed of Felicie's death in December 1944. In 1981, she earned the *Bundesverdienstorden* from the West German government, a special distinction awarded to persons who opposed the Nazi regime.

The question before the Commission for the Righteous, which discussed this case in 1994, was whether the still-living Elisabeth Wust merited the Righteous title, as one of her sons asked of Yad Vashem. The consensus among commission members was that the romantic relationship between the two woman, one Jewish, the other not, was not the critical issue at stake. The question to be asked was whether there was sufficient evidence to confirm that Elisabeth Wust, after she learned of Felicie's Jewishness, continued to host her in her home—in other words, continued sheltering a fleeing Jew thereby consciously risking her own safety? The answer to that was affirmative. Moreover, after Felicie's arrest, and her own confrontation with the Gestapo, Elisabeth placed herself under additional jeopardy by sheltering three more Jewish women. Here, Elizabeth's humanitarianism was unquestionably the principal motivation, and she was awarded the Righteous title.[14]

Left:
Felicie Schrader
in 1941;
Right:
Elisabeth Wust
in 1943

Refik Veseli

The Albanian Photo Shop Clerk Who Saved His Jewish Employers

In June 1990, Gavra Mandil, living in Israel, addressed a letter to the President of then-Communist Albania — a country with whom Israel had no diplomatic ties. "Your Excellency, President Ramiz Alia, I was born in Yugoslavia in 1936 to a Jewish family," Mandil opened his letter to the Albanian head of state. He continued with the story of the family's flight from the Germans to Albania, a country which the Germans eventually also occupied in September 1943. "In those dark days, when danger and death were all around, the small and brave Albanian people proved their greatness!. . . Each Jewish family found shelter within an Albanian family — and at the risk of their own lives, they saved and protected their guests." As is confirmed by other accounts, almost all of the 2,000 Jews in that small Balkan country were sheltered by the local mostly-Moslem population, during the one-year occupation by the Germans. In his letter, Mandil described his family's rescue by a certain Refik Veseli and his parents, and he asked the President's permission for Mr. Veseli to be allowed to visit Israel, so that he could be properly honored by Yad Vashem.

Three years earlier, Mandil nominated Veseli for the Righteous title. In his testimony to Yad Vashem, Mandil related how, in 1941, as a five-year-old child, he fled with his family from Belgrade, the city of his birth, following the German invasion of Yugoslavia. Arriving in Pristina, Kosovo province, he and other Jews were interned by the Italians who for a time ruled this region, but were otherwise not physically harmed. A year later, the Italians moved the Jews to Albania, also under Italian control, where they lived in relative security until the country's occupation by the Germans in September 1943. Before that, the Mandils had employed as an apprentice in their photography shop, in Tirana (the country's capital), a 15-year-old Albanian, named Refik Veseli. When the Mandils felt threatened by the presence of the Germans, the now 16-year-old Refik decided to come to their rescue, by spiriting them out of Tirana, and leading them during several nights' ride on the back of donkeys, to his parents mountain house, in the small village of Kruja. "Refik's parents, who had never seen or heard of us before," Mandil states, "accepted our family and another Jewish family into their home saying that 'only over their dead bodies would the German Nazis get to us!'"

At first, the adults among the Jewish group were hidden in the barn's attic, whereas the children were allowed to mix with the host family's numerous children. The situation became especially dangerous toward the end of the war, when communist partisans, led by Enver Hoxha, engaged the Germans in stiff combats, who in turn intensified their search of partisans and Jews. Upon the end of the war, the Mandils moved back to Yugoslavia, where they were joined by Refik Veseli, who came to resume his photography apprenticeship, which lasted two years. In 1948, Veseli, an accomplished photographer, returned to Albania, and the Mandils moved to Israel.

In 1988, Yad Vashem acquiesced to Mandil's request, and awarded the Righteous title to Refik Veseli and his parents, Vesel and Fatima. "I am addressing you personally, Mr. President, the Albanian government and your Foreign Ministry," Mandil wrote in 1990, "to permit Refik and Drita Veseli to take this journey to Israel for this important occasion." Added to the urgency of the request was the fact that Gavra's two children were to be married in the summer of 1990, so "it would be a wonderful opportunity to enable Drita and Refik to attend our children's wedding and combine the official visit with the family's joy."

Left: Veseli and Mandil in 1943.
Above: Refik Veseli today.

To the surprise of Mandil, the President of communist-ruled Albania acceded to Mandil's plea, and the two Veselis arrived in Israel in July 1990, to be feted in a dignified ceremony at Yad Vashem, the first Albanians ever. Soon thereafter, Albania opened its doors to visitors, and with the demise of communism, most of the remaining Jews moved to Israel. As a result, more information became available on how the small Jewish community in that country was saved with the help of a majority of the Albanian people—mostly of the Islamic faith. The survivors told how, during the German occupation, many (some say, most) Albanians vied with each other for the privilege of hosting fleeing Jews in their homes, an ethic obligation which they claimed had its roots in the Islamic religion. Since Refik's recognition, fifty additional Albanians have joined the ranks of the Righteous.[15]

Mustafa and Zejneba Hardaga

The Bosnian Angels of Mercy

In the late hours of February 10, 1994, I waited tensely at Ben Gurion airport, near Tel Aviv, for the arrival of Zejneba Susic-Hardaga, on a special flight from war-torn Sarajevo, Bosnia. Next to me were Tova Rosenberg, whose family was saved by Zejneba and her husband, as well as Israeli government and Yad Vashem dignitaries. As the waiting time dragged into the small hours of the night, my mind went back to over a year earlier, to December 31, 1992. Sitting in my office at Yad Vashem, I turned on the radio and heard of an additional severe rocket strafing of Sarajevo by the Serb militia from the adjacent hills. I then reflected on Zejneba Susic's visit to Yad Vashem in June 1985, when Yugoslavia was still a united nation, and the moving ceremony during which she planted a tree in her family's name, and placed a flower in the Hall of Commemoration over the slab bearing the name of Jasonevac, the concentration camp where her father was imprisoned and died for helping Jews.

I wondered how she was now faring in that war-torn city? Placing a call to Tova Rosenberg, the former little girl in the Kavilio family, whom the Hardagas sheltered in their home, I was told that Zejneba desperately needed medicine for her heart condition. As Israel had no diplomatic representation in Bosnia, my mind searched for an agency through whom the vital medicine could be provided. The idea then struck me to contact the Joint Distribution Committee (JDC) office in Jerusalem, as the sole Jewish organization with outlets in all Jewish communities (including Sarajevo), and thus capable of providing the urgently-needed medicine. I was referred to Pauline Shomer—a Project Coordinator, who was attentive to my request to use the JDC connection in order for Yad Vashem to send the medicine to Mrs. Susic. As it turned out, the medicine would only be a partial solution to her problem. She needed to be evacuated from Sarajevo in order to assure her well-being, indeed her survival.

The story really begins on April 14, 1941, with the German invasion of Yugoslavia, spearheaded by a savage air bombardment of the major cities in the country, including Sarajevo. At the time, Mustafa Hardaga, a Muslim by belief, owned a building in which Josef Kavilio operated a firm manufacturing sewage steel pipes. Over the years, a friendly relationship had developed between both sides. When the Germans bombed Sarajevo, Josef, his wife Rivka, and their two children, Benjamin and Boena (today Tova) fled into the woods. After the German air raid, the Kavilios returned to their home, only to see it in a state of ruins. They then considered taking up residence in the steel pipe factory. Stopping to see Mustafa on the way, he insisted that they come and stay with him. Zejneba recalls:

> We found them destitute. We brought the whole family, Josef, his wife and two children to our home. This was the first time that an outside man slept in our home. For us women, who veiled our faces according to our religion and tradition – this was forbidden. But we welcomed them with the following words: "Josef, you are our brother, Rivka – our sister, and your children – our children. Our house is your house; feel at home here just as you would in your own home.[16] Our women will not hide their faces before you, since you are family. Today, when your lives are in danger, we shall not forsake you."

The Hardagas were observant Muslims, and the women covered their faces before strangers. Never before had a strange man stayed over at their home. Along with Mustafa's family, the household also included his brother Izet and wife Bachriya.

With the German occupation of the city, conditions for Jews worsened. The old synagogue was looted and the 400-year-old Torah scrolls committed to flames. "I watched this terrible sight, hidden behind a curtain in my host's home," Josef recalls. After a brief stay with the Hardagas, Josef, fearing the worst, had his family moved to Mostar, which was under Italian control, and relatively safe for Jews, while he stayed behind to liquidate his business which the pro-Nazi authorities ordered him to "aryanize," that is, turned over to non-Jewish hands. Bosnia was then ruled by the Croatian Ustase regime, which collaborated with the Germans in the persecution of Jews, and especially of the large Serb minority. After a while, Josef was arrested on the charge of sabotage, and imprisoned.

It was now the winter of 1941-42, and a heavy blanket of snow covered all major roads, making it impossible for Kavilio and other prisoners to be moved to the infamous Jasenovac concentration camp. Instead, chained by their legs, they were taken out to clear the snow on major roadways. One day, Josef noticed a veiled woman standing at a distance and weeping. It was Zejneba's sister. Hardly controlling her tears, she ran home to Zejneba. From that moment, and for a whole month, Zejneba brought food to Josef, who was working outside the prison, in quantities which sufficed for his prison mates as well.

Josef eventually made his escape and returned the Hardaga home, where he was again welcomed and nursed back to health. Not wishing to further endanger his charitable hosts (their home stood across the Gestapo head-quarters in Sarajevo, and at night Josef could hear the screams of prisoners undergoing torture in their cells), he decided to escape and join his family in Mostar. When that city came under direct German rule, in September 1943, the Kavilios fled into the mountains and joined up with Tito's partisans. After the war, the Kavilios returned to Sarajevo, where they were again welcomed by the Hardagas, who hosted them until they found a proper dwelling. They then learned of the arrest of Zejneba's father Ahmed Sadik for hiding the Jewish family Papo in his home. Imprisoned by the Ustase, he died in the Croatian concentration camp of Jasenovac. The Hardagas returned to Josef Kavilio the jewelry and other valuables which he had left with them for safekeeping. The Kavilios then left for Israel. When Mustafa died, Zejneba remarried and assumed the name of Susic. A daughter, Aida, born from this marriage, was added to Zejneba's other children, who eventually emigrated to other countries. In 1984, Josef Kavilio nominated his erstwhile rescuers for the Righteous title, and the following year, Zejneba Susic was feted in a ceremony at Yad Vashem, in her and her family's name, after which she returned to her native country. In the meantime, Josef Kavilio passed away while Zejneba, widowed from her second husband, lived in Sarajevo with her married daughter Aida.

Sitting comfortably in my office, on this last day of 1992, I now felt a terrible urge to help this woman in her moment of need. Following my appeal to Mrs. Shomer, of the JDC office in Jerusalem, their European representative suggested that Zejneba be taken out of Bosnia and brought to Israel. Upon his suggestion, Yad Vashem drafted a letter to the President of Bosnia, asking him to allow her to leave for Israel. As it turned out, Zejneba refused to leave without her daughter Aida, the latter's husband, Branomir Pecanac, and their daughter Stela, as Zejneba was totally dependent on them. Yad Vashem interceded with the Israel Minister of Absorption to grant Zejneba's relatives the status of state-supported immigrants. In January 1994, Absorption Minister Yair Tsaban finally granted this concession, and the four Hardagas landed in Israel in early hours of February 11, 1994, to a tumultuous welcome by representatives of the Israel government, Jewish organizations, and Yad Vashem — as well as the Kavilio family and friends. A month later, Zejneba Susic was awarded Israeli citizenship in the presence of Prime Minister Yitzhak Rabin. She died in October of the same year, at the age of 76, and was laid to rest in the private cemetery of Beit Zayit, a Jewish settlement, at the feet of the hill on which stands the Yad Vashem memorial.

Zejneba's daughter saw in her rescue and arrival in Israel the hand of God, and after much thought and reflection decided to convert to Judaism, together with her husband and daughter. They assumed new names: Sarah and Moshe Pecanac and daughter Ruth. Asked by the rabbinical council, which studied her request, why she wished to go through with the converson, Sarah responded that — if my mother risked her life for Jews — "it is only natural that I should want to become Jewish. It is an honor for me to belong to this people." In addition, soon after her arrival here, Sarah asked not to remain a public charge, but be gainfully employed. I again interceded, and Yad Vashem agreed to use her language skills for work in the archives department. "This invitation was the greatest honor for me," Sarah Pecanac stated. "For this is a sacred place, a place which remembers the past, the history, for the sake of the future. My work is mainly technical, but I feel that every page that I touch has a story behind it, and every name that I write has significance." From time to time, she appears before audiences. "I try to explain to people life under wartime conditions, and of the tremendous significance for us of Israel's help. Only Israel received us — four people with one suitcase and many difficult experiences. There are still many people who suffer in the world, and it is important to help them. In this way, I should like to continue the work of my mother."

Zejneba's rescue from war-torn Bosnia and her arrival in Israel, in the company of her daughter and son-in-law, was one of the proudest moments of my work at Yad Vashem. During one of the worst periods in Jewish history, Zejneba's family had sheltered a Jewish family. When Zejneba found herself in distress, the State of Israel reciprocated by offering shelter and a safe haven to her and her immediate loved ones. A moral debt had been repaid — in an especially significant way.[17]

Left: Zejneba Hardaga with her children and with the child Tova (seated), during the war. Above: Hardaga arrives at Ben-Gurion Airport in Israel in 1994, greeted by Tova Rosenberg.

Chapter 5

Subterfuge Methods

Public servants and persons in authority in the Nazi establishment could, if they so wished, subvert the rules and regulations affecting the Jews, and reinterpret them in such a way as to create a loophole through which Jews could escape the Nazi net. Unfortunately, not many availed themselves of this possibility. The few who did were able to save numerous Jews—if not permanently, then at least for long periods of time, thus affording the trapped Jews time to ponder and plan alternative escape routes. Similarly for diplomats of neutral countries stationed in places where Jews were being deported to concentration camps. They could issue passports or documents, which listed the threatened Jews as nationals of their countries, and thus affording them protection from deportation. In this chapter, we will illustrate several such cases.

Hans-Georg Calmeyer

How a German Official Saved 3000 Dutch Jews Under the Noses of the SS

One of the clearest examples of how a German official, wielding much authority, could subvert Nazi anti-Jewish policies is that of Hans-Georg Calmeyer. During the war years, he filled a top post in the German administration of the occupied Netherlands — a position which spelled the difference for many Jews whether or not they were to be deported to concentration camps.

Born in Osnabrück, Germany, in 1903, to a father who served as a judge, and having lost two brothers, who fell in battle in World War One, Hans-George Calmeyer studied law, and eventually opened his own practice in his hometown. In 1933 he ran afoul of the Nazis, who took power that same year, when he pleaded the case of communists on trial; also angering local Nazis when he refused to dismiss a Jewish employee. As punishment, he was disbarred for a year. For a while, he thought of leaving for the Netherlands, where his aunt lived after marrying into a Dutch family. In May 1940, he participated in the German invasion of the Netherlands, in an air force unit. Soon thereafter, Dr. Stüler, a hometown acquaintance, who presently worked in the German administration of occupied Holland, invited Calmeyer to head a section in the *General Commissariat for Administration and Justice*, which dealt with matters arising from the antisemitic measures of the new overlords of this country. More specifically, to examine and decide on doubtful racial cases. Why so?

On January 10, 1941, the Nazi governor of occupied Netherlands, Dr. Arthur Seyss-Inquart, issued an edict which required of all Jews to register with the authorities. This regulation applied to anyone with as much as one-quarter Jewish blood (by Nazi definition); that is, even a person who for all intents and purposes was a practicing Christian, but his records showed him to have at least one Jewish grandparent. Not to mention any person who, at the time, was registered with the Jewish community; he was now obliged to identify himself and be subject to anti-Jewish measures. A provision in that edict stated that the *General Commisariat* was the sole authority on the decision in questionable racial cases; in others words, whether a person was to be classified as fully, partly, or non-Jewish at all. This was the task assigned to Calmeyer's department.

In the Nazi judicial system, there were several categories of semi-Jews/semi-Aryans. A person with two Jewish and two non-Jewish grandparents was classified as a *Mischling Grade A*, and was not to be immediately

deported, although he was to be deprived of many rights. A person with
only one Jewish grandparent was a *Mischling Grade B*, and was to be treated
more favorably, and perhaps eventually be integrated into the general non-
Jewish population, depending on his physical features and other criteria.
A person with three Jewish grandparents was considered fully Jewish, and
liable to deportation, irrespective of his current religious affiliation. In
Germany, the decision on doubtful racial cases was the sole prerogative of
the Führer, of Hitler alone, who indeed decided on several hundred such
cases, before Germany's entanglement in an ever-widening war, in 1942,
placed a lid on all such reviews. In occupied Holland, Calmeyer asked and
was granted the authority to decide on such issues, whenever appeals were
received by persons who claimed that they had been erroneously registered
as Jews.

Before continuing, the reader should be cautioned that the Netherlands
occupied a special status in the eyes of the Nazis, which paradoxically
resulted in a harsher occupation than other occupied West European
countries. The Dutch were considered a lost Germanic tribe, soon to be
brought back into the Aryan fold, headed by Germany. Hence, in preparation for this great event, the population was to be cleaned of all "undesirable" racial elements — namely, the Jews. A full military and civilian occupation was imposed on the country, with Nazi overlords appointed over
various Dutch ministries, and a free hand was given to the German police,
the SS and other Nazi security agencies. These were supported by a native
collaborationist movement — the NSB, and its paramilitary militia.

Returning to Calmeyer's work — if Jewish women could show that their
son was the product of an illicit relationship with an Aryan, the son could
be classified as "half-Jewish," and spared immediate deportation. Similarly,
if one could show that some of one's forefathers were really not Jewish, they,
the offspring grandchildren, now facing deportation to the camps, could also
hope to benefit from a temporary lapse of their deportation until their status
had been clarified. Calmeyer took a lenient approach when faced with such
doubtful claims, and the word soon spread that Calmeyer was willing to
stretch to the limit his acceptance of questionable documents in order to
allow one to claim he or she was not a full Jew, perhaps even an Aryan, and
should therefore be exempted from deportation, and his valuables and
goods, which had been impounded, returned. This went to such great
length — causing Jacob Presser, in his magisterial book on the Holocaust in
the Netherlands, to wryly note that it was sometimes said that the Jews
suffered from not having an Eleventh Commandment: "Thou shalt not
convert thy grandfather and thy grandmother from Judaism."[1]

In this work of racial reclassification, Calmeyer was seconded by a team
of trustworthy aides, carefully selected to keep knowledge of the deceitful

nature of some of the methods employed from falling in the hands of the SS and the Gestapo, who wished nothing more but to wrap up Calmeyer's whole operation. Dr. Gerhard Wander, also an attorney by profession, and an officer in the German army, stationed in the Netherlands, was one of Calmeyer's closest aides. His duty consisted of preparing legal opinions on the status of Jews and Jewish firms which were in the process of being Aryanized; that is, forcefully sold, at a laughable low price to a German trustee board — as well as assist Calmeyer in his racial reclassification. Some of the cases handled by him were similar to the one of Mrs. Polak, who claimed that her late departed Jewish husband was not the father of her four children, whose real father was an earlier first husband, a certain Muller, whom she never married, and who was now probably dead. The proliferation of such incidents led Wander to once remark ironically: "I never suspected that Jewish women are so unfaithful." Dr. Benno Stokvis, one of the Dutch attorneys who pleaded on behalf of Jewish clients, related how Wander provided him with papers confirming the Aryan credentials of his Jewish clients, including his own fully-Jewish mother. At their first meeting, however, Wander was irritated with Stokvis, and he pointedly asked him: "Dear colleague, why are you making such major efforts to turn Jews into Aryans?" Not losing his cool, Stokvis replied: "You are mistaken. I am not changing Jews into Aryans. I only want to prevent you from transporting to the East Jews who are in truth Aryans." Wander then laughed. "Now the ice between us was somewhat broken. We looked at each other, and from this moment we knew that we understood each other well."[2]

In another confrontation with Wander, Stokvis related the case of a Russian Jewish woman who claimed to be in truth the daughter of fully Aryan parents, but as an orphan was adopted by a Jewish family, and then married a Jewish man. Wander suspected foul play and ordered a full examination of this case. He was able to locate a document signed by seven rabbis who confirmed the woman's Jewish ancestry, and Wander was about to refuse the petition. At which point, Stokvis pounded his fist on Wander's desk and raising his voice, exclaimed: "Since when, Dr. Wander, is a statement by seven rabbis considered authentic in the Greater German Reich?" Wander was dumbfounded, and he gave in.

This was not the only occasion on which Wander proved difficult. At the same time, Stokvis adds that "he was always there for me. He helped whenever he could. In more than 20 cases that I brought before him, he strove to reach favorable decisions." He closed his eyes before clearly false ancestry documents presented to him. He was a good and honest person, "a rescuer of people, out of love and compassion of fellow man." As suspicions mounted against Wander, he was recalled for active duty and sent on to the Russian front. Evidently, his experience in Holland opened his eyes to the inhumane designs of his government, and caused him to desert from his unit, and clandestinely return to Holland, where he joined the Dutch underground. The Gestapo waylaid him on an Amsterdam street, in January 1945, and in a shoot-out, killed him. He is the only German buried in a Dutch Underground cemetery in Leenen, on Dutch soil. Wander was recognized as a Righteous.[3]

Ever suspicious of the machinations of Calmeyer's team, SS chief Rauter finally persuaded Nazi governor Seyss-Inquart to agree, in June 1943, to a complete reexamination of the "Calmeyer Jews," as many of them had been found to have pronounced Jewish features. Calmeyer had already previously been cautioned not to add more names to his protective list, after December 1942, but he kept adding people beyond this deadline. Up to 1943, the Nazi governor withheld from clamping down on Calmeyer's work, not out of love of Jews, but as a result of a struggle for power within the Nazi establishment. As a representative of the Nazi party, Seyss-Inquart was no doubt privy to the ongoing rivalry in Berlin between Goebbels (representing the party) and Himmler (head of the SS), as each wished to gain the upper hand in an eventual succession to Hitler. Consequently, Seyss-Inquart had an interest in keeping the SS at arm's length, and this played into the hands of Calmeyer, who worked for the Nazi governor. However, in 1943, a Dutch genealogist and Nazi firebrand, named Ludo Ten Cate who had assembled much information on Jewish birth records from newspaper birth announcements, marriages and deaths, was assigned to examine Calmeyer's files. Ten Cate prepared a report, in which he noted Calmeyer's mistakes, which he turned over to SS chief Rauter, who then asked Seyss-Inquart for a thorough investigation of Calmeyer's work — a demand rejected by the Nazi governor. Luckily for Calmeyer, Ten Cate was removed from the Dutch scene, after he had embroiled himself with the SS, and was sent to the front. At the same time, the pressure on Calmeyer from the SS did not let up. By January 1944, Calmeyer's office had investigated 4,787 doubtful racial cases, of which 2,026 (or 42%) were declared as only half-Jews, and 873 (or 18%) as quarter Jews or Aryans. In other words, 2,899 Jews had been saved from deportation. At the same time 1,868 cases (or 39%) were rejected. But even here, Calmeyer gave them sufficient advance warning and ample time to seek alternative ways of rescue, such as hiding.[4]

Calmeyer also created additional categories of Jews, whose deportation was to be postponed, such as the "Blue Knights" (based on the blue marking on their cards in Nazi files) — a group of privileged Jews which included 13 former members of the Dutch Nazi party (up to a time, the Dutch Nazi party had admitted certain Jews in its ranks), several persons married to non-Jews who had sons fighting on the side of the Germans, a German Olympic champion, and several more celebrated Dutch Jewish persons. Calmeyer was less successful with the largest category of exempted Jews — the Portuguese Jewish community. They were descendants of Jews exiled from the Iberian peninsula in the 16th century, which in an earlier age produced the great philosopher Spinoza, but who now numbered much less than their fellow Dutch Jews, who were of middle- and east-European stock. The leaders of this proud community, anxious to save themselves from deportation, hired a genealogist who, after a thorough study of that community's racial components, concluded that they were not of Semitic origin, and should therefore not share the fate of their Hebraic but non-Iberian co-religionists. Calmeyer saw a chance to save this community of 4,000 persons, who were kept in separate quarters at the Westerbork transit camp, until their fate had been decided. He urged that they be allowed to leave for Portugal, in exchange for Germans and Dutchmen held by the Allies. Rauter of the SS was not prepared to consider even an initial release of 400 such Jews, whom Calmeyer argued were definitely non-Semitic, and insisted that the whole matter be resolved in favor of their deportation. Playing for time, Calmeyer prepared a memorandum for Himmler with whom the ultimate decision lay. Finally, a committee of Nazi experts came to inspect these Jews in Westerbork, in February 1944 (by this time, the rest of Dutch Jewry had already been deported to the death camps in Poland), who were paraded before the Nazi team. Their decision was unanimous: "A subhuman race." The die was cast, but Calmeyer succeeded in having them diverted to Theresienstadt, where their chances of survival was considered better than Auschwitz. Unfortunately for them, after a brief stay in Theresienstadt, they were all subsequently deported to Auschwitz, where most of them were gassed. [5]

One of the Dutch persons working for Calmeyer was a young attorney, Jaap van Proosdij, who moved to South Africa after the war. In his testimony to Yad Vashem, he listed some of the errands he did for Calmeyer, whom in hindsight he did not evaluate highly. Proosdij felt that Calmeyer was not a bad person; that he knew that a negative decision would have serious, probably fatal, consequences for the persons involved, and this awareness moved him to decide favorably. At the same time, one was never certain of him. At times, he seemed to be sincerely interested in wanting to help, but "he was certainly not a person whose mission was to help and save people." Although not anti-Jewish, he was neither pro-Jewish. He would help as long as he could keep the fearful SS at a safe distance from his operation and himself. Some persons involved in this conspiracy of rescue were unknown to Calmeyer. Such as the medical student Cornelis Teutscher, who landed a job as a genealogist in the office of the Dutch Public Records, in Haarlem. He helped persons associated with Calmeyer (but probably without Calmeyer's personal involvement) with various falsified birth and baptismal records, which made it easier for Calmeyer and his trusted German team (principally Gerhard Wander and Heinrich Miessen), but also the young Dutch law graduate Jaap van Proosdij, carry on their work of subterfuge, largely undisturbed.[6] Considering the scope and depth of the German occupation of the Netherlands, and its control of all facets of the people's lives, it is no less than miraculous that a German team, working out of the offices of the Nazi governor, was able to save close to 3,000 Jews, by the judicious use of subterfuge, and by profiting from the Nazi governor's aim to keep the SS operation in Holland at arm's length, and not allow them total control of the occupied country, and thus strengthen the Nazi party's position vis-a-vis its chief rival—Himmler's SS.

Presser, the aforementioned historian, who judges harshly the German civilian and military administrators in Holland, and no less so the heads of the *Joodse Raad*, the Jewish Council (considered by many a pliant tool of the Germans) which carried out instructions handed down by the SS, has only kind words for Calmeyer. In his study of the Jewish Holocaust in the Netherlands, Presser states that although Calmeyer knew that many Jews were trying to pull the wool over his eyes, he let them go unpunished. "He went to endless trouble to prove helpful to all petitioners. There is no doubt that hundreds of Jews owe their lives to him." He would go to great length to look for loopholes in cases which seemed hopeless. After the war, he described his position to that of a doctor in a lonely isolated post, with only 50 doses of medicine to treat 5,000 severely ill patients. He could not save all, so he saved the few that he could. Jews claiming to be the illegitimate offspring of non-Jewish fathers had become so much the fashion, with Dutch lawyers besieging his office with pleas for their Jewish clients, that if he were to accept all such claims, his whole rescue operation would have been undermined. "The writer of this work, for one," Presser underlines, "has not the least doubt that Calmeyer was skating on exceedingly thin ice, that he was working under duress and that, had he gone any further than he did, he would, in fact, have jeopardized what little help he was able to give to the Jews."[7]

After the war, a downhearted Calmeyer returned to his law practice in Osnabrück, but he suffered from pangs of conscience at not having done enough to save, and he felt dejected at the mild sentences meted out to former Nazi criminals. In a 1965 letter to Presser, he wrote: "Every action—whatever we did to help, was too little, too little. . . I am to this day filled with despair. Being in despair, maintaining the feeling of despair—that is the only dignified and worthwhile attitude to adopt." Then, speaking in the third person, he added:

At that time, he was already in the same despair as he is today. At that time, he already understood that every effort and every action was vain and insufficient. However, he acted and failed to act; whatever he did and failed to do — he did everything out of a burning heart. . . The [Good] Samaritan is not permitted to ask whether the man he helped was worthy of that help. The person who was helped only represents the high number of those who had to be helped.[8]

The most authoritative historian of the Netherlands during World War Two, Leo de Jong, and the Dutch Holocaust historian, Joseph Michman, both petitioned Yad Vashem to nominate the already departed Calmeyer to the Righteous title. When the case came up for consideration at the Commission for the Righteous, opinions were divided. After several spirited debates, the majority sided with de Jong and Michman — that the rescue of close to 3,000 Jews under the noses of the Nazis, by a person whose job was quite the opposite — to enforce Nazi racial regulations; that such behavior, at considerable risk to the man, made such a person worthy of the Righteous title — and so it was resolved.[9]

Hans-Georg Calmeyer

Alfred Rossner

The German Hemophiliac Who Died Attempting to Save Jewish Laborers

Another German official, stationed in Poland, also tried subterfuge to save his several thousand Jewish workers, but failed in that endeavor which also cost him his life. "It took me a very long time to confront my memories of Alfred Rossner," Henrietta Altman, one of Rossner's beneficiaries, stated in her 1994 deposition. It was a daunting undertaking, she continued, to recreate the atmosphere of Nazi rule in her hometown of Bedzin, Poland, during the dark days of the Holocaust. "It is almost impossible to resurrect the memories, without being affected by the perspective, created by time and emotional distance." But try, she had to.

The story takes place in Bedzin (pronounced Bendzhin), part of a cluster of cities centered around Zaglebie (pronounced Zaglembie), in the coal-rich southwestern Silesian region of Poland. Before the war, Bedzin was known for its many traders and small firms, mostly Jewish-owned, which produced a variety of goods. On the eve of the war, in 1939, the city counted 27,000 Jews, about 50% of the total population. Some 15,000 more Jews were forcefully moved in from surrounding localities during the initial period of the German occupation. German rule was celebrated with the torching of the main synagogue in Bedzin, only days after their arrival, which also consumed nearby houses, and cost the lives of several dozen Jews. This was followed by the confiscation of all Jewish businesses; those considered essential for the war-effort were either sold to private German entrepreneurs or placed under direct control of the SS, which appointed German administrators (known as *Treuhänder*, i.e., trustees) to operate and manage them.

The largest of these enterprises or factories (sometimes referred to as "shops") was managed by Alfred Rossner. At its height, he employed some 10,000 Jews in his two factories, which produced mostly uniforms, but also boots, for the German army. Each such worker was allowed to protect two members of his or her family from deportation. For a time, holding a special "shop" pass was the best insurance against the ravages of the SS, but only for a while. Tradesman, such as tailors, furriers, shoemakers and mechanics had no problem to be accepted in these factories, especially when they brought along their own machinery. Those lacking tools who wished to be accepted had to pay a certain fee, which with time grew to great proportions, and was transacted through Jewish section managers in Rossner's factories. This, of course, led to malpractice, with some section chiefs enriching themselves by exacting stiff entrance fees. As Henrietta Altman's (born

Szpigelman) teaching skills were not considered "essential" by the Germans, she managed to be admitted into Rossner's factory thanks to her aunt's connection with a relative of one of the section managers, and was assigned to sew buttons on uniform trousers.

It was rumored that Rossner had been brought in from distant Berlin by Arieh Verlager, one of Jewish section chiefs, who once operated a textile firm in Berlin, in which Alfred Rossner worked, and who thought it in the best interest of the Jewish workers to have such a person as chief manager. Rossner, whose hemophilic condition disqualified him for army service, readily accepted Verlager's proposition. The SS approved his nomination, in spite of his earlier association with the outlawed Socialist party. During his three-year managerial tenure of his two factories, he tried as best as he could to save them from deportation to the death camps. In this, he was not as successful as his other counterpart in Cracow, the famous Oskar Schindler. At the same time, in contrast to other German-appointed managers, who only thought of ways to enrich themselves, Rossner cared principally for his workers, and exerted himself to save them. Through his personal involvement during many crucial moments, including tense stands-off with SS, many Jews were able to avoid arrest and deportation and remain under the beneficent care of Rossner, and thus eventually survive.

One should bear in mind that, in contrast to Schindler, Rossner was not the proprietor of his shops but was responsible to the SS, who supervised his day-to-day activities. This reduced his flexibility and freedom of action in comparison with other Germans, who as independent entrepreneurs had greater freedom of action, and could exert themselves to save their Jewish workers, if they so wished. Most didn't. To curry favor with his SS overlords, Rossner entertained and bribed them generously with custom tailored uniforms, and hand-picked material for coats and suits, for them and their spouses. To the SS, he explained that since his physical disability prevented him from serving the Fatherland on the front, he would exert himself to exploit highly-valued Jewish labor to produce war-essential goods, such as uniforms and boots. This ploy did not stop the SS from eventually taking away all of his workers, with the exception of those who, with his help, had in the meantime managed to make good their escape.

Henrietta, then known as Henryka (or Kicia), and today affectionately called "Kitia" by her friends, was visibly taken aback when she first met him, as he called her into his office to inquire about her work. He was a slight figure of man, with fleshy jowls, and wore a blue jacket (which he later turned over to one of his Jewish workers, when he noticed her trembling from cold). What struck her in particular was his visible limp, due to his hemophilia, and his missing teeth. As she came to know him more, she was surprised by his affinity to the Yiddish language, taught to him by one of his Jewish section chiefs, who read to him in Yiddish some of the works of the famed Shalom Aleichem. As to his care for his workers, one of them — Edward Retman—remembers Rossner often addressing the workers in a friendly manner, and that he "made one feel at ease in his presence." To facilitate the conditions of his workers, circumstances permitting, he hired as personal aides Germans who may have been card-carrying members of the Nazi party but who, like him, were prepared to go to great length and do whatever they could to protect the Jewish workers.

Rossner's help became prominent during SS killing and deportation raids. There were three major ones in Bedzin: in May and August 1942, and on August 1, 1943 — which signaled the final liquidation of the city's Jews. During these terrible raids, Rossner personally intervened to try to save as many Jews as possible; some by claiming that they were part of the "essential" workers of his factories; others, by simply adding them to his workers. At the start of the second major action, in summer 1942, Rossner had himself driven, in his one-horse buggy, in the streets of the Jewish neighborhood, shouting in Yiddish: "Jews, don't be stupid; don't go when they call you!"[10] The intention was for the people not to voluntarily give themselves up for the Nazi euphemistic "resettlement" call — even if their names were on the deportation list. In another such raid, Rossner placed himself astride the marching Jews. "When he saw me pass," Yocheved Galili recalls, "he pointed me out to the SS man as one of his "essential" workers. Yocheved grabbed her sister's hand — who did the same to her cousin, and so on, until six women formed a chain. A heated debate ensued between Rossner and the SS man, who insisted that only Yocheved be allowed to go. As she left the column, she dragged with her the other five women. During the melee of pushing and beatings, the six were able to sneak away. "To this day, I don't understand how this all happened. Rossner's men covered our escape, and we fast found ourselves hidden in Rossner's offices."

An even more dramatic story is that of Karola Baum. During the August 1943 action, she hid with her family in a coal basement. Somehow, luck was with her and she was not apprehended. When the sun had settled, she tried to leave, but was inhibited by the sight of the streets filled with soldiers, and sidewalks littered with corpses of dead Jews. She finally was able to sneak out of the ghetto, barefooted, and headed to the non-Jewish side of the city. "I was left on the street. I then decided to sneak away and head to Rossner's home. I looked terrible: dirty, with leg wounds, and frightened." After Rossner's Polish governess allowed her in, he stepped out of his room and said that she was welcome to join the others Jews hiding in his factory. "In simple words, he said that I could wash up and eat, and asked his governess to help me." After a night's stay in his home, she was taken by Rossner to the factory. During the same Nazi action, Cesia Rubinstein had been rounded up and was standing in line to be deported. As they waited, Rossner suddenly appeared with a German assistant, and the two began fetching young Jewish people, including herself, whom they quickly moved into the factory, where they were safe from harm. "There I was now in the factory together with about 50 young Jewish people working again. Rossner went on treating us friendly." Kitia Altman related in her deposition that when he initially learned of this SS action, Rossner almost went mad, shouting: "They have betrayed me, they have betrayed me!" He then ran out of his office to frantically search for Kitia's cousin, Aron Ehrlich, with whom Rossner was in touch on underground-related things, and was known to be hiding in one of the ghetto bunkers. He finally spotted him on the railway station platform, about to be loaded on one of the cattle wagons. When Rossner returned to his office, he relayed to the anxious Kitia his failure to save her cousin. "He grabbed my arm and said: 'that's how I grabbed Aron's arm and begged the SS man: grant me only this one Jew.' He was brutally pushed away." On Rossner's orders, several trucks loaded with fabric were sent to the doomed ghetto. Under the layer of clothes, people were hidden and smuggled into Rossner's two factories. After the final great liquidation raid of August 1943, there were now only 600 workers left, out of an original 10,000. This small number was to be reduced further, to a mere fifty, and they too would be deported.[11]

In his maddening efforts to protect his workers, Rossner had to contend with both the SS and with the Gestapo-controlled Jewish council, headed by Moniek (Moshe) Merin, whose office was in nearby Sosnowiec. Merin saw himself as a new Moses, who would rescue, perhaps not all or most but at least a fraction of the Jewish community in his area. He justified his cooperation with the Germans before his people, as in his 1943 speech, in the following words:

I am in a cage, confronted by a raging, hungry lion. I stuff flesh down his throat, human flesh, my brothers' and sisters' flesh. . . Why? Because I am trying to keep the lion in his cage, so that he doesn't get out and trample and devour every one of us at once. . . I shall not let the youth distract me from my bloodstained labor. . . Let history judge me![12]

In his zeal to placate his SS masters, Merin often complained to them of Rossner's tactics in protecting his factories' workers and their families, thus sabotaging Merin's efforts to fill the SS quota of Jews to be deported. In Kitia Alterman's opinion, it was a typical Catch 22 situation. "The workshop, which belonged to the SS and was managed by a non-SS was saving Jews from deportations by making them 'essential' to the war economy. The same SS demanded from the Judenrat 'delivery' of Jews, which the Judenrat

was unable to meet because they were protected by working for Rossner."
In her estimation, this situation, where a German appointed administrator
was in conflict with a German-appointed Jewish council, was to be found
only in Bedzin.

On top of the protection of his workers during SS killing raids, Rossner
was also implicated in clandestine work. Kitia recalls meeting in Rossner's
office a Jewish underground man, working with the Polish railways, who
discussed with Rossner the hijacking of a German military wagon, loaded
with military boots, so this merchandise could be sold on the black market,
to help finance the underground. In addition, he had some of his workers
sent to Germany, under new false identities, for household related duties,
thus assuring their survival. In the words of Edward Retman: "It was his
money that sent the illegal transports to Hungary and Romania via Vienna.
This was a big secret and none of us knew any details, except that he was
involved." Kitia Altman, who was privy to Rossner's plans, remembered
being told by Rossner that he counseled people in his factories how to
organize themselves, so that they could give refuge to a greater number of
Jews (including old people and children) fleeing SS killing raids.

Rossner took a special interest in Kitia Altman, and wished to rescue her
at whatever price. On one occasion Rossner came up with a daring proposition of opening up a branch office, in Paris of all places. Since Kitia knew
some French, he proposed that she join the pilot group. This idea "literally
took my breath away," in Kitia's words. Nothing came of it, and Kitia
believes that Rossner was testing her discretion — whether she was able to
keep a secret. On another occasion, Kitia was called into Rossner's office and
introduced to a man dressed in an SS uniform. "I have never been in such
proximity to an SS man and it was frightening." As it turned out, the plan
was for her to accompany this man to Vienna, armed with false credentials,
where arrangements would be made for her continued care. Rossner
explained to her all the precise details:

> I'll go to Katowice. I'll be in a box filled with straw, in a furniture van. After
> the control, I'll get a signal, the box will be opened, I'll make a dash into the
> ladies' toilet (the van will stop in front of it) and change into different
> clothes, which will be in a bag in the box. I have to make sure every bit of
> straw is removed from my hair! I'll change, put on a hat and step out,
> carrying my gloves in my right hand. . . I'll be approached by this officer,
> take his arm and together we will board the train to Vienna.

Kitia could hardly catch her breath in disbelief. It seemed to her like a
film script for a cloak and dagger story. In the final account, the plan fell
through, not through any fault of Rossner, but because Kitia could not bring

herself to leave her parents behind. When she relayed the escape plan to them, her mother sobbingly told her: "My love, we want you to survive, to live. We understand, perhaps this is the only way. But you must know that the day you'll go, you'll sign our death warrant." She resigned herself to staying on. Eventually, her father perished in a death camp, but her mother survived the Holocaust. Another plan, also hatched out with Rossner's complicity, was for Kitia to join a group of Jewish persons on an escape plan. Rossner had already prepared special clothing for Kitia. This too fell through, due to Kitia's hesitation about the plan, coupled with the doubtful reliability of the people involved. She proved to be right, as some of the persons in this escape conspiracy backed out at the last moment.

In spite of Rossner's delaying tactics, the SS kept reducing his work force, and finally decided they had had enough of him, and had him arrested, at the end of 1943. The charge was the 90 gold watches found in his uncle's home. Kitia Altman is not sure whether these watches were part of the payments by well-to-do Jews in Bedzin to his Jewish appointed section chiefs, in return for their names to appear on his worker list (some of whom did not perform any work in his factories), or whether he kept these watches for safekeeping. Conflicting reports were received about his fate. For a time, it was believed that he would be released. Then, in January 1944, his aunt came with the sad news: "They hanged him because he helped Jews." By that time, there were only 50 people left in the factory; they too would be deported.

Rossner had a premonition about his fate. He once told Kitia that the war would last for several years; "You'll survive, but I won't," for the Germans would certainly kill him. One friendly Gestapo man once offered him a membership ticket in the Nazi party, which Rossner turned down. To Kitia, he gave the following justification: "If I stay alive, no one will ever believe me I wasn't a party member. I don't know for how long I can protect you all." Kitia's final assessment of the man is to link his physical disability with his affinity of the persecuted Jews. He had tried to outmaneuver the SS, and failed. In her words: "It is not a story of spectacular rescues and achievements, but a story of desperate attempts. . . My survival, I believe, was largely due to Alfred Rossner," not only to him, but "Rossner was the most contributing factor." Edward Retman, another of his survivors, credits him with possessing a "noble character," and a sincere attempt to help Jews survive. "He always treated us as human beings, in the full sense of the word." Another witness, Karola Baum states emphatically: "One can say that he risked his life and position and saved me. Retman feels that "Alfred Rossner's name should have a place among those of the other Righteous Gentiles," to which Kitia adds: "He paid with his life and the few whose life he touched want his story to be told and his name to be properly honored."

In May 1945, immediately after the war, Henrietta (Kitia) Altman promised to herself one day to tell Rossner's story. Post-war vicissitudes kept her from fulfilling that vow until 1994, when she submitted a lengthy testimony to Yad Vashem, which was supplemented with testimonies of other beneficiaries of Rossner's aid. A year later, Yad Vashem added his name to the Righteous honor roll.[13]

Alfred Rossner

Kalman Horvath

The Hungarian Officer Who Saved by Conscripting Jews for Forced Labor

Could the Righteous title be attributed to someone who conscripted Jews for forced labor? Generally speaking — no. In one exceptional case, however, the decision was to be otherwise. The story takes place in Hungary, during May and June 1944, when the deportation of Hungarian Jews to Auschwitz was in full swing — an operation personally supervised by SS chief Adolf Eichmann, and with the collaboration of the Hungarian gendarmerie. The country had been occupied the preceding March 19 by German troops. Although nominally an ally of Nazi Germany, the Hungarian government had by 1944 become a puppet regime of Germany with only a limited scope in local and international affairs. Eichmann with his Hungarian accomplices immediately took themselves to the task of destroying the country's over 700,000 Jews. The decision was to leave Budapest for the last stage, and begin by emptying the Hungarian provinces of all Jews, and deport them directly to Auschwitz, where additional gas chambers and crematoria were built to cope with this new and sudden large influx of Jews. Within the space of two months, in May and June, over 400,000 Hungarian Jews were deported to Auschwitz, where most were gassed upon arrival. Simultaneous and in tally with the large-scale deportations, Laszlo Ferenczy, the head of the Hungarian gendarmerie, at the request of his German masters, signed an edict, on May 5, 1944, prohibiting the further conscription of Jews into labor battalions — earlier formed to force all able-bodied Jewish men to perform hard labor duties on or near the Russian front, in which the Hungarian army was engaged. Those already drafted, and present on Hungarian soil, were to be converted into prisoners-of-war and treated accordingly. With few exceptions, most non-Jewish military commanders of these units treated their Jewish laborers harshly, denying them the minimal necessities for the performance of strenuous physical assignments, and not a few of these laborers died or suffered impairment to their health. It was now forbidden to further conscript Jewish men to these labor battalions, to avoid that these units serve as an escape valve from deportations to Auschwitz.

As the large scale roundup of Jews continued unabated, an Hungarian major suddenly made his appearance, in June 1944, in the Jewish ghetto of Miskolc, and ordered all Jewish males to assemble in the main square. Convinced that this was a deportation rollcall, hundreds of Jewish males hastily and dejectedly gathered outside as ordered. The officer then quickly passed before each of the men, and began conscripting them into the labor battalions. This was a surprise to the men, since the drafting into these units had been rescinded the previous month. To their queries, Major Kalman Horvath told them that he was doing this, not because he needed them for labor assignments, but to prevent them from falling into Nazi hands, and be deported; in short, he wanted to save their lives. For this purpose he drafted men above and below the officially permissible ages (18 to 48) for duty in the labor battalions. As the then 15-year-old Imre Lebovits recalls, Horvath told him that this was the only way he could rescue them from the Germans. Another young conscript, Pal Foti-Friedländer, recalls how the day previous to Horvath's arrival, Hungarian gendarmes had rounded up a group of Jews of Miskolc in a brick factory.

> It was a frightful night. Shooting, shouting, cattle wagons arriving. In the morning a MIRACLE happened: an army officer, named Capt. Kalman Horvath (I only learned his name at a later date) ordered every man – from the age of 15 to 65 to gather in the courtyard. . . At this moment the commanding officer of the gendarmes reprimanded Captain Horvath, threatening him for interfering with 'his Jews!' The miracle was that Horvath ordered his soldiers to surround our Company with rifles drawn – ready to protect us, shouting back to the gendarme commanding officer: 'These men are enlisted in the army's labor force. . .' Turning to us, he gave the order: 'Quick march! Towards the exit gate'. . . That 1944 summer morning in the brick factory remains unforgettable for me. . . Captain Kalman Horvath enlisted us in the army's labor force; with this, he gave us a chance to survive the Holocaust. . . My mother, Mrs. Lajos Friedländer and my sister Marta were deported to Auschwitz.

Similar confirmations are replicated in the testimonies of other men, conscripted by Horvath. Yitzhak Steinberger, who eventually became a physics professor at the Hebrew University in Jerusalem, stated how impressed he was with Horvath when he appeared before them in the brick factory. He addressed the frightened men and boys in the third person, which in Hungary is a polite and courteous form, hardly to be compared with the humiliating treatment at the hands of the gendarmes who were guarding them. "I was 16, thin, small, with big glasses and a limp. When my turn came to face Horvath, he asked me about my occupation. I was a high school student, but I claimed being a cobbler's apprentice. Horvath did not even blink and he let me enlist. . . At least half of the recruits in our unit 107/318 were either below or above the draft age." The men were taken to nearby Jolsva, where they were assigned to various units. Steinberger, together with many others spent days doing absolutely nothing. Some were assigned cleaning up ruins from air raids, or moving ammunition from one storehouse to another. "I fully believe Horvath's word that his aim was to save lives," Steinberger categorically stated.

Another witness remembered him telling the men who were over 50, and physically fit, to declare that they were 45, and for 15 year old boys to register as 18 year olds. In the words of Paula Neuman, whose father and brother-in-law were drafted and saved from deportation: "he saved whomever he could." Similar incidents took place in other ghettos. In Mezorsat, Horvath ordered all men, aged 16 to 60 to step forward. "My mother, instinctively pushed my 14-year old brother forward," Yeshayahu Keinan remembers. Horvath overlooked his young age. 14-year-old Haim Krauss hesitated whether to enlist. Horvath told him bluntly: "Here it is I who decides who is young and who is capable. You are definitely capable for the place I am sending you." "I was drafted," Krauss stated, "and as it turned out, this saved my life." Shraga Shemer, then a 15-year old frightened lad, equally recalls Horvath's words to the gathered men, that whoever wanted to save himself from deportation was invited to join the labor service, without regard to age and health. "I remember him telling us that the conscription is in order to save us from the Germans and to show the world that the Hungarian army still includes decent men." Another witness, Rabbi Yaakov Yules, recalls a similar visit by Horvath in Tisafird, Transylvania, and his drafting of men, as low as 14 years of age into the labor battalions. Rabbi Yules considers Horvath a man of conscience who placed the welfare of the threatened Jews above his own.

Alexander Grossman, another person saved by Horvath's action, had known him from earlier days in the military. Horvath told Grossman that by enlisting as many men as possible into labor battalions, he was playing for time. In his words: "whoever gains time, gains lives." The number of persons thus conscripted by Horvath ran into several thousand. Some fell into the hands of cruel commanders, but most remained at leisure and unharmed, while the deportation of other Jews continued apace. When the more strident pro-Nazi Arrow Cross movement snatched power on October 15, 1944, most of the those drafted by Horvath had already made plans for their further flight. Thanks to Horvath, they were given a respite of four full months to plan their escape, some by crossing over to places already controlled by Soviet troops; others (here too with the help of Horvath), by joining up with Slovak rebels operating in the north of the country; still others, by arranging their admittance into Budapest-located "protective homes," flying the flags of neutral countries, and some by joining up with clandestine Zionist organizations in Budapest. Horvath had allowed them this breathing spell — as he had earlier told his friend Grossman: "Whoever gains time, gains lives."

When the case came up for consideration before the Commission for the Righteous, the issue on hand was whether conscription into labor battalions which, previous to 1944, was a punitive measure against the Jewish population, could in this instance be considered as rescue and its author honored as a Righteous. Of equal importance was in what way Horvath jeopardized his standing in the military, and perhaps his personal safety, by flouting orders which prohibited the further enlistment of Jews. Some argued that, granted that his intentions were honorable, it was not clear whether his action was in violation of government policy—in light of the confusion which prevailed in various quarters on the conscription of Jews in the labor battalions due to conflicting instructions from above. Hence, one could not say with certainty that he was at risk for disobeying orders. In fact, no punitive measures were taken against him, and in August 1944, he was sent to the front on regular duty. Those arguing in favor of recognition pointed out that, whatever the instructions, Horvath overstepped his mandate and that, moreover, the number of persons involved (running into several thousand) was also of significance. Above and beyond these considerations, the Commission pondered on the man's motivations. Was he principally concerned with the deteriorating situation at the front and, hence, the need to beef up the labor battalions, or was his action prompted solely by humanitarian considerations? Obviously, the fact that he conscripted persons above and below the permissible ages, with many not in the best state of health, was an indication that the proper performance of physical labor assignments was not his main concern. The additional fact, that he had to face-off the gendarmes, known for their blatant antisemitism, who tried to forestall his action, even to the point of Horvath threatening them with arms in hand, also pointed in the direction of the humanitarian motivation. When one added to this his involvement in encouraging many to flee and join up with Slovak partisans—the welfare of the trapped Jews loomed as the greater concern for Horvath than any other consideration. The fact that he was not punished nor reprimanded during the chaotic days which followed the seizure of power by the Arrow Cross, was no proof that he stood under no risk of personal jeopardy. All these factors (including the number of Jews saved) added up towards a favorable consideration of the man's meritorious conduct; that his actions during the critical days of mass Jewish deportation to the camps demonstrated his acting above and beyond to try to save as many Jews as possible within the briefest time. Under other circumstances, conscription into the Hungarian labor battalions would not be considered an act of rescue; in this particular case, it definitely was. After lengthy spirited debates, the Commission for the Righteous voted to award the Righteous title to Kalman Horvath.[14]

Giorgio Perlasca

The Italian Who Saved Thousands of Hungarian Jews by Posing as a Spanish Diplomat

In December 1987, a letter was received at Yad Vashem from a woman living in Berlin, who introduced herself as Professor Eveline Blitstein-Willinger, who stated that six months earlier she had learned of the existence of Giorgio Perlasca, a 79-year-old Italian, who as the man in charge of the Spanish legation in Budapest, Hungary, had saved thousands of Jews. She continued: "To my astonishment, nobody knows his name, nobody thanks him for what he did." She concluded with a plea: "We are asking you to honor this great man with a noble soul, before it is too late."

In fact, the name of Perlasca was well known to students of the Holocaust in Hungary. As early as 1948, Eugene Levai, in his pioneering study of the Holocaust in Hungary, had included the name of Perlasca among the group of ambassadors from certain neutral countries, stationed in Budapest, who had appealed to the pro-Nazi Arrow Cross regime in Hungary in late 1944, to cease or at least curtail and lessen the vicious anti-Jewish measures of the regime. In these documents, Perlasca's first name appeared as Jorge, which is the Spanish version of the Italian Giorgio — his real name. Randolph Braham, in his 1981 two-volume seminal study of the Holocaust in Hungary also mentioned Perlasca as a person who, as Chargé d'Affaires, had become the *de facto* man in charge of the Spanish legation, after the departure of the Spanish ambassador Angel Sans-Briz, in late 1944, in light of the approach of the Soviet army. What was not known to Yad Vashem historians was that the man who had collaborated with Wallenberg to save the remnants of Hungarian Jewry was not a Spanish national, but an Italian passing for a Spanish citizen and, moreover, very well alive and residing in Padua, Italy.[15]

Before arriving in Budapest, in 1942, as the representative of an Italian firm dealing in meat packaging, Giorgio Perlasca had led quite an adventurous life. In the 1930's, he served in the Italian army in two campaigns: the Abyssinian war of 1935-36, and the Spanish Civil War, in 1936-37. To the end of his life, he remained fond of the earlier style of Italian Fascism, which he felt did good for the country; that is, until Mussolini allied himself with Nazi Germany. In 1941, while on a business tour in Yugoslavia, he witnessed the brutal and inhumane Nazi measures against Jews, a sight which was replicated in Hungary, when that country came under the Nazi boot, in March 1944. A sensitive chord awakened in Perlasca's heart, but which did not immediately translate itself into action. The opportune moment had not yet presented itself.

In the meantime, in September 1943, the Germans, now in full control of Italy, had installed a new and more virulent form of Fascist regime. Perlasca and other Italians in Hungary refused the new government's call to return to Italy. When the Germans invaded Hungary on March 19, 1944, to force their ally to stay on their side, Perlasca felt threatened, and he fled for refuge to the Spanish legation.

Why the Spanish legation? Years earlier, at the end of the Spanish Civil War, as a token of gratitude by the victorious Falangists to Italians who fought alongside them, Perlasca had been handed a certificate promising Spain's assistance in the future, should he ever need it. Producing this letter to the Spanish minister, Angel Sans-Briz, Perlasca was housed in a villa which enjoyed extraterritorial status. However, after a short stay there, Perlasca left and found himself interned in a transit camp, awaiting a decision by the new pro-German government in Hungary whether to force him back to Italy. Making his escape, he stealthily returned to the Spanish legation in Budapest, and again sought its assistance. After some hesitation, Sans Briz issued him a Spanish passport, and a letter specifying that Perlasca had been granted Spanish citizenship. His first name now appeared in the Spanish form — Jorge. It was a fateful date — October 15, 1944, not only for Perlasca, but for Hungary and its remaining Jewish population. On that day, the Germans removed the country's ruler, Admiral Horthy, and installed the pro-Nazi Arrow Cross leader, Ferencz Szálasi, who also seconded as a fanatical antisemite, and a reign of terror was unleashed on the streets of Budapest against the city's Jews.

Up to then, some 440,000 Jews from the country's provinces had already been deported to Auschwitz and mostly gassed. Now, it was feared that a similar fate would befall over 200,000 of the country's remaining Jews, living in Budapest. Previous to the October 15 coup, the Spanish legation, following the example of the Swiss and Swedish embassies, had issued "protective letters" to many Jews claiming a Spanish ancestry, and housed several hundred such persons in houses flying the Spanish flag. Now, with Budapest in a state of turmoil, and the Spanish legation in need of additional hands, Sans Brinz invited Perlasca to stay on, to look after the needs of the Jews in the Spanish protective homes. He was handed a certificate identifying him as a member of the legation staff.

Perlasca addressed himself with vigor to his new task. More persons were admitted into the Spanish protective homes, and Perlasca went as far as staging a confrontation with József Gera, a top Arrow Cross official, over the illegal invasion by one of these homes by a band of Arrow Cross militiamen.[16] After listening to Gera's harangue against the Jews, Perlasca reminded him that he was a representative of a government friendly to Hungary. That, if Hungary would be on the losing side of the war, as it seemed in late 1944, persons like Gera would need alibis to shield themselves from prosecution as war criminals. At this, Gera changed his attitude, and promised that the inhabitants of the protective homes would no longer be molested. It was no secret that not a few Arrow Cross officials hoped to be granted asylum in Spain upon the expected collapse of Nazi Germany.

As the Soviet army closed in on Budapest, Sans Briz, as other many diplomats, left for Switzerland on December 1, 1944, promising to send Perlasca a visa from there. However, Perlasca decided to stay on and became the *de facto* chief diplomatic representative of Franco's government in the beleaguered capital without, one should add, any official accreditation by his superiors. Perlasca took the liberty of issuing more protective letters. These certificates, backdated to the period when Sans Briz was still in Budapest, stated that such-and-such person had requested permission to move to Spain and that, while awaiting departure, the person and his family had been placed under the protection of the Spanish government.

Perlasca then presented himself before the Hungarian authorities, announcing that Sans Briz had left, not permanently but to communicate more easily with Madrid from Switzerland, and in the meantime had charged Perlasca as his personal representative at the legation. "You are speaking with the official representative of Spain," Perlasca exclaimed at the Ministry of Foreign Affairs, and warned of retaliatory measures by the Franco regime against Hungarian citizens and interests in Spain, if Spanish interests in Hungary were to be violated, which included any harm befalling the persons huddling in the Spanish protective homes. Hungarian Foreign Minister, Gábor Kemény assured him that Spanish interests would be respected. However, bands of the Arrow Cross militia were beyond disciplining, as they wildly roamed the streets, and in frustration at the Russian shelling of the city, exacted vengeance on countless Jews, whom they indiscriminately shot and dumped their bodies in the Danube river. Edith Weiss related how she was led with a group of Jews toward the banks of the Danube, when suddenly Perlasca appeared on the scene. "He was mesmerizing. In this forceful, powerful way of his, he told them to go away and leave us alone . . . Perlasca had such authority, he was so strong, that there was no way anyone could contradict him. They simply went away."[17]

To better protect his Jewish wards, Perlasca increased his rounds at the protective homes, and the several thousand residents living in overcrowded conditions had gotten to know him well. He notes in his diary, for December 16: "To better defend our wards, I've decided to let myself be seen as often as possible. . . to visit the houses twice a day and to spend a little time in each one. To attract attention, I drive around in the embassy's Ford with a Spanish flag flying."[18] With the city under siege, food became a luxury and Perlasca arranged with a baker to provide his wards with hard-to-get provisions. In addition, in consultation with the Papal Nuncio, Monsignor Angelo Rotta, and the Swedish special emissary, Raoul Wallenberg, Perlasca helped draft petitions to the Hungarian government asking to ease the inhumane measures against the Jewish population. In one such memorandum, signed by Perlasca and the representatives of the Vatican, Sweden and Portugal, the Hungarian government was warned to exclude children (who are "absolutely harmless beings") from being closeted in with Budapest's remaining Jews in a special restricted ghetto. Hungary was reminded that "every civilized people respects children, and the entire world would be terribly surprised if it were to learn that Hungary, a country with a noble and Christian tradition, has taken action against minors." The diplomats asked that children be turned over into the care of the signatory diplomats. To the Vatican representative, Angelo Rotta, a fellow Italian, Perlasca disclosed the truth of his faked appearance as the Spanish Chargé d'Affaires. Rotta advised Perlasca to keep the secret to himself.[19]

On January 6, 1945, with shells constantly raining down on the streets, Perlasca joined Wallenberg, and Zurcher of the Swiss legation, on a last-ditch mission to Ernö Vajna, the Minister of Internal Affairs, to threaten dire reprisals by the victorious Allies if the Hungarians and Germans were to go through with their plan to torch the Jewish ghetto, after evicting the inhabitants of the protective homes. In Perlasca's words: "I told him that burning down the ghetto with seventy thousand people inside would be an evil deed that the world would never forgive." Speaking to Vajna in private, Perlasca then warned that if the Spanish protective persons were removed, he would urge his government to take immediate action against the three thousand Hungarian citizens currently residing peacefully in Spain. At this, the Hungarian Minister backed off. Perlasca insisted that the guarantee not to harm the protective homes should also be extended to the Swiss and Swedish homes. "I told him that Wallenberg and Zurcher were waiting outside and that I would not consider myself satisfied unless he offered them the same assurances." Vajna conceded, and "I went out and briefly informed Wallenberg of the result."[20]

In the meantime, the Hungarian government mounted its pressure for full Spanish recognition of the Arrow Cross regime — not merely *de facto* but also *de jure*. Feigning a personal interest in the matter, Perlasca counseled patience, assuring the Hungarians that Madrid was still favorably considering the whole subject. In fact, Madrid was not at all aware of any such proposal, nor of Perlasca acting as its representative in Hungary. As far as Spain was concerned, its legation in Budapest was merely in the hands of caretakers, and without any diplomatic accreditation. Fortunately for

Perlasca, thanks to the chaotic situation prevailing in Hungary (parts of which had already been overrun by the Red Army), the government there had its hands full with more pressing and urgent matters than a checkup of Perlasca's credentials.

When asked later why he acted at such considerable risk to his person, Perlasca replied: "Because I couldn't stand the sight of people being branded like animals. Because I couldn't stand seeing children being killed... I don't think I was a hero. When it comes down to it, I had an opportunity and I took advantage of it... All of a sudden I found that I had become a diplomat, with a lot of people who were depending on me. What do you think I should have done? As it turned out, I think being a fake diplomat was a big help, because I could do things that a real diplomat couldn't do."

As a non-diplomat, he felt himself free of the constraints (such as etiquette, hierarchies, and one's career) which usually restrict one's freedom of action. To another questioner, he replied in like manner: "I saw people being killed and, quite simply, I couldn't stand it. I had the opportunity to do something, and I did what I could." He then added a statement, voiced by many other rescuers of Jews, "Anyone, in my place, would have done what I did."[21]

He was especially fond of retelling the story of how he had saved two brothers about to be forced on a train for deportation to the camps, after insisting that they were in the care of the Spanish legation. A German major, in charge of the operation, refused to release the boys, and in the confrontation with Perlasca, he drew his pistol on him. At this point, an SS colonel arrived on the scene and gestured to the other officer to let the boys go. That colonel then turned to Perlasca and said: "You keep them. Their time will come." Wallenberg, who was standing nearby, turned to Perlasca and told him that this SS colonel was no other than the notorious Adolf Eichmann.[22]

With two staff persons at his side, "Jorge" Perlasca remained in charge of the Spanish legation from December 1, 1944 to January 16, 1945, when Soviet troops occupied that part of the city. On that day, residents of one of the Spanish protective homes drafted a letter addressed to Perlasca, in which they thanked him "for all that you have done for us, saving us from certain death," and the courage, self-sacrifice and risks undertaken in this effort. Fleeing the Spanish legation (Spain was considered an adversary state by the Soviet Union), Perlasca was accosted by Russian soldiers and was forced to help dig up dead bodies buried in the snow and rebury them. Escaping from this labor unit, he made his way to friends, who helped him eke out an existence. The reconstituted Jewish community in Budapest afforded him another document, in which gratitude was expressed to him for his rescue efforts during the Szalasi regime. "Your activity on behalf of Jewish citizens made it possible for several thousand of them to save their lives," the letter read. In April 1945, on the eve of Perlasca's return to Italy, former residents of one of the protective homes gave him the following letter, written in French:

> *We are sorry to learn that you are leaving Hungary to return to Italy, your native land. On this occasion we wish to express to you the affection and gratitude of the several thousand Jews, persecuted by the Nazis and the Hungarian Fascists, who were placed under the protection of the Spanish legation. We shall never, never forget not only your tireless day-and-night work to shelter and nourish us, but also your tender care of the young, old and sick, in a way which words fail to express. We shall never forget that as a person who on many occasions encouraged desperate people, you dealt with us with great wisdom and courage, when our situation was so hopeless, and we know how many times you risked your own security and life to save us from the hands of the murderers. Never, never shall your name be removed from our prayers. We pray to God to bless you, for only He is capable of rewarding you.*[23]

Sadly, after returning to Italy, Perlasca was forgotten. While other diplomatic rescuers in Budapest and elsewhere were honored and feted, this business-representative-turned-diplomat, who risked being defrocked at any moment, with the consequent danger to his life, but overlooking such risks stayed on his post, until he was assured that his Jewish wards were safe and sound — this man received no recognition, and his whereabouts in Italy were

lost. In fact, no one bothered to check, until his accidental discovery, in 1987, by Dr. Blitstein-Willinger's close circle of friends. Since then, in addition to his honoring as a Righteous by Yad Vashem, he received honors by the Hungarian and Spanish governments, and various organizations. He died peacefully in August 1992, at the age of 82 and laid to rest in Padua. Over his tomb is an inscription in Hebrew, which reads:"Righteous Among the Nations."[24]

Giorgio Perlasca

Selahattin Ülkümen

The Turkish Consul in Rhodes Who Saved 50 Jews by Declaring Them Turks

When, in 1989, Mathilde Turiel learned that her rescuer, the former Turkish diplomat Selahattin Ülkümen, was living in retirement in Istanbul, she informed Yad Vashem of her rescue story. In her testimony, she described how this man was instrumental in saving her from the Germans during a most critical moment. Born in Turkey, Mathilde moved in 1933 to the island of Rhodes when she married a man holding an Italian citizenship. The two sons born to them held dual Turkish-Italian citizenship. Italy captured the island from Turkey in 1912, and consequently many of the several thousand Jewish inhabitants opted for Italian citizenship, and allowed their Turkish ones to lapse. By the time the Germans took over control of the island from the Italians, in September 1943, the Jewish community had dwindled, through emigration, to some 1,800 persons — almost all of them Italian nationals.

At the time, Selahatttin Ülkümen was the Turkish consul-general on the island, and going about his business, representing Turkish interests, which included Turkish nationals living in Rhodes. Suddenly, on July 18, 1944, with German forces in full retreat on all fronts, and as defeat loomed larger than ever, the Nazis decided not to forego the opportunity to liquidate the small Jewish community on that distant island, from which one could see the Turkish shore. On that day, the SS ordered all Jewish males to present themselves the following day at a certain assembly point. The women were in turn also ordered to show up, with the threat that if they failed to do so, their husbands and fathers would be shot. "As I was about to give myself up," Mathilde Turiel relates, "I was met by Mr. Ülkümen at the door [of the assembly point]. This was the first time I had ever seen him. He told me who he was and that I should not enter. He instructed me to wait a few blocks away while he went in to attempt to release my husband and save us from imprisonment," on the strength of her Turkish origin, and her two sons' Turkish citizenship.

Emilia Tarika experienced a similar encounter with the Turkish diplomat. Born into the Mizrahi family, in Turkey, she also married in Rhodes a man holding Italian citizenship. When she heard that the Turkish consul-general was exerting himself to save from deportation persons claiming Turkish nationality, even of a dubious nature, she decided to approach him. "Totally despondent, I decided to seek out the consul, although he lived far away, and there was no transportation due to the lack of fuel. I went by foot, when suddenly a car stopped by me, and the consul asked me why I was so upset. I explained to him the situation, and he calmed me." He instructed Emilia to gather all persons claiming Turkish descent in front at a certain hotel in Rhodes town, for he had arranged a meeting there with the German commander to discuss the fate of the Turkish-Jewish nationals. When Ülkümen left the meeting, he told the tense group of several dozen women, that he had succeeded after a long and tense debate to free them and their already imprisoned husbands. "Only someone who ever trembled in the presence of the SS," Tarika underlined, "is capable of appreciating the courage of Mr. Selahattin Ülkümen, who placed himself before the evil Nazi beasts, and snatched Jews from their claws, and this was a humanitarian and courageous deed done only by the few."

Ülkümen briefly told them to show up at 6 p.m. in front of the building where the Jews were held, in order to be reunited with their liberated husbands. And so it was. Close to 50 persons were thus freed from deportation, literally at the eleventh hour. The rest of the close to 1,800 Jews were taken by boat to the Greek mainland; thence by train over a long, arduous and painful 1,000 kilometer journey in cattle wagons, via Serbia, Croatia, Hungary and Slovakia—to the Auschwitz death facility, in Poland, where with a few exceptions, they were all herded into the gas chambers. In their psychotic mania, it was important to the Nazi leadership, that in spite of the ever dwindling resources in a losing war—to commit soldiers and railway stock, so as not to allow the small distant Jewish community of Rhodes, who had not taken sides in the war, to remain alive. The Turkish diplomat had managed to save only a handful.

Mathilde Turiel emphasized that only about 15 men and women were in truth Turkish nationals, but Ülkümen added 25 to 30 more people "who he knew were no longer Turkish citizens since they had let their citizenship lapse." Not satisfied with Ülkümen's claim that the group of Turkish nationals included more than the original 15 persons, the SS insisted that he produce documents to that effect. At this point, Ülkümen claimed that under Turkish law, spouses of Turkish citizens were also under Turkish jurisdiction, irrespective of their own citizenship," a point contested by some persons familiar with Turkish law at the time. Not wishing to offend Turkey, a country still neutral in the war, the Germans relented and released the close to 50 Jewish persons on Ülkümen's list.

Responding to the appeal of Mathilde Turiel, and other beneficiaries who survived thanks to Ülkümen's magnanimity and courageous action, Yad Vashem awarded the Righteous title to the retired Turkish diplomat, in 1989—the only Turkish person decorated with this honor. In the words of the chairman of the Commission for the Righteous: "Fifty Jews state, 'I am alive thanks to him; had he not intervened—I would not be alive.'" A year after his recognition, Selahattin Ülkümen visited Israel, and planted a tree in the Avenue of the Righteous, at Yad Vashem. His, and the other cases in this chapter, is further proof of how public servants in various capacities could, if they wished, reinterpret existing laws and regulations in such a way as to make it possible for Jews to elude capture and death at the hands of the Nazis.[25]

Selahattin Ülkümen and Mathilde Turiel at a reunion in New York

Chapter 6

Rescuers Who Were Punished for Showing Compassion

As pointed out in our introductory chapter, the risks facing would-be rescuers of Jews were serious, including even the loss of life. While no estimate exists on the number of rescuers who suffered martyrdom after being apprehended in the act of help, from the available documentation it is clear that among them are to be counted persons from all occupied European countries. More than a few rescuers were the object of physical assault by their own countrymen, either during or, as in the already related case of Jonas Paulavicius, in the immediate postwar years. Some rescuers, who disobeyed instructions from above and afforded help to fleeing Jews were penalized by their own governments, such as in the case of Aristides de Sousa Mendes, the Portuguese consul-general in Bordeaux, France. Although told in clear terms not to issue transit visas to Jews, he disregarded these instructions and issued the visas to thousands of Jews stranded in Bordeaux, and wishing to leave the city in advance of the arrival of the Germans, in June 1940. Recalled to Lisbon, he was ordered to face a disciplinary board, which decided to strip him of his title, dismiss him from his country's diplomatic service, and deny him severance payments to which he was entitled for many years of service to his country. The Swiss authorities, likewise moved harshly against Major Paul Grüninger, commandant of the St. Gallen police border post, facing Austria. He had allowed thousands of Jews, fleeing from Austria, which after March 1938 had been annexed to Nazi Germany, in spite of instructions to the contrary. Placed on trial, he too was dismissed from the police without pay, and with the forfeit of any severance payments. Both these rescuers were awarded the Righteous title.[1] In the following select stories, we tell of rescuers who either died or suffered severe physical abuse at the hands of the Nazis, as well as one story of a rescuer killed by his own countrymen for refusing to expel a group of Jews whom he had admitted for shelter.

Heinrich List

The German Farmer Who Paid with His Life for Sheltering a Jew

In March 1992, a letter was received from the Israeli embassy in Bonn, Germany, informing Yad Vashem that a group of high school students from Michelstadt would be visiting the memorial the following month, and wished on this occasion to hand over a Gestapo report on a certain Heinrich List. The two high school teachers leading this group of students also inquired whether the late Heinrich List could, on the occasion of their visit, be awarded the Righteous title. Some time earlier, the two teachers had come across a book on the Jewish community in Michelstadt, which included a report on the tragic case of Heinrich List in the nearby village of Ernsbach. This prompted them to inquire further with the inhabitants of the village on the List story, but found themselves stonewalled. Most people either feigned ignorance or lived under the spell of *Denunziationstrauma*, that is, they all suspected everyone else as being the one who had betrayed List to the police. During the Hitler period, the villagers were known to be staunch supporters of the Nazi party. The off-handed attitude of the villagers stimulated the teachers to seek more information elsewhere, and for this they turned to the regional police archives, which were located in the city of Darmstadt, and this is what they uncovered.

Heinrich List, a farmer in Ernsbach, Hessen province, had fought in the First World War, and during the Second World War had a son serving in the German army. Before the war, List had done business with a certain Ferdinand Strauss, in Michelstadt, who dealt in textiles. The Jewish community there counted some 150 persons. None returned to Michelstadt after the Holocaust. During the large-scale *Kristallnacht* pogrom of November 10, 1938, Strauss had been arrested, but he made his escape and fled to an uncle, living in Frankfurt. In November 1941, sensing the noose tightening ever stronger around the neck of the Jews in that city, he fled again — this time to his former business acquaintance, the farmer Heinrich List, in Ernsbach, who immediately admitted him. Strauss was kept hidden on List's farm until the latter was betrayed to the authorities, in April 1942. The informer was a farmhand, a Polish forced laborer, who after an altercation with List, decided to report him to the village mayor for sheltering a Jew. At first, the mayor did nothing, and for a month kept the information to himself, until people in the village began to gossip about a Jew in List's home. Sensing the handwriting on the wall, Strauss fled in time, and eventually was able to cross into Switzerland, from where he continued to Jamaica. Back in Ernsbach, with the village a beehive of gossip about the mysterious Jew in List's home—the mayor fearing arrest on the charge of withholding evidence decided to inform the police, who passed it on to the Gestapo, who in turn acted immediately by arresting List, nominally a card-carrying member of the Nazi party, on April 17, 1942.

At first, Heinrich List denied having harbored a Jew on his farm. But faced with the foreign laborer's statement, and the grilling of Heinrich's wife, he admitted to the "serious" offense. In the signed confession, List reported that one day, in November 1941, Ferdinand Strauss appeared at his home, and told him that his uncle in Frankfurt had died, and his aunt had poisoned herself. Since he was now alone, he asked to be allowed to stay just for a few days, but List, in fact, decided to shelter him for an indefinite period. Strauss was treated as an equal by the Lists, even sharing their dining table, together with the Polish laborer. However, whenever people visited, Strauss hid in a side room, until the visitors had left; the Pole did not have to do so. The following is from the Darmstadt police blotter on List's interrogation:

Question: *For what reasons did you admit the Jew Ferdinand Strauss and afford him shelter?*
Answer: *Because we knew each other well since childhood, and he was now all alone.*
Question: *Why did you not report him to the police?*
Answer: *I was not aware that I had to report him to the police. At no time was I motivated to hide him due to opposition to the regime. Only because we knew each other well, and previously we entertained good business relations. I felt compassion toward him and so I hid him.*

Showing compassion to a fleeing Jew was not a mitigating excuse in Nazi Germany; in fact, it was a serious offense. In the words of the police investigator, who analyzed the case:

He must without any doubt be considered a friend of the Jew. I arrived at this conclusion, based on the fact that it was otherwise impossible to hide a Jew in a village of 298 inhabitants [without the others knowing of it]. *I therefore take the position that he knew perfectly well what he was doing and what this implied. In my opinion, he kept* [the Jew] *from being apprehended and jailed in full conscience and foreknowledge of the deed's implications.*

The die was cast for Heinrich List. After several weeks imprisonment in Darmstadt, the 60-year-old defendant was sent to Dachau on July 17, 1942, where he died (or was murdered) three months after his arrival — on October 10, 1942. He was survived by his wife Marie, and a daughter, Margarethe. To add to Marie's sorrow — her son, Jakob, a soldier in the *Wehrmacht*, was reported missing in 1944, on the Russian front. Immediately after the war, Ferdinand Strauss, safely established in Jamaica, wrote to Marie List, suggesting financial assistance to offset the difficult conditions prevailing then in the war-torn country. Marie politely turned down the offer, without disclosing to him the fate of her husband. Strauss died in 1983.

Upon arrival at Yad Vashem, in April 1992, the German high-school students turned over the incriminating police records of Heinrich List, which had been neatly preserved in the city archives of Darmstadt. That same year, his name as well as of his wife Marie were added to the list of the "Righteous Among the Nations." The following year, the Righteous medal and certificate of honor were awarded to the List grandchildren by the Israeli ambassador, in a ceremony in the restored synagogue in Michelstadt, and in the presence of local dignitaries. Thus, a German rescuer, who paid with his life for sheltering a Jew, had been accidentally discovered during a cursory search in the archives of a German city by two high school teachers, who were preparing their students for a first visit to Israel.[2]

Left to right: Margarethe, Marie, Heinrich, and Jakob
List around 1920-21.

Ilse Sonja Totzke

The German Woman Who Openly Defied the Nuremberg Laws

Another similar accidental discovery is that concerning Ilse Sonja Totzke. The story first appeared in a book by Robert Gellately, entitled *The Gestapo and German Society*,[3] which was based on police and Gestapo records in Würzburg on the enforcement of Nazi racial policy and measures taken against offenders. On pages 180-184 there appeared the story of Ilse Sonja Totzke and her bitter fate. The footnotes indicated the police file numbers that could be obtained in Würzburg. The Würzburg city archives responded to Yad Vashem's request for more information, which came in the form of a batch of 72 Gestapo reports — more than anything originally anticipated. Upon receipt of the rich documentation, I was stunned by the tenacity, persistence, and thoroughness of the Gestapo in enforcing Nazi laws against fraternization with Jews, and of the extraordinary courage of a lone young German woman who took a stand against such a policy. What follows is based on the neatly assembled documentation by the Gestapo to justify the persecution of a sole person.

In June 1936, for reasons left unexplained, the Gestapo began to screen Totzke's mail. Nothing apparently further happened until September 27, 1939 (with Germany already at war), when her landlord informed the Gestapo on the "suspicious" behavior of Miss Totzke. In the words of the informer, he had rented an apartment to Miss Totzke on the outskirts of Würzburg. She claimed to be a music student, but showed no particular interest in her studies, and in light of her fraternizing with two or three Jewish men, he suspected her of being opposed to the Nazi regime. He was sure that she did not wish be part of the German *Volksgemeinschaft* (a Nazi term signifying a racial community of people), although he could not remember hearing her make anti-German remarks.

In March 1940, another informer, who lived across Totzke's home, also reported her "unusual" behavior, such as making sure that no outsiders knew her address. Her mail box, moreover, was always empty; she did not get up for work but slept until midday, remained closeted indoors, and only stepped out at night. More seriously — she was not returning the Hitler salute in response to a similar greeting. In summary, there was something definitely suspicious about her, coupled with the fact that she consistently avoided contacts with her neighbors. This second informer was instructed by the Gestapo to watch Totzke's movements and continue reporting her "suspicious" behavior.

Several months later, three additional informers added their own reports on Totzke, which this time included her anti-Nazi views and her "crazy" ideas. Fritz Friedrich, who claimed to know her for four years, charged her with being an individualist, who absolutely refused to be part of the German *Volksgemeinschaft*. An additional complaint, in July 1940, by a certain Theresia Kraus, reported Totzke's definitely anti-German, pro-Jewish and pro-French views (the war with France had just ended in a stunning German victory). Again—she declined to respond to the Hitler salute, kept to herself, left her apartment only at night, returning at dawn the next day ("our dog barks when she returns"), and from time to time received the visit of a 35-year-old, Jewish-looking woman. Mrs. Kraus was asked by the Gestapo to keep a close watch over Miss Totzke's movements. In the meantime, the Gestapo satisfied itself with censoring Miss Totzke's mail.

Close to a year later, on May 2, 1941, an additional informer reported to the Gestapo that Totzke was in violation of the anti-fraternization laws with regard to Jews, in that she was entertaining a very close relationship with a 15-year-old Jewish girl named Schwabacher. This time, the Gestapo decided to act and Totzke was called in for an interrogation, while simultaneously undertaking a search of her apartment. During her lengthy interrogation, on September 5, 1941, Miss Totzke told of her past and present life. Born in 1913, in Strasbourg, to Protestant parents (her father was an orchestra director), the family moved back to Germany, in 1919, after Strasbourg reverted to French sovereignty. After her mother's death, in Mannheim, Ilse moved to Ludwigshafen and took up studying music in Würzburg. A traffic accident in 1935 produced a severe migraine. Medical costs, support of her two step-sisters (her father had remarried after the death of Ilse's mother), and other expenses ate up the money she had inherited after her father's death in 1934. She admitted having contact with Jews in the past, but it was mostly restricted to leasing dwellings in Jewish-owned apartments. She did, however, entertain a special relationship with the Jewess Ottenberg. As for her fraternization with Else Schwabacher, whom her parents knew from the Strasbourg period—she was actually not Jewish, Ilse claimed, but merely married to a Jewish man who had already left for America. Insofar as her pro-French sentiments was concerned—it amounted to merely taking French lessons with a certain professor. Otherwise, she took no interest in politics. At the same time—and here the courageous character of this woman came to light—she wished to make it clear that she did not agree with the regime's treatment of Jews. "I cannot agree with the measures in this regard." She was not a communist, but simply believed that every decent person was to be afforded equal treatment by society, without regard to one's ethnicity. She was undoubtedly quite aware that this last statement represented a open challenge to the Nazi regime.

During her interrogation, Gestapo agents raided her home, and subsequently reported on some of the "subversive" literature found, including: *The Mother*, by Sholom Asch; *Jewish History*, by S. Müller; *Theodor Herzl – a Biography*, by Alex Bein; *Palestine Diary*, by Manfred Sturmann; and *The New Crusade*, by Benjamin Disraeli.

Seven weeks later, on October 28, 1941, Totzke was invited for another session with the Gestapo, and made to sign a statement, which reiterated information given during her previous interrogation. Asked again concerning her relationship with Else Schwabacher, Totzke repeated her previous assertion that this woman was definitely non-Jewish, but married to a Jew, who left for America two years ago. "I admit having contact with her, but she is an Aryan, nee Else Klose. . . I have no contacts with Else's in-laws, who live on the ground floor whereas Else lives on the first floor." Asked again on her views with regard to the Nazis, she disclaimed any interest in politics. "At the same time," she repeated for the second time, "I find the measures against the Jews as unjust. I wish to emphasize I am not a communist. Every decent person is acceptable to me, irrespective of one's nationality." She was then made to sign a statement that in the event of further fraternization with Mrs. Schwabacher, and additional complaints by neighbors on her non-German disposition, "I will face the possibility of immediate arrest and transfer to a concentration camp." A month thereafter, on November 3, 1941, the Würzburg Gestapo was informed by its Nuremberg head office (following a directive from Berlin) that, in light of recent cases of public fraternization between Aryans and Jews, all non-Jewish offenders were to be arrested and transferred to a concentration camp for a stay of up to three months. The Jewish person, in such cases, was to be immediately removed to a concentration camp.

Over a year later, in February 1943, the Würzburg municipality informed the police that Ilse Sonja Totzke had apparently left for Berlin, but did not leave a forwarding address. Then, on March 4, 1943, the Mulhausen (Mulhouse, in the French annexed area) Gestapo reported that the Swiss custom authorities had the previous week arrested Totzke, together with a Jewish woman, named Eva Ruth Sara Basinsky (a Berlin kindergarten teacher), on the charge of illegal crossing of the border, and had turned both over to the German border police. In her statement, at the time of her arrest, Totzke repeated the biographical sketches she gave in previous Gestapo interrogations; that she was born in 1913 to a father who was a musician, and a mother was a stage actress. She then added that after continuing to have contacts with Jews, in spite of Gestapo warnings, and upon receiving a summons to report to the Gestapo in December 1942, fearing arrest, she decided to flee to Berlin. Before that, she confided to a certain Mrs. Strauss, an Aryan married to a Jew, of her decision to flee to Switzerland. This lady asked her, when in Berlin, to extend greetings to a certain Ruth Sara Basin-sky, through her son. This is how she got to know this woman in September 1942. In Berlin, Totzke boarded in private rooms, and once stayed overnight at Basinsky's place, in clear violation of the law forbidding non-Jews to be hosted in Jewish-assigned homes. Then, in early January 1943, she left for Strasbourg. After a night's stay there, she continued via Mulhausen to Sonnheim; then via Colmar to Münster (in Alsace), where for three days she reconnoitered the border area with Switzerland. Secretly returning to Würzburg, to fetch her clothes, she traveled via indirect routes to Berlin, to look up Mrs. Basinsky to invite her to flee with her to Switzerland. However, in Berlin, she learned that Basinsky had been arrested and placed in a Jewish transit camp. The day afterwards, she waited for many hours in front of that place until she made contact with Basinsky, and urged her to join her on a flight to Switzerland. After two more hurriedly-arranged meetings, Basinsky allowed herself to be persuaded. As for the reason for wanting to flee Nazi Germany, Ilse Totzke minced no words, and made the following telling statement:

> I already thought for a long time to flee Germany, since I did not feel comfortable under the regime of Adolf Hitler. Above all, I find the Nurem-berg laws unacceptable, and for this reason I considered my relations with the Jews whom I knew to be justified.[4]

She then gave a precise, day-to-day account of her flight toward the German-Swiss border, in the company of Basinsky. After arriving in Stras-bourg, on February 26, the two women proceeded by train via Mulhausen to Durmenach, the last stop before the border. They then headed in the evening on foot toward the Swiss border. "I knew this way from summer 1942, during my vacation in Alsace. Already then, I checked out the flight route toward the border," Totzke stated in her deposition. Late at night, between February 26 to 27, the two women crossed the barbed-wired German-Swiss border, near Neumahle, only to be apprehended by Swiss customs officials. In spite of their pleading that they no longer wished to remain in Germany, they were returned to the border point at dusk. That same evening, the two women tried a second crossing at a border point without barbed wire. After aimlessly walking two to three hours inside Switzerland, they were again arrested by Swiss custom officials. This time, the Swiss were less benign, and they handed the women over directly into the hands of German border officials. Wishing to relieve Mrs. Basinsky of complicity in this escape attempt, Miss Totzke placed all the blame on her own shoulders.

I was not asked by anyone to take the Jewess along. I only felt
compassionate toward her and wished to free her from deportation. It is
I who persuaded her to join me. For this, I did not receive from Basinsky
or anyone else any payment. In addition, I was not helped by anyone to
carry out my flight plan. I should like to repeat, that I wished to flee
Germany, since I am opposed to National Socialism. Above all, I cannot
approve of the Nuremberg laws. I had decided to let myself be interned in
Switzerland. I have no wish to further live in Germany, under any
circumstances.[5]

On March 13, 1943, the Würzburg Gestapo ordered her internment in
a concentration camp, noting, in a lengthy report of the case, that with Totzke
one deals with a lazy person; that despite her denials, she was probably
involved in other attempts to take Jews across the border; that she was
definitely opposed to Nazism, the Hitler regime and the Nuremberg laws;
that her motivation in helping Basinsky was "compassion" — to help her
avoid deportation. She is a "Jew-woman" (*Judenweib*), the Gestapo official
concluded, and in light of her behavior, she is beyond redress. On May 23,
1943, Gestapo headquarters in Berlin approved Totzke's incarceration in
Ravensbrück camp, where she arrived on the next transport — on June 4,
1943.

When this bulky and neatly arranged Gestapo and police report was
placed before the Commission of the Righteous, in March 1995, it had no
trouble awarding Totzke the Righteous title, while at the same time
wondering what had befallen this heroic woman after her arrival at the
infamous women's camp of Ravensbrück. I immediately asked our embassy
in Bonn to help us learn of her fate. "If still alive," I wrote, "she should be
84 years old. If not, we should like to have the address of a relative or nearest
friend." I was then informed that, according to records which reached the
embassy, Ilse Totzke was sent from Ravensbrück to Auschwitz; then
returned to Ravensbrück, and liberated on April 26, 1945 — when the camp
was captured by the Russians. Her further whereabouts were unknown.

Ilse Sonja Totzke, the lone courageous woman, who in 1943 declared
that she could no longer live in a Germany headed by Adolf Hitler, and in
which Jews were persecuted, and true to her innermost conviction, tried to
flee the country and take along a Jewish women, whom she had accidentally
met while passing through Berlin — survived the horrors of two
concentration camps. That in itself, is a source of great consolation. Although
no further information is, as of this moment, available on her postwar fate,
her name proudly adorns the Righteous Honor Roll at Yad Vashem.[6]

Adelaïde Hautval

The French Woman Physician, "One of the Most Remarkable Persons Humankind Has Ever Known."

At times, even expressing sympathy for Jews, let alone extending help, could land a person in a concentration camp, as was the case with Adelaïde Hautval of France. Her story became a *cause célèbre* when on April 29, 1964, she took the stand during a highly-charged trial in a London court, in the case of Wladyslaw Dering versus Leon Uris. In his best-selling novel, *Exodus*, the famed author and movie-script writer had inserted a paragraph in which he charged Dering, a Polish prisoner-doctor at Auschwitz, with performing surgery, without proper anesthetics, on ovaries and testicles of Jewish women and men, after they had been sterilized with X-ray by SS doctors. The purpose of these experiments was to find out the correct dose for producing sterility, which would then be applied on a mass basis so as to eliminate, by failure of reproduction, "undesirable" races and ethnic groups, such as half- and quarter-Jews.

After the war, Dering had fled arrest to England. After being briefly detained, he left for Somaliland, where he acquired British nationality, and in 1960, on the Queen's birthday, was made an Officer of the British Empire, in recognition of his medical services to the natives of this then-British colony. He then returned to England, where he set up a private practice. He was now suing the American author for defamation of name, and sought redress through an apology and the payment of a stiff fine. In his testimony, Dering admitted to having performed numerous ovaries and testicle removing operations in Auschwitz, at the request of Dr. Schumann, a German military doctor, but claimed innocence in this otherwise malpractice action. In that infamous place, Dering claimed, "all law, normal, human and God's law were finished. They were Germans' law." If he refused to perform them, he claimed, he would certainly be killed. "To refuse would be sabotage. That meant only one thing in the camp." Moreover, by himself performing the removal of sterilized ovaries and testicles, he at least took care that it be done efficiently, instead of allowing the SS doctors of doing such surgeries in a "butchery" manner. In addition, Dering claimed in his defense, had he not performed these despicable operations as ordered, the Germans would simply have killed the patients. The surgeries were done with the use of an anesthetic in the form of a spinal injection ("I used the same method in Somaliland in 15,000 operations"), which according to Dering gave the patients a lease on life. Hence, Uris' depiction of Dering's behavior was wrong and defamatory, let alone an insult to the plaintiff's respectable doctoral career. So went his argument, which Dering presented in a haughty and self-righteous manner, and without expressing any regrets or showing compassion toward the hapless victims of these experiments.

Leon Uris' defense counsel presented an array of witnesses to contest Dering's claim that the experiments were conducted in a proper medical manner, and with great attention to the victim's care, as well as his claim that refusal to perform these experiments would have resulted in death to the recalcitrant doctor. Dr. Alina Brewda, a fellow doctor-prisoner at Auschwitz, was a witness to Dering's operations. "As I entered through the corridor of Block 21, I heard screaming. . . I saw two men holding a screaming girl on a couch and a second one was crying. Dr. Dering was washing his hands in the anteroom." Brewda's task, as instructed by the German doctor Schumann, was to calm the hapless young women during and after the operation. She also testified that the girls had not been given morphine injections; that the whole operation was done at terrific speed (about ten minutes); that Dering did not wash his hands between operations, nor were the instruments sterilized. It was as though he was operating on corpses, she added. Some of the women indeed died soon thereafter from the pains of the operation. Amos Carmeli, one of those operated upon, came from Israel to testify. He told how he was strapped to a table for the removal of his testicles, after the needle injected in his spine broke, and Dering ordered the injection of another needle. Through all this, Dering's behavior was not that of a doctor, but of a brutal and uncaring person, such as his facetious remark to a complaining victim that he should be thankful, for at least he would not be committed to the gas chambers.

As to Dering's claim that he had no choice in the matter, Dr. Dorota Lorska stated that one could bypass the orders of the SS in such a way as to avoid punishment. "I know of many who did not carry out their orders. . . in the first place, Dr. Hautval." Dr. Brewda too told of how she tried to invent lies to avoid participating in these heinous experiments; that many prisoner-doctors acted likewise, and none were punished. The German historian Hans Seraphim testified that after a 12-year search through the records and available evidence, he failed to bring to light a single death sentence imposed on members of the SS or police for refusing to carry out extermination orders. Finally, when the gynecologist Professor Nixon recited in court the Hippocratic Oath: "I will abstain from abusing the bodies of men and women, either free or slave," there was an icy silence in the courtroom.

Adelaïde Hautval appeared as the star and final witness for the defense. Her testimony of her refusal to perform surgical operations on women prisoners in Auschwitz contrasted sharply with Dering's opposite behavior. Born in Hohwald, eastern France, in 1906, she qualified as a medical doctor at Strasbourg University. She then practiced medicine and psychiatry.

During the German invasion of France, in May 1940, she fled the Alsace region to the interior of the country. In April 1942, she was arrested for trying to cross the demarcation line inside France without a permit, to attend her mother's funeral in the Alsace region. Imprisoned in Bourges, she witnessed the arrival of a large number of Jews. "I protested to the Gestapo the treatment of the Jews. . . I told them I knew that in the occupied part of France they were treated like inferior beings and many things were denied them. For example, they could not travel on the subway; and could not sit in the first carriage." In response to her complaint, she was told: "As you wish to defend them, you will follow their fate." She was originally slated to be freed on July 5, 1942, but due to her pro-Jewish complaint, she was given a cloth, on which was written "Friend of the Jews," and was told to sew it on her coat. Moved to Pithiviers camp, she witnessed the deportation of Jewish parents, separate from their children. In November 1942, she was transferred to Romainville prison, and on January 24, 1943, she was placed on a convoy of French non-Jewish women prisoners for Auschwitz, where she arrived after a three-day journey.

After a three-month stay in Birkenau, she was transferred to Bloc 10, in Auschwitz, which was reserved for experiments. Among the German doctors, there was Clauberg who selected married Jewish women, on whom he practiced sterilization by inserting a caustic liquid in the uterus, causing great pains to the victims. Dr. Schumann's experiments were worse, since they were performed on 16- and 17-year-old Jewish girls, through the irradiation of their genital organs via X-ray. To check the results, the ovaries were removed, and sent to laboratories. Learning of the presence of a woman prisoner-doctor in Auschwitz, Dr. Eduard Wirths, the camp's chief SS doctor, invited Hautval to practice gynecology. "I asked him what kind of work it was. He did not answer me." Hautval was suspicious, having already heard of the sterilization experiments. "I wanted to know what kind of experiments these were, and so I accepted." She was assigned to help Dr. Clauberg in Bloc 10, where she also met Dr. Dering. When she noticed the experimental methods there, she immediately objected. Dr. Wirths' brother, also a physician, came to inquire. "He said he was surprised that a doctor who was practicing psychiatry could consider objectionable a method which was a selection to preserve the race. I answered that this was very arguable and also that this was a method which necessarily caused abuse. He talked to me about the Jewish question, and I answered him that we had no right to dispose of the life and destiny of others." She was then told to report directly to Dr. Eduard Wirths.

Entering his office, Dr. Wirths asked her why she refused to cooperate in the experiments. Hautval replied that it was contrary to her conception of a doctor. To which he said: "Can't you see that these people are different from you?" Hautval answered him: "There are several other people different from me, beginning with you." She was forthwith ordered back to Birkenau, and advised to stay low. She worked in the Revier, the camp's medical dispensary, which was a far cry from a regular and fully equipped dispensary. There she was told by a German woman prisoner that there was talk of her return to Bloc 10 and of forcing her to participate in the experiments. Hautval replied she would rather commit suicide. Luckily for her, this plan came to naught. To fellow prisoner-doctor, Dr. Lorska, she confided: "The Germans will not allow people who know what is happening here to get in touch with the outside world, so the only thing that is left to us is to behave, for the rest of the short time that remains to us, as human beings." Nothing further happened to her. To the court's question: "Were you ever punished?" Hautval replied: "No, I was never punished. I refused afterwards to carry out experiments for Dr. Mengele and they said, 'We cannot force her to do what she does not want to do.'" In August 1944, she was moved to Ravensbrück camp. When liberated by the Russians, on April 28, 1945, she was part of 50 women survivors out of an original convoy of 230 women to this camp from Auschwitz. She then returned to France.

In his summation of the trial to the jury, Frederick Lawton, the court presiding judge described Adelaïde Hautval as:

> one of the most impressive and courageous women who had ever given evidence in the courts of this country, a most outstanding and distinguished person. She had stood up to the Nazis four times and made it quite clear what she was and what she was not prepared to do. . . She gave a reply to Dr. Wirths which I expect would live in jury's memories for many years – a devastating reply.

Judge Lawton further noted that fear is no excuse for murder or causing serious injury. That there comes a point when one must say "I will die rather than do this." The jury handed a verdict in favor of the plaintiff, Dr. Dering, but awarded him the sum of only one-half penny, the smallest denomination in currency – in effect, a vindication of the defendant author Leon Uris. A year later, in May 1965, Adelaïde Hautval was awarded the Righteous title by Yad Vashem, and a year thereafter, she visited Israel and planted a tree in her name in the Avenue of the Righteous. During the ceremony in her honor, she stated: "This return of the people of Israel to their own country is an accomplishment which concerns not only you, but the world at large. It has been ardently awaited also by non-Jews. Israel has always played a gestating and fermenting role, because of which it was hated or respected. Its mission in the world continues to exist, and may Israel remain faithful to this mission. The entire history of this people demonstrates the primacy of spiritual forces, and hence its undertakings cannot but be successful."

Reminiscing in a 1972 article on the Dering trial, she noted that this case demonstrates what can happen to a man, an ordinary doctor, when he participates in a process leading to the degradation of man. She then added her own reflection on what took place in Auschwitz:

> *I'm sure that all the terrible things in the world begin with small acts of cowardice. At Auschwitz, for instance, we prisoner-doctors had to face this terrible question of the selections: that is, we were asked by the SS to decide which patients were too ill or weak to be able to work properly, and if we selected these patients we knew perfectly well that they would be dispatched immediately to the gas chambers. . . I myself refused to write the words 'unfit for work' on any medical papers. And what happened was that another prisoner-doctor did it on my behalf in order that I shouldn't have my own head chopped off. . . Some of the prisoner-doctors felt themselves obliged to make the selection after all so as to be sure that only those who were really likely to die anyhow would be chosen.*

Dr. Adelaïde Hautval

What happened inside Auschwitz, and her role as a prisoner-doctor in that infernal place, continued to trouble her mind and conscience to the end of her life. Returning to her medical practice, she spoke out against the "arrogance" of doctors, many of whom regard themselves as "superior beings," who know everything, and treat their patients as if they were "complete morons." She also complained about the sorry treatment of the elderly in modern societies. In her opinion, it was sort of a "selection" all over again. "People who have worked all their lives, who have brought up children, are suddenly to be denied elementary care because they've reached the age of 70 or 75: it's unthinkable. Primitive tribes treat their old people better. They would never let them rot away in institutions."

As to her own life philosophy — one should try and remember the good things. "I think we ought to love life too much to remember only the hatred and bitterness of the past." When she died in 1988, Judge Moshe Bejski, who succeeded Landau as chairman of the Yad Vashem-appointed Commission for the Righteous, and himself a Holocaust survivor, lauded her as "one of the most remarkable persons that mankind has known. . . When I visited her, in Groslay [France], three years ago, she told me she did not think she had the right to hold the Righteous title, for such a title is reserved to God alone, and not to mortal beings." Adelaïde Hautval's severe punishment — two harrowing concentration camps — was for her sole "transgression" of rejecting the inhumane treatment of Jews. In the Nazi world of lawless justice, being branded a "friend of the Jews" meant having to bear more suffering at the hands of the Nazis.[7]

Stefan Sawa

Killed by His Own People for Sheltering Jews

The following story is of a Polish rescuer whose humanitarianism was repaid with assassination at the hands of some of his own people. In February 1990, Zevi Selinger asked Yad Vashem to bestow the Righteous title to the late Stefan Sawa. In his testimony, he disclosed that the mysterious death of his sister Dina, in a hiding place arranged by her rescuer Stefan Sawa, had given him no rest for over 40 years. According to Selinger, his aunt Sofia's (father's sister) friendship with Stefan predated the war period. When the Selinger family was forced into the Kielce Ghetto, Stefan stole food and clothing for his friend's family inside the ghetto. In August 1942, the Germans liquidated most of the Jews in Kielce, allowing only a small group to survive as forced laborers in a German factory (known as Hasag), including members of the Selinger family. When the Germans began to liquidate this surviving group in 1943, the Selingers managed to flee. Some headed to Warsaw, armed with false identities, and others were moved by Stefan Sawa to a secret hiding place in an isolated village house (Brzechowie), outside Kielce. Among the hiding persons were Zevi's sister Dina and his aunt Sofia. There the group of five Jews remained hidden for a year's time.

Zevi Selinger was not part of this group of hiders, but joined his father, who lived under an assumed identity in Warsaw. Concerned for his son's safety in this large metropolis, Zevi's father arranged, through the Polish underground to which he belonged, for Zevi to be joined to his relatives in the secret village hideout. But after a few days there, the Polish woman-associate of Stefan objected to his further stay, and had him returned to Warsaw. Thanks to being expelled by this irate woman, Zevi's life was paradoxically saved. His father, back in Warsaw, wondering why he was not getting any further news of his daughter and sister, learned of a tragedy that occurred in that isolated village house, through the underground conduit. On February 16, 1944, the house was raided by unknown armed persons, who torched it with its occupants, killing the five Jews inside, including the rescuer Stefan Sawa. Zevi's father's determination to investigate this tragedy was thwarted during the tumultuous conditions of the war. In August 1944, during the Polish uprising in Warsaw, Zevi's father fell in battle. Immediately after the war, Zevi and his mother returned to Kielce to learn more about their loved ones' mysterious death, but this time their efforts were frustrated by the intense antisemitic atmosphere reigning in Kielce, which erupted into a pogrom against the returning Jews, in July 1946. Before hurriedly leaving Kielce, and Poland, for Israel, the two Selingers managed to learn that the dastardly act was committed not by Germans but by Polish armed men.

For over 40 years, Zevi Selinger kept silent. Then, in 1989, in a sudden passionate upsurge, he decided to try to unravel the identity of the authors of that criminal act. Returning to Kielce that year, he undertook a tedious ten day investigation, with the help of a local journalist. He found the torched home's location, and interviewed formed residents of the village who recalled the tragic event. A relative of Stefan Sawa finally rounded out the missing details, giving Zevi the near-precise sequence of events, as follows.

In early 1944, a unit of the Polish underground (the Home Army), headed by a man known by the code-name "Barabash" searched the house. Finding hidden Jews, they told Stefan Sawa to have them expelled — or else! As Sawa related to his sister-in-law, the partisans justified their demand by arguing that the Germans would exact punishment on the whole village if they found the Jews hidden in that home, and therefore one had to be rid of them. Sawa assured his sister-in-law that he was going to reason with his Polish compatriots on their next visit and ask for a postponement, telling them that since the Germans were losing the war, they had their hands tied with other pressing matters than a few hidden Jews, if it ever came to that. If he failed to convince them — he would try to buy them off. His aim was to play for time. Tragically for Sawa and his hidden wards, when the partisans returned to the house and discovering that Sawa had not heeded their warning, they torched the building, and all its occupants including Sawa who died in the inferno. "I feel terribly bad," Zevi related, "that the deed was performed by the same underground to which my father belonged, and fell in one of its operations." The Germans themselves came to investigate the strange fire, but were stonewalled by the silence of the village residents. After a while, Stefan's mother was notified of her son's death. She came, wrapped her son's torched body, as well as the six hidden Jews, and buried them all in one grave, bearing her son's name. Presently, Zevi Selinger asked for Stefan Sawa to be recognized as a "Righteous Among the Nations."

As I listened to Zevi's emotional account of the tragic death of his sister and aunt, I could not help but also be moved, and frankly upset that Jewish persons fleeing the Nazis should lose their lives not at the hands of the principal culprits, the Germans, but of Polish antisemitic partisans — themselves fiercely resisting the Nazi occupant of their country. At the same time, my responsibility as a Yad Vashem associate required of me not to be satisfied with eyewitness accounts over 40 years after the event, but to seek additional reliable verification of the particular Polish partisan's participation in this criminal act, before recommending Yad Vashem's stamp of approval of the story. When I shared this concern with Selinger, he told me that during his recent trip to Poland, he learned that in 1946, the Polish police had undertaken an investigation of this tragic incident. I therefore suggested to him to try, on his next voyage to Poland, to locate the relevant official archival data. True to his word, Zevi Selinger was able to acquire a copy of the official Polish investigation of this case, which had resulted in the trial in 1951 of "Barabash" and his accomplices, who received jail sentences.

Armed with this additional information, the Commission for the Righteous had no reservations in awarding the Righteous title to Stefan Sawa, a Polish knight of the spirit of the highest caliber, killed by his own kinsmen for the "sin" of harboring Jews. Zevi Selinger's persistence to acquit himself of a moral debt, through Yad Vashem, to the man who tried to save his sister and aunt, and several other Jews, had been vindicated. Several years after Sawa's recognition, in 1991, Zevi Selinger passed away.[8]

Chapter 7

Sheltering Children

Jewish children faced an unimaginable fate during the Holocaust. In stark contrast to other ethnic groups persecuted by the Nazis, Jewish children were the only ones specifically singled out for extermination, for the simple reason of having been born, and in order to avoid the perpetuation of the Jewish people. Some one and a half million Jewish children, most of whose traces are lost, perished in the Holocaust, since they accompanied their parents into the gas chambers or met their death in various forms of brutal killings. An estimated several tens of thousands of children survived in hiding, either in private homes, or in various lay and religious institutions. While there, they underwent psychological pains; first, of being separated from their parents for reasons not fully — if at all — understood by these tender minds. Many interpreted this as no less than abandonment, as being considered undesirables, not to be loved by their own parents. They then had to undergo another psychological test — the rigors of readjusting to new names, religions and cultural environments; this, at an age when love, affection, and trust are indispensable elements in a child's development. But these children found it hard to understand why they were being brutalized for no offense on their part. After the war came the pains of another readjustment; this time, of having to leave newly-found homes, where they basked in the love and affection by foster parents and their families, and readjust (again for reasons they did not understand) to new names, religions, and cultural environment, and accompany family relatives, who had suddenly appeared out of the mist and claimed them as their own.

The traumas experienced by the children, at an age crucial to their mental and psychological formation, have left an indelible mark on their lives. Most decided to turn their back on their wartime experience, and erase it from their memory — at least, in the immediate postwar period. Many decades later, the youthful memories resurfaced and began to haunt them. With children and grandchildren of their own, they had matured sufficiently to try to master the hidden and buried childhood pains, and come to grips with their past. This meant rediscovering the ones that had risked their lives in order to save them from the Nazis and the flames of the Holocaust. The following stories are but a selection of these former children's rediscovery of their hidden and painful years, culminating in finding recognition for their rescuers through Yad Vashem's program of "Righteous Among the Nations." We begin with stories where rescuers and rescued children searched and found each other, many decades after the war. Then, several stories of a renewed meeting between both parties after a long lapse. Finally, two stories of rescued children who were adopted and raised as non-Jews, and who suddenly felt a strong urge to uncover their original Jewish family roots; in one such case—a Jewish child turned Catholic priest. We end with an edifying story of a rescued child who, at first, decided to sever all links with her painful past; then, after many years, found the strength to pick up the threads of her early years.

A transport of Jewish women and children arriving at Auschwitz.

Hein R. Korpershoek and Wibo Florissen

Two Dutch Men Save a Jewish Girl by "Kidnapping" Her

In November 1985, Hein Korpershoek, a consulting geologist working in Brazil, was preparing to attend an exhibit in his honor in his native country, the Netherlands, consisting of wartime posters, cartoons and pamphlets he had drawn for the Dutch underground. As his mind wandered back to his wartime activities forty years earlier, he started thinking about the little Jewish girl he had saved from the Nazi grip, virtually at the eleventh hour. He began to wonder what had become of her. He had learned that after the war she was taken to Israel by her parents. So he drafted a letter to the Israeli consul-general in Rio de Janeiro, asking for his help to locate the girl, and perhaps obtain from her some photos and personal testimonies that could be used as background material for the exhibit in Amsterdam. "I would be most grateful," Korpershoek concluded his letter, "if you, through official Israeli channels or otherwise, would be willing and able to help me in this quest."

Korpershoek was referring to a dramatic episode of his underground life, during the German occupation of the Netherlands, when he and a fellow underground operative volunteered to save a Jewish child. The drama began on Sunday, November 28, 1943, when Ans Van Dam, a medical student, whose semi-Jewish background exempted her from deportation, frantically appeared at the home of her friend, Mrs. Morling, in Hilversum, with the terrible news that the daughter of her Jewish friends was about to be picked up by the Germans. Miss Van Dam learned of this after she was asked by the child's parents, Nathan and Elisheva Dasberg (themselves in hiding), to look up their daughter, Miriam, who was kept in a private boarding house, in the heart of Amsterdam, and bring her a gift on her third birthday. Arriving there, Ans learned from the pension mistress that several days ago she had been visited by the German Security police, the dreaded SD, an arm of the Gestapo, who had immediately identified the young child by her looks as Jewish. Taking the woman's husband as a hostage with them, they promised to return in a few days to pick up the child.

Instead of returning to the Dasbergs with the bad news, Van Dam hurried to her friend, Mrs. Morling, who was linked with the underground, and with tears in her eyes asked for her help to avoid the child's capture by the Germans. Wibo Florissen, a 20 year-old Dutch underground operative, who happened to be visiting Mrs. Morling, overheard the story and immediately alerted his 17-year-old colleague, Hein Kopershoek. They both decided on a plan to snatch the child, before the Nazis could lay their hands on her. Hein, who specialized in the fabrication and falsification of documents, immediately set himself to work. He prepared identification papers for himself and his friend, posing as Nazi SD agents. The following day, the two rendezvoused with Ans Van Dam in Amsterdam, whence they proceeded to the pension house, in the center of town, while Ans was told to stay behind, and be on the lookout several blocks away.

It was Monday, 7:15 a.m., when Wibo and Hein, dressed as Nazi police agents, with Gestapo-styled hats properly pulled down over their forehead, appeared in front of the pension house. Furiously banging at the door of the pension, they shouted: "Security Police! Open Up!" They presented their credentials before the frightened lady of the house and, pushing their way past her, they entered the lobby, where some of the boarders had gathered. They told the residents to return immediately to their rooms, or else! Shouting and speaking in a disrespectful tone, the two then said that, as promised, they had come to pick up the small Jewish "creep." The lady of the house—wishing to verify that the two men were not impostors, and mindful of the threat by the real Gestapo agents not to give the child away until they had returned—picked up the phone, saying she wanted to confirm the two men's identity with a call to the main German police station. Wibo and Hein immediately grabbed the receiver out of her hand and, cursing at her and threatening violence, told her they knew perfectly well what game she was up to—she wished to alert her underground friends. Continuing to shout insults and threats, they grabbed the little girl, had her dressed up, and immediately whisked her out of the house. Hurrying a few blocks away, where Van Dam was waiting tensely, they placed the child in her care and disappeared. The whole thing had lasted barely a few minutes.

The two underground operatives then hurried to a friend, where they hid for several days, while the child was turned over to a family for hiding in the Limburg province in southern Netherlands, where she remained until 1945. The Dasberg parents, who knew of the child's location, came to fetch her after the war, and in 1948 the family emigrated to Israel. Miriam eventually settled on a kibbutz, married, and gave birth to six children.

Back in Amsterdam, when the real Gestapo agents appeared at the pension as promised, they were furious to learn that the Dutch underground had outsmarted them, and snatched a Jewish victim from their hands. Under questioning by the Gestapo, and fearing for her husband's life, who was being held as a hostage, the pension mistress gave out the name of Ans Van Dam, who had visited her prior to the arrival of Wibo and Hein. Ans was tracked down in Amsterdam, arrested and deported to Auschwitz, where she served in a medical capacity, and luckily survived. She too moved to Israel, and has made her home in Jerusalem where she is a practicing physician.

Other than the rescue operation itself, the other details regarding the Dasberg family were unknown to Korpershoek when he wrote to the Israeli consul-general in Rio de Janeiro. The consul-general communicated the request to his colleague in The Hague, who luckily knew of the Dasbergs' move to Israel, and contact was established between both sides within a relatively short period. Writing to Miriam's father, in March 1986, and introducing himself as one of the two men who carried out the rescue operation, Hein underscored the importance he attached to his participation in the rescue of the three-year-old child. "The kidnapping, if I may say so, of your little girl was the highlight of my underground activity, and the most cherished memory of a life filled with many shades and adventures. If one needs to be thankful for anything, it is I, myself—for having had the opportunity to carry it out." Hein continued by expressing his frustration that the Dutch people had not done more to save its Jewish population (close to 80% of which were deported and killed). "I am thankful that I was privileged to erase something of this disgrace." The Dasbergs reciprocated with words of thanks and appreciation, and expressed the wish of the family to meet Korpershoek on a visit to Israel.

This wish was fulfilled a year later, in 1987. On a visit to Yad Vashem, and standing next to the little girl, now a mother of grownup children, Hein

Above: Hein Korpershoek.
Right: Poster by Korpershoek,
titled: "Miriam's Rescue."

Korpershoek was awarded the Righteous medal and Certificate of Honor and planted a tree in the Garden of the Righteous. That same year, Hein was also honored in Amsterdam, in a special exhibit of his wartime posters and cartoons, organized by the Dutch National Museum and the National Institute for War Documentation. For this exhibit, Hein prepared a hand-printed linoleum cut, depicting the rescue of Miriam — a copy of which was made available to Yad Vashem. Wibo Florissen, his friend and colleague in this rescue operation, was also awarded the Righteous title. Rescuer and rescued, living in two countries, thousands of miles apart, had found each other again, thanks to a fortuitous event — an invitation to an exhibit of wartime posters in a third country — formerly, the home of both rescuers and rescued.[1]

Pierre-René Delvaux, Marie Taquet-Mertens and the Chateau Jamoigne

The Belgian Headmistress Who Was Mother and Rescuer to 80 Jewish Children

In a yet another remarkable story of the renewal of lost contacts, a group of former hidden children were reunited with their headmistress and instructors who operated a children's home during the war years. The renewal of contacts was prompted by Pierre-René Delvaux, who wrote to Yad Vashem, in 1985, asking for assistance in trying to locate the dozens of Jewish children who were sheltered in a children home, in an isolated place, in the Ardennes region of Belgium. Delvaux then explained the difficulty facing him, and what made him decide to look up the children:

> During the war, I was privileged to participate in the rescue of some sixty Jewish children in the Queen Elizabeth Home, in Jamoigne-sur-Semois, in the Luxembourg province of Belgium. . . I'd like to locate and renew contact with the Jewish children hidden in this home, but find myself faced with an almost insurmountable problem, due to the fact that on the one hand, these children bore a false name (quite an unavoidable necessity!) and, on the other hand, being myself wanted by the Germans, I also carried a false name – Pierre Milet, and the children called me 'Mr. Milet.' You will, therefore, understand the difficulty facing me. Perhaps you can help me?. . . I am sixty-two years old; I am retired for reasons of health, and I would very much like to find them again. Since the end of the war, I think of them every day, for in a certain way they are my children.

Before anyone in the Yad Vashem Department for the Righteous had time to suggest how best to respond to this request, Delvaux, as it later turned out, had already, through responses to a newspaper announcement, made much progress and quickly located 14 of the children. To Jacques Funkleder, one of the former hidden children, Delvaux mentioned how he had created a children choral, and taught them Bach songs while on hikes outside the children home. He asked Funkleder to help him locate as many of the other children. In his communication to the former children who responded to his call, he proposed a novel idea:

> Would it not be a good idea to create an association of former persons from Jamoigne? Would this not be an occasion to collect all our testimonies concerning those years, so as to transmit to our descendants what tran-

spired to us, by every one of us writing one's personal testimony, relying on one's memory? I know this is a sensitive issue, for to most of you it is painful to talk about your parents and loved ones. In fact . . . in hiding you, we replaced, although not quite, your parents. I confess that I constantly carry within me a certain paternal feeling towards you, a feeling which for over 41 years has not weakened. It is, moreover, the reason why I have not ceased to try to find you.

Following the renewed interaction between Delvaux and his former wards, some of these placed a request to have the headmistress of the Jamoigne home, and many of the instructors, recognized by Yad Vashem as Righteous Among the Nations. As more material flowed to Yad Vashem on this episode, the curtain rose to reveal a rescue operation of considerable magnitude. The Chateau du Faing, as the building was originally known, was located in the village of Jamoigne-sur-Semois, some 10 kilometers east of Florenville. It was originally owned by a Catholic order and inhabited by nuns. In 1941, Belgian Queen Mother Elizabeth acquired the building, and transformed it into a home for feeble children of parents in prison, or in the military — but also for Jewish children on the run. With offices in Brussels, operations were coordinated by Princess Jean de Merode, on behalf of the Queen Mother, and Mrs. Yvonne Nevejean, who headed the country's national child welfare organization (*Oeuvre National de l'Enfant,* or *ONE*). Marie Taquet-Mertens and husband Emile were appointed administrators of the home. As Delvaux testified: "When I arrived in end March 1943, as instructor, there were 60 Jewish children. This number increased after November 15, with 12 additional Jewish children, bringing to a total of 73 children."

Jacques Funkleder and his brother were brought to Jamoigne in May 1943 by Ida Sterno, an operative of a Jewish clandestine organization (*Comité de Défense Juif,* or *CDJ*), dedicated to the rescue of Jews. On the way to the distant chateau, she urged the boys to adopt non-Jewish sounding names, such as: *Van Humbeek* instead of *Funkleder.* Jacques recalls "the extremely painful and heartbreaking moment for our mother to see her children being taken to an unknown place." At the train station, they were joined by other children. Arriving in Jamoigne, the first days were difficult ones, trying to adjust to new and strange surroundings, and away from one's parents. "However, the smile of Mrs. Taquet, as well as her husband. . . instilled confidence in us from the start, and we found there so much warmth, that for us the chateau became a vacation camp." The staff also helped to ease the pains of separation from parents, and the children soon got accustomed to a boy scout regimen, including finding solutions to problems, communal singing, camaraderie and sport activities. Upon returning to the chateau after an outing, the children would sing in unison hymns in praise of Jamoigne, while Mrs. Taquet waited for them, standing on the top staircase at the chateau's entrance. She verified to herself that all the children (including the Jewish ones, who were well known to her) were present and accounted for, before dismissing them to their quarters. What's more, before lights were turned off at bedtime, Mrs. Taquet made a habit of making the rounds of the bunks, and giving every child a small kiss, "just as mother would have done." Thus reassured of the headmistress' motherly care, all were permitted to close their eyes. "In this enclosure," Jacques notes, "we did not feel that we were persecuted; we felt safe in the midst of non-Jewish children."

Danger, however, lurked from sudden German raids, one which took place in September 1943. Luckily, one of the staff workers had discerned the Germans approaching through the forest, and sounded the alarm. All the children, Jewish and non-Jewish, were quickly gathered in the large ground-floor hall. A German officer point-blankly asked Mrs. Taquet: "Are there any Jewish children here?" She responded quietly: "Wouldn't this be very risky for us to do?" The officer bowed and left. In addition, during the summer vacation period, when the non-Jewish children were sent home to their families, glaringly exposing the presence of the Jewish children, the solution found was to take them to a nearby village for a month's stay, where by contrast to Jamoigne they felt unsafe and in danger of detection. "What a joy, what a holiday, when we returned to the chateau, and seeing the reassuring smile, filled with warmth, of Mrs. Taquet, her husband Major Taquet (as he was affectionately called), as well as the instructors." The days passed with worry until liberation time, in September 1944, and the return of some of the children to liberated Brussels. Those not yet claimed by their parents or relatives had to endure the Battle of the Bulge, which raged around them in December 1944, and during which the children were closeted in the chateau's caves for a full month.

In September 1987, during the celebration of the first reunion of the Jamoigne children, Pierre-René Delvaux greeted the assembled guests with a reading from Psalm 124: "Let Israel now say — if it had not been the Lord who was on our side, when men rose up against us, then they would have swallowed us alive, when their anger was kindled against us. . . Blessed be the Lord, who has not given us as prey to their teeth!" That same year, based on the evidence on hand, the 89-year-old former headmistress, Marie Taquet-Mertens and her late husband Emile were admitted into the ranks of the Righteous. Also recognized were Pierre-René Delvaux, the initiator of the search for the Jamoigne children, and six of his instructor colleagues.

During a visit to Yad Vashem the following year, former hidden children reminisced on their stay in Jamoigne. "It was, to my mind, a happy period, for I do not remember anything embarrassing or unpleasant," David

Inowlocki recalled. Recollecting his memories from that early child period, he continued: "I think I was traumatized by the separation from my parents, so I tried not to think about anything, just to hitch on to this hope for life which the place offered to me. . . in order to keep one's head above water."

Dov Shaked, another Jewish Jamoigne resident, arrived there at age 10 from Germany under the name of *Albert Mandier*. Refugeed in Belgium, his family had arranged with a clandestine organization to take him to an uncertain hiding place—this, after Dov's older brother was picked up and deported to Auschwitz. In Jamoigne, Dov remembers sleeping in large hallways housing several dozen children. Night pots were placed in the corners for use at night, which were frequented by the children. "I knew there had to be more Jewish children, but Mrs. Taquet cautioned me not to talk about it, and not to develop close ties with the kids whom I suspected of being Jewish."

Akiva Kaminsky, born in 1936, recalls suddenly being told, in 1943, that he and his brother were to be taken away immediately from a Jewish children's home to a new home. Before leaving, he was given a new name—*Camée*. "All my previous identifying papers were burned." Arriving in Jamoigne, "I found there, for the first time since I can remember, a warm and loving home."

Jewish children were told to attend church services on Sundays, but Mrs. Taquet reassured them that it was part of the cover-up, so they should not be concerned about it. "The period I spent in Jamoigne was the best time of my childhood," Akiva states emphatically. Especially reassuring was Mrs. Taquet's habit of passing each night by everyone's bedside and blessing everyone "with a good night wish and kiss." For a forlorn Jewish child, in the Nazi world of 1943-44, after a traumatic separation from his parents, and not understanding why he was being hunted like a dangerous animal, such daily nocturnal smiles and kisses by the person who held the key to his survival, represented a tremendous psychological boost.

On May 15, 1998, the Jamoigne children held another reunion; this time to celebrate the Yad Vashem honors to those awarded the Righteous title. On this solemn occasion, Andrée Geulen, who had earlier also been awarded the Righteous title for her role in conveying many children to new temporary homes, including Jamoigne, evoked in touching words her introduction to the world of children rescue:

I was then a young woman; not better, nor worse than others. Life had kept me isolated from the major upheavals around me; I did not know unhappiness. Then, suddenly, I found myself, a young teacher, confronted with this tragedy which befell you. I could not accept it. I met you; I came looking for you at your homes. You placed your little hand in mine (the

*other hand held on to the large suitcase, with all the treasures prepared
with tears by your mothers), and we left on our journey. . . for a long time
now I wanted to say to you 'thank you,' for having taught me for all of
my life the immeasurable stupidity of racism. . . Never again have I felt
such exaltation, such satisfaction, except when raising my own children;
no other work has filled me with such pride. Imagine what this represented
for a 20-year-old woman, to go to sleep at night, and think – another five
children saved; another five children spared deportation. . . I loved you then
so much; I still love you as much today.*

**Reception in honor of Madame Taquet. Left: Daniel
Inowlocki, one of the children she had saved.**

A commemorative plaque was placed on one of the walls of the Jamoigne home, recalling the saving of some 80 Jewish children behind the thick
walls of the chateau. During those dark years for civilization, in occupied
Belgium, Jewish children penned words of thanks, comfort and hope for
their non-Jewish benefactress, Mrs. Taquet (who died in 1989 at age 91);
words collected in a special album presented to the Chateau's headmistress – such as the following paean by Gideon Glinoer (then known as
Jules Kayser), and brother Philippe:

*Oh, dear Madame Taquet/ Truly, it is not you who has raised me/ When
I was hardly born./ But, now when I need to be saved/ It is you with your
great love/ Who nourishes me, who looks after me/ And cares for me as her
own child/ And she continues to care for me all the time./ Yes, all this,
Madame Taquet/ You have done for me/ On the occasion of Mother's Day/*

Permit me to write a few sentences/ And, wish you the best of happiness/
This I wish you with all my heart.[2]

It is hard to imagine that words like these, inspired by feelings of love, thankfulness and hope, appropriate for different circumstances, were written by a Jewish child while sheltered in a chateau, in the dense Ardennes forest, in the year 1944, while outside the chateau's protective walls, Jewish children were being relentlessly hunted and delivered to the gas chambers and crematoria.[3]

Franciscus & Hillegonda Snel

The Son of a Fallen Soldier Repays a Debt to Dutch Rescuers

Rummaging through his late father's papers, Uri Cohen became more aware of a particular unfinished business that his father had left undone—a moral debt to his Dutch rescuers. Shlomo Cohen had been called up to the colors during the Six Days War in June 1967, and had fallen in battle. Before that, he had begun assembling written material on how the Snel family had assured his survival, while the Germans had his parents murdered in a concentration camp. Shlomo's death had grounded this special assignment which he had committed himself. Over a decade after his father's death, the now grownup Uri, himself a soldier in the Israeli army, was determined to accomplish what his father had left undone. As he studied his father's records, the story of his rescue took shape. He then turned to Yad Vashem, and asked, in the name of his fallen father, that his rescuers be awarded the Righteous title.

Shlomo, or Sallo as he was known in Holland, was born in 1936 to Annie and Philip Cohen. In 1942, to save the three children in the Cohen household from deportation to the camps, they were dispersed among different families. "I don't know where my father was sent first," Uri stated, "but when he arrived at the Snel household, in June 1943, it was after six months of wandering between seven families." Franciscus and Hillegonda Snel were a recently-married couple who lived in Utrecht, and operated a bicycle repair shop, which was attached to their house. Arriving at the Utrecht train station, to be introduced to his new hosts, the timid Sallo asked the waiting Mrs. Snel if she was sure she really wanted him since he had a wetting problem. She immediately realized to what extent the seven-year old child needed comfort, warmth and love.

At first, Sallo remained indoors until a proper story could be concocted to explain to neighbors the presence of a seven-year old child in the home of a recently married couple. Even close relatives were not told of the newcomer. When guests appeared, Sallo hid in a closet or other hiding place. The Snels realized that this situation could not go on indefinitely, so they dyed Sallo's hair blond and took him out for walks in the park. But here too, as added precaution, Sallo was made to leave first and head toward the park, where he would then "accidentally" meet Mrs. Snel, who left her home a few minutes after the boy's departure. Back at home, Sallo received private school lessons, so that he could pick up on his schooling immediately after the war.

When his parents failed to turn up, at the war's end, in May 1945, the Snels considered adopting him, as a brother to their new-born girl. However, in September 1945, a relative of the Cohen family suddenly appeared, accompanied by Sallo's elder brother, Menachem. They were determined to take the orphaned boy with them on their way to then-Palestine, together with his sister, who had also survived. After finishing his army duty in 1960, Sallo, now known as Shlomo, returned to Holland and spent time with his former adoptive rescuer family. He communicated with them frequently and was assembling data on his rescue, when the Six Days War intervened, and Shlomo fell in battle.

"These late years," his son Uri wrote, "it is I who is maintaining contact with the Snel family. . . I visited them twice, and they visited me in Israel. These are people with a great love for human beings and for Israel." As they were planning another visit to Israel, Uri asked that the Righteous title be awarded them on that occasion. "I regard this as the fulfillment of my father's last will," Uri underlined. "As a citizen, I am proud that our people do not forget to thank those who did not fail us during those terrible days." Recognition was bestowed on the Snel couple by Yad Vashem in 1983. The following year, the Snel children planted a tree in their parents name in Yad Vashem, in the presence of Uri Cohen and his father's close relatives. The Cohens felt relieved, having acquitted themselves of a long-standing moral debt, and at the same time cementing the bond with the Snel children, whose parents saved their loved-one — the fallen Shlomo.[4]

Uri Cohen with members of the Snel family during a tree planting ceremony.

Hajrija Imeri-Mihaljic

Honoring a Gypsy Rescuer

As Kosovo was being torn by civil war, Esther Levy began to think about her late rescuer, the gypsy woman Hajrija. She wondered how her family was faring in that troubled region of Yugoslavia. Back in 1988, Esther told her story to a Yad Vashem interviewer, and three years later, her rescuer was awarded posthumously the title of "Righteous Among the Nations" — so far the only gypsy person to earn this honor.

At the time of the German invasion of Yugoslavia, in April 1941, the family of little Esther, born a year earlier, resided in Pristina, the capital of the Kosovo region. Fearing the pro-Nazi Croatian regime, which had taken control of this area, Esther's parents fled to the hills to join up with the partisans, leaving the little girl in the care of her grandmother. During the preceding year, the Baruchs had hired a nanny, a gypsy woman named Hajrija Imeri, who lived in a nearby village, to help out with household chores. With Esther's parents gone, Hajrija came often to visit Esther's grandmother, and look after the child's needs. Soon thereafter, Hajrija learned that Esther and her grandmother had been picked up by the authorities and moved to a labor camp. She quickly hurried there and met the frightened grandmother, who pleaded with her to take the child away with her. "Please guard her and care for her as your own child. If her family returns, they will take her back; if not, keep her as your own daughter." Quickly leaving the camp (Kosovska Mitrovica), Hajrija took the one-year-old child to her tribal village, and joined her to her own five children. She gave the child a new name, Moradia, and treated her with special kindness. At night, the Imeri family spread out hay on the floor, and all lay down to sleep, with Moradia tucked in between the other children—always in between, for added security. "I talked and acted like a regular gypsy child," Esther recalls.

After several years, towards the end of the war in 1945, Hajrija felt she had to disclose the truth to Moradia. One day she told the child: "You know, your name is really not Moradia, but Esther Baruch, and I am not your true mother. Your mother was Bokica, and she probably died fighting with the partisans." This disclosure meant little to little Moradia, as she was comfortably ensconced in the surrounding gypsy society. She also remembered the day when, as a four year old, and standing barefooted, she was shown the boy who it was decided would later be her husband. However, soon thereafter Hajrija's husband became embroiled in a feud with a neighbor over a parcel of land, and the neighbor decided to tell the police the Imeri-Mihaljics were illegally keeping a Jewish child. Josef Jospovich, who in 1945 worked for the Jewish community in Pristina, remembers being asked by the police to accompany them to the village of Ade, where a certain gypsy woman was keeping a Jewish child. Arriving there, in the company of several other Jewish community workers, they were introduced to Hajrija and her six children. Josef immediately noted that one of the children had a lighter complexion than the others. Hajrija was asked: "Is it true that you are hiding a Jewish girl?" Hajrija readily admitted, but added: "I am not hiding her. She is mine!" She then disclosed the story of the Baruchs, and of the grandmother who had turned the child over to her for safekeeping. Upon this, the police decided to take the child with them. Esther recalls that as she was being led away, Hajrija followed them, weeping hysterically. "Don't take the child; her parents are not alive. Please, don't throw her away. I am taking care of her, and I love her." Esther-Moradia also wept bitterly, pleading, "I love her; she is the only one I know." The police disregarded Hajrija's pleadings and told her to return home.

In Pristina, Esther-Moradia was turned over in the care of a nursemaid, until her further disposition could be decided. The child was dirty and her hair was covered with lice. She resisted when they tried to replace her gypsy dress with other clothes. She also refused to taste the food prepared for her, and instead gobbled up the two boiled eggs that Hajrija had secretly tucked inside her dress as she was being led away. Not knowing how to respond to the child's uncontrollable behavior, she was sent to a child center in Belgrade, the country's capital. However, there too she refused to cooperate, and communication with her proved extremely difficult because no-one understood the particular gypsy dialect spoken by the child. Contacting the local Jewish community, they learned that a certain woman had some knowledge of gypsy talk, and she was asked to come over. She grabbed the child, and asked her in gypsy language for her name. What happened next is best told by Esther Levy herself:

> *Like a parrot, I repeated what I was told; that my mother was Hajrija, but that I had another mother who was already dead, and her name was Bokica, and I mentioned the other names of my family. As I was talking, the woman fell flat on the floor and passed out. When she regained consciousness, she said: 'I have found my daughter. This is my daughter.' I always have tears in my eyes when I tell this part of the story.*

It turned out that Bokica had survived the war and had remarried, having lost her husband. This revelation did not change Esther-Moradia's attitude, as she refused to accompany that strange woman to her home. "I did not want to come with her; I wanted nothing from her. She had a difficult time with me, for I was very difficult and refused to listen. This lasted for two years." The child refused to eat, and was literally starving herself. Bokica at first thought that perhaps the child suffered from a throat infection, which prevented her from swallowing the food, and consulted a doctor, who reassured her that the problem was strictly psychological.

In the meantime, Bokica visited the gypsy woman in the village, to thank her and support her, and she continued to remain in touch with her. One day, Hajrija came to Belgrade to see for herself how the child was doing. By then, the child had already become accustomed to her mother, to her new clothing, new food, and new lifestyle. Esther panicked, fearing that Hajrija had come to take her back to her village, and began to weep. Hajrija cuddled the child in her arms and calmed her fears. She only came to reassure herself that Esther was really in the care of her mother, not some children's institution. She had brought along a basked filled with various fruits, in case the child was hungry. The two embraced.

In 1948, Bokica, her husband, and Esther left for Israel. Esther later learned that Hajrija had died in poverty, and in a state of abandon by her nearest kin, and that there was no forwarding address for her children. She turned to Miriam Aviezer, a Yad Vashem associate, also from Yugoslavia, to help her locate Hajrija's family, in spite of the near-chaotic conditions in Kosovo, so as to tell the Imeri-Mihaljcic family that Hajrija, of blessed memory, has been proclaimed a hero by the Jewish people (the only gypsy person so honored), and her name was engraved in stone in the Garden of the Righteous, at Yad Vashem, for her heroic part in saving a Jewish child during the Holocaust—the least Esther could do to repay a moral debt to her rescuer.[5]

Joseph and Yvonne Smeesters

A Belgian Rescuer's Attempt to Keep a Hidden Child

In 1992, Joseph Schreiber, in Israel, received the following letter from a Jean-Paul Smeesters, in Belgium:

> You don't know how happy I am to have found you. You are my
> "wartime brother." I loved you much, and I still do. If you only knew
> how much I searched to find you. . . without success; from one disap-
> pointment to the next. . . Thanks to Mr. Schapiro I know you are alive
> and living in your own country. This is amazing! I have much to tell
> you, from 1942 till today. . . You were my little brother. . . A son was
> born to me in 1956. I named him Michel, after you. . . I end this first
> letter by telling you, my dear Joseph (I always think "Michel"), how
> happy I am to have found you, my little brother. A fraternal kiss.

This letter ended a long separation and rupture between two families: rescuer and rescued. The story began in Antwerp, Belgium, where Joseph Schreiber was born in 1941 to his parents Yaakov and Yetta – the sixth child in the family. What happened afterwards is not too clear. It seems that the family was arrested by the Germans and taken to the Malines transit camp for deportation to the concentration camps. The Germans, however, allowed a certain Jewish woman to take little Joseph and place him in a Jewish orphanage. After a while, he was fetched by an operative of the clandestine Jewish Defense Committee, and brought to the home of the Smeesters, in Waterloo. Evidently under the impress of the traumatic separation from his parents, the boy arrived at the Smeesters with an unsteady walk and a speech impediment. He was evidently still in a state of shock, and in need of a comforting and loving hand. His benefactors did not disappoint him – as he stated in his deposition: "I was received by the family in the warmest way as a son in all respects; I was doted on and spoiled – more than the other children."

After the war, Joseph's mother began looking for her son, and finally was able to locate him in the Smeesters home, now residing in Uccle, outside Brussels. At first, the Smeesters claimed that the boy had already been returned to the clandestine Jewish organization which had originally brought the child to them. As this could not be confirmed by this organization, Joseph Smeesters, a notary public, finally admitted to the boy's presence but reacted angrily, claiming that the publicity of having sheltered a Jewish child would place him in danger from pro-Nazi elements still in circulation. As for the boy, Smeesters refused to return him, claiming a strong affection toward little Joseph which had developed over the war years. He counseled the boy's mother that as the Smeesters had found consolation in the boy, after the death of their daughter during the war years, she too should find consolation in her survival and that of her five other children who remained in hiding during the war (her husband was deported and did not return). This answer infuriated Mrs. Schreiber; she adamantly insisted that her son be returned to her. She eventually lodged a complaint with the police, who raided the Smeesters home and forcefully took the weeping child away, and returned him to his mother. This occurred in 1947, after a struggle lasting two years.

The Schreiber family eventually moved to Israel, with Mrs. Schreiber severing all ties with the Smeesters. After her death, Joseph attended a Hidden Children Conference, in 1992, in Israel; there, a certain Mr. Shapiro took it upon himself to try relocate the family which had showered him with so much love during five crucial and tender years in the child's development. The result was the previously-mentioned letter by one of the Smeesters children. In this communication, Jean-Paul also informed Joseph that Joseph, the family head, had long since passed away, whereas mother Yvonne was in a nursing home in Switzerland, and due to her advanced age had lost all memory of the war years.

Marie-Astrid, another of the Smeesters' four children (the first, Christiane, died in 1944 after a four-year bout with diabetes), sent Joseph wartime pictures, to remind him how he was doted on and loved by the whole adoptive family. Her sister, Monique, also wrote Joseph how, at a recent family gathering, they had wondered what had become of little Joseph, as they went over the war years' pictures—"suddenly this miracle!" Joseph, thereupon, turned to Yad Vashem and asked that his rescuers be awarded the Righteous title.

Things did not go smoothly at the Commission for the Righteous during the debate on this case. On the one hand it was clear that the feelings of affection and closeness by the Smeesters toward Joseph were genuine, and that he was well treated while with them. At the same time, some commission members felt that Joseph Smeesters' behavior after the war demonstrated a strong egotistical streak and a troubling lack of understanding of the feelings of a mother toward her child, especially after all doubts were removed that the child which had come to them under the name of Oscar Pollack was none other than Joseph Schreiber. The rescued person had every right to be appreciative and thankful toward his benefactors but, in light of Mr. Smeesters' insensitivity toward Mrs. Schreiber, prolonged over two years, he should not awarded the highly-prized title of "Righteous Among the Nations."

Other Commission members saw it a bit differently. Granted that

Smeester's postwar behavior was morally
inexcusable, there was no proof that he
originally admitted the distraught child
into his home with the intention of not
returning it. In the words of one member:
"We are faced with a question of principle. Should we judge the person strictly
on the basis of the rescue operation, or
also include his personality and characteristics as they became evident years
later? Do we award the Righteous title

Right: Joseph Schreiber
Below: The Smeesters family
with little Joseph

to a person whom we consider to be noble-minded, or rather to a person who
during a certain time and a certain moment did a noble deed?" Even on the
question of the person's personality — the fact that he refused to return the
child may be an indication not of a flaw but rather of strong affection and

love of the child whom the family received in a sorry and frightened state, and who was now happy and fully at home with them.

Other members disagreed with this viewpoint. Failure to return a child to its proper mother, after she had been forced to part with him in order to ensure the child's survival, was a cruel act—so went this argument. Moreover—the resolve to retain the child may be considered a form of compensation to the rescuer, and he should therefore be denied the Righteous title. At this, a woman Commission member demurred, adding that one should take into consideration the wishes and feelings of the rescued person—the former child himself; what he desired and wished the Commission to do. "He too has feelings toward the person who rescued him, as well as to his own mother. He is the deciding factor—not us." At the end of several spirited debates, the Commission acted to vote for the inclusion of the late Joseph Smeesters and his living wife Yvonne among the Righteous. By refusing to return the child to his natural mother, the Commission was of the opinion that the rescuers' ultimate motivation was concern with the child's welfare—hence, they deserved recognition. After learning of Yad Vashem's decision, the gratified Joseph Schreiber journeyed to the nursing home in Switzerland, and planted a loving kiss on the cheeks of his benefactress; to a person who had restored his feelings of love, self confidence and hope. To the children of Yvonne Smeesters, Joseph Schreiber has been, and continues to be affectionately considered as their little "wartime brother."[6]

Franciszek and Stanislawa Kaczmarek, and Charlotte Rebhun

Who Am I?

After the war, Penina Gutman had repressed memories of her childhood years during the Holocaust. But these came to haunt her many decades later. In recent years, she was suddenly overcome by a terrible urge to find out more about the lost years of her early life: who were her parents and the people who had saved her? Stumbling upon a newspaper announcement on the availability of a list of children in a Jewish children's home, in Otwock, Poland, and dizzyingly remembering that she had spent some time as a child in that place, she ordered a copy of this list, and was startled to see her name on a list of children who had been returned by a certain unknown Polish family who had sheltered her during a critical phase of her childhood.

Based on this minor but important information, and determined to pick up the additional threads of her story, Penina left for Poland to locate her wartime benefactors. Luck was with her, for at the Jewish Historical Institute, in Warsaw, she was able to trace further documentation of her rescue. It turned out that during the last year of the war and for three years thereafter, she had been kept by a certain Kaczmarek family, who lived in Sierakow, near Poznan. After some wrangling, Penina was able to establish contact with Janina and Bogdan, two of the family's five children. From conversations with them, and the records at the Jewish Historical Institute, she was able to piece together part of the puzzle of her early childhood. In October 1944, after the Germans had crushed the Polish rebellion and expelled the Warsaw population, she was found abandoned in a railway station, in Milanowek, near Warsaw. She was then one and a half years old. To inquirers, she gave her name as Barbara Rebhun, and stated that she lived in Warsaw. Underground people turned her over to the Kaczmareks, who eventually settled in Sierakow. Little Barbara stayed with them until April 1948, when she was taken by a Jewish organization to Otwock, and then turned over to a Jewish family, in Lodz, who adopted her and took her with them to Israel.

Needless to say, the visit of Penina-Barbara Gutman was for the Kaczmareks a total and, at the same time, pleasant surprise, since they recalled how their late parents had brought the little girl into their household over 50 years ago. "I found a warm and loving family," Penina wrote, "who cherished my memory with love and yearning." In January 1997, Franciszek and Stanislawa Kaczmarek were posthumously honored with the Righteous title. An important segment of the puzzle had been found. However, Penina Gutman remained restless, since she still knew nothing of the earlier period of her childhood — her natural parents, and what caused her to be found, abandoned and alone, in a remote town not far from Warsaw. She decided to take up the search for the Rebhuns — the name which was etched in her memory, and remained the only clue to a possible previous biographical record. She placed ads in newspapers, and turned to the International Red Cross for any information of a family with the name of Rebhun.

Again, and for second time, luck was with her. For, unbeknownst to her, a certain Wolfgang Rebhun was simultaneously looking for the little girl his family had sheltered in Warsaw during the war years. His and her inquiries with the Red Cross crisscrossed each other, and both quickly linked up with each other. As Wolfgang later wrote to the astounded Penina, he was born in 1927 in Berlin, to a Jewish father, Max Rebhun and a non-Jewish mother, Charlotte. During the Nazi government's orchestrated *Kristallnacht* pogrom, of November 1938, Wolfgang's father was expelled to Poland. His mother and the rest of the family (Wolfgang and his sister Adele) followed suit, in early 1939. The Rebhuns settled in Warsaw, and with the German occupation of Poland, they moved into the Warsaw Ghetto. In 1942, they fled the ghetto and lived on the non-Jewish, or Aryan side. Father was eventually arrested and sent to Treblinka, where he perished. Mother was then approached by Jewish persons with a request to look after their 9-month-old child. "Mother agreed on the spot," the then 15-year-old Wolfgang remembers. Besides the little girl, whose family name none of the two Rebhun children remember, their mother also sheltered other Jews in their apartment. Young Wolfgang joined the Polish underground and took an active part in the Polish Uprising of August 1944. "Adele and myself played a lot with you," Wolfgang noted, "and took you out for walks. When you began to run and to talk, I always said to you, 'your name is Barbara Rebhun.'" This explains the recollection Penina has of this name; she was, of course, too young to remember her original name.

After the suppression of the Polish uprising, in October 1944, Wolfgang, on the verge of being shot, was spared by an SS man who placed him on a train for Mauthausen; his mother and slightly younger sister were taken to Czestochowa, in southern Poland. Somewhere, during these chaotic and unforeseen peregrinations, little Barbara was separated from them. In January 1945, Wolfgang made his escape from Mauthausen, and remained in hiding in Vienna until the end of the war. Returning to Berlin, he was reunited with his sister Adele, who sadly informed him that their mother was executed by the SS on May first, one day before the fall of Berlin. Wolfgang's inquiries with his sister, who was recovering from wounds, about little Barbara produced no results. Determined to make an orderly life for himself, Wolfgang married and raised three children, and was now a grandfather. Adele also married, but was without children.

In March 1997, barely a year after her meeting with the Kaczmareks, Penina Gutman visited Germany and met with her other benefactors. On this occasion, Wolfgang showed her photos taken during outings in Warsaw, when little Barbara was in the care of his mother. In December 1997, at Penina Gutman's request, Yad Vashem responded, for the second time, and the late Charlotte Rebhun was awarded the Righteous title. The following year, in a moving ceremony at Yad Vashem, the two Rebhun children were awarded the Righteous medal and certificate of honor, bearing their mother's name. A second and major element of the puzzle has been assembled. What is still missing is the last, and for Penina Gutman perhaps the most important — the identity and fate of her parents. It is hoped that, as this book goes to press, Penina Gutman, alias Barbara Rebhun, will finally have uncovered the last piece of her childhood puzzle — her original name, that of her natural parents, and what became of them.[7]

Penina Gutman and the children of Charlotte Rebhun
from Germany.

Piotr and Emilia Waszkinel

The Double Life of a Rescued Jewish Child

Another rescued Jewish child had even greater difficulties establishing his true origins. When his quest was crowned with success, he was already a Catholic priest in his native Poland. In 1993, he visited Israel for the first time, for an emotional get-together with the Orthodox Jewish person who claimed to be his lost father's brother. Afterwards, he came to Yad Vashem, and in an emotional testimony, mingled with tears, gave a dramatic account of the discovery of his Jewish roots. Following are excerpts of this man's unusual story.

My name is Romuald-Jakub Weksler-Waszkinel. I am listed as born on February 28, 1943, although in truth it was a month later that my Jewish mother placed me under the window of my Polish mother. My Polish mother told me I was born on March 23rd, since this was the day when she picked me up. According to the Russian writer Lermontov, one cannot express in words what is hidden deep in the human soul. There are things that a person wants to leave to himself. Perhaps, I should want these to be revealed after my death.

During the war, we lived in a place near Swieciany. I was always afraid of Swieciany, afraid to go there, for reasons unknown to me. At the end of the war, we left and moved to Paleska, near Olsztyn. I was always closer to mother than father. I always clung to her dress for fear that she would abandon me. I did not want to be alone. I was a cry-baby, who held on to her dress and followed her everywhere. I guess, subconsciously, I was afraid they would leave me. My sister, Janina, was born in 1952.

At school, I was accepted and I was a good student. I wish to emphasize that I never had any problems; no one connected me with Jews. In Paleska, I finished elementary and high school. I was a good student and very active socially. I was invited to many parties with my accordion, where I played, sang and danced. The high school years were the happiest years of my life. My parents loved me dearly. My father, Piotr Waszkinel, a plain locksmith, sold a cow in order to buy me the accordion. I was not really spoiled, just loved, for at times father was capable of unleashing his belt and giving me a wacking.

I looked different from the others. I had black hair and dark skin, but inside I did not feel different from the other children. At times they would say to me: do you know that your father is really not your father? I would answer: You're stupid. When I was six, one day in the summer, on my way home, I suddenly heard screams behind me: 'Jew, Jew, foundling,' followed with loud jeering. I took this very seriously. Coming home, I burst out crying. I told mother in a whimpering and stuttering voice: "They called me a Zyd. 'You're a Jew; you're a foundling.' I asked mother what is the meaning of Zyd? After a pause, she said: 'Don't pay attention to those stupid words. You should disregard them.' This was my first encounter with antisemitism. At the time, I did not know what a Jew meant. However, in high school, which was the happiest time of my life, I never encountered antisemitism.

I was 17 when I graduated high school. At home we were very religious, always attending church. Christianity was to my parents like air for breathing. I prayed together with them. During my last year at school, a priest came to teach us religion. I told him if I passed the exams, I wanted to study for the priesthood. In fact, as a child, I wanted to be a priest. When I told father about it, he tried to talk me out of it. I wondered why. He told me: 'Listen, you know that I go to church and pray, but one does not have to become a priest to believe in God. Think it over. Have you considered what it means to become a priest? Are you aware how hard it is?'. . . I replied: 'I don't know, and I'll go there to find out. Going there doesn't necessarily mean I must become a priest'. Father said: 'Going there, you'll have to become a priest; or else, it would be something immoral.' Father wanted me to become a doctor. That was his dream. One has respect for a doctor. 'You will have a family. A priest's life is difficult.' He was stubborn on this point.

Learning of my intention, my mother, Emilia, said nothing, just ran about the house and wept. I did not understand why. She said: 'Do what you want to do; this is your life, your fate. Do what you want to do. Only, be careful you do not regret it.' So, I did exactly that. This was around September 1960. I was then 17 when I entered the seminary. Then something strange happened with father. He wrote me saying he wanted to come and see me. When he came, he looked very sad, and was silent. He went into the chapel and stood in front of the Madonna. Suddenly, he fell on his knees and began to weep. I did not understand why. I had never seen him weep like this before. At home, he was always quite a tough person, and here he was weeping. I felt sorry I had caused him such pain. But what did I do wrong? After all, he loved me so much! He had never caused me harm! He then got up and left without saying a word. I asked him: 'Papa, are your sick?' 'No,' he replied, 'I am fine. Everything's fine. I have come to terms; do what you want to do.'

This was on a Sunday. On Thursday, I received a phone call informing me of my father's death. He had slipped while walking down a staircase, and fell hitting his head. I had a gut feeling I had caused his death. I decided I would not continue my studies at the seminary, and told my mother about it. She responded: 'You must not say this. You did not kill anyone. You must return. Go.' I went to my supervisor and told him I couldn't stay on, for father did not want me to be here, and I felt responsible for his death. He replied: 'If in another two or three months you still feel that way, come back and I will return your papers, and you can leave. You are now in shock, and you mustn't do anything rash.' So, I stayed on. After two months, I no longer wanted to leave. I took my priestly vows on June 19, 1966, which coincided with the celebrations of 1,000 years of Christianity in Poland.

Before taking the vow, I was called in by my supervisor-bishop, the then-rector, who suggested I be baptized. This greatly surprised me. Had I not been baptized at birth? With my own eyes, I saw the baptismal certificate. He insisted. This raised doubts in my mind; something here is not all right, not as it should be. I told the bishop my parents prayed every day, and on Sundays they attended church. How can one imagine that such parents would raise a child who had not undergone baptism, an act of such importance to a Christian?' The bishop said: 'I know things from certain sources which I cannot reveal. There is no smoke without fire.' I said: 'That is generally true, but sometimes it is caused by human stupidity. Perhaps it is due to jealousy. I know for sure that I was baptized.' The discussion then turned unpleasant, and he simply threw me out of his office. I thought, this is the end for me. I will be expelled. Upon leaving, I said: 'I will find the baptismal certificate,' to which he replied: 'One can falsify baptismals.' I said: 'In the case of a Jew — yes. But why would it be necessary to falsify one for me?' This incident was quickly forgotten, and I was transferred to Lublin Catholic university to continue my studies. I chose for my doctoral thesis the philosophy of Henri Bergson, the son of Jewish parents from Warsaw (again a Jew in my life!) At the time, I read a lot on Jewish life in Poland, and on Jewish life during the war.

It was only in 1979 that I first learned of my Jewish origin. I worked at the time as an assistant at Lublin university. I had bought an apartment and moved my mother and sister to Lublin. All this time, I had the feeling that there was something about me which was being hidden from me. First of all, I did not resemble anyone around me, not even my family. This appeared quite odd to me. In addition, the thought that the truth was being kept from me was quite unbearable. There was this incident at school about my baptism. Then, my nose which became more prominent as I grew into manhood. When I looked at my profile photos, I noted the difference between me and the others around me. I walked around with the feeling that there was something special about me, which made me different from my family, from their way of thinking and their genetic characteristics.

By then I was already a priest, and I was dedicated to Jesus, a Jew, a native of Israel, who loved his country and the people living there deeply. I wanted to be able to love like him. Every time I asked my mother about

*my origins, she would say: 'Don't I love you?' In 1979, mother became
ill and was admitted to a hospital. I was told that the blood transfusion
was not having an effect. They would try one more time, and if the results
proved negative, then, in consideration of her age, I was told to expect the
worst. Surprisingly, the body reacted favorably to the infusion and she
recovered. She was released, and lived for another ten years.*

*I then looked for an opportune moment to confront her with the doubts
about my origin. One evening, after supper, mother seemed very
forthcoming, so I decided to go on the attack. She let out a cry. I said,
'Mommy, let it go, release it, finally. After all, it concerns not only you,
but me as well! I have a right to know. You must tell me. This is a
beautiful chapter in your life, and I will not love you the less.' So she said,
'Come, let's go to your room.' I remember the candle burning in the
darkness. I was alone with my mother. My sister, who was already
married, lived elsewhere.*

*She wept as she told me that I am a child of Jewish parents. I had
previously suspected that only one of my parents was Jewish: my father
or my mother, but not both! I was not prepared for this. She continued,
'I had to lie about you to protect you.' My Jewish father was a tailor in
Swieciany, and did some work for the Germans. Mother occasionally
visited my father's workshop and told him about a certain Russian girl
which she had temporarily taken care of (she was then childless). My father
suggested that she could take another child. She then came into the ghetto
to speak with my mother (she always spoke about my mother with much
appreciation and love). I had another brother, named Shmuel. When he
was 4 or 5, he was turned over to a Lithuanian family, who returned him
to my mother – perhaps due to fear, or because the money ran out. My
mother was then pregnant with me. So my Jewish parents felt that they
wanted at least to make sure I survived. My Jewish mother, whose name
was Batya, said to my adoptive mother: 'My lady, you constantly say you
believe in Jesus.' So using all of her persuasive powers in order to save me,
she continued, 'Take this child in the name of Jesus, in whom you believe
so much. Perhaps, this small boy will one day become a priest.'*

*[At this point the priest wept]. Towards evening, my mother placed
me on the porch window sill of my Polish parents. As prearranged, my
Polish mother watched from the window, waited for 15 minutes to allow
my mother to leave, then opened the window, and there I was, all silent.
My mother stepped out and screamed for all to hear: 'A child, a child.'
People started to gather and stare. They unraveled my clothing, and
noticed I was not circumcised. So everything was fine. Only one onlooker,
a shoemaker, felt otherwise. He ran about, shouting: 'It's a Jewish boy; I
will catch his mother.' And he began to run in the direction of the ghetto.
But by then, my Jewish mother had already managed to leave safely.*

Several days later, my Polish parents went to the birth registration office and announced they had a foundling. My mother said: 'I want this boy; I found him; it belongs to me; I want to keep him.' I was properly registered, and a birth certificate was issued in the name of Romuald Waszkinel, son of Piotr and Emilia. All the neighbors knew that my Polish mother had not given me birth, but did not know the identity of my true biological parents. My parents, it seems, perished in the Vilna Ghetto, shot to death either in Ponary or Klooga. I was later told that my mother visited me three times before she disappeared. As for my brother Shmuel, I have no idea about his fate. I keep hoping he is alive, and I will see him one day.

When this story was revealed to me, I felt tremendously gratified that I was a Jew. This feeling came to me as a volcanic eruption, full force. Being Jewish caused me great joy. But this joy was mixed with pain. Why? Why did my father, a modest tailor, have to be killed? What was my little brother guilty of? He was not capable of harming anyone. What sin did my mother and the six million commit?

Romuald-Jakub Waszkinel with his Israeli uncle, in front of the Honor Wall bearing the names of his rescuers.

After this revelation, I embraced and kissed my mother, wishing to thank her in the name of my Jewish mother and father. The first moments after this disclosure were difficult ones. That evening, I did not sleep. I asked of God that my parents should come to me in my sleep, so I could see them. This did not happen. So I felt more and more torn inside, for I wanted very much to know my family's name. This is when I met Sister Klara Jaroszynska, in 1979. She told me how she had saved Jews. I told her all I knew about myself. She visited Israel several times. While there, she discovered there's an association of Swieciany survivors, headed by a Mr. Kuversky. After hearing the particulars about my parents (he being a tailor, etc.) they immediately said; 'Why! It's Weksler.' They showed her my mother's photo, taken at a Zionist gathering, to which she belonged. I have no photo of my father. 'I looked at her eyes, and saw my own eyes. All my life I searched for some resemblance. I immediately started crying. I had no doubt this was my mother. Here in Israel, on Friday, I visited a synagogue for the first time. The next morning, I put on a Tallith [praying shawl]; I prayed, was called up to the Torah, which I touched like a real Jew. Everyone shook my hand. It was wonderful. I wept like a dumbfounded person.

For my uncle there are two separate religions. For me there is only one religion. I simply believe that Jesus the Jew did not come to abrogate the law. 'Not an iota or line will be changed.' For me, this is the continuation of my Judaism. I love this people, in spite of my being Polish. Poland is my homeland, as it was for my parents. At the time, there was no Israel. Poland is my Israel, but everything Polish to me includes my Judaism. I
am a Jew, and no one has the right to chase me out of Poland, which is my homeland. For a people is first of all a language; culture is spirit, not flesh and blood. I am deeply rooted in the culture in which I was raised.

People often say that Hitler murdered Jews using Christian hands. There is much truth in this for, in general, Europe, so they say, was Christian. And that Christian Europe did not behave properly, and still doesn't. For me, the main problem is that this Christianity should remain faithful to Jesus, for it seems to me that if someone kills Jews, he spits on Jesus, on the roots of Christianity. Hence, the humiliation of Jews is the humiliation of Christianity; it is simply insulting one's own foundations, one's own mother. Thus, antisemitism is ipso facto anti-Christian. This, one has to understand. When we mock Jews, we disparage the most precious value of Christianity.

My fervent wish is for my Polish parents to merit the same recognition given to other rescuers of Jews. They saved a Jew, not a Catholic priest. They deserve this recognition. This is my greatest wish, and I hope to be able to achieve it.

After learning of his original family name, Romuald Waszkinel applied before a civil court for a slight correction to his name—adding his Jewish name to his Polish one. He now appears as Romuald-Jakub Weksler-Waszkinel (Jakub, in memory of his biological father, since he does not know the name given him at birth). His uncle would have preferred for Romuald-Jakub to revert to his parents' Jewish faith. To this, he replies by pointing to the Star of David with a cross in the middle, which he wears around his neck. "I am the Star of David with the cross inserted. That is my life as I see it. The cross is love. Without love, it is the Roman gallows." He would like to resemble Jesus, "if only a little." As for the nomination of his rescuers to the Righteous title — two women, friends of his late mother, as well as his uncle, gave testimony and confirmed the rescue of the son of Jakub and Batya Weksler. These made possible the awarding of the Righteous title to Piotr and Emilia Waszkinel, the rescuers of Father Jakub-Romuald Weksler-Waszkinel. At a ceremony at Yad Vashem, in 1995, which was attended by survivors from Swieciany, the city of his birth, he shed tears and wept as he uncovered the name of his rescuers, his adoptive parents, in the Garden of the Righteous.[8]

Genia Pajak

A Coming to Terms With One's Traumatic Childhood Before Life's End

For some children, the traumas associated with the Holocaust years were too painful to bear, and in order to avoid going mad, they felt constrained to erase (or at least try to) the psychological pains associated with the memories of that period, including the persons who had miraculously saved them. Some adamantly resisted any ties and connection with persons living in a place associated with their youthful sufferings — even with their rescuers, such as in the following story.

"I am not the person that was rescued," begins Henrietta Altman's touching letter to Yad Vashem, sent in 1982 from Australia. In fact, the rescued person, a first cousin of Henrietta, lived in Israel but could not bring herself to confront her painful youth and, therefore, although she supported the nomination of her rescuer for the Righteous title, she pleaded not to be involved in the requisite procedures, including the submission of a written or even oral testimony. It was left to her cousin, in distant Australia, who was also a party to the rescue story, to fill in all the details (as she also did in the previously-mentioned Alfred Rossner story).

"It was a hot day at the end of that July 1943," in the Bedzin Ghetto, in Poland — begins Henrietta's testimony. The ghetto was buzzing with rumors of a large scale final liquidation raid of the Jewish population by the Germans. On the eve of the war, the city counted 27,000 Jews. Now only several thousand were left, and their turn had come. Henrietta (or Kitia, as she is affectionately known) had befriended a Polish lady, who lived not far from the ghetto, and who had helped Kitia's family with extra food, which she had bartered on the black market in exchange for clothing, bed linen, and other items, provided by the starving Jewish family. On this July day, Genia came running to Kitia's room with the terrible news, which she had gotten from a reliable source (her female friend whose lover was a German soldier) — a soon-to-be final liquidation of the ghetto's Jews was to take place. "I want to save you!" Genia, trembling, pleaded with Kitia. Kitia searched Genia's eyes and finally said: "Dear Geniusiu, I am young and healthy and I'll survive. But there is a child in my family whom I love dearly, the eight year old daughter of my beloved auntie." The child was Tamara Cygler, born in 1935 to Samuel (a painter) and Rachela (a dental surgeon). In those hellish days, Jewish children had little chance to survive. They, together with the old and the sick, could not contribute to the German war economy, and would therefore be immediately killed.

Genia agreed to save the child, "without a moment's hesitation," in Henrietta's words. Time was of the essence, so the next day Genia took the child with her for a three day trial period. The child's parents had never heard of Genia, but Kitia begged them to trust her with the child for at least a few days, just to see how it would work out. When Genia returned with the child, the mother parted from her six-year-old daughter, with the words: "this is your aunt Genia; you'll go and stay with her for a few days." She bent down, and kissed the child's head. It was the last time she and her husband were to see their daughter.

Returning to her Spartan-furnished home, Genia immediately set to work on obtaining proper credentials for Tamara, including a birth certificate, on the claim that the child was hers from a previous out-of-wedlock affair. Tamara Cygler became Bogusia Pajak, a fourth child to Genia's three natural children. "I think, that every child in the ghetto was taught that a day might come when he or she would get a new name, and a new 'mama,'" Henrietta Altman notes in her testimony; "that they shouldn't cry or talk about their real parents and never, ever admit they lived in the ghetto and are Jewish." Now came Tamara's turn to pass this searing and traumatic test.

A few days later, the final curtain came down on Bedzin's Jewish population, with the dreaded liquidation raid of August 1, 1943, claiming among its thousands of victims Kitia's parents (her mother, luckily, survived the concentration camp ordeal) and other members of her family. The whole city was swarming with German soldiers, making sure that no Jews eluded their death trap, including those in hiding on the non-Jewish side of the city. Stricken with fear, Genia quickly dressed Bogusia and told her to hurry to one of the addresses that Bogusia's mother had given Genia in case of emergency. The first one was the child's former governess, from prewar times. After being twice rebuffed, she returned home, and afraid of being an annoyance to Genia, she climbed into the attic on the building's last floor, and fell asleep. She kept herself warm by cuddling up to a rabbit, which one of the building's tenants was breeding, in time for the Christmas dinner.

When morning dawned, Bogusia half-hearted knocked on Genia's door. The frantic woman immediately tucked her into a warm bed. After this incident, Genia decided to send the child to friends on a farm. From there, Bogusia passed through several hands, and ever new readjustments. In the meantime, back in the ghetto, the last few hundreds of the city's once numerous Jews, including Kitia, had been locked in a factory that produced uniforms for the German army. In late 1943, there was a knock on the factory's outer gate; there stood Genia with the child. "Laughing and crying, we kissed and embraced through the grill," Kitia recalls. "Now you can see with your own eyes that she is well," Genia reassured her friend. Another meeting was planned. This time, the remnant of the Jewish workers swarmed to see a Jewish child still alive, this late in the Holocaust. Kitia notes her impressions of the others and her own inner feelings:

> *They all wanted to touch and embrace a Jewish child! The only hope for a future!. . . Everybody wanted to say something to her as if to leave an important legacy in the child's hands. . . Words that were beyond comprehension of the child's mind – but perhaps they would remain in a small cell, perhaps they would be stored in the child's memory until a day when they would storm out of the depths of a nightmare and cry out for the whole world to hear: 'Do not let it ever happen again – to anybody!'*

The child reacted to this quite differently. Terrified at the sight of emaciated-looking people rushing toward her, fervently touching and kissing her, as they blurted out words with an intensity that frightened her – she withdrew and sought shelter in Genia's arms, whispering in her ears: "Promise me, promise me, that I'll never have to be a Jew again!"

Kitia was one of the lucky few to be released by the Germans to the Red Cross, weeks before the war's end, and she arrived safely in Sweden. From there, she wrote to Genia, asking about news of the child, but received no response. It was only in November of that year that postal services with Poland were restored, and with it news that Bogusia was well. After Genia dutifully handed over the child to Kitia's mother, she again passed through several hands, until she was eventually taken to Israel, where she reverted to her original name (but dropped the final "a," to give it a Hebrew sound, "Tamar," the fruit of the palm). Under new sunny skies, she grew up, married and brought two children into the world. With her new life came a resolve to draw a line, and in the interest of sanity, cut all connections linking her with her past ordeal, including that of her rescuer, Genia Pajak. Fervently intent on integrating herself in the heroic and Maccabean spirit of the new nation of Israel, she rejected all remembrance of her childhood period, and with the exception of her beloved cousin in Australia, all links with people of those painful years. As Henrietta (Kitia) Altman noted in her 1982 statement: "It seemed, the only way for her to handle her life was to deny the past."

As for Genia Pajak, the poverty-stricken woman, who for almost three years had cared for a strange child, while all this time knowing and fearing that one day she would have to relinquish her to her people – this good-hearted woman had to make yet another sacrifice. In Kitia's words: "She had to be denied the pleasure and joy of participating, even from afar, in her growth and development into womanhood and motherhood." Although pained by this, she did not bear a grudge against the child, now a woman in her own right. "I tried to explain to her," Kitia sensitively adds, "that though in a sense she had given her the gift of life for a second time, she must now stand back, so the child could fully benefit from it." A day before she died, in 1974, Genia asked Kitia for a picture of Tamar-Bogusia. Six years thereafter, Kitia asked that the child's benefactress be admitted into the ranks of the Righteous, without requiring Tamar to come and testify, as is generally required — a step for which she was still psychologically unprepared and unwilling. As Tamar's husband informed Yad Vashem, any reference to her past during the Holocaust, caused his wife tremendous psychological pain. He asked on her behalf not to insist on her participation in the nomination procedure. Yad Vashem acquiesced, and based on Henrietta Altman's elaborate testimony, and other relevant documentation, awarded the Righteous title to the late Genia Pajak.

The story does not end here, for some two decades after Pajak's induction into the Righteous Hall of Fame, Tamar underwent a slow but steady reawakening and a coming to terms with her past. It may have been triggered in 1991, when she received a letter from the museum curator in Bedzin, informing her of plans to exhibit her father's artistic drawings, and soliciting information about her father and his relatives. This time, Tamar reacted differently and, surprising herself, responded affirmatively. As she wrote to her cousin in Australia: "Perhaps now that my father has been recognized as a painter, I have been given a new identity; the one I've denied for so many years." A dried-up well had suddenly burst open, and was now gushing forth with unhindered vigor.

In preparation for the exhibit in Bedzin, Tamar visited her cousin in Australia to learn more about her background and her parents. "She would jot down everything I said," Kitia remembers. Back in Israel, Tamar confirmed that her father's painting exhibit "had pulled a trigger inside me and in the last three weeks I remember so much that I forget to eat." She had, indeed, tried to collected her thoughts on paper, in a memoir which has recently been published in Australia. In April 1993, eleven members of Kitia's family attended the opening of the exhibit of Samuel Cygler's paintings, some of which were sent on loan from an Israeli museum with Tamar's help. Tamar walked again through the streets of the former ghetto, and visited the others spots in the Bedzin linked to her childhood. Tragically, that same year she died, at age 58, after suffering a stroke. Before that, however, she had managed to put her new thoughts on paper.

Tamar began her memoirs with reflections on her father who perished in Mauthausen, a month before liberation. She noted: "How is it possible for people to vanish without a trace, yet art can endure forever?" She continued by readily admitting her previous determination to forget her past.

"But the past would not die. It returned – from the beginning." She then
recounted, step by step, the terrible events inside the Bedzin Ghetto, as it
went through its death throes at the hands of the Germans. Included is a
dramatic episode when, in July 1943, she was hauled on a cattle train
together with her parents, but they managed to jump, and return to the
ghetto, with only minor wounds. The shots of the guards on the train had
missed them. These events filled her with fear of people. Instead – "I loved
cows, dogs, grasshoppers, even snakes don't repulse me." While in the care
of Genia Pajak, she invented fairy tales, which she told other children, not
without trepidation, for fear that this would lead to someone checking on
her past, and discover who she really was. She relates her thoughts as a
hunted child:

> I am a Jewish child and children like me are condemned to death by the
> Germans. I don't know why this is so and I don't understand it. All I know
> is that I must never disclose the truth about who I really am to anyone if
> I want to stay alive. And I want to live so very much!

Then, there was that terrible night, when the Germans were looking
for Jews in hiding, and Genia put a cross around Bogusia's neck and sent
her to seek temporary shelter with another person. She tried the house of
Basia, a friend of her mother. But she was not home, and her husband
refused to let her in. At another home, also an acquaintance of her mother,
she was told: "Get lost at once or I'll call the Gestapo! Out! Now!" She finally
passed the night in the attic of Genia's home, in the company of a rabbit. "I
felt the beat of his heart and the warmth of his trembling body penetrated
my skin." The warmth of the rabbit's body put her to sleep. Returning home,
Genia exclaimed: "You were lucky; the cross saved you." Tamar thought
to herself: "No, the rabbit did." She was then sent to stay with other people,
for her own protection, and she moved from place to place. A disconsolate
thought became etched deeper in her mind. "I learned this about life: you
meet people and later they disappear forever." She witnessed Genia's
husband's brutal beating by the German police on suspicion of aiding the
partisans; she also came down with a severe case of typhus, from which she
recovered very slowly. Food was in short supply wherever she went. In one
place, she stole the food reserved for the house dog. The dog, it seems, took
it in stride. Summarizing her thoughts before passing from this world Tamar,
however, gave expression to a new sense of confidence:

> Life can be seen as a continuous chain of links between people. There are
> some who give you love, friendship and warmth, and there are others to
> whom you in turn bestow these feelings. . . I did not lose my love for, or

faith in, humanity. On the contrary, I have always encountered wonderful human beings, everywhere. My faith in humanity has been strengthened by years of experience. . . . All that I have received, I have passed on in my own way to others.

A tree grows at Yad Vashem, bearing the name of Genia Pajak. It was planted in a ceremony which Tamar, at the time, found it mentally difficult to attend. The paintings of Tamar's father are exhibited in a city, in Poland, which witnessed the destruction of her immediate family and thousands of others Jews. Tamar left behind a husband and two grownup children. One cannot help but wonder whether her renewed preoccupation with her distant past might not have opened unhealed wounds, and indirectly contributed to her untimely death. Hopefully, this was not the case. Her memoirs remain a testimony of the resurgence of memory after a lapse of close to fifty years, and of a renewed confidence in the bonds of love and humanity, reinforced by the love, care and understanding of the two important women in her life: her beloved cousin, Henrietta (Kitia) Altman, and her courageous rescuer, Genia Pajak.[9]

Wartime photo of Genia Pajak with daughter Sonia, and (left) Tamara Cygler.

Chapter 8

Clergy in Various Robes

There is an ongoing scholarly debate on the role of the church hierarchies during the Holocaust; what they did, or failed to do, to stop Nazi Germany from implementing and carrying out the murder of the Jewish people. Questions are being raised regarding the heads of Catholic as well as various Protestant denominations in countries close to or where the mass killings took place. While this debate goes on, there is no denying that more could have been done by the head of the Catholic church at the time, Pius XII, and most of the cardinals and bishops in countries with a large Catholic following, such as Germany, Austria, France, Belgium, Poland, Lithuania, Slovakia (where Josef Tiso, a Catholic priest, was head of the Fascist state, and consented to the deportation of Jews to Nazi concentration camps), Hungary, and Croatia. This is equally the case for the heads of the Protestant churches, particularly in Germany, where a major wing of the church, the German Christians, toed the Nazi line, including its virulent antisemitism. There were also instances of open or silent collaboration by heads of churches in some of the countries, either under occupation or allied with Nazi Germany. At the same time, in all countries under German occupation or its influence, stories have surfaced of priests, pastors, monks and nuns, of all colors and shades, who sheltered Jews or provided them with false credentials, so as to assure their survival. In many, if not most of these cases, lower-ranking clerics among the rescuers did not necessarily seek the consent of their elders, and of the church hierarchies, before deciding on extending aid to Jews, for they felt that such behavior was derivative of their Christian faith. In this chapter, we have selected a sample of such rescuers.[1]

Abbé Simon Gallay

A Personal Search Leads to Discovery of Many Clergy Rescuers

In 1984, a man walked into my office at Yad Vashem, and presented himself as Father Bernard Boisson. He had just completed a religious tour of duty in Israel and was returning to France. Before leaving, he decided to visit the tree of a relative in the Avenue of the Righteous. He was satisfied with the tree's growth and before leaving came to bid farewell. As we exchanged parting words, a sudden thought flipped through my mind. Remembering the story told and retold by my parents of a certain priest who had helped us cross the Franco-Swiss border during a critical phase of our flight from the Germans, and being now informed that Father Boisson's new assignment would be near that crossing site, I asked whether he could assist me in locating that French priest. Although his name was unknown to my family, my mother had provided me with some helpful identifying hints which I passed on to Boisson. Hopefully, he was still alive; if not, I should at least have the satisfaction of visiting his gravestone. We shook hands, as Father Boisson promised to do what he could.

In November 1982, when I was appointed head of the Department for the Righteous at Yad Vashem, I had written to my parents, in New York, asking them for a detailed account on the help received from that unknown priest. Responding, my father wrote that in September 1943, when the Germans occupied the Italian zone in France, my parents felt the time had come to leave Varse, an off-the-beaten-track village, outside of Grenoble, where under the Italian occupation we lived in relative security, and head toward the Swiss border. We were then a family of six children, plus my maternal grandmother. Taking along the three eldest children (myself – then 6 years, and my two sisters, Annie, 7, and Leah, 4), and leaving my father behind with the rest of the family, my mother whose appearance was less Jewish-looking than my father, left on a hazardous and uncertain journey toward the resort town of Evian-les-Bains, where we had previously been informed that a priest, code-named Mr. Lebain, would help us flee across the border. As she related to me in her letter: "Arriving there, I knocked at a door near the church. A woman came out and led me into a room and told me to wait. A little while later, a man appeared. He was handsome, tall, with blond hair and blue eyes." Next to him stood another priest, a bit older. In a weeping voice, my mother related our precarious situation, and pleaded for his help. We were immediately led to a religious home, where the nuns gave us something to drink and a room to pass the night. Several days letter, the priest returned and told my mother: "Now, it's time." "I was crying and wanted to give Mr. Le Bain my wedding ring in return for his good deed," my mother related, "but he said to me, 'My dear lady, keep the ring, just remember me.' I remember him to this day – his lovely and friendly face." A coded telegram was sent to my father, and he arrived with the rest of the family (my siblings, Frieda and the 10-month-old twins, Mania and Simon, and my grandmother). After several days, we were instructed to head to Thonon-les-Bains and from there by bus to a village, to rendezvous with a *passeur* (border smuggler) who would be waiting for us in a certain bistro. This man and his companion then led us across the barbed-wired border under the cover of night. Leaving us on a small ridge, on the Swiss side, we were told to wait until a Swiss border patrol would spot us. Since our party included small children, it was felt (or rather, hoped) that we would not be turned back. And so, indeed, it happened, and we were safe and sound inside Switzerland.

I had kept with me my mother's story, waiting for an opportune moment to make an effort to locate and identify the benevolent priest who helped us elude the Nazis. A short time after my meeting with Father Boisson, I received a letter from him suggesting that I write to a certain Father Gallay, in Annecy, for further information. I did so, and in November 1984, I received the following response.

> Yes, it is I who took care of you at Evian and arranged your passage to Switzerland. I helped many Jews cross into Switzerland, but I was not alone in doing it. The passeurs included Yves Roussey, shot by the Germans, Jacques Moulard – deported for one year. . . I was encouraged in this work by Abbé Albert Simond (deceased), Abbé Camille Folliet (deceased), Abbé Jean Rosay, deported to Germany. He did not return. I must point out those who worked with me, for I would not have been able to do much all by myself. Thank you for writing to me. If you need more information, ask me. Sincerely yours, Simon Gallay.

I was stunned, not having expected such a straightforward affirmative response, quite so soon. I was, moreover, not familiar with the other priestly persons who were involved in the rescue of Jews.

In addition, my doubts concerning the true identity of the "Mr. Lebain" in my mother's testimony were not allayed. Was it really the same person as Abbé Simon Gallay, previously of Evian-les-Bains and now living in a Catholic retirement home, in nearby Annecy? Responding to him politely, I asked for further clarifications on my family's passage to Switzerland through his help, as well as a wartime picture of him.

Some months later, my colleague Dr. Eva Fleischner, who had come to
Yad Vashem to research French clergy rescuers of Jews during the war, was
leaving for France to pursue her research. She cheerfully agreed to my
request to meet with Abbé Gallay, and elicit more information from him. In
October 1985, she wrote to me that after a lengthy conversation with Gallay,
"there is *absolutely no question* but that he is the one your mother remembers. . . He clearly remembers your mother's offering him her ring." As for
the mystery of "Mr. Lebain" — it was Gallay's superior, Abbé Albert Simond,
who was called by the people 'Mr. Plebain,' a man of the people (from the
Latin 'plebs' — people), apparently a title sometimes popularly attached to
a rural pastor. This Simond was probably the older man standing next to
Gallay during the encounter with my mother. "Everything fits," Fleischner
concluded; "there were only these two priests in Evian during the war. . .
I believe I can say, mission accomplished. . . I am glad I could do this for
you — you can put aside *all* doubt."

Soon thereafter, I also received a positive response from my mother, who
recognized the wartime photo of Gallay's face, as the man who calmed her
fears and refused to accept her wedding ring as a token of her gratitude to
him. The die was cast — I had found my rescuer! Soon thereafter, Yad
Vashem awarded him the title of "Righteous Among the Nations," and on
May 6, 1990, I attended a ceremony, in Annecy, where Gallay was awarded
the Righteous medal and certificate of honor by Israeli Ambassador Yitzhak
Aviran, in a ceremony attended by local Christian and Jewish dignitaries.

By design or coincidence, the Gallay discovery also led to the uncovering
of more information from other sources, which amplified the scope played
by Gallay and some of his colleagues in the rescue of Jews. Gallay's story
shed light on a larger rescue operation, involving a host of Catholic clergy,
some of whom eventually were also awarded the Righteous title.

For instance, from the testimony of Sister Aline (Josephine Treblet), who
during the war years served as a nun at the *Soeurs Infirmières de Saint-Joseph*,
in Evian — we learned more about Abbé Albert Simond, the Curé (or head
priest) of Evian, under whom Simon Gallay served as vicar. Together they
sheltered many Jews in the presbytery, and cared for them before arranging
their safe passage into Switzerland. Gallay was especially active in planning
these flights across the border. "He exhausted himself on account of this,"
Sister Aline recalls, "and often worked nights to arrange a passage — to the
point of falling asleep the next morning in church." She also mentioned a
certain Abbé Pierre Mopty who often came to help out. He had a canoe
which he used to take people across Lake Léman, the waterway separating
France and Switzerland – doing the rowing himself. Another witness, Louis
Girod, who lived in Douvaine during the war years, but often visited nearby

Evian to see his mother, knew Mopty as a man of action, who often traveled to distant places to fetch Jewish children. Girod also remembers when Gallay entrusted him with 300,000 francs, which Girod was to turn over to a *passeur* in Douvaine, for distribution to other *passeurs*, probably to take Jews over the border.

As for Abbé Simond, Mrs. Zemboul Abouaf (born Molho), who with her husband lived in Evian during that period (they were protected for a time from deportation, due to their Turkish nationality), related that in the spring of 1943, Simond learned that the French pro-Fascist Milice was about to torch the local synagogue. Hurrying there in time, together with another priest (probably Gallay), he fetched the two Torah scrolls, and took them to his presbytery for safekeeping. After the war, the two Torah scrolls were turned over to the Jewish community.

My family probably also crossed paths with Erica Stevens, formerly Sternschein, and her husband. Fleeing from Nice, in southern France, they arrived in Evian and took up residence in an hotel. Told to refer to the church presbytery, they were received by Simond, who promised to help, but were told to wait a few days since he was at the time busy with another family with children (probably mine) who were staying in the presbytery and were about to be taken across. An alternative plan was to have them taken by Abbé Mopty across Lake Léman by boat. However, Mopty was apprehended by French customs officials together with three fleeing Jews in his boat, and the plan had to be abandoned. Instead, Erica and her husband were spirited across the Swiss border with the help of a priest in the nearby town of Annemasse.

Another witness, Ruth Lambert, told a most fascinating story about Abbé Mopty. Close to Christmas 1943, she was part of a group of volunteers (including Andrée Salomon, of the Jewish children welfare organization known as OSE, and Abbé Albert Gross, a Swiss Catholic chaplain, working on behalf of Caritas-Suisse) active in ameliorating conditions of foreign-born Jewish internees in French detention camps. They had just arrived in Rivesaltes, one of these infamous camps, and had settled down on the floor, in a room without any furniture, when there was a knock on the door, and a young priest with a black umbrella, and a big smile, entered: "Bonjour, I am Abbé Mopty. I am here to save Jews. . ." The three were stunned. Mopty then explained that he was sent on a mission to fetch three Jewish persons (father, mother and son), in Rivesaltes, who were sought by the Gestapo, and help them cross into Switzerland. In this instance, the French authorities acquiesced to demands for the release of these persons to Mopty's care. Several days later, Mopty and his three companions showed up at the Evian harbor. He requisitioned a suitable canoe, and all four boarded it in the direction of the Swiss shore, where Abbé Gross was already waiting to receive them. Returned alone, Mopty replaced the canoe. It turned out that the boat belonged to the local police chief! No one had noticed. He continued to be much involved in rescue operations, and once told Lambert: "Doing what God wants is the only undertaking which gives me rest." He, as well as Simond and Gross, were awarded the Righteous title.

Gallay later wrote to me more on his life and activities. Born in 1913, the 10th of 13 children, he was ordained into the priesthood in 1937. That year, he was sent to Evian to serve under Albert Simond, the local curé. During the war years, many fleeing Jews sought his help. Crossings into Switzerland were generally done via mountain passes. Gallay never himself undertook such mission. "I did not have the time and I did not know the region well." He used three professional *passeurs:* The brothers Yves and Raymond Roussey and Jacques Moulard. He believes that one of them took my family across into Switzerland in the mountain region, from the side of Bernex. Jacques Moulard was eventually arrested and deported to Germany, but luckily survived. The brothers Roussey were also arrested, but were not as fortunate as Moulard. Taken for questioning in nearby Annemasse, they were later shot by their German guards, near Douvaine, in reprisal for an attack by the resistance on a German convoy. As for my family, in Gallay's words — "they came to me one evening: father, mother and six children. The mother offered me her wedding ring so that we re spond affirmatively." Gallay declined the ring. "There was among them a 5-year-old boy [I was actually six at the time]. I think he carried in his arms a smaller child. We acted."

Once Gallay was almost arrested by the Gestapo, when a certain woman came to him ostensibly to seek help. "Mr. l'Abbé, your brother is a prisoner in Germany," she said. Gallay knew this was true, but he immediately became suspicious. From whom did she learn this? He had never seen her before. He was sure she was sent by the Gestapo to entrap him, and he gently showed her to the door. In 1945, Gallay took up a new post in nearby Douvaine. Much later, the tension of the war years caught up with him, and in 1965, he suffered from severe depression, which forced him to seek medical treatment in Paris. He finally retired in Annecy in 1982. Summing up his career as a priest, Gallay reminisced: "I always try to take an interest in the life of people. I love all the world. I love every human being. I don't have enemies. Those who are cross with me and consider me their enemy are wasting their time. Myself, I love them and am always ready to be of assistance to them."

Thus, a story which began with a lone personal quest of one's family rescuer led to the unfolding of a string of other rescuers, of Catholic clerics in southern France who acted in unison to save Jews; to the addition of valuable testimonies by survivors, and to the adding of more names to the list of "Righteous Among the Nations" at Yad Vashem.[2]

Abbé Simon Gallay, with the author (1990). *Author's photo*

Anna Borkowska

A Nun with a Broken Heart

Far away from France, in distant Lithuania, a nun was wondering how to help Jews on the run. That extraordinary woman's story had almost been forgotten when, in 1984, the well-known Israeli man of letters, author, thinker, poet, and Holocaust fighter Abba Kovner was told that the Polish nun who had helped him and his beleaguered comrades during the early phase of the Holocaust in Lithuania, and was believed no longer to be among the living, a woman to whom he had dedicated a poem entitled "My Little Sister" — was indeed alive and living in Warsaw. That year, he wrote to Yad Vashem, asking that this 85-year-old woman be awarded the Righteous title. "In my name, and in the name of the Vilna fighters, I ask you to please award the title of Righteous Among the Nations to Anna Borkowska, who is to be counted among the courageous woman of World War Two."

The story unfolds in Kolonia Wilenska, near Vilnius (or Vilna, its former name under Polish rule, presently the capital of Lithuania), where Sister Anna Borkowska served as Mother Superior in a convent consisting of a small group of Dominican nuns. Shocked by the horrible massacres of thousands of Jews in the Ponar forest, not far from her convent, in the summer months of 1941, she invited a group of 17 members of an illegal Jewish pioneering group to hide in the convent for brief spells of time. Soon thereafter, the convent of nine nuns was bustling with activity, for the youthful Jewish men and women were plotting, behind the secure walls of the Dominican convent, an eventual uprising in the Vilna Ghetto.

"They called me *Ima* (mother)," Anna Borkowska fondly remembered. "I felt as if I were indeed their mother. I was pleased with the arrival of each new member, and was sorry that I could not shelter more of them." Recalling those who passed through the convent walls, Anna mentioned Arieh Wilner: "I gave him the name 'Jurek'" — the code-name under which he was to be known for his exploits in Warsaw, where he eventually perished during the Warsaw Ghetto uprising of April 1943. As a member of the *Hashomer Hatzair* (Young Guard), an ultra-socialist wing in the Zionist movement — he held to Marxist opinions. "Two different worlds met," she stated. "Nevertheless, we found points of contact, or rather bridges, since each one of us wished to be able to look into the other's soul. . . In our discussions we tried to escape from the monstrous reality into the world of ideas. In spirit 'Jurek' was the closest to me." Then, there was Abba Kovner, the moving spirit of the Vilna underground—"my right hand."

Kovner presided over the conclaves in the convent where plans were hatched for an uprising in the Vilna Ghetto. Until these plans could mature, Kovner and his 16 colleagues worked side by side with the convent nuns in the fields. There was also Tauba, "who loved life so much, gentle, pleasant," and later died during an attack on a German convoy. Margalit, who worked in the kitchen while shedding tears for her lost child; Mrs. K., who was torn by terrible doubts—could God be good if such monstrosities were allowed to happen? She was to die during the Warsaw Ghetto uprising in April 1943; Michas, who had, previous to his coming to the convent, remained hidden for many weeks in a hole in an attic without light and air, and was pale "as a holy wafer." While in the convent, he helped during the harvest and got tanned. He too did not survive the Holocaust.[3]

To conceal the group's activities from the eyes of suspecting neighboring peasants, ever watchful of the unusual comings and goings of the convent, all protégés were given nun habits and thus they cultivated the nearby fields. In this departure from monastic rules, it is reported that Mother Anna had the support of her superior in the Vilna archdiocese. A former Jewish refugee in this convent calls it "the only spark of light that shined in the general darkness; the only place where one found brotherhood and human compassion. The Mother Superior had become elevated in the hearts of those who stood in her presence to the symbolic image of the ideal person." In the convent cells, Kovner issued his famous clarion call of rebellion, the first of its kind in Nazi-occupied Europe, which opened with the ringing words: "Let us not be led like sheep to slaughter!" This manifesto, secretly printed in the convent and distributed inside the ghetto on January 1, 1942, served as inspiration to many ghetto and partisan fighters.

When the time came for Abba Kovner and his comrades to return to the ghetto (they told her, "If we are to die, let us die the death of free people, with arms in our hands"), Anna Borkowska rushed to join them. "I want to go with you to the ghetto," she pleaded with Abba; "to fight and fall with you... Your war is a holy war. Even though of Marxist orientation and free of religion, you are a noble people for there is religion in your heart. A great God—now you are closer to Him than I." Kovner told her she could be of greater help by smuggling in weapons. The noted Yiddish poet Abraham Sutzkever relates: "the first four grenades... were the gift of the Mother Superior, who instructed Abba Kovner in their proper use... She later supplied other weapons." In her postwar account of this episode, Anna Borkowska wrote: "Among the whole ocean of small and gray events in life, these moments, when one was gambling for a big stake, were the most beautiful and valuable. Such moments occur only once in a lifetime."[4]

As suspicions mounted, the Germans had Anna Borkowska arrested in

September 1943, the convent closed and the Sisters dispersed. One nun was dispatched to a labor camp. Surviving the Holocaust as a fighting partisan and moving to Israel, Abba Kovner sought after the war to reestablish contact with her, but was misinformed that she had passed away. He then immersed himself in work to forge ethical and moral foundations for the newly-established State of Israel. Four decades after the war, he learned that Anna Borkowska was alive. In 1984, suffering from an incurable disease to which he would later succumb, Kovner rushed to her side in a nondescript tiny Warsaw flat and presented her with the Yad Vashem medal of "Righteous Among the Nations." She wondered: "Why do I deserve this honor?" He movingly replied: "You are Anna of the Angels."

During the ceremony in her honor, he learned that the trauma of the war years had caused her to relinquish the life of a nun. When her turn came to speak, turning to Kovner, she hesitatingly asked: "Isn't it right, that you were always a believing person?" "Yes, indeed," Kovner replied, somewhat confused. He then turned to the audience gathered in her honor, and said: "In the days when the angels hid their faces from us, this woman was to us Anna of the Angels — not the angels that we invent for ourselves, but angels which help us build our lives for an eternity." He had dedicated a poem to her, which begins with the words: "My little Sister! Nine Sisters look at you with anxiety, as one looks at the sands in the desert." A year later, Abba Kovner planted a tree in her honor at Yad Vashem. At last, a long standing wish had been fulfilled. He had seen once more Anna Borkowska and bid her a last farewell, before he was to pass away.[5]

The poet Abba Kovner presents the "Righteous Among the Nations" scroll to Anna Borkovska.

Elizabeth Skobtzova (Mother Maria)

The Martyrdom of a Russian Nun in Paris

Before the war, Elizabeth Skobtzova, a nun in the Russian Orthodox church, operated a charitable network in Paris for Russian political refugees of the Communist revolution. Her story became known to two Holocaust historians — Léon Poliakov, whose sister was provided with a false certificate by Skobtzova which helped her and her husband to survive, and Georges Wellers, who added valuable information about the help his family had received from her. Who was this rather unknown (other than among small circles) Russian nun, who suffered martyrdom at the hands of the Nazis, dying in Ravensbrück concentration camp, to where she was sent after being implicated in the "offense" of aiding Jews?

She was born Elizabeth Pilenko, in 1891, in Riga (then part of the Russian Empire), to a father who served as chief prosecutor and a mother who was a descendent of a French officer in Napoleon's army. While still a child, the family moved to Anapa, on the Black Sea coast, where her father specialized in viniculture. After his death, in 1905, the family moved to St. Petersburg. There, Elizabeth took an interest in poetry, and wrote *Scythian Shards* and *Ruth*, which were well received in literary circles. Her first marriage with Dimitri Kuzmin-Karavaev, a lawyer, produced a child, but the marriage soon disintegrated, and the two parted ways. When the Russian Revolution broke out in March 1917, Elizabeth was a staunch supporter of the Social Democrat party (known by its initials SR). Furious at Bolshevik leader Leon Trotzky for forcefully closing the SR party Congress, she decided to assassinate him, but was dissuaded by her party colleagues. Instead, she was sent back to her youthful town of Anapa, on the Black Sea, to spread the revolutionary cause there, and was elected the town's mayor. With the capture of the town by the White forces of General Denikin, she was arrested and placed on trial as a left-wing revolutionary. With the help of her defense lawyer, she was able to sway the court president, Danilo Skobtsov (a former schoolmaster), to dismiss all the charges. The two eventually married. When Anapa was overrun by the Red Army, the couple fled to Turkey and Yugoslavia; thence to France, where they arrived in 1923. In the meantime, she bore Danilo a son and a daughter.

Upon the death of her four-year-old daughter, in 1932, Elisabeth underwent a religious transformation, which led her to the decision to become a nun in the Russian Orthodox Church. Taking her vows, she adopted the name "Maria," and became known as "Mother Maria." She chose not to withdraw from the world but instead dedicate herself to the cause of the needy, especially from among the Russian emigrants in France. This led her to open a dormitory in Saxe, outside of Paris, which included a free kitchen. In 1935, the Russian Orthodox Church purchased for her a building on Rue de Lourmel, in the 15th district of Paris, which became the base of her charitable work. Another home, in Noisy-le-Grand, near Paris, served as a convalescent home. Part of her work also included helping free Russian emigrants (there were altogether some 40,000 of them in Paris alone) who were mistakenly committed to insane asylums, and secure for them suitable employment. In these activities, she was seconded by Father Dimitri Klepinin, also a Russian emigrant, who, while already married and father to a child, had opted for the priesthood and was ordained in 1937.

With the German occupation of France, in June 1940, Elizabeth Skobtzova, or *Mère Marie*, turned her attention to needy Jews. She began by making the free kitchen available to Jews; then, by providing temporary shelter at her Lourmel center for those fleeing the authorities, until other arrangements could be made for them — to the point that the Lourmel center was often referred to as the "Jewish Church." In this, she cooperated with various clandestine Jewish organizations. In May 1942, when the forceful wearing of the Yellow Star by all Jews was enacted by the Germans, she countered with a celebrated poem, which she entitled *Israel*. It reads as follows:

> *Two triangles, a star*
> *The shield of King David, our forefather*
> *This is election, not offense*
> *The great path and not an evil.*
>
> *Once more is a term fulfilled*
> *Once more roars the trumpet of the end*
> *And the fate of a great people*
> *Once more is by the prophet proclaimed.*
>
> *Thou art persecuted again, O Israel*
> *But what can human ill will mean to you,*
> *You, who has heard the thunder from Sinai?*[6]

Two months later, in July 1942, during the giant roundup of Parisian Jews at the Winter Sports Stadium, she made her way in the closely-guarded stadium to spirit out two Jewish children, hidden in trash bins. At night, in her tiny and modestly furnished room, she expressed her innermost thoughts in a diary, in which she clearly alluded to her charitable work, as in the following entry:

There is one moment when you start burning with love and you have the inner desire to throw yourself at the feet of some other human being. This one moment is enough. Immediately you know that instead of losing your life, it is being given back to you twofold.[7]

Towards the end of 1942, she was warned that the Gestapo was on her trail, but she took no notice of this. In fact, she dismissed all suggestions to cease helping Jews; she could no longer change course, she stated, since her work was led by an invisible hand. On February 3, 1943, she was arrested by the Gestapo, together with her son, her mother, and Father Klepinin. She readily admitted to helping Jews, including the issuing of false baptismal certificates and to transferring funds to Jews in hiding. A Gestapo man named Hoffmann lashed out at Maria's mother: "You educated your daughter very stupidly. She helps Jews only." To which the old woman replied: "This is not true. She is a Christian who helps those in need. She would even help you, if you were in trouble." The Nazi was furious: "You will never see your daughter again." It is also reported that this Gestapo agent offered Klepinin his release in return for a promise not to help Jews again. Klepinin's answer was: "I can say no such thing. I am a Christian, and must act as I must." The enraged Hoffmann struck Klepinin across his face and screamed. "Jew lover! How dare your talk of those pigs as being a Christian duty!" Recovering his balance, Klepinin raised the cross from his cassock and facing Hoffmann quietly said: "Do you know this Jew?" Another blow by Hoffmann landed Klepinin on the floor.[8] The Gestapo decided to deport Mother Maria, her son Yuri and Klepinin to concentration camps. Maria arrived in Ravensbrück; in that infamous place, ravaged by hunger, disease, and torture, she finally succumbed on March 31, 1945, only weeks before the camp's liberation, and her body was consumed by the crematoria flames. Her son Yuri died previously, in Dora camp, alongside Father Klepinin, who also perished.

Maria Skobtzova's charitable help to Jews is brought out in various testimonies and documentation. Holocaust historian and survivor Georges Wellers testified that he was arrested in 1941, and was imprisoned on French soil for close to three years, before being sent to Auschwitz. While in the Drancy transit camp, his friends turned to Skobtzova and Klepinin, who, in 1942, issued false baptismals for Wellers' wife, and membership certificates in the Russian Orthodox Church. This exempted her children as well from deportation. When SS officer Alois Brunner became suspicious of Anne Wellers' non-Jewish credentials, she took flight and went into hiding with her children. Brunner ordered that she be found at all cost. When this proved unsuccessful, Anne's husband, Georges, was deported to Auschwitz, in June 1944. This two-year respite (he could not be deported until the issue of his wife racial status had been fully cleared up) eased his survival in Auschwitz. In his words: "I am convinced that all four of us remained alive thanks to Father Klepinin and Mother Maria. I also know that thanks to their admirable action in favor of Jews, of which my family is but one example, both were arrested, deported, and perished. May their memory be immortalized."[9]

On October 12, 1945, a memorial service was held in a Parisian synagogue for Skobtzova, with cantor and congregation in tears over her tragic end.[10] Maria's widowed mother, Sofia Pilenko, was aided by the American-based Jewish labor union ILGWU, which kept an office in Paris. Mother Maria and Dimitri Klepinin were both awarded the Righteous title in 1985. During a visit to Yad Vashem, Klepinin's daughter planted a tree in each name.[11]

In her prewar writings, the following statement by Mother Maria was found which perhaps sums up her life's philosophy:

At the Last Judgment, I will not be asked whether I satisfactorily practiced asceticism, nor how many bows I made before the divine altar. I will be asked whether I fed the hungry, clothed the naked, visited the sick and the prisoner. This is all that will be asked.[12]

Above: Elizabeth Skobtzova arrives in Paris in 1923 with her children. Right: Mother Maria (center) in Noisy, mid-1930s.

Angelo Rotta

A Prince of the Church and of Humanity

As the Hungarian regime, an ally of Nazi Germany, cowed to Hitler's demand to be rid of its Jewish population, there were no doubts in the mind of Monsignor Angelo Rotta, the Vatican's ambassador to Hungary, what his response should be — unconditional opposition to these heinous measures, and immediate steps to alleviate the plight of thousands of Jews. He tried to stem the anti-Jewish measures, both during the rule by the moderately pro-Fascist regime of Horthy, as well as later on during the savage reign of terror of Szálasi, head of the pro-Nazi dreaded Arrow Cross movement. Together with other diplomatic colleagues, such as the Swedish diplomats Carl Ivan Danielsson and Raoul Wallenberg, the Swiss Carl Lutz, the Spanish Angel Sans-Briz, and the Italian Giorgio Perlasca, he exerted himself, above and beyond his mandate, to contain the regime's measures against the Hungarian Jews and stop their deportation to the death camps.

With the German occupation of Hungary on March 19, 1944, and the first news of the roundup of Jews in various parts of the country, Rotta made his voice heard. He pleaded with the government of Admiral Horthy (still the titular head of the country) to at least moderate the anti-Jewish measures, and respect the personal, and — in his view — God-given natural rights which all people share. In a written memorandum to the Hungarian Foreign Ministry, on May 15, 1944, Rotta noted that the very fact that people are persecuted only because of their racial origin constitutes a violation of the natural law governing all people. If God gave people life, he argued, no mortal man was allowed to take it away or deprive them of the means of existence. Although at first mostly concerned with the plight of baptized Jews, he later also pleaded the cause of all Jews, without distinction.

On June 18, 1944 Rotta reported to his superior, Cardinal Maglione, the Vatican Secretary of State, on the start of deportations of over 300,000 Jews to the camps, which he noted were probably extermination camps, and where those unable to work would not be expected to survive. For the second time, Rotta urged direct intervention by the Vatican so as to halt the deportations. It took another month for Pope Pius XII to write directly to Horthy. This, together with appeals by neutral countries and international agencies, had the desired effect, and the deportations were stopped in July 1944. Aware of the Church's sensitivity toward baptized Jews, Dominic Sztojay, who then headed the Hungarian government, assured Rotta on July 25 that in the future converted Jews would be exempted from any anti-

Jewish measures, Rotta rejected this bait, and asked for a further relaxation of the "really Draconian regulations applied to Jews," baptized or not.

Rotta was also annoyed with lack of action by the head of the Catholic church in the country, Cardinal Justinian Serédi, whom he visited on June 8, 1944, and reproached him for not energetically opposing the government's anti-Jewish measures. Seredi replied that a pastoral letter read from the pulpit would not help but result in greater harm to the interests of the Church in Hungary. In addition, as a rejoinder to Rotta, Seredi remarked that the fact that the Holy See still maintained diplomatic relations with Nazi Germany, was wrongly interpreted by many people with respect to the Vatican's position vis-à-vis the persecution of Jews.[13]

Following rumors that the deportation of Jews was about to resume, Rotta, as the doyen of the diplomatic corps, together with the Swedish ambassador Danielsson, called on Reményi-Schneller, the deputy prime minister, on August 21, and handed him a note, on behalf of the neutral countries, expressing their concern regarding the possible resumption of the deportations. The ambassadors underlined that they were well aware "what deportation in most cases means, even if it is cloaked under the description 'work abroad.'" The note went on to denounce the "inhuman" treatment of Jews, since "it is quite inadmissible to persecute people and to drive them to death simply because of their ancestry." The Portuguese and Swiss Chargé d'Affaires also appended their signatures to this note.[14]

The respite experienced by the Jewish population in Budapest, after the large deportations had emptied the provinces of over 400,000 Jews, who were delivered to the gas chambers of Auschwitz, came to an abrupt end on October 15, 1944. On that day (after the defection of neighboring Romania to the Allied cause, and with Russian troops already on Hungarian soil), Horthy declared a cease-fire. The Germans were prepared for this move; they had Horthy arrested, and installed a new government, headed by the pro-Nazi and intensely antisemitic Ferencz Szálasi, head of the Arrow Cross movement and militia. On that day, a reign of terror was unleashed on Buda-pest's population of over 200,000 Jews and any remaining Jews outside the capital. The new government also announced that it would no longer honor the "protective letters" (*Schutzpass*) previously issued by the ambassa-dors of the neutral countries, including the Red Cross and the Vatican. These documents, originally used by Carl Lutz of the Swiss legation, and copied by Raoul Wallenberg, representing Sweden, stated that the person whose name and picture appeared on it, was under the protection of that particular government, and should therefore be exempted from any harm. This protective device had now been nullified by the country's new rulers. Rotta realized that immediate forceful action was necessary if the remaining Jews were to be saved.

On the day of the Arrow Cross takeover, Rotta visited the new foreign minister, Gábor Kemény, whom he urged to use moderation on the Jewish issue. Six days later, he met with the new head of state, Szálasi, and exacted from him a promise not to resume the deportations and to honor the protective letters issued by the neutral countries.[15] With the Jews in greater danger than ever before,[16] Rotta continued to freely distribute protective letters to whomever turned to him for help.[17] However, one could not place much trust in promises by the Szálasi regime, in light of the worsening military situation. In fact, the authorities had declared open season on Jews (and in many cases, even those with protective letters), who were either killed when caught on the streets, or taken to the ice-cold Danube riverbank, chained to each other, and shot in the head. Similar to the example of several other neutral embassies, Rotta's Nunciature opened two dozen houses, and hoisted a Vatican flag over them, thus gaining extraterritorial rights over these premises in which several thousand Jews were sheltered.

As conditions deteriorated further for the Jews in Budapest, Rotta invited his diplomatic colleagues to a meeting, which resulted in a new memorandum handed to Szalasi on November 17. In it, the ambassadors of five countries restated their complaint that in spite of promises to the contrary, the deportations were resumed and were being carried out "with such brutal severity," deserving the condemnation of the whole world. The ambassadors had in mind the Death March which had just begun, and in which well over 20,000 Jews were driven on foot, and in inclement weather, toward the Austrian border, a distance of 200 miles, where they were to be turned over to the SS. The roads were littered with the corpses of many who, exhausted, fell by the roadside or were struck down by Arrow Cross men and the Hungarian gendarmerie. The ambassadors noted that the excuse that the Jews were being driven for work-related assignment was belied by the fact that even small children, old men and invalids were included. Clearly, no work was meant here. "On the contrary, the brutality with which the removal is being carried out makes it possible to foresee what the end of this tragic journey will be," the note went on. On behalf of the signatory ambassadors, Rotta requested that the government revoke the decision to deport the Jews, and see to it that those already deported be afforded sufficient food, shelter, medical and religious care, and the respect of their lives. Rotta was not naive enough to believe that the fiercely antisemitic regime of Szalasi would be impressed by pleas embellished with humanitarian considerations. Hence, a warning was added—a threat of the possible retaliation by the countries at war with Hungary, including the warning that "all Hungarians abroad would be exposed if the deportation and annihilation of the Jews is continued; not to mention the fact that in the event of an occupation of Hungary, the occupying bodies could apply the same methods to the Hungarian people." Other than Rotta and Danielsson, the signatories included Harald Feller, for Switzerland, Jorge (Giorgio) Perlasca, for Spain, and Count Pongrácz, for Portugal.

On Christmas Day 1944, with the Russian army already besieging the capital and pelting it with artillery shells, diplomats of the neutral countries assembled again — for the last time — in Rotta's residence for another petition to the Arrow Cross regime. This time, the ambassadors addressed a plea not to force children to be caged inside a ghetto which the government had planned for the remaining Jews in the capital.

> *We hear it asserted that the Jews are Hungary's enemies, but even in wartime justice and conscience condemn all hostile activities directed against children. Why then compel these innocent creatures to live in a place which in many ways is like a prison; where the poor little ones will see nothing but the misery, suffering and despair of old men and of women who are being persecuted simply because of their racial origin? All civilized peoples show consideration for children, and the whole world would be painfully surprised if traditionally Christian and chivalrous Hungary wanted to take action against the little ones.*[18]

Furthermore, in view of the continuing violation of human rights by the government and the failure to honor its promises with regard to the treatment of Jews, Rotta informed the Foreign Ministry that he would not go to Szombathely, where the Hungarian government had moved, but would remain in Budapest, so as continue to oversee the assistance which the Nunciature was affording to thousands of Jews during the last and dying phase of the Arrow Cross regime in the capital city.[19] Rotta indeed stayed during the dreadful siege which lasted until the city's full capture on February 12, 1945 (a month earlier, on January 16, 1945, the Russians occupied the Pest part of the city).

It is to be noted that Monsignor Angelo Rotta is the only Vatican nuncio to be awarded the Righteous title. In the evaluation of this case, the Commission for the Righteous was impressed with his personal and, one may add, emotional involvement in the rescue of Hungary's Jews. From the start, he saw through the mist, and realized the dangers facing the country's Jews, which compelled him to press, warn and threaten with no letup. He went further than merely complying with Vatican instructions, such as not satisfying himself with verbal protests to the Hungarian government, but drafting strongly-worded memorandums to the authorities, with frequent use of the word "protest," instead of the usual "concern." Twice, he urged a direct intervention by the Pope, and in one communication (June 18, 1944) he actually demanded that this be done. He tried to activate Cardinal Serédi and the Hungarian episcopate (Hungary is two-thirds Catholic), and in his reports to Rome he expressed his disappointment with Serédi's inaction.

In addition, as the doyen of the diplomatic corps, he acted as a catalyst and took the lead in several appeals to the government. In his petitions, he never overlooked the plight of non-baptized Jews, and in time he avoided all distinctions between both categories. Clearly, while following Vatican policy, Rotta went beyond his mandate, bending the rules whenever necessary in order to save lives. His behavior is to be contrasted with the lackluster attitude of the other heads of the Catholic church, both in Hungary and elsewhere. He, moreover, issued thousands of protective letters, evidently at his own discretion, and had several thousand Jews sheltered in houses flying the Vatican flag. To Nina Langlet who, together with her husband Valdemar, represented the Swedish Red Cross in Hungary and actively helped Jews in various ways, Rotta disclosed that he had received permission from the authorities to issue no more than 2,500 protective letters in the Vatican's name, but he had in fact issued over 19,000 such documents.[20]

Rotta's involvement in the rescue of Jews became even more pronounced during the November 1944 Death March — as reported in the testimonies of Ujváry and Baranszky. As a Red Cross official, Sandor Ujváry was sent to Rotta to fetch blank protective letters, so as to fill them in with names of persons on the infamous Death March of November 1944. When Ujváry told Rotta that many of the people carried forged baptismal certificates, the Nuncio replied: "What you are doing, my son, is pleasing to God and to Jesus, because you are saving innocent people. I give you absolution in advance. Continue your work to the honor of God.[21] The second witness, Tibor Baranszky, was a 21-year-old seminarian when in October 1944, at the request of a Jewish woman, a neighbor of his family in Budapest, he went to the Nunciature to ask for a protective letter. Brought before Rotta, the Monsignor asked him whether he was prepared to immediately go to a nearby cement factory, where Jews were being held by the authorities, and fetch persons who held Vatican protective letters. Baranszky managed to free 40 persons. Impressed with the young man's success, Rotta without further ado appointed him as his secretary and made him responsible for the department dealing with the protected persons. In this capacity, he distributed hundreds of protective letters, and cared for the 3,000 Jews in the Vatican homes.[22]

As to the personal risks resulting from Rotta's humanitarian action, his high position was no guarantee against harm from the radical elements within the Arrow Cross militia who, with the approach of the Russian armies toward Budapest, dropped all pretenses of respect for law and order, and were not beyond harming diplomatic representatives. They probably would not have attempted anything against Rotta himself, though they once raided his premises, looking for anti-government persons. However, Rotta could not be too sure of this, well aware as he was that the Arrow Cross officers were privy to his involvement in the rescue of many Jews. Furthermore, not to be minimized is the likelihood of mistreatment of a person representing the Vatican by the liberating Soviet troops. All of these point to the courage of this man in staying in the besieged city until the safety of the Jews in the protective houses had been assured with the capture of Budapest by Russian troops. All the data on the man's behavior and action prompted the Commission for the Righteous to award the Righteous title to Monsignor Angelo Rotta.[23]

Monsignor Angelo Rotta
© *Ungarisches Museum für Zeitgeschichte*

Chapter 9

Death Marches

As the fortunes of war turned sour for Germany, the remaining Jewish concentration camp inmates were taken on forced marches towards the German border. As these German retreats occurred during the winter months of 1944-45, the undernourished and thinly-clad prisoners were made to walk in inclement weather and subzero temperatures, causing thousands to fall or be shot for failing to keep up with the others, and left to die by the side of the road. Hence the term "Death Marches." A few made their escape, and were sheltered by persons whom they approached and pleaded for help — as in the following stories.

Erwin and Gertruda Moldrzyk

Rescue of Two Sisters on the Verge of Collapse

In January 1945, the two Dafner sisters were part of a column of prisoners, marching in deep snow, after the Germans had them evacuated from Auschwitz, due to the approaching front. In this Death March many fell, shot by the SS guards for failing to keep pace with the straggling column, in subzero temperature. Anna-Sima Dafner was already ill and had a fever; her sister Malka was helping her trudge in the deep snow, hoping against hope to survive this terrible ordeal.

The two sisters were born in Sosnowiec, Poland. There were five children in the Dafner family. The father operated a stationery store, which was confiscated by the Germans. Both parents perished in the Holocaust, together with a married sister and a brother. A third sister, Pola, was deported to a labor camp in Markstadt, Germany. In 1942, during the final liquidation action in the Sosnowiec Ghetto, the two sisters were hiding in a bunker. Chancing a risk, they decided to approach a woman in Katowice, a distance of 8 kilometers from the ghetto, who had once been their nursemaid. Anna Ptosza welcomed them with open arms. At a later period, she acquired for them false credentials, under which they appeared as *Volksdeutsche*, that is: ethnic Germans, of the lowest category of this kind, but which still afforded them some protection by the Germans. With these documents, they were sent to the Breslau (today Wroclaw, in Poland) region, in Upper Silesia, to help German families with household chores. As *Volksdeutsche*, both girls were urged to register in the Hitler Youth movement.

All went fine until March 1944, when Anna Dafner's supervisor, pleased with her performance and behavior, decided to surprise her by upgrading her *Volksdeutsche* status. It turned out the town in Poland she had given as her birthplace had no record of her. Anna and Malka were promptly arrested, and after undergoing brutal interrogations, broke down and admitted to being Jewish. The two sisters were immediately dispatched to Auschwitz. Upon arrival there, their hair was razed and they were assigned to digging and hauling stones. Luck was with them again, when the camp administration, short of qualified translators from Polish into German, assigned the two sisters to this special unit, and their lives were momentarily spared. Then came the terrible Death March of January 18, 1945. Malka, then 18, stole her sister Anna-Sima, then 20, out of the camp dispensary, and placed her in the middle of the five persons assigned by the SS to each row of marchers, so they could support her in case she fell. "During the march,"

Malka remembers, "we stepped on bodies; there was constant shooting. The snow reached our knees."

That first evening, they reached an abandoned school building, in Jastrzebie-Zdroj, and the Germans ordered a rest period. "I looked for a way to escape, since I realized I could not go on," Malka writes. Her sister Sima adds: "My feet were badly frozen and swollen and it became almost unbearable to continue." In the lavatory, there was a small window. "I took my sister (I don't remember how I was able to lift her)," Malka adds, "and pushed her out of the window. Then I climbed over. Luckily, no one noticed us. I pulled my sister like a sack of flour, until we reached the first shed."

The two completely exhausted sisters hid in the barn until a farmer approached to milk the cows. "We fell over him and begged him to let us stay until the transport had passed through the village," Sima notes, adding: "Without hesitating, he embraced us with kindness, took us into the house and introduced us to his wife and two children, girls aged 10 and 2 years." At first the two sisters were hidden in the barn for three days, until the danger of searches by SS guards for stragglers of the march had passed. The Polish hosts, named Erwin and Gertruda Moldrzyk, then gave them a hot bath, and burned their prisoners' clothes. At first, they gave them only water and sugar, until their bodies could readjust to regular food. The two women helped out with various farm chores. They wore a shawl to cover their shaven heads, and a shirt with long sleeves, to cover the tattooed camp number on their arms. Neighbors and friends of the Moldrzyks were told that the two strange women were actually cousins of theirs, who had fled their home due to the advancing Red Army. As to the behavior of the host family, in the words of Sima, "I had no doubt all along they knew we were Jewish because the entire transport was known to be Jewish, but they never asked us nor did they ask us for money; they just treated us as if we were their own children. They knew they were risking their lives." By late March 1945, the village was emptied of its inhabitants by the Germans, due to the approaching front. However, the two sisters remained behind by hiding in a cellar.

When they were liberated by the Russians, their ordeal was not over. They were immediately suspected of being spies for the Germans (for why would the Germans evacuate all the village inhabitants save the two girls, the Russians reasoned?) and were made to undergo intensive interrogations by the Soviet secret police (NKVD). Upon news of Germany's surrender, on May 8, 1945, they were told the "good" news that they would not be further harmed, but simply expelled to Siberia. The two sisters decided to act immediately. They managed to escape, and eventually made their way — Malka to Israel, and Sima to the United States.

In July 1988, forty-three years after her miraculous escape from the Auschwitz Death March, Sima returned to Poland, together with her husband (himself a Holocaust survivor), first to locate the tombstone of her mother; then, to find her benefactors. Arriving at Jastrzebie-Zdroj, they were told that this once small town was now a city of 120,000, as a result of the nearby coal mines which were employing thousands of workers. Sima began asking about the little school house on a hill (which earlier served as the base of her escape route), overlooking the main road. To her dismay, she was told there were some 35 schools in the city. Not giving up, she inquired with local residents on the Death March trail, and soon enough she found the school house. It was Sunday afternoon, persons were streaming out from church, and Sima approached them with questions about the wartime school building. She was finally directed to an old farm house behind a certain apartment building. Quickly going over there, Sima and her husband were disap-pointed to find the farmhouse abandoned. What ensued is best told in Sima's words:

> As we kept asking aloud if someone lived there, a young man came to the window looking out from the fourth floor apartment and asked me what we were looking for. Again, I explained that in 1945 I escaped from the transport and was hiding here with this family. He responded, "wait a minute, wait a minute," and a lady came to the window and asked the same question — what we were looking for? I explained again and suddenly she burst out with a scream asking me if I was Hilda. I told her no, I was Anna; Hilda was my sister — it was Malka's name. She began screaming and crying, asking us to come up to the apartment quickly. This was the elder of the two girls, the 10 year old. . . The scene of how we fell over one another is indescribable. She embraced me as if we were real sisters.

By coincidence, the younger Moldrzyk sister showed up too, coming back from church, and immediately realized who Sima was. Father had passed away, but mother Gertruda was alive and was away visiting her sister. Sima was told that the Moldrzyks had felt deep remorse for leaving the two Dafner sisters behind during the town's evacuation. They had heard rumors that the Russians had killed them. As a remembrance of the stay of the two sisters in their home, the Moldrzyk sisters told Sima that for many years, every Sunday, they would light candles for Sima and Malka near the monument for the Death Marchers, erected after the war. In fact, they invited Sima to cross the street and see for herself the candle still flickering from that day's lighting, plus some flowers placed besides the candles.

The Moldrzyks and the Salzbergs (Sima's current family name) reminisced for seven hours before parting. This chance miraculous reunion led to the tightening of relations between both sides. "We are in correspondence," Sima underlines, "and my sister and I would love to show our appreciation and would be very proud and touched to bring this beautiful lady [the elderly Mrs. Moldrzyk] to Israel to be honored by Yad Vashem on behalf of the Jewish people. I could sit for days and days," Sima adds, "to tell the story of the almost three months we lived with the family. I have no doubt that without their help and sacrifice, and this had to be an act of God, I and my sister would not have survived."

Erwin and Gertruda Moldrzyk were indeed awarded the Righteous title, in December 1988, and the following month Mrs. Moldrzyk planted a tree at Yad Vashem in her husband's and her own name. Sima's search for her rescuers had miraculously paid off, when the daughter of her rescuers recognized her from a fourth floor balcony — even after a separation of 43 years![1]

Konrad and Regina Zimon, and Daughter Stefania

Escape and Shelter during the Auschwitz Death March

On the eve of January 17, 1945, Michael Goldman was among the 14,000 inmates of Auschwitz whom the Germans evacuated on a Death March to head off the approaching Soviet army. "The column stretched for many kilometers," Michael recalls. "We walked the whole night, in snow and terrible cold, surrounded by armed SS men. Those whose feet failed them were rolled over to the side of the road and shot to death by the murderers." That evening, they covered 100 kilometers. "The shots never ceased."

At the start of the war in 1939, the 14-year-old Michael fled with his parents, brother and sister, from Katowice eastward towards Przemysl. After the city's capture by the Germans, all of his family members were deported and murdered in Belzec. Orphaned and alone, Michael survived the brutalities of the local SS commander who administered him 80 lashes for a supposed dereliction at work. He was eventually sent to Auschwitz, where he performed various labor duties in the German firms, including the I. G. Farben firm, which exploited the camp's huge reservoir of cheap and expendable labor. Presently, he was part of a straggling column, marching in deep snow. After a short rest, on the outskirts of Gleiwitz, they were loaded into open transport wagons, stuffed like sardines, with hardly room to breathe, without food or water, and with the snow constantly falling. After a two-hour ride, they were told to disembark, and the march on foot resumed. "I felt I was at the end of my strength," Michael relates, "and rather than fall, I preferred to try to escape, risking being shot in the attempt, but nevertheless not to give up on the idea."

Towards evening, they approached a village, which they later learned was called Wielopole. People lined the main streets and some wept as they watched the distraught and haggard faces of the dwindling marchers. At an opportune split-second moment, Michael slipped away and hid behind some of the villagers. With him was a fellow Auschwitz prisoner, Hanan Ansbacher (originally from Berlin), and the two were joined by a third man, Eli Heiman. The three quickly headed to an open courtyard behind one of the houses, mounted the attic of the barn and buried themselves in the hay. "We did not know whether the household people had noticed us," Michael recalls. A little while later, they heard voices speaking in German, coming from the direction of the courtyard, which they gathered were SS men searching for escaped marchers. Shots, interspersed with the howling of dogs and loud voices in German, reverberated throughout that night, as the SS searched for escaping marches with the help of torch lights.

Early the following morning, they suddenly heard the footsteps of someone mounting the ladder leading to the attic. "I was sure we had been discovered," Michael relates, "and they were about to sniff us out from the hiding place. For myself, I decided I would not leave, and preferred to be killed right there." To their surprise, instead of SS men, the face of a girl appeared, who placed a jug and a loaf of bread, and left. Fearing a trap, the three men maintained their distance from barn's opening. Then, overtaken by hunger and thirst, they crept toward the exit and quickly fetched the bread and the jug, which contained fresh milk. The men gulped down the food, without for a moment removing their eyes from the outside doorway. The same girl returned that afternoon; she then asked for the men's identity. Fearing to disclose they were Jews, the men identified themselves as Poles from the local Silesian region. The girl did not question them further, but introduced herself as Stefania, and added that she lived with her parents, and her six-year-old sister. Her father, she said, was a railroad worker. Her only request was for the men to maintain silence. She continued feeding the three, twice a day, for a whole week, and also disseminated news on the progress of the war.

A week later, on January 25, 1945, the village was liberated by Soviet troops. The three men were then allowed to be hosted in Stefania's family household, where they met her parents, Konrad and Regina Zimon. But after a three-day stay, in light of a possible German counteroffensive, the Russians decided to evacuate the village population. The three men helped the Zimons to pack vital provisions. On this occasion, Regina Zimon told them that when the SS came in search of the escaped marchers and asked her whether she had seen them, she had pointed them in the wrong direction, and they left. After accompanying the Zimons for part of the road, the three parted with them, and continued toward Cracow, which had already been liberated. Michael enlisted in the Soviet army, saw action in combat, and was wounded twice. Immediately after the war he left for Palestine via Germany and Italy.

In 1949, Michael Goldman, under his new family name, Gilad, enlisted in the Israel police, where he served for 14 years. When the Nazi war criminal and Holocaust architect, Adolf Eichmann, head of the Gestapo Jewish section, was captured in Argentina in 1960, and brought to Israel to stand trial, Gilad headed a special team in the police which assembled the documentation for the prosecution. After the sentencing, he witnessed the execution, the burning of the body, and the spreading of Eichmann's ashes in the Mediterranean sea.

At the same time, the memory of his rescuers never left him. As he admitted in his testimony: "Throughout all these years, I tried to find my rescuers." All his letters were returned unopened, and marked "address unknown." In 1989, on a visit to Poland, he learned that the village Wielopole had been incorporated in the city Rybnik, in Upper Silesia. He went there, and was reunited with his rescuers, after a lapse of 44 years. Konrad and Stefania were well-advanced in age, and daughter Stefania was married and a mother to four children. The meeting was very emotional, with the two elderly Zimons weeping incessantly. "We sat for many hours and recounted our wartime experiences."

As to the fate of the other marchers of Michael's column — they were led to a nearby forest about 1.5 kilometers from the village, and were mowed down with machine gun fire. A monument now stands on that spot. Michael and his two friends had been saved in the nick of time. A year after his dramatic reunion with his rescuers, their names were added to Yad Vashem's honor roster of "Righteous Among the Nations."[2]

Michael Gilad visiting his rescuers, Regina and Konrad Zimon.

British POWs in Germany

Saving One Jewish Girl

This Death March rescue story begins with a frantic call, on October 21, 1988, from Richard Woolfe, producer of a London BBC TV program named *Hearts of Gold*. He was about to enact a reunion between a rescued Jewish woman and a group of British POWs who had been imprisoned in a lonely POW outpost in what was then Germany (East Prussia). As he explained to me in his letter:

> *The program, called "Hearts of Gold," celebrates great acts of kindness. The men have no idea that they will be the center of our program and that they are to be honored – indeed, they think that I am making a special documentary about the last War. Their names are Roger Letchford, George Hammond, Tommy Noble, Stan Wells, Alan Edwards, and Bill Keable. . . They have received absolutely no recognition or award for their life-saving risk. We shall record this program on Thursday, 3rd November, and it will be broadcast the following Saturday 8 p.m. I sincerely hope that Yad Vashem will agree with us that these gentlemen are worthy of the title "Righteous Gentiles". . . We need a decision as soon as possible.*

The necessary documentation, including the testimony of the saved Jewish person, Sarah Rigler, and the diary kept by a British POW, William Fisher, were swiftly dispatched to Yad Vashem for an evaluation by the Commission for the Righteous. Before the Commission's eyes unfolded a life-and-death drama of a Jewish family, taking place on an ice-cold and snow-covered road straddled with corpses of Jewish women, led on a Death March by their German captors, in January 1945.

Sarah Rigler was born in 1928, in Siauliai (also known as Shavli), Lithuania, to Samuel and Gita Matuson, and had an older sister, Hannah, born three years earlier. During the short-lived Russian occupation of 1940-41, Samuel was kept in jail as a "capitalist" (he owned a leather factory). Released three weeks before the German invasion, of June 22, 1941, he was executed by the Germans, together with other prominent Jews, three days thereafter. Gita and her two daughters withstood the terrible deprivations in the Shavli Ghetto, until July 1944, when they were transported to the Stutthof concentration camp. Shuffled from one camp to another, in November the women prisoners were led on a forced march toward the Baltic coast. Lightly clad, with clogs instead of shoes, very little food, and ravaged by lice, hundreds of people lost their lives during the Death Marches. Sarah recalls the sorry state of the marchers:

We were about 1,200 women when we started in late November with only about 300 left in January 1945. . . We walked a whole day, clubbed by the German guards who were watching us, and led into barns for the night . . . We had not eaten in weeks, the snow underfoot was dirty but that was our only water; we were not human beings anymore. We were so hungry we even ate food prepared for pigs – potato peels and manure. My mother at that point had frozen hands and feet. . . My sister Hanale was wearing a very thin coat, bare feet in clogs, with a thin blanket to keep out the bitter cold, and she was also in bad shape. We were at the end of the line being beaten by the guards to hurry up. I felt I had to do something drastic to get us a piece of bread.

Passing the village of Gross Golemkau, near Danzig (today Gdansk), Sarah, at the point of physical collapse, asked her mother to give her the diamond ring which she secretly carried in her dress, in the hope of exchanging it for bread. "I took the ring, my mother wished me luck and we parted. That was the last time I saw my mother and sister alive." Sarah slipped out of the line and hid in a nearby barn. She was soon discovered and chased back to the straggling column. But Sarah decided to try again; pushing her way through the large crowd of onlookers, she ran into another barn and crouched silently in a trough, not knowing what to expect and do next. Her only thought at the time was that "my mother is not going to see me shot, as punishment for running away; they can kill me, but not in front of my mother." After a while, a man entered the barn. Thinking him to be either a German or a Pole, Sarah told him that if he wanted he could kill her, right there and then. To her total shock, the man introduced himself as a British POW – which she later learned was Stan Wells. He calmed her fears, and returned a while later with some food. "The cows were nibbling on my hair and nose; I was in their way, and I was busy eating." Stan told her that she was in a German-owned farm, and she should therefore momentarily remain hidden in the trough. He was part of a small group of 10 British POWs who had been taken from a nearby POW camp to perform farm chores; they were temporarily housed in another farmhouse barn, part of which had been slightly refurbished to accommodate the small group of POWs. Stan at first inquired with a fellow Russian woman prisoner whether her people would be prepared to admit Sarah with them. When the response was negative, and after consulting with his POW buddies, Stan decided to smuggle Sarah into their makeshift compound, and hide her upstairs in the hayloft of the barn, next to the room where they were staying. Covered in an army overcoat, brought to her by one of the men, and walking in the midst of the other POWs supposedly on their way back from work, Sarah was smuggled into the British POW compound.

Quite by coincide, William Fisher, one of the British POWs, kept a diary, and on January 26, 1945, he made the following entry:

> *I have seen today the filthiest, foulest, and most cruel sight of my life...* *At 9 a.m., this morning, a column straggled down the road towards Danzig – a column far beyond the words of which I am capable to describe. I was struck dumb with a miserable rage... They came straggling through the bitter fold, about 300 of them, limping, dragging footsteps, slipping and falling, to rise and stagger under the blows of the guards – SS swine. Crying loudly for bread, screaming for food. A rush into a nearby house for bread resulted in one being clubbed down with a rifle butt, but even as she fell in a desperate movement, she shoved the bread she'd gotten into her blouse... 27th January, temp -15⁰C... Stan comes to me after dinner and tells me a Jewess has got away and he has her hiding in cows crib. I suggest moving her to loft over camp. Plenty straw and the chimney from our fire will keep her warm.*

Stan Wells recalls that when he found her in the cow's crib, "she looked like a bundle of rags." George Hammond adds that inside the rags "was a girl who didn't even look like a human being." Some could not recognize her as a young woman. She was all skin and bone, covered with cuts and bruises and very frightened of the men.

The men immediately attended to Sarah's medical needs; ointment to stop the bleeding of frostbitten feet, and paraffin to remove the lice on her body. They then bathed her. "All I had was a dress with a very big red Jewish star on the back of it, a thin coat and a blanket. I was very sick – I had diarrhea." For the next three weeks, the men nursed her back to health, and gave her a new set of clothing. "I owe them my life," Sarah states in her testimony; "ten British prisoners of war who jeopardized their own meager existence to save one Jewish life." After four weeks, and in the face of the Russian advance, the Germans had the men moved out of the area. Before that, however, the British rescuers had made arrangements with local people to look after Sarah until the Russians had taken over. Thus, her life had been spared.

After the war, Sarah found out that her mother and sister had not survived the Holocaust. Since then, Sarah has added to her middle name that of her sister – Hannah. Moving to the United States, and settling in New York, Sarah became active in various communal affairs. In 1969, she was able to trace her rescuers through the British War Department, and both sides have since met at annual reunions. Writing 43 years later, Sarah tried to explain:

> *"Living in America with a loving family and secure, how can I explain the fear and loneliness I felt at that time. The men took an extraordinary risk, as a unit. Had I been discovered, I would certainly have been shot. . . I had nobody and no one would have known had I been killed. I would just have been another one of the six millions but they [the British POWs] had much more to risk and it was close to going home. They could touch freedom."*

Her testimony ended with an appeal: "I pray that Yad Vashem will after 40 years give them their highest (and richly) deserved honor—that of Righteous Gentiles."

The former POWs were quickly awarded the Righteous title, in time for the surprise reunion on live television. In March 1989, four of the former British POWs visited Israel, together with Sarah Hannah Rigler, and planted a tree in the Garden of the Righteous, at Yad Vashem. Asked why he and his army buddies risked their lives to save her, Alan Edwards replied: "It was just one of those things. What else could we do? We couldn't turn her back to the Germans. They'd have probably killed her like they did all the others. We didn't think about it being dangerous—you don't in war time. Anything you can do against the enemy, you just do." George Hammond still refers to her as "our little sister."[3]

Left: The British POWs, with Sarah Rigler and the author, during the tree planting at Yad Vashem. Right: Alan Edwards, Royal Engineers, 1939.

Chapter 10

Those Who Did Not Qualify

A mong the persons involved in the rescue of Jews are to be counted some who were not attributed the Righteous title. This, as in the previously-mentioned case of Kurt Gerstein, has mainly to do with the overall record of the person during the Nazi period, including cases of some who saved but also harmed Jews, and others whose rescue mission was colored with questionable intentions. In one striking case, the Righteous title was denied to a person who caused the death of an innocent person, not during the Holocaust, but afterwards. In another case, the earlier attribution of the Righteous honor had to be annulled to a recipient who, it turned out, was not the veritable author of a rescue deed. Following are a few of these relatively isolated cases.

Jean-Marie Musy

Rescuing Jews to Benefit Himmler!

On November 1, 1944, former Swiss President, Jean-Marie Musy, arrived
in Berlin to be met by SS general Walter Schellenberg, head of the SS counter-
intelligence, and closest aide of SS chief Heinrich Himmler. The party
proceeded to Breslau, where the three closeted themselves in Himmler's
private train, to listen to Musy's proposal for the saving of Nazi Germany
through the rescue of the remaining Jews. The linking of the two ideas
seemed at first preposterous and even outrageous, but there was a logical
twist to this idea. If, as Musy proposed, Germany were to agree to free the
remaining six to eight hundred thousand Jews still held imprisoned in its
concentration camps (now reduced to mostly mainland Germany and
Austria), this perhaps could constitute a first step of opening a channel of
communications with Great Britain and the United States for negotiating a
separate cease-fire with them, in order to allow Germany to marshal its
dwindling forces to stem the Russian steamroller on the eastern front.
According to this fantastic idea, which was fed by antisemitic notions of a
preponderant Jewish influence, if not outward control, of American and
English policy-making, the USA and Great Britain would not be averse to
a separate peace with a Nazi Germany headed not by Hitler, but the powerful SS chief Himmler.

Negotiations with the Nazis in the hope of freeing some Jews from
deportation to the camps was nothing new, although with very limited
success.[1] Several months before Musy's meeting with Himmler, a first group
of hundreds of Jews had arrived from Hungary (a country under German
occupation since March 19, 1944) to Switzerland, via Bergen-Belsen camp — a
voyage to freedom arranged between Reszö Kasztner, representing the
Zionist organization in Hungary, on the one hand, and SS chiefs Kurt Becher
and Dieter Wisliceny, acting with the consent of Himmler, on the other hand.
In the summer of 1944, Himmler toyed with the idea of freeing up to one
million Jews in return for receiving ten thousand trucks and other badly-
needed necessities, but nothing came of it.[2] Presently, a group of U.S. and
Canadian-based Orthodox rabbis, anxious to save rabbis and seminarians
trapped in Nazi-dominated Europe, were searching for a proper person to
act as intermediary for negotiations with the SS leadership. Organized as
a rescue committee (*Vaad Hahatzalah*), it referred this quest to its Switzerland-
based affiliate, which was headed by Isaac and his energetic wife Recha
Sternbuch. Joining them in the search of a suitable candidate was Reuben
Hecht, the Swiss representative of a militant Zionist breakaway organization

(the Revisionists).[3] They found the right candidate, in the person of Jean-Marie Musy. In the two decades preceding the war, Musy had made a name for himself as an ardent defender of traditional Catholic and conservative values. He was alarmed by the rise and spread of communism, which he saw as the main threat facing Western civilization. This led him to view with favor and even support the Fascist takeover in Italy under Mussolini, which he hoped would be replicated in other countries, including his own—Switzerland. Although not a racist in the Nazi sense of the term, he viewed Nazi Germany an additional strong bulwark against the spread of communism in Europe, and favored an anti-communist alliance of European nations, headed by Germany and Italy and, after the fall of France, including the Vichy government of Pétain. In that effort, he undertook many trips to Berlin, where he cultivated friendly relationships with some of the Nazi leadership, including SS chief Heinrich Himmler.[4]

It is also possible that the news that filtered into Switzerland of Nazi excesses against conquered populations, and especially the mass killings of Jews, caused Musy to become disenchanted with Nazi Germany, although he continued to view communism as a greater danger. At any rate, on several occasions when asked, he readily agreed to intervene to effect the release of persons imprisoned by the Nazis, including Jews. This brought him to the attention of the Sternbuch couple, who, backed by Reuven Hecht (the sole non-orthodox member on the Swiss Orthodox Rescue Committee), decided to approach Musy, in the fall of 1944, with the idea of offering top Nazis huge sums of monies in return for freeing as many Jews as possible. Musy, who had served twice as President of the Swiss Confederation, and enjoyed easy access to top SS officers, including Himmler, and who as a staunch Catholic was sensitive to the plight of innocent persons, seemed to be the right person for this kind of transaction. He readily agreed to the mission, but his motivations were not what the Sternbuchs and Hecht had in mind. By the fall of 1944, with the German army in full retreat, and the Allies poised to invade Germany, there could be no doubt that Germany would soon lose the war, and face occupation by the Allies, which included the Soviet Union. The threat of a communist takeover in Europe (Musy's constant "bête noire") now seemed more real than ever. If only Germany could negotiate a separate peace with the USA and England, so as to free its dwindling forces to contain the communist steamroller in the east—these thoughts ran through the minds of not only Musy, but of not a few leading echelons in the Nazi hierarchy, including SS boss Himmler. Musy felt he had a brilliant idea how to bring this about. If he could persuade Himmler to free the 600 to 800,000 remaining captive Jews, as a gesture of good will, the road could be opened for separate negotiations with the Western Allies. This idea appealed to the distorted minds of the Nazis, who believed that the Jews controlled the policies of the USA and England, and would therefore grab at this opportunity to save their captive brethren, even at a price of ditching their Soviet ally. At any rate, Musy felt that it was worth a try, and he was willing to sound Himmler out on this. The Sternbuchs agreed to subsidize Musy's trip inside Germany, and place at his disposal a vehicle with Red Cross markings (to avoid becoming a target by strafing Allied planes, who by then had gained full control of Germany's skies).

At his meeting with Himmler, on November 1, 1944, the latter remained noncommittal, but he agreed to study further the exchange idea. The two met again in mid-January 1945, during which Himmler ordered the release of Recha Sternbuch's two brothers, and instructed his aide Schellenberg to seek a favorable outcome of the negotiations with Musy. The tentative agreement reached included: the immediate release of 1,200 Jews, who would be directed toward the Swiss border (with Musy seeing to their admittance into the country), the further freeing at 14-day intervals of similar numbers of Jews; the deposit of 5 million Swiss Francs (equivalent to 1.5 million U.S. dollars) by the U.S.-based Orthodox Rescue Committee in a special Swiss account in the combined names of Musy and Sternbuch, which was eventually to be turned over to the Red Cross for help to German civilians after the cessation of hostilities; and favorable press reports in the West on Germany's humanitarian gesture which, hopefully, would lead to secret negotiations between both sides. The danger for Himmler was obvious; he would be acting behind Hitler's back (who it was known was violently opposed to any talk of separate negotiations, and even more so, to releasing Jews), with everything that this implied for a man who had sworn an unbending and unconditional allegiance to his Führer. Himmler, who at first asked for hardware, such as trucks, for use by the military, in return for the freeing of Jews, by late 1944 realized that such an exchange was out of the question. He was now prepared to think in terms of a political deal, advantageous to Germany and to himself, as a possible alternative to Hitler.

The first group of 1,200 Jewish prisoners left Theresienstadt camp, and reached the Swiss town of Kreuzlingen on February 7, 1945. The fortunate Jewish inmates had been carefully selected to include persons of good health, favorable appearance, and not privy to Nazi dissimulation plans of making Theresienstadt appear as a model camp for misleading Red Cross inspection teams. The Nazis even produced a propaganda film called, "The Führer Grants a City to the Jews," showing the Jewish inmates of the camp in relatively comfortable quarters, and enjoying the pleasures of a rich and varied cultural life, including a football team. Jewish inmates who had been pressed into this deceptive film operation were not included in the transport, for fear they would disclose the true nature of the camp. Before crossing into

Switzerland, they were ordered to wash and spruce up; the men were handed suits and neckties, and the women dresses, even makeup. They were treated to sumptuous meals, including cakes — all this to mislead the outside world as to the true nature of Nazi treatment of Jews in their concentration camps.

At this point, however, the whole plan fell through, due to a combination of several factors. On the Jewish side, the leading Swiss Jewish community head, Sally Mayer, was opposed to the whole Musy idea, which he viewed with great suspicion. As the representative of the U.S.-based Joint Distribution Committee (JDC), the leading Jewish agency which distributed funds for various rescue purposes, he was negotiating separately with SS officers, such as Kurt Becher, for a different resolution of the fate of Jewish prisoners in Nazi camps. He felt it was better to arrange for the camps to be turned over to the International Red Cross, which would care for improving the lot of the prisoners, instead of having them moved to the Swiss border under war-time conditions, with Allied planes strafing everything that moved on the roads. Although he favored negotiations with the Nazis in the hope of saving Jews from death, he was opposed to helping the Nazis in any way whatsoever, including a public relations operation to show them in a more favorable light. Some observers speculate that Mayer may also have feared that a sudden large influx of Jews in Switzerland would spur antisemitic feelings among the population. On the German side, Schellenberg's rival, Ernst Kaltenbrunner, the most powerful man in the SS establishment, second only to Himmler, was opposed to the whole Musy idea and decided to scuttle the plan, by leaking word of it to Hitler, and topping it with a false news coating: that, as part of the agreement with the Allies, 300 top SS officers would be offered refuge in neutral Switzerland. Upon hearing of this, Hitler flew into a tantrum, and fuming with rage ordered that any SS officer involved in these negotiations was to be shot on the spot. This was more than the ever-vacillating Himmler could stomach, and he informed Musy that he was abandoning the whole idea.

In spite of this setback, Hecht was convinced that the Musy initiative produced other beneficial results, such as Himmler's cancellation of Hitler's orders that all remaining Jews in the camps were to be annihilated before surrendering to the Allies. "This in my opinion," Hecht emphasized, "is Musy's greatest achievement, for it saved most of the last Jewish camp inmates." Some claim that the Musy initiative created a favorable climate which facilitated rescue initiative of other representatives of neutral countries, in the closing days of the Third Reich, such as the negotiations by Swedish Count Folke Bernadotte, which resulted in the liberation of women inmates in the notorious Ravensbrück camp. Others dispute the Musy influence on these later developments which in their opinion was the result of last-ditch efforts by the Nazis (with defeat staring them in the eyes) to curry favors with the soon-to-be victors.[5] The controversy on the merits of the Hecht/Sternbuch/Musy rescue initiative continued to reverberate in the postwar years, with the three accusing the Swiss Jewish establishment of lending a hand in the scuttling of what could have evolved into a major rescue operation, and others rejoining that the whole initiative was doomed to failure from the start, due mainly to Himmler's own prevarication, of not wanting his name linked to a rescue operation of Jews, and the bad conscience of betraying his master on a most sensitive issue of the Nazi platform.[6]

In 1987, Dr. Reuben Hecht, presently a leading Israeli industrialist (he headed the giant Haifa grain silo), formally asked Yad Vashem that the Righteous title be awarded posthumously to Jean-Marie Musy, who had died in 1953.[7] Countering the claim of those who pointed to Musy's pro-Fascist and traditional antisemitic views, Hecht wrote: "How otherwise could it have been possible for anyone to bring about such an achievement with the Nazis, as Musy did, unless he was close to Himmler's general thinking." As also underlined by Dr. Benjamin Pragai-Gilad, another Israeli pro-Musy partisan: "Who else should the [Swiss-based Rescue] Committee members have chosen for the negotiations with Himmler? A Quaker, a representative of the World Jewish Congress, or rather someone who already had connections with this master murderer?" According to Hecht, Musy was prompted primarily by his religious conscience "which did not give him any rest," and he was shocked when he learned the crimes his friends had committed. As for his antisemitism, it was of the traditional conservative type, and did not go so far as to deny Jews their legal, moral and human rights; certainly not to murder them. As an emissary of the Rescue Committee, "he dedicated all of his energy and time to his interventions for the benefit of the persecuted Jews." At home, he represented a district known for its antisemitic clamor; hence, his pro-Jewish intervention was certainly not meant to gain him votes. As against those claiming that, faced with the fall of his Fascist friends, he was seeking an alibi, to prevent any actions against him after the war, Pragai counters, that Musy committed no crimes, and he was a citizen of a country which had remained neutral throughout the war; he, therefore, did not have to fear any repercussions for his prewar pro-Fascist sentiments. His actions, therefore, had to be explained strictly as deriving from religious and humanitarian considerations. A totally contrary opinion was proffered by the leading Holocaust scholar, Yehuda Bauer, who expressed dismay that Musy was even being considered for the Righteous title. One had to acknowledge that Musy caused the rescue of 1,200 Jews, Bauer added, but so did other, less contradictory personalities, such as Eichmann and Becher, who were instrumental in permitting over one thousand Jews to leave for freedom, as a result of negotiations with Kasztner, representing the Zionist Federation in Hungary. Were they too to be viewed as suitable candidates for the Righteous title?

The Commission for the Righteous, too, was not easily swayed by the pro-Musy arguments. It was pointed out that Musy's anti-immigration stance both before and during the war (that is, up to 1944) had strengthened the Swiss resolve to close its doors to Jewish refugees fleeing the Nazi terror. Moreover, despite Musy's postwar disclaimers of any ulterior motives save the humanitarian one in his secret tête-à-tête negotiations with Himmler, in light of his pro-Fascist past, and his anti-communist obsession, the question as to the real purpose of these meetings could not be entirely divorced from what may have been Musy's ultimate objective: to save Nazi Germany from utter collapse, so as to prevent a communist takeover in its stead; and to achieve this through a separate negotiated settlement with the Western Allies at the expense of the powerful Eastern one. The price for this would, among others, be an immediate cessation of the killings of the Final Solution, so as to endear a new and post-Hitler Nazi leadership to the West.

The whole idea seemed fanciful, but for persons on the brink of panic, intent on saving their necks, the most fantastic idea suddenly becomes a Machiavellian possibility. Moreover, since the "risk" factor, in the sense of a personal jeopardy to the rescuer due to the fear of arrest by the authorities, did not exist here since Musy's rescue endeavor followed a formal invitation by the SS leadership, the "motivation" factor was of ultimate importance; namely, the question whether it was the rescue of Jews or the saving of Nazi Germany from ultimate doom? The uncertainty concerning Musy's real purpose in reaching out to Himmler, coupled with his outspoken pro-Fascist and pro-Nazi Germany stance throughout the 1930's and well into the war years, ultimately prevailed upon the Commission to decline Hecht's request for the Righteous title to the late Jean-Marie Musy. At the same time, the Commission underlined Musy's role in effecting the release to freedom of 1,200 Jews, an act which, in the Commission's eyes, merited acknowledgment and appreciation to the man.[8]

Alfons Zündler

Saving at a Price while Causing Harm

What about a rescuer who jeopardized his life, but whose help may have
been tainted by personal gain of a morally questionable nature? Would he
qualify to the Righteous title? This question arose in 1993, when Elma
Verhey, a respectable Dutch journalist, interviewed in Munich, Germany,
Alfons Zündler – a former German SS guard at the Dutch Theater in Amsterdam, which had served as a collection and transit point for some 60,000
Dutch Jews on their way to the concentration camps. Survivors testified that
this former SS guard had exerted himself to facilitate their escape from the
Dutch Theater, as well as of other persons, and therefore merited the
Righteous title by Yad Vashem. One witness recalled how, as a 17-year-old
girl, she had turned to Zündler to have her 15-year-old sister released from
the Dutch Theater, and he complied. This witness was a child care worker
in the Creche, the former day-care center, across the Theater, where children
of those arrested were kept, until they were rejoined with their parents, when
the latter were deported – and they were therefore momentarily exempted
from deportation. Another witness told how she was arrested with her whole
family and brought to the Theater. She too was released, thanks to the
intercession of Zündler.

Still another witness related that when her father suddenly appeared
on the scene, when she and her family were arrested in their Amsterdam
home by the Germans, an SS man, who later turned out to be Zündler,
scolded her father with the word: "We have no need for curious Gentiles.
Get out of here." The father did not grasp the cue [i.e., to leave the place, and
thereby save himself], and followed his family to the Theater, where he tried
to get them released. When the police van on its way to the Theater stopped
to pick up some more arrested Jews, Zündler, who sat with them, urged the
mother to get out with the child, on the excuse that the child needed to
urinate. She was afraid that this was just an excuse for shooting her in the
back, and she remained in the van. She and her family were eventually
released – she believes through the intervention of Zündler.

An additional woman witness told how an SS man appeared on the train
wagon where she was about to be deported and told her point blank to get
off. Leading her along the railway track, he told her to continue in the
direction indicated by him. She too suspected that it was just an excuse to
shoot her in the back. Nothing happened, and she continued walking – all
the way back to her home. Later, she learned through her husband that this
man was Alfons Zündler.

Yet another woman witness testified how she begged Zündler to have her father released from the Theater. After some reflection, he decided to let the two go. Several more witnesses equally confirmed that they were saved by this strange SS man, who was in charge of the SS guards at the Dutch Theater, which had been converted into the main assembly point for Amsterdam Jews on their way to the concentration camps. Here, it seems, at long last was the first case of a totally altruistic SS man, presently living in retirement in Munich, who perhaps merited the title of "Righteous Among the Nations."

As news leaked out in the Netherlands that the Commission for the Righteous was deliberating this case—at first, influenced by the favorable reports on this man, a storm broke out among many circles in the Jewish community, with persons taking sides for and against Zündler. Additional evidence gave quite a different picture of the man and his actions. It may, or may not, have been strict coincidence that almost all those who testified in his favor were women in distress. It turned out that Alfons Zündler, had an obsessive attraction for the female kind, especially the young and good looking, and could not resist responding kindly to their pleas. Especially worrisome, insofar as the Righteous title was concerned, was the evidence that he had sought sexual favors, at least from some of the women, as a condition for their and their family's release from the Theater compound. In some cases, no such conditions were stipulated; he had simply yielded to the requests of the opposite sex, although here too, the promise of a sexual compensation at a future date was never too distant from his mind—as in the case of one of the female witnesses who testified in his favor, and related the following story.

After her release from the Theater and return to her home, she stood in the kitchen when she suddenly felt someone behind her placing his hands over her eyes. She also felt the pistol on his belt. As she turned around, she was shocked to see it was the SS guard at the Theater—none other than Alfons Zündler. She immediately told him to dismiss any ideas of illicit relations. He calmed her fears, and said he had not come for this, but just to talk. He then apologized for his being in the SS; it was not of his own will. His police unit had been forcibly incorporated in the Waffen-SS (the military combat section of the SS), and sent to the Russian front, where he had sustained a serious wound and hospitalized. When he first noticed her at the Theater, she reminded him of a former girlfriend; that is why he decided to help her. He then returned for daily visits for a whole week, where he and the woman held long discussions. It was quite out of order for an SS man to cultivate a relationship, of whatever sort, with a Jewish woman—in her own home. Interestingly, she notes that during these visits, she made sure there were two other men present. Before the last visit, he promised to have

her parents released. He kept his word. Equally indicative of Zündler's state
of mind, as far as women were concerned, is the testimony of a then-14 year
old girl, imprisoned in the Dutch theater, to whom Zündler "spoke very
softly and kind to me." To her as well, he told of his wound at the front and,
consequently, of his assignment as a guard. He added that she reminded
him of his sister, who also had blonde hair. He then arranged her release.
He had not asked any favors in return.

Other persons added their recollections of the man's weakness for
beautiful women. "Naturally, he had some doings with the women. He was
young and handsome, and the girls loved him," stated one witness. "He was
a beautiful man, a Don Juan. The woman loved him — Jewish or not; it did
not matter to him." He was good-looking, in his twenties, tall and slim, and
sported dark hair. Lex van Weren, one such witness, stated that Zündler had
an obsession with feminine beauty. He liked to drink, but he was particularly
attracted to women. Among the *Joodse Raad* (men of the German-appointed
Jewish council, in the Dutch Theater), van Weren added, "it was common
knowledge that Zündler sleeps with Jewish women, at least once a week.
We used to see a young lady go upstairs, and we would say to each other:
'There goes another one.'" Van Weren was told by a lady acquaintance that
Zündler tried to fix a meeting with her. She did not tell him whether she
accepted. "One could bribe Zündler not only with sex but also with liquor,
linen, choice fruits, sweets and such. I once went to fetch for him candy, and
handed it to him, in return for being able to take a walk with the Creche
children." This was confirmed by another Jewish Council worker, Jacques
van der Kar, who added that Zündler sought out young women in the hall
(where the newly-arrived arrested Jews were lined up). Some women offered
themselves willingly in the hope of escaping deportation. Van der Kar
related how he unsuccessfully tried to stop a young woman from walking
up the staircase to Zündler's office (where he kept a couch), by intimating
to her that her freedom could be arranged by other means; such as, through
help from the Jewish underground operating in the Theater, but she refused
to listen. As stated, Zündler was also not averse to other forms of bribery,
such as liquor and choice chocolate and candy. Although he also released
Jewish prisoners (especially women) without exacting favors in return, the
many testimonies received in this regard left no doubt to his penchant for
sexual favors and other forms of bribery.[9]

More troublesome for consideration to the Righteous title was Zündler's
participation in raids on Jewish homes, when he was enlisted to beef up an
occasional shortage of German manpower. Several witnesses saw him leave
the Dutch Theater armed with a rifle, board a police van accompanied by
Dutch and German policemen, and return with captured Jews. Here too, he
occasionally freed some Jews, when he was not observed. Indeed, he did not

fit the brutal type of other SS men. On the contrary, he at times showed compassion for those arrested, releasing a few, and treating the others non-violently. Although most witnesses believed Zündler was the best of the lot, others saw him as a wolf in sheep's clothing .[10]

Zündler's cooperation with Süskind and his clandestine organization in facilitating the flight of many Jews from the Theater compound was well established. The German guards at the Theater were co-opted in this conspiracy of rescue, but this was in return for hefty bribes in the form of choice liquors, sweets, garments and women, as well as payoff money received through Dutch underground channels.[11] Zündler, as head guard, participated in these endeavors and cooperated closely with Süskind.[12] However, in contrast to the other guards, he may have gone the extra mile, and in some instances also acted out of humanitarian considerations. He is reported have lent his SS uniform to a Jewish operative in the Theater, to help him in his clandestine activity.[13] In one incident, he wished to consult one of Süskind's men in the Theater, and failing to see him, decided to free a woman, by taking her across the street to the Creche, whence she continued the following morning to her home.

To complicate the picture further, in May 1943, Zündler was arrested together with several other SS guards, and tried by an SS court for violation of racial laws (*Rassenschande*, the "shaming" of blood, in the Nazi vocabulary). The Nazi charge sheet and the minutes of the trial have been lost, but top SS officers in the Netherlands, on trial after the war, reported on the disciplinary measures taken against the Theater guards for sexual misconduct with Jewish female prisoners. The titular SS head of the Theater, Aus der Fünten told of several such intimate encounters by his men. A report by SS prosecutor A. Arlt told of a particularly severe breach of racial misconduct, when a Jewish woman was forced to dance naked before the German guards, who had gathered for a drinking orgy, in which Zündler also participated, and which resulted in intimate contact with the hapless woman, against her consent—although, the SS report noted, it could not be classified as rape. Two of the guards, including Zündler, were sentenced to death. In Zündler's case, due to his wartime record, and his injury on the Russian front, the sentence was commuted to ten years imprisonment, which he spent in a special punitive section of the Dachau concentration camp.[14]

In February 1945, Zündler was conscripted back in an SS division, to help stem the advance of the Allies during the closing months of Nazi Germany, and he surrendered to the British army two months later.[15] Earlier, while in prison, and years later, Zündler continued to insist that his arrest was due to his involvement in the flight of Jews from the Theater, not—in his words—to trumped-up sexual misconduct charges. However, most Jewish witnesses (both those who speak in his favor and others opposed to him) link his arrest to dealings with Jewish women—that he was either arrested during an intimate act with a Jewish woman; or, a woman with whom he had slept, then freed by him, was later picked up on the street, and implicated Zündler in her release.

With all this accumulated material on hand — when the Commission for the Righteous resumed its debate on the Zündler case, after a lapse of over a year, the portrait of the man was quite different and more convoluted than at the start. On the question of whether Zündler was conscripted or enlisted in the SS, the answer was twofold. His police unit was indeed integrated in the Waffen-SS by order of Himmler. At the same time, after Zündler recuperated from his wound, he joined the notorious SD branch of the SS, an act which was strictly voluntary. Furthermore, as the man in charge over the German guards in the Dutch Theater, he willy-nilly bore responsibility for the deportation of thousands of Jews, who passed through the Theater's gates. Moreover, his participation in the forcible roundup of Jews from their homes made him an additional instrument in the Final Solution, whether his heart was in it or — as the evidence shows, it was not. On the other hand, he cooperated willingly with the German-appointed Jewish heads at the Theater in their rescue conspiracy. However, here too, many if not most of his involvements—and those of the other guards - was in return for some favors. Zündler's sexual licentiousness and obsessive attraction to young females led him down the slippery road of tying his rescue participation with the sexual submission of many, if not most, of his female companions.[16] He must have been quite aware that the Jewish women who, ostensibly, willingly submitted themselves to him—did so because of his position of authority in the Theater compound. Whatever the ultimate cause of his arrest—sexual "misconduct," as defined by the Nazis, or allowing persons to escape from the Theater, as he claimed, or perhaps a combination of both—for thousands of Jews, Alfons Zündler was one of the SS man on the spot who made possible their deportation to the death camps.

As one Commission member noted, Yad Vashem is principally a memorial for the six million martyred Jews, and Zündler's involvement, as a person ultimately responsible to the SS unit headed by Eichmann, who dealt with the deportation of Jews, cannot be overlooked. The fact that his participation in the rescue efforts of the Jewish administrative personnel in the Theater was, in many instances, linked to securing personal favors, including sexual relations with captive women, placed an additional cloud over his record. Bearing all this in mind, the Commission resolved to acknowledge Zündler's role in freeing some Jews from eventual deportation, in a special letter to him, but to decline the morally-significant title of "Righteous Among the Nations" as inappropriate in this case.[17]

Andrei Sheptitzky

Collaboration with the Enemy?

One of the most vexing cases, with respect to the Righteous title, that has taxed the minds of people at Yad Vashem, as well as elsewhere, concerned Andrei Sheptitzky — a person, unique in many ways, of historic and religious significance to his people, as well as endowed with a special charm and keen intelligence, attributes which could not fail to leave an impression on those who came to know him and deal with him — Jews and non-Jews alike.[18] During the war years, Sheptitzky served as Metropolitan, or head, of the Uniate church in western Ukraine, a Catholic variant church for Ukrainians who desired a distinct and more Slavonic expression of the church's rites, as well as separation from the Polish Catholic church with its pronounced Polish nationalism. During the Holocaust, Sheptitzky was credited with saving a certain number of Jews.

In 1991, Kurt Lewin told Yad Vashem about his survival thanks to Sheptitzky's intervention. After his father's murder by rampaging Ukrainians in Lwow, in July 1941, Lewin was admitted by Sheptitzky for hiding in one of the churches' monasteries, disguised as a monk.[19] Lewin was later to meet Rabbi David Kahana, who was hiding in the Metropolitan's private library. Zvi Barnea (formerly Chameides) also related how in September 1942, as a ten-year-old boy, he was brought by his father, Rabbi Kalman Chameides, to Sheptitzky's official residence, near the Uniate's church imposing St. George's Cathedral.[20] As Rabbi Chameides informed the venerable Metropolitan of the bitter fate of the Jews in Lwow, Sheptitzky comforted the rabbi with the words: "after the storm the sun always shines." Several days later, Zvi was admitted to a Uniate church orphanage; thence, to various monasteries, where Uniate monks assured his safety. He was later joined by his younger brother, Leon, and met other Jewish children in hiding, including Nathan Lewin, Kurt's brother.

Other Jews were helped with false credentials, under which they appeared as Greek Catholics, and were thus able to live openly as non-Jews. Oded Amarant, another child beneficiary (born 1935), confirmed being brought by his uncle to Sheptitzky, who then placed the boy in the care of one of the monks. In one of the church's orphanage, in the village of Univ, he met several other Jewish children in hiding, including Leon Chameides, as well as the 1938-born Adam Rotfeld. Likewise for the 1931-born Ludwig Podoshin, who was sheltered by a Uniate priest, whereas his parents were hidden in Sheptitzky's private library. Lili Pohlmann and her mother Cecylia

Stern were also helped by Sheptitzky's church to find hiding places in several convents in the Lwow region. Her immediate benefactor was Helena Witer, better known as Sister, or Ihumena (Abbess) Josefa, of the Uniate church, who watched over Jewish children brought to her care in her convent and children's home, in nearby Lyczakow.[21] In addition, a group of Jewish adults was sheltered in a shoe shop, operated by Uniate monks, in Lwow, where they worked shoulder to shoulder with the monks in manufacturing shoes and boots, commissioned by the German army.[22]

The most thoroughgoing of these favorable accounts appeared in the testimony of Rabbi David Kahana.[23] As one of Lwow's prewar prominent rabbis, he had met the Metropolitan on official occasions. He also learned of Sheptitzky's interest in the study of Hebrew, and the welfare of the city's Jews, especially the poorer elements, whom he occasionally supported with donations — especially on the eve of the Passover holiday. During the Holocaust, Kahana first sought out Sheptitzky in August 1942 to ask him for the favor of hiding Torah scrolls, as well as the possibility of hiding Jewish children. The Metropolitan remained noncommittal on the matter of the children but, at the same time, assured the rabbi that his home would remain open for any Jews fleeing the Nazis and seeking shelter. If they knocked on his door, they would be admitted, he emphasized. Several days after this visit, the Jewish ghetto in Lwow experienced one of its worst days, when close to 7,000 Jews were massacred. Kahana, who luckily survived this killing raid by hiding in a cellar, came to see Sheptitzky for the second time, and related to him the terrible events of the recent days in the ghetto. "I could discern that the man was shocked. Many tears flowed from his eyes as he listened to my litany on the liquidation in the Lwow Ghetto."

On Sheptitzky's orders, Rabbi Kahana was temporarily sheltered in the Metropolitan's private library; he then returned to the ghetto. In his testimony, Kahana lists the various religious monasteries and children's homes, where Jews (adults and children) found refuge — in Lwow and environs, including Lyczakow, where Abbess Josefa hid Jewish children in her orphanage. Kahana fled to Sheptitzky's residence for the third and final time in June 1943. He was again sheltered in the library, and an artificial wall was constructed to hide his presence. The rabbi's wife and young daughter were hidden elsewhere and separately by Sheptitzky's church. After several weeks' stay in the library, Rabbi Kahana was moved for his safety (German officers and officials often came to visit Sheptitzky) to one of the nearby monasteries of the Uniate church, where he was cared for with the utmost attention and compassion by several monks.[24] He was then brought back to Sheptitzky's residence, and returned to the library. Sheptitzky again asked Kahana to relate to him in detail news of the liquidation of the city's Jews. "I sat up with him until the late hours of the night," Kahana related. "The

Metropolitan was completely broken by my words. From time to time, he wiped off tears from his eyes. He was deeply shocked." Returning to his cell in the library, the rabbi was met by the 11-year-old Nathan Lewin, the son of the martyred rabbi, Ezekiel Lewin, who had been brought in from one of the monasteries. Together, they shared the secluded place in the library. In November 1943, Kurt, Nathan's brother, joined them. Abbess Josefa brought news of Kahana's wife and daughter who were in hiding and were in good hands. Thus, Kahana survived until the city's liberation by the Russians in July 1944.

It would seem from the previous account that Metropolitan Andrei Sheptitzky, the eminent spiritual head of a church counting millions of followers in Western Ukraine (parts of which once formed the eastern regions of Poland) would automatically merit recognition as a Righteous. However, the story proved to be much more complicated and problematic than at first sight, since Sheptitzky was also an important political figure in the Ukrainian national movement. This movement was known for its fierce antisemitism. It clamored for independence from Russia, in partnership — for lack of a better choice — with Nazi Germany. For a better understanding of this point, the political and social context in which Sheptitzky operated needs to be clarified.

Sheptitzky's main base was Lwow, a multi-ethnic city, with the largest groups being Poles, Jews and Ukrainians, in that order. In 1931, the Jews amounted to a third of the city's population — close to 100,000. This number swelled to about 160,000, when the Germans swept in on June 30, 1941. From the start of the German occupation, one "action" (the Nazi term for deportation and killing raids) followed another relentlessly, until the Jewish community was totally decimated. These killing raids by the SS were actively supported by many Ukrainians, in and out of uniform. Between June 30 and July 7, about 4,000 Jews were massacred by German units, with the assistance of the Ukrainian auxiliary police. On July 25-27, some 2,000 Jews were murdered, under the slogan of revenge for the death of Petlura (a Ukrainian national hero) in Paris many years ago. All told, some 30,000 Jews are estimated to have been murdered in this massive pogrom wave during the first few months of the Nazi occupation.[25] This was followed by a whole sequence of unending killing raids, beginning October 1941, with the establishment of a Jewish ghetto (for which the slums of the city were chosen). During the "bridge" action, Ukrainian and German guards on duty at the entrance and exit to the ghetto (near a bridge, hence its name), robbed and killed all who aroused their suspicion, anger or greed. These and other random killings, up to December of that year, cost 10,000 Jewish lives — all these with the participation of the Ukrainian militia and gendarme.[26] In March 1942 came the liquidation of the "non-social" elements; in other words, those on the welfare list. Some 15,000 were killed, here too with the active participation of Ukrainians.

In June 1942, came the "Blitz" action, killing 6-8,000 Jews. Smaller killing raids followed during the summer months. Then came the "great action" of August 1942 on the ghetto Jews, during which some 60,000 Jews were deported to the Belzec death camp or the nearby Janowska labor camp, in an orgy of extremely cruel and inhumane methods. In November 1942, some 15,000 more were killed, either on the spot, or murdered in the Belzec death camp. In December 1942, Germans and Ukrainians, using grenades to flush out hiding persons, killed numerous Jews. There were now only 23,000 Jews left in the ghetto, out of an original population of 160,000. In January 1943, Germans and Ukrainians deported an additional 4,000 Jews to Belzec camp. Many died or were torched to death, when they refused to obey orders by Germans and Ukrainians to leave their homes. Another killing raid in March 1943 netted several thousand more.

On June 2, 1943, the Lwow Ghetto was officially liquidated; many were killed and several thousand moved to Janowska camp, on the outskirts of Lwow. Finally, on November 23, 1943, all Janowska camp inmates were brutally murdered, and the city was festively declared as *Judenrein*, "clean of Jews." A large population of 160,000 Jews had been decimated within a 2 ½ year period — all this with the active participation of many Ukrainians, and under the watchful eye, and literally under the window of the most venerated religious and political figure in town, Andrei Sheptitzky — a strong supporter of the Ukrainian cause.[27] Tens of thousands of other Jews filled dozens of German forced labor camps, with Ukrainians serving as auxiliary guards, until the camps' liquidation in 1943. Close to 30,000 Jews at times filled the Janowska camp alone, on the city's outskirts, many of whom were brought in from outlying regions, and who underwent unimaginable cruelties and killings, until the full extermination of the camp's inmates in November 1943.[28]

An untold, but small, number of Jews sought refuge on the Aryan side of the city, by hiding in private homes, with Poles and Ukrainians. Ukrainian nationalists were divided in their allegiance among several factions, some of which even fought against each other. However, all wreaked vengeance on the Polish population and its organized underground (the Home Army), against pro-Soviet partisans, and especially against all Jews, on whom open season was declared. Those discovered in hiding (in private homes or forest lairs) were either killed on the spot, especially by armed men of the Bandera faction, or turned over to the Germans.

News of this ongoing reign of terror on the city's Jews constantly reached Sheptitsky's ears at the Uniate church compound, on Mt. Jur, in the heart of the city. Kurt Lewin, in a 1991 letter to Yad Vashem, wrote that "visiting priests told of frightful events taking place in their parishes. . . In some villages Jews were killed by their neighbors before the 'final solution,' had begun. . . Jur was deeply disturbed that the outrage perpetrated against the Jews was carried out with the assistance of a large segment of the Christian population." Rabbi Kahana also recalled that when he first went to see him, in the summer of 1942, Sheptitzky asked him for details on what was happening inside the ghetto — details that touched him deeply. His response, however, to these unprecedented terrible events has been and is still open to debate among survivors and Holocaust scholars.

To understand the man's reaction to this large-scale murder of the Jewish population in his city, a brief biographical sketch is in order. Born in 1865, as Roman Aleksander Szeptycki, into an old Polish noble family, but with Ukrainian roots, the family divided its allegiance between Polish and Ukrainian causes. His maternal grandfather, Aleksander Fredro, was a known Polish playwright, and his younger brother, Stanislaw Szeptycki, became a general in the Polish army and Polish Minister of Defense in 1923. However, Roman Aleksander chose to identify with the Ukrainian cause. After studying law and theology, Roman, now known by his adopted religious name "Andrei," was ordained in the priesthood in 1892. In 1899, he was nominated bishop of the Greek Catholic church in Stanislawow, and in 1900, he was installed as Metropolitan (the equivalent of archbishop), with headquarters in Lwow. In 1907, Pope Pius X extended Sheptitsky's jurisdiction over all Greek Catholic churches in the Russian empire, in the hope of spreading the Catholic faith there (he traveled incognito in various Russian cities for that purpose). Another brother, Kazimierz, also joined Andrei into the Greek Catholic church (also known as Uniate), assumed the name of Klementyi, and was appointed head of all Uniate monasteries, as well as eventual head of Uniate churches in Russia and Siberia — a prospect seemingly made possible by the German invasion in 1941.

However, uppermost in Andrei Sheptitzky's mind were the national aspirations of his adopted Ukrainian people. Throughout the war years, he remained the incontestable leading religious-spiritual figure in Ukrainian society in Lwow and eastern Galicia. As the head of the Uniate-Catholic church, he was the most prominent religious figure in his area. As a political man, he was president of the Ukrainian National Council. Even with the national movement rent by divisions, his own stature was not harmed, and he was accepted and applauded by all the factions. Although suspicious of the Poles, the communists loomed in his mind as the personification of a double evil — against both God and the Ukrainian people — and he therefore looked forward to a German-Ukrainian alliance, which would ensure an independent Ukraine.[29] This passionate national goal, which had witnessed so many setbacks, undoubtedly colored his political activity, and was reflected in his reaction to the Nazi occupation of Ukraine, and the ambivalence of this response vis-à-vis the Jewish tragedy surrounding him. As a Christian clergyman, he remained faithful to the traditional Christian theological antisemitism. Thus, his often-reported friendliness toward Jews was colored by ulterior considerations, as the following passage, in a surprisingly frank prewar admission of his true motives gives ample testimony:

> *When I face assembled Jews, who are ready to listen to me, I cannot avoid considering them as fellow men exposed to eternal perdition. That is why I consider it my duty to take advantage of this opportunity to convey to them at least one word of the Lord's revelations. I accomplish this while talking to them. Indeed, I do it in their tongue and language. . . This is the only means to bring the represented truth closer to the listeners' souls . . . And if in the soul of any amongst them there is a spark of religious sentiment, it might be kindled under the influence of the uttered words of the Holy Scripture. . . Every thread of Christian love for one's fellow man which links the faithful with non-believers may become by the Grace of God, an opportunity for bringing them nearer to Christ's teaching.[30]*

Several years later, in a communication to Rome in which he bewailed the Nazi killings of Jews, he added the "comforting" afterthought that perhaps this was part of a greater divine plan, for "among the massacred Jews there are many souls who converted to God, because never through the centuries have they been placed in a situation as they are in the present, facing for months on end the possibility of a violent death."[31] The theological approbation of the cruel fate of the Jews at the hands of the Nazis came out again in an intimate conversation with David Kahana, the rabbi he was sheltering in his own residence. As related by Kahana, Sheptitzky asked him, late one evening: "Have you ever reflected and asked yourself from whence this hatred and inhumane persecutions against the Jewish people, from earliest times to this day? For what reason?" He then quoted from Matthew 27:25, where the assembled Jews at the crucifixion site are reported to have exclaimed that Jesus' blood be "on us and our children." "If you will reflect and take into consideration this passage from the New Testament," the venerable Metropolitan told the subdued rabbi, he would surely understand what was happening to the Jews. Shortly thereafter, agonizing over the pain he had caused the frightened rabbi, Sheptitzky apologized to him: "In this grave situation, when the Jewish people is bleeding profusely and bearing the sacrifice of hundreds of thousands of innocent victims, I should not have mentioned this subject. . . Please forgive me." He regretted having added to the rabbi's pains – not the religious justification of the persecution of the Jewish people, a theology from which he evidently did not detract.[32]

What makes it more troublesome and puzzling to understand Sheptitzky, is the fact that for the first seven months of the German occupation, while the killing of Jews continued unabated in Lwow and environs with the active participation of many Ukrainians—who looked up to him for spiritual and political guidance—he remained silent. Finally, in February 1942, he wrote to SS head Himmler, protesting, not the killing of Jews, but the use of Ukrainian militia in that sordid undertaking. There is no record of Himmler's reaction to this letter. Some claim he wanted to punish the Metropolitan, but was dissuaded by his aides from harming a person, held in high esteem by the Ukrainian population, and who was being cultivated by various German agencies to cement a closer collaboration with them.[33]

He was more outspoken in a later communication to the Vatican, on August 29, 1942—after the dissipation of hopes of immediate Ukrainian independence, and the ongoing enslavement of the local population to suit German military needs. In this letter, he expressed his horror at the "regime of terror that is becoming more intolerable every day;" a regime that "is perhaps even more evil than the Bolshevik. . . It is almost diabolical. . . It is very simply as if a pack of raving or rabid wolves had fallen upon a poor people." The Nazis, he continued, represented "a caricature of every idea of civilization and order. . . hatred of everything good and beautiful."[34] To Dr. Frederic, a French East European expert who worked for the Germans, Sheptitzky reproached the Germans for their inhumane behavior toward the Jews, and told Frederic that a young man had confessed to him to having murdered 75 Jews in Lwow in one night alone.[35]

All these protests, however, were voiced in private; the Ukrainian populace in Western Ukraine who equated Jews with the hated communists mistakenly believed that the venerable Metropolitan was heart and mind with them as they committed the worst excesses against the Jews in their midst, with no dissenting voice emanating from Sheptitzky. However, in November 1942, Sheptitzky wrote a pastoral letter under the heading: "Thou Shalt Not Kill," in which he decried the random killings of innocent people. To the Jews' dismay, they were not mentioned by name, and the letter's wording was such that to many it appeared a condemnation of random political killings. According to one historian, the pastoral letter was primarily directed against the almost anarchistic civil-war-like conditions which prevailed in the region; against the bloody clashes between Polish and Ukrainian nationalists, coupled with the internecine warfare among Ukrainian factions themselves.[36] He may also have had the Jews in mind, as his supporters claim, but for the unsophisticated masses, many of whom participated in the massacres of Jews, this had to be clearly spelled out if it were to have any impact on them.

His hesitancy to speak publicly against the massacres of Jews, even when they were taking place under his own window, was exemplified in the story of Rabbi Ezekiel Lewin, the chief rabbi of the large Jewish community in Lwow. The martyred rabbi's son, who heard it from Sheptitzky himself, relates that, as the anti-Jewish riots spread in Lwow on June 30, 1941, the first day of the German occupation, Rabbi Lewin rushed to Sheptitzky's residence and pleaded with him to intervene against the rioting mobs:

> 'I have come to your Excellency, in the name of the Lwow Jewish community, and in the name of half million Jews living in Western Ukraine. You once told me: I am a friend of the Jews. You always underlined your friendship to us. I now ask you, at this most dangerous moment, to give proof of your friendship and prevail upon the masses that are running wild and attacking us. I beg you to save the thousands of Jews, and the Almighty will reward you.' Sheptitzky asked him to stay in his residence until the riots had passed. My father responded: 'My mission is over; I came to ask on behalf of the people, and I return to them, for it is there that I belong, and may God help me.' Saying this, he left.[37]

Rabbi Lewin was caught by the rioting Ukrainian mob and beaten to death. The silence of Sheptitzky, who at the time also held the influential post of Chairman of the Ukrainian National Council, at the riots which cost the lives of 2,000 people, including the city Jews' chief rabbi, could only have been misinterpreted by his followers as, at the least, a silent assent of this act. Sheptitzky was undoubtedly caught between his sincere desire to stop the massacres of Jews, and his lifelong passionate goal to gain independence for his beloved Ukrainian people which, in the context of the Nazi-Soviet war, called for some form of collaboration with Germany, even if it was headed by Adolf Hitler. This conviction was also shared by the leaders of Ukrainian national movement, which was split into the two rival factions of Stepan Bandera and Andrei Melnik. In the eyes of many Ukrainians, and to some extent Sheptitzky himself, Jews were associated with the earlier Soviet suppression of national Ukrainian aspirations, and "Judeo-Bolshevism" became an indissoluble and tragic catchword, justifying the terrible excesses committed against the whole Jewish population.[38]

In January 1940, before the German invasion, Professor Hans Koch and Dr. Otto Waechter of the *Abwehr* (German military intelligence) and Nazi governor Hans Frank's office respectively, came to Lwow to elicit Sheptitzky's support for the creation of a Ukrainian Legion to help the Germans in the forthcoming invasion of the Soviet Union. Sheptitzky agreed to these plans and two Ukrainian battalions (*Nachtigall* and *Roland*) were formed. Both were under the religious guidance of Ivan Hryniokh, a military chaplain appointed by Sheptitzky. They marched into Lwow with the German army.[39] On that day, which coincided with a three-day pogrom of the Jewish population, Sheptitzky in a printed pastoral letter to the Ukrainian people proclaimed: "We greet the victorious German army as a deliverer from the enemy." In the words of historian Shimon Redlich, Sheptitzky's response to the German invasion "was positive and even enthusiastic."[40]

During the "Petlura Days" pogrom, starting on July 25, 1941, Sheptitzky, overlooking the blood bath of Jews in his city, called on the Ukrainians to assist and cooperate with the Germans. In late August 1941, as the killings of Jews in Lwow intensified, Sheptitzky in a dispatch to the Vatican, stated categorically that "we are indeed obliged to support the German army, which freed us from the Bolshevik regime, so that it can bring this war to a positive conclusion, which — God granting — will eliminate atheistic and militant Communism once and for all." Still favoring an alliance with Germany, in February 1942 Sheptitzky, as chairman of the National Council, added his signature, together with Ukrainian nationalist leader Melnyk and others to a letter addressed "to His Excellency, the Führer Adolf Hitler." The letter protested German reluctance to include more Ukrainians "in the armed struggle against their traditional enemy," and assured Hitler that the "leading circles in Ukraine" were still willing to cooperate with Germany "in order to establish the New Order in Ukraine and throughout Europe." There is little doubt that Sheptitzky knew that in Hitler's mind, the New Order meant a Europe without Jews. This letter, however, which was stopped by the German censor in Lwow and never reached Berlin, drew a sharp German reaction — the dissolution of the National Council, headed by Sheptitzky, and the postponement of any further discussions on an independent Ukraine. Still unwilling to abandon hopes for a German-Ukrainian rapprochement, Sheptitzky spoke in secret conversations with Nazi officials about the unique opportunity granted to Germany to split the Russian empire into single nation-states, including an independent Ukraine.[41]

By mid-1942 Sheptitzky was fully disillusioned with Nazi Germany. Some 250,000 Ukrainians had been forcefully transported to work in Germany. There were compulsory food deliveries, and hunger was spreading. Yet, in the following year, he surprisingly supported the creation of an Ukrainian SS division. In advance of this, Sheptitzky was visited by a delegation of German officials, including SS, to seek his support in this endeavor. They correctly judged that the creation of this unit depended on Sheptitzky's support. Due to health reasons, he could not participate in the oath-taking ceremony, but referred this task to his coadjutor Bishop Josef Slipyi. Sheptitzky, however, appointed five military chaplains, one of whom gave a sermon on the struggle against Bolshevism, during a mass celebrated for these SS soldiers. It is reported that some 70,000 — much more than the required number — signed up for the SS Galicia division, which was officially created in late 1943. During the existence of this division, it was involved mainly in the pursuit of anti-German dissident elements as well as Jews in hiding in the forests. Sheptitzky died in November 1944, four months after the Germans were driven out of Lwow and the city had reverted to Soviet rule.

Sheptitzky's case was hotly debated in a dozen sessions of the Commission for the Righteous. While some favored recognition, pointing out his role in the rescue of Jews in his church's institutions, strong opposition was voiced by some historians, as well as Holocaust survivors from Ukraine, who pointed out his dubious role in cementing an alliance with Nazi Germany and his support of the creation of the Ukrainian SS division. Those favoring his recognition argued that only the rescue part, not the political orientation of the man, should be taken into consideration. As for his welcoming of the Germans as liberators, this was in line with his realistic appraisal that Germany represented the only force capable of saving his people from the tentacles of Stalin's Soviet Union. If some misinterpreted this as a license to kill Jews, this blame should not placed on Sheptitzky's shoulders, for he never publicly said anything disparaging about the Jews. Finally, if a man of the stature of Rabbi Kahana, who after the war held the post of head chaplain in the Israel Air Force, later chief rabbi of Argentina, and finally, a member of the Commission for the Righteous — if such a person added his petition to those of other beneficiaries of the Metropolitan's aid, for saving his life, and that of his wife and daughter, then the Commission should respond favorably.

Countering these pleas were those who opposed the nomination, and they advanced the following arguments. Sheptitzky could not be viewed (as would be the case with most other candidates to the Righteous title) as simply a plain and private person, to be judged by only one facet of his activities, and without regard to his importance in the community wherein he resided and which he served. As Metropolitan of the Uniate Church in West Ukraine, he was to his millions of followers a miniature-Pope figure. One, therefore, could not separate his rescue action, which is to be acknowledged, from his other and particularly political involvement for the simple reason that the importance of the man stemmed not merely from his elevated religious post, but also, and in particular, from his political role as one of the principal protagonists of the Ukrainian cause. This is also how he, and not merely others, viewed himself. In addition, if he never spoke out against the Jews, he also never publicly condemned these killings, at a time when such a public denunciation may have produced an impact on his followers, many of whom were bloodying their hands with Jewish victims. Instead, he made public his repeated calls for cooperation and collaboration with the Germans, and added his signature to an appeal to Hitler for a greater military collaboration with the Ukrainian people, at the time when the Germans were involved in the mass murder of Jews right under his window. Finally, especially troublesome was his support for the creation of an Ukrainian SS division in 1943, and appointing a close aide as head chaplain for this unit; this, after he had been confronted with evidence from all quarters of the great misdeeds of this murderous organization (see his own letter to the Pope the previous year). Consequently, according to this argument, awarding this man the most prestigious and morally-significant honor of the Jewish people to non-Jews, would seriously undermine the prestige of such a dignified honor. In a final marathon debate, in 1991, the Commission reaffirmed its previous decision to decline the Righteous title to Sheptitzky.

Sheptitzky was evidently torn between his moral and humanistic values and his passion for the Ukrainian cause. Hence, in his relations with Jews during the Holocaust, according to Holocaust historian Redlich, Sheptitzky yielded "a complex picture of diverse and often contradictory reactions;" that one finds in his attitude "complexities, tensions, and conflicts."[42] Redlich furthermore adds that when Sheptitzky heard of the hysteria which had caught the masses during the initial anti-Jewish riots, he realized that there was nothing he could do to stop them. The question, however, is not whether he would he have succeeded or not, but whether he made the effort, especially since in Redlich's own words, Sheptitzky "was outside the range of punishment by the Germans."[43] Hansjakob Stehle, another historian, in a book dedicated to the memory of Sheptitzky, asks: "What was it that had moved the Metropolitan, despite his deep abhorrence of Nazi rule, once again to give his blessing to collaboration with the German regime, even under the SS symbol. . . What motivated him, just one year before the total collapse, to support the formation of a Ukrainian SS division?"[44] Whatever the answer, one cannot blame an institution dedicated to the memory of Holocaust victims for its unwillingness to award its most precious honor to a man who lent a hand to such an endeavor. At the same time, those whose lives were spared, thanks to Sheptitzky's intervention, have every right to hold him in their highest esteem.[45]

Willi Friedrichs

Killed Innocent Person after the War

What of a rescuer who caused physical harm to a person—but not during the Holocaust, only afterwards, and the event having nothing to do with the Holocaust? Would the Holocaust-period rescuer still qualify to the Righteous title? That question came up sharply in the case of Willi Friedrichs.

During the war, Friedrichs was a German civilian working for the German Todt firm, in Brest-Litovsk, in occupied Belarus. There he met and rescued Lea Kirschner. In her testimony she described the loss of her parents and brother in Nazi-instigated killing raids. While on forced-labor duty in a German-operated knitting shop outside the ghetto, she befriended a Polish family, who promised to help her if she were to flee the ghetto. This moment of distress came in October 1942, during a German killing raid on the ghetto's remaining Jews. After hiding for three days under the floor of her home, Lea slipped away and made her way at night to the Polish home. "My appearance shocked them all, as they knew that sheltering a Jew was punishable with the death penalty," she recalls. They told her to hide in a ruined building until they had time to contact a good-hearted German they knew, who would come to fetch her. And so, indeed, it was. After nightfall, someone called her name from the dark and asked her to follow him. Passing German patrols, the man, who identified himself as Willi Friedrichs, led her to his house, which he shared with a convinced Nazi. He was going to introduce her as his Polish girlfriend, and asked her to play the role. At his house, Lea met two more Jews, the physician Dr. Begun and his 16-year old daughter, who were hiding in a room below the ground floor. Friedrichs, she learned, was a civilian auto mechanic, on hire with the German Todt company, which the German military had contracted for various engineering-related projects. In the meantime, Friedrichs had managed to spirit the Jewish doctor and his daughter to safety. As for Lea, Friedrichs arranged with a friendly Pole to acquire for her new credentials, under which she appeared as Irena Lutowska.

During the three months Lea spent in Willi's house, she had several close calls with the Gestapo and SS, who twice searched the house for her (as a suspicious Polish woman living in a house assigned for Germans). She was, however, able to hide elsewhere in time. During that period, Friedrichs treated her, in her words, "in an exceedingly polite, friendly and patient way, in spite of the danger I presented to him," making no improper romantic advances on her. Eventually, with her new credentials, Friedrichs was able to find for her work in a Todt affiliate in Kobryn, some 50 kilometers from

Brest-Litovsk. From there, she was moved to Munich, as a housekeeper for a German family, until the end of the war. She met Friedrichs again briefly afterward, then eventually made her way to Israel, where she settled in a kibbutz, married and became a mother to four children. After the war she had lost contact with her German benefactor.

Twenty years after the war's end, in 1965, Lea (now known as Ben-Horin) wondered how her rescuer was coping. Not knowing his address, she wrote to Yad Vashem, asking for help to try finding the man who had saved her life during the Holocaust. "I should like to make great efforts in order to find him," Lea added, "since I owe him a lot. . . [and should] thank you much if you were to succeed to help me find the man." Unbeknownst to her, Willi Friedrichs had at the same time contacted the Israel diplomatic legation in Cologne, to help him locate a certain Irena (Lili) Lutowska, one of the several Jewish persons he had helped during the Holocaust. It did not take long to piece together the missing parts of the puzzle: Irena Lutowska was none other than Lea Ben-Horin.

Willi Friedrichs wasted no time in posting a letter to Lea Ben-Horin. He related to her that after the war he had returned to his family in Hanover, to a wife and four children who had since grown up, married, and raised their own families. He then disclosed to her the shocking news that in 1950, due to severe financial troubles, he and his brother-in-law had decided to rob a bank mail clerk. When that person put up a fight, Willi's brother-in-law fled the scene, leaving the short and lean Willi to tackle with the stocky mail clerk. As the two toppled to the ground, a shot rang out from Willi's gun, critically wounding the mail clerk, who eventually died. Willi Friedrichs was promptly arrested, and sentenced to life imprisonment. "I don't want in any way to excuse the deed, which was the result of a deep despair," Willi remorsefully told Lea. He had deeply regretted the act, which caused the death of an innocent man. "As you know, I am a weak person, not tall, whereas the teller was 1.90 meter tall. I did not fire at him intentionally, but only after an uneven struggle." He now asked of Lea to send a request to the German authorities, through his attorney, asking that he be pardoned.

Lea Ben-Horin was both overjoyed and shocked: happy at having reestablished contacts with her erstwhile rescuer and stunned at the tragedy which had befallen him. In her letter to him, she gave him news about her current life; that she was happily married, with a husband and four children. "We live in a kibbutz. If you don't know what a kibbutz is like, I am prepared to explain. My eldest daughter, age 18, has finished high school and is now in the army. Here, girls must serve for 20 months." Her other younger children were still in school. Sadly, her ten-year-boy was stricken with polio as a baby, but had since gained the use of one leg. Besides, he was a smart and a lively boy. "As a person who risked his life to save me," she added at the end of her letter, "you are close to me, like a member of my own family."

She then decided to do anything in her power to effect Friedrichs' release from jail, where he had already spent 15 years.

Lea Ben-Horin followed up her deposition to Yad Vashem with an appeal to the President of Israel, and to various German and Jewish dignitaries, including the presiding judge at Friedrichs' 1950 trial. This man, Dr. Blankenburg, of Jewish origin, who had spent time in a concentration camp during the Nazi period, replied that he regretted that Friedrichs' humanitarian help during the war years was not disclosed during his trial, for this would certainly have had a mitigating effect on the man's sentencing. Friedrichs' attorney had learned of his client's wartime humanitarian record, only nine years after his client's sentencing. It was only then that the attorney initiated the pardon plea.

An additional favorable statement regarding Friedrichs' help during the war was received by Yevdokia Timoshenko, a Jewess, living in Leningrad. She told how after working for Friedrichs for six weeks doing household chores, he helped her flee with her child to another city to avoid her arrest, disguised as the wife of man serving in the Red army. Moments before the departure, he slipped money into the pocket of the child's coat. He also arranged for Yevdokia's mother to join her in her new place. Although she appeared under a non-Jewish identity, Yevkodia was certain that Friedrichs suspected the truth, but did not raise the issue, nor did it affect his "humanity and magnanimity." She also added her plea for a pardon and an early release for the man, who had already spent 16 years behind bars. "I am personally prepared to help Friedrichs; I feel it is my obligation, for we owe him our lives."

With regard to Friedrichs' imprisonment, his attorney, in his appeal to the Hanover state judicial authorities, contrasted his client's plight with other prison sentences. A former Nazi who, without reason, shot two released concentration camp prisoners, was given a 15 year jail sentence, and has since been pardoned. Likewise, a man who had murdered his stepbrother in his sleep for monetary reasons had received a life sentence, and was released after serving 16 years in jail. These rather lenient sentences, Heins argued, should be contrasted with Friedrichs' harsh sentencing for the accidental shooting of a man, an act which his client deeply regretted.

Yad Vashem's response to Lea Ben-Horin's petition was two-fold: satisfaction that she had found her wartime rescuer, coupled with deep regret that the man who had risked his life to save hers and others had allowed himself to become entangled in a criminal act which had cost of the life of an innocent man. In the meantime, the pardon pleas addressed to the Hanover District Court resulted, in 1966, in the reduction of the sentence to 20 years imprisonment. In other words, Friedrichs was to be released four years hence, in 1970. This did not satisfy Lea Ben-Horin and she enlisted the aid of Israel Shiloni, a fellow kibbutz colleague, who added his appeal for

Friedrichs' immediate release from jail, simultaneous with a request to have him awarded the Righteous title.

In his letter to Yad Vashem, in April 1967, Shiloni told how he had left Germany in 1939, as a first step before fetching his family. But the war intervened, and Shiloni, who fought with the British army, learned after the war that his mother, wife and two children were murdered in the Holocaust. Said Shiloni: "Had a man like Friedrichs been around, I might have one of my beloved ones with me today. But there was no second Friedrichs." This explains his voluntary engagement to effect the release of this Friedrichs, who had spent 17 years of his life in a German jail. Shiloni added: "I doubt that it would give me satisfaction to hate all the Germans. To love this German, however, to be grateful to him and support him in his difficult fate – this is my consolation." He had already paid sufficiently for his guilt.

As to the claim by some people that "we can only deal with 'clean' people," Shiloni added the following biting rejoinder: "The 'clean' people thought only of themselves and their families at that time, but this simple worker did what his heart dictated to him." This was not the case of a criminal type, Shiloni continued, but of a man who in deep despair committed a criminal act." A *Baal Teshuva* [a Hebrew term for a repentant sinner] has a higher place than a *Zaddik* [a Righteous person]. I therefore ask for Yad Vashem to write to Germany — perhaps the last straw in the effort for his full release."

Yad Vashem acceded to this request, and in a matter-of-fact letter wrote to the judicial authority in Lower Saxony, acknowledging Friedrichs' help to Jews during the Holocaust. This had the desired effect — Friedrichs was granted a pardon, and was to be released on December 1, 1968 — two years ahead of time. Lea Ben-Horin and Israel Shiloni then turned to the matter of the Righteous title for Friedrichs, and here his advocates found themselves stonewalled. As Lea Ben-Horin was told, the Righteous title requires not only a personal risk on the part of the rescuer, but the person's general behavior must also be taken into consideration — an allusion to the regrettable incident in 1950 in which Friedrichs caused the loss of an innocent life. One advocate for Friedrichs' recognition, an attorney by profession, argued that most law professionals concede that, with a person's end of a prison term, the debt for whatever felony or crime committed had been requited, and no one had the moral right to impose on the freed felon an additional social form of punishment. "On the contrary, society has an obligation to pave the way for that person's return to a normal existence, as if nothing happened." This should include expressing society's gratitude for his wartime humanitarian exploits, through the Yad Vashem-sponsored Righteous program. "Will we now shut our ears to the calls of conscience by denying Friedrichs the honor which we award the other Righteous?" the attorney ended his plea.

Yad Vashem Board member Gideon Hausner, who prosecuted Adolf Eichmann seven years earlier, responded to this by remarking that if Friedrichs had not committed the criminal offense he would certainly have earned the Righteous title. However, this was not a question of a man's return to a normal life in society (as argued by the attorney), but of awarding him a high honor – the highest honor, indeed, awarded by the Jewish people to non-Jews. Here, one must take into consideration the message that Yad Vashem wishes to send to the public at large – of the Righteous as role models, as examples of human conduct others should imitate and replicate. The cloud hovering over Friedrichs' head placed Yad Vashem in a predicament, which the Commission for the Righteous would have to seriously examine and debate.

The Commission devoted two sessions to this thorny issue, and decided, in January 1969, by majority vote to decline the Righteous title to Willi Friedrichs. In the Commission's eyes, it was not a question of limiting the Righteous title to persons free of personal faults, for such an approach would, indeed, scuttle the program. Hence, the examination was limited to the man's action and behavior during the Holocaust years and, in particular, his initiative and personal role in the rescue operation. At the same time, Yad Vashem could not shut its eyes to deeds committed by a rescuer before and after the Holocaust period, especially if it involved physical harm, let alone the taking of an innocent life. Totally overlooking such an act, which had already gained wide publicity, and awarding the author of such an act with a morally-significant title would make a mockery of the whole Righteous program. This Yad Vashem could not allow itself to do.

This decision notwithstanding, Lea Ben-Horin's kibbutz, in conjunction with the association of former residents of Brest-Litovsk, paid for Willi Friedrichs' visit to Israel, together with his wife, in February 1970, and hosted him at a celebration in his honor at Lea's kibbutz. At this occasion, Willi Friedrichs was warmly received, and his benevolent rescue action lauded and applauded, to the relief of the man and to Lea Ben-Horin, who had struggled so hard to effect the man's release from prison. He was, however, denied the Righteous title.[46]

Willi Friedrichs and Lea Ben-Horin during his visit to her kibbutz.

Mathias Niessen

Others Saved, Not Him; Title Annulled

In another case, a person wishing to enhance his political ambitions imputed to himself the authorship of a rescue act. In 1980, Marlene Grüneberg, in Cologne, Gemany wrote to Yad Vashem regarding the rescue of a Jewish couple by a father-and-son team, one of whom currently held an important political post in one of Cologne's district municipalities. She had heard the story from her late husband, who was the son of the late rescued Jewish couple. According to this story, the Grünebergs were arrested in October 1943 and taken to a transit camp in Bocklemünd, in preparation for their deportation to Theresienstadt. Josef Niessen, a worker with the German railways, alerted his son Mathias, who was serving in the German air force and stationed in southern France. Mathias Niessen immediately flew into Cologne on a military plane, which he piloted, in order to assist his father in snatching Dr. Albert Grüneberg (formerly a medical doctor with the German railways and a friend of Josef Niessen) along with his wife Philomene out of the camp. With the liquor which Mathias had brought with him from France, father and son (dressed respectively in train worker and military uniforms) were able to turn the guards at Bocklemünd drowsy enough to make possible the escape of the two Grünebergs. The plan succeeded, and the Niessens sped off with their wards to a nearby village for hiding. Fearing arrest by the local Nazi chief, named Zilliken, the Grünebergs were moved to several alternative places and cared for by the two Niessens almost until the end of the war. Dr. Grüneberg died in March 1945, while still in hiding, and was secretly buried. Mathias, from his distant army base, had sent food packages to his father for the hidden persons.

Marlene had heard the story from the Grünebergs' son, whom she married after the war, and who had also passed away. As for Mathias Niessen, he was presently an important political figure both in the Social Democratic party, as well as on the Cologne metropolitan board and, moreover, a mayor of one of its district municipalities. He presently upheld and confirmed Mrs. Grüneberg's account; she was also affiliated with the Social Democratic party. Based on this, and some additional information, the Righteous title was awarded to Mathias Niessen and his departed father Josef.

The ink had hardly settled on the Certificate of Honor which, with a special medal, was awarded to Mathias Niessen by the Israeli ambassador in a public ceremony in 1981, when some people began to question the authenticity of the rescue authors. The honoree's own nephew contested his uncle's role in the rescue operation, claiming that the man had no part whatsoever in it. The question of the rescue's true authors assumed a new dimension when radio journalist Heiner Lichtenstein protested plans to dedicate a commemorative plaque in memory of Arnold Zilliken, formerly an important local politician, charging him with personally seeking out Jews in hiding in Worringen, a township where Zilliken acted as the local Nazi boss. Lichtenstein was supported in his petition by Marlene Grüneberg and Mathias Niessen, who were political opponents of Zilliken's Christian Democratic party, and who stated that since they feared Zilliken's Jew-hunting, the Niessens were forced to move the Grünebergs to a different hiding place, after the two had spent some time in hiding in Worringen. Zilliken's widow and daughter countered by suing Lichtenstein for defamation of Zilliken's name, and bringing forward witnesses who challenged Niessen's claim of being the author of the Grünebergs' rescue.

According to one of these witnesses, the real authors of the rescue operation were Bill Bochanek and Agnes Schneider who, upon learning of the Grünebergs' arrest, in October 1943, immediately hurried to the Müngersdorf train station, where the two were held (not the Bocklemünd camp, as claimed by Niessen), and succeeded in spiriting both out. The Grünebergs were first taken for temporary hiding in Mrs. Schneider's home; then, in the cellar of Hans Krause's home, whose family were Dr. Grüneberg's prewar patients. From there, they were again moved to several other locations, finally to a hiding place in the Nippes section of Cologne (Niessen's current fiefdom). Three days after the area's liberation by U.S. troops, in April 1945, Albert Grüneberg died of food poisoning (caused by consuming army k-rations), and was buried by Krause in a local cemetery. This contrasted with Marlene Grüneberg's earlier statement that her father-in-law had died in March 1945, while still in hiding. More damaging for Niessen was the testimony of one of his former air force colleagues, who stated that Niessen was not stationed in southern France as claimed by him, but attended a flying course inside Germany, and that he was not given leave in 1943 to fly home on an army plane.

In addition, Marlene Grüneberg could not remember whether she married Rolf, the Grünebergs' son in 1952 or in 1955. At any rate, she could not have heard of the rescue story from Rolf's mother Philomene, who died in 1949, which was before Marlene met Rolf, who had since also passed away.[47] The weight of evidence turned against the defendants Niessen and his political protégé. When Mrs. Grüneberg refused in court to disclose the name of the peasant family where the Grünebergs supposedly were hidden in Worringen, she was declared in contempt of court, and fined. Finally, in July 1987, Mathias Niessen admitted in court that he had lied about his involvement in the rescue operation, and that his version was pure fabrication. The court thereupon imposed a stiff fine on him, which also led to Niessen's forced resignation from the Cologne municipality, followed by his Social Democratic party's condemnation. Soon thereafter, Niessen returned to the Israeli ambassador the medal and certificate of honor he had received four years earlier. He also gave a letter of apology, where he took full responsibility (exonerating his co-worker Marlene Grüneberg) for the misrepresentation of the facts, and asking for Yad Vashem's forgiveness for his abuse of the Righteous program. Yad Vashem obliged, and annulled its previous positive decision in this matter—the first such instance in the program's history.

The Niessen affair exemplifies a situation in which the Righteous title was abused for political gains. Paradoxically, it also demonstrates the high prestige accorded to this title in Germany, the country where Nazism was born and which presided over the Final Solution. Mathias Niessen's fall from grace was due to a large extent to the civic courage of a group of persons (including a member of his own family) who were outraged by the misuse of this honor by a person who did not merit it at all.[48]

Oskar Ebers

I Am a Jew — The Righteous Honor is Reserved For Non-Jews

The final story dealing with the question whether certain rescuers merited the Righteous title, has a somewhat titillating ending. In 1983, Yehoshua Ben-Ami wrote to Yad Vashem concerning his Hungarian rescuer. In his testimony, he related that in October 1944, together with a friend, he escaped from a Labor Battalion,[49] and fled to Budapest. Soon thereafter, on October 15, 1944, the pro-Nazi Arrow Cross movement staged a coup d'état, with the help of the German military, and unleashed a reign of terror on the Jewish population in Budapest.[50] Ben-Ami's sister linked the two up with her friend, who was engaged to a certain Oskar Ebers. The two escapees, together with Ebers' fiancee hid in Ebers' home for several days. Ebers then arranged a hiding place for the group, including ten more Jews, underneath the stage of a theater under construction, and provided them with food and other necessities. After a while, the hidden persons were able to obtain refuge in one of the Spanish protective homes, and thus survive the Holocaust in Hungary.[51] Ben-Ami presently learned that Ebers had settled in the United States, and asked that the Righteous title be awarded to his rescuer.

When the case came up for examination at the Commission for the Righteous, a spirited debate arose whether the Righteous title, which was designed for non-Jewish rescuers of Jews, should be attributed to a person whose mother was Jewish and his father non-Jewish. It was pointed out that the rescuer had been raised in a non-Jewish environment, and was probably a Christian in practice, even if not thoroughly devout. The fact that the Hungarian authorities did not conscript him into the Labor Battalions, in which even baptized Jews were drafted, and was not forced to wear the identifying Yellow Badge, was proof that Ebers was non-Jewish in the eyes of the authorities, even though according to Jewish religious law (*Halacha*), he was still considered Jewish because of his mother's Jewish origin. As pointed out by a Hungarian-born Commission member, in Hungary there were no fixed and established rules; persons in mixed marriages decided among themselves in what religious tradition to raise their children. This argument was countered by others who stated that his Jewish side may have motivated him to extend help to his distraught distant brothers-in-need; hence, in the act of helping, he may simply have seen himself as a Jew aiding fellow Jews. The Commission resolved to award him the Righteous title, since it could not be proven whether the rescuer saw himself as Jewish — probably not, due to his exemption from any form of anti-Jewish restrictions. The case in favor of his recognition was even stronger for, as pointed out by one Commission member (himself a Holocaust survivor), with the SS and their Arrow Cross henchmen unleashing a reign of terror on the country's Jews, it was best for a person like Oskar Ebers to do everything in his power not to jeopardize himself by acts which would have exposed his partly-Jewish origin. In the words of the Commission chairman: "A person with butter on his head, does not take a walk in the sun." Since Ebers acted otherwise, and notwithstanding his safe status as a Christian, he acted to save, thus also risking exposing his Jewish paternity, he definitely merited the Righteous title.

Over a year later, Oskar Ebers decided to visit Israel, and preparations were made to allow him to plant a tree at Yad Vashem, when an urgent call was received by his former ward, Ben-Ami. He had just learned from his American visitor that he considered himself fully Jewish, and therefore did not wish to be listed among the Righteous. Invited to Yad Vashem to explain this apparently change of heart, Ebers stated that he was indeed raised without any religious attachment, neither Jewish nor Christian, since his parents were fully secular persons. However, when, as an adult he was refused work and membership in a sports club because of his semi-Jewish paternity (he claimed two Jewish grandparents), he decided to throw his lot with the Jewish people, and extend them his help, as a fellow or semi-fellow Jew. Furthermore, when he emigrated to the United States after the war, and married for the second time (both his marriages were with Jewish spouses), he decided to formally convert to the Jewish faith. To his surprise, he was told by a New York rabbi that he need not convert, since according to Jewish religious law, he was already a Jew. "I feel and consider myself a Jew in all respect," Oskar Ebers declared at Yad Vashem, "and when I die, I wish to be buried in a Jewish cemetery." In fairness to the deserving non-Jewish rescuers, he did not wish as a Jew to be included among them, and asked for his name to be removed from the Righteous list. The Commission for the Righteous thought it best to comply with the man's wish.[52]

Concluding Thoughts

E lie Wiesel has recently stated that as a result of Hitler, man is defined by what makes him inhuman. This quite pessimistic assessment of man has, of course, a lot to draw on—the Holocaust being the most extreme example in support of this statement. At the same time, the example of thousands of persons who risked their lives to save Jews, during that same terrible period, is proof that the last word on human behavior has not yet been said.

At Yad Vashem, the purpose of the Righteous program was and remains to single out persons who, irrespective of their private opinions and inclinations, stood morally firm when faced with the challenge presented by the Holocaust. By saving Jews, in spite of the tremendous risks to themselves, they sustained the image of man as a moral, caring and compassionate being. Consequently, they, rather than the perpetrators and the bystanders, should serve as role models for future generations. They teach us that the individual person, when left to himself, can draw the right moral lesson, if and when called upon. This is not an abstruse philosophical statement, based on theoretical reflections of idyllic and utopian societies, but rather on the actual examples of thousands of men and women from all walks of life and professions — literate and illiterate, blue and white collar workers, who acted in like manner and upheld the principle of the preciousness and sanctity of every individual's life. When approached and challenged to extend a helping hand, they did not shirk responsibility, but responded affirmatively to the call of distraught persons. Hence, the philosophical and psychological significance of their humanitarian response. According to the French-Jewish philosopher Emmanuel Levinas, true ethics begins with turning towards and responding to the other, leading to a commitment to caring for the other person's needs. This, to Levinas, is the essence of a true morality - the concern for the other's well-being occasioned by the face-to-face encounter. Such an ethic became concretized in the deeds of rescuers of Jews during the Holocaust.[1]

The massive documentation available on the Holocaust (such as Raul Hilberg's magisterial study *The Destruction of the European Jews*) clearly establishes that this murderous act was carried out as official government policy, with the participation of an obedient bureaucracy, and men in uniform. In other words, man the killer during the Holocaust was a person who blindly adjusted his behavior to that demanded by his superiors, or his society. On the other hand, man the rescuer followed blindly only his own conscience, even if it meant risking his own life. One may thus infer that when man acts on his own, and not at the behest or influence of others, he need not be the irresponsible egotistical and aggressive being portrayed by

Hobbes and Freud. Quite the opposite, man the savage manifests himself in situations like the Holocaust, when he abdicates his individuality and acts according to the will and volition of others.[2]

The purpose of this book was to highlight this positive aspect of human behavior; the sparks of light which cracked the darkness of the Nazi world. These sparks represent glimmers of hope, helping us confront the Holocaust, and not lose hope in ourselves as responsible and caring beings. The hope is that the stories of the Righteous will be creatively used as role models, for the mending of a world torn asunder by strife and senseless killings. As stated by Dutch rescuer Johtje Vos:

> *My father had died during the first year of the war, and when my mother came to visit me and saw we were hiding Jews, she was upset and said, 'You shouldn't do it, even though I agree with what you're doing, because your first responsibility is to your children.' I told her, 'That's exactly why I'm doing it.' I thought we were doing the right thing, giving our children the right model to follow.*[3]

Stefania Burzminski, from Poland, who together with her sister saved a large group of Jews, put this thought as follows:

> *You have to show people a good example. Who will teach people humanity if they see only killing and nothing else?. . . When there's chaos in a country, it's very easy to be a bad boy or bad girl. But to be good is very difficult.*[4]

One such "good example" took place in the hell on earth that was Auschwitz. In concerns the story of Primo Levi, one of the greatest narrators of the Holocaust experience, who in December 1943 was arrested, in Turin, by the Italian Fascist police and deported to Auschwitz. In June 1944, he met an Italian mason, not a prisoner, but a civilian worker of an Italian construction firm which had been contracted to build several structures in one of the camp's subsidiary locations. Understandably, the Italian workers benefited from more privileges than the ragged prisoners of Auschwitz. They were paid for their labor, had Sundays off, enjoyed one or two weeks of vacation, and could exchange letters with people in Italy as well as receive additional food and clothing packages.

By pure coincidence, Levi was picked by his Kapo (prisoner supervisor) to help out two Italian masons he had never seen before, at their work location. One of these workers was Lorenzo Perrone. Irritated at Primo Levi's sluggish handling of the cement, Lorenzo uttered some words in Italian, and was surprised to learn that the man was from Turin, Italy — not far from Lorenzo's home town of Fossano. At that moment, something was born in

Lorenzo's heart — a commitment to assure the survival of Primo Levi in this most terrible concentration camp.

Three days later, and every day thereafter, for the next six months, Lorenzo brought Levi a military mess tin full of soup, and told him to bring it back empty before evening. Lorenzo found a way to secretly scrape the leftovers from the cauldrons of the Italian worker's kitchen, when everyone was asleep at three o'clock in the morning, and bring it the next day to Levi at the work site. For added security, Lorenzo would leave the mess tin in an agreed-upon hiding place under a pile of boards. A slice of bread was sometimes added to the daily soup. Levi is sure that without it he, as a person not inured to the hard labor under the conditions of the camp, would not have survived.

In addition, Lorenzo made it possible for Levi to communicate with his mother, who was in hiding in Italy. In *Moments of Reprieve*, Levi writes: "I had gotten hold of a sheet of paper and a pencil stub, and for many days I had been waiting for the opportunity to write the draft of a letter which I meant to entrust to [Lorenzo] so he could write it, sign it as if it were his, and send it to my family in Italy. . . We were strictly forbidden to write. . . If I could think about it for a moment, I would find a way to devise a message that would be sufficiently clear to the recipients but at the same time innocent enough not to attract the censor's attention." Lorenzo agreed to this device, and Levi penned a message to his mother, which was addressed to a non-Jewish woman friend of his.

A little while later, Levi received a letter from home, "an unprecedented event." This was followed with a package, addressed to Lorenzo, sent by Primo's sister and mother, both in hiding in Italy. The package contained ersatz chocolate, cookies, and powdered milk. "To describe its real value, the impact it had on me. . . is beyond the powers of ordinary language," Levi wrote after the war. "That unexpected, improbable, impossible package was like a meteorite, a heavenly object, charged with symbols, immensely precious, and with an enormous momentum." If the real purpose and author of the letter writing had been uncovered, both Levi and Perrone would have been in immediate danger of their lives. Not to forget that it was forbidden for a prisoner to even speak with a contracted civil laborer, let alone for both to conspire to communicate with the outside world.

Lorenzo also gave Primo a "rag of clothing" to wear under his prisoner uniform. [In return, the first thing Primo brought Lorenzo after the war was a vest, knitted especially for him out of goat's hair.] Lorenzo adamantly refused to discuss any sort of reward for his help to Primo, not even a promise of help after the war. He only agreed to Levi's pleading to allow his worn boots to be repaired at the prisoners cobbler's shop. This is as far as he would go in benefiting from any reward for his magnanimous help, because, in the words of Levi "he was good and simple and did not think that one did good for a reward."

Primo Levi was amazed by Lorenzo. "A man helping other men out of pure altruism was incomprehensible, alien, like a savior who's come from heaven." It was difficult to penetrate Lorenzo's inner thoughts and motivations and communicate with him, for he was not very talkative, and he kept to himself. At times, he could also be irate and unresponsive. "I offered to have some money sent to his sister, who lived in Italy, in exchange for what he did for us, but he refused to give us her address."

When the Germans disbanded the foreign labor camp, on January 1, 1945, due to the approaching front, freeing foreign non-Jewish laborers to go wherever they pleased, Lorenzo together with a colleague decided to march out on foot back to their homeland. With the help of schematic maps and the stars, they made their way at night, in the direction of the Brenner pass which they crossed after a four-month walk. On the way, they stopped in villages where they hired themselves out as masons. In mid-May 1945 (the war having just ended), still on foot, Lorenzo reached Turin, and headed directly to Levi's mother, to whom he brought news about her son. A month after the end of the war, Primo Levi (released in Auschwitz by the liberating Russians) wrote to a friend in Italy: "I've had no news of the marvelous Lorenzo Perrone, but it's probable he's safe... No one knows what I owe that man; I shall never be able to repay him."

The impression Lorenzo made on Levi's thinking may be garnered from the author's words in *If This Is a Man*:

> *Why I, rather than thousands of others, managed to survive the test, I believe that it was really due to Lorenzo that I am alive today; and not so much for his material aid, as for his having constantly reminded me by his presence, by his natural and plain manner of being good, that there still existed a just world outside our own, something and someone still pure and whole, not corrupt, not savage, extraneous to hatred and terror... for which it was worth surviving... His humanity was pure and uncontaminated, he was outside this world of negation. Thanks to Lorenzo, I managed not to forget that I myself was a man."[5]*

On one occasion, Lorenzo Perrone told Primo Levi, "we are in this world to do good, not to boast about it." It is the hope that the lessons of the Holocaust will not be restricted to the terrible misdeeds of the perpetrators, but that these lessons will also be drawn on the good deeds of the thousands of persons, who acted in like manner as Lorenzo Perrone.

Left: Lorenzo Perrone; right: Primo Levi (wartime photo)

Appendix A

The Jewish Connection

The title of "Righteous Among the Nations" is, of course, reserved for non-Jews who risked their lives to save Jews from the Nazis and their collaborators during the Holocaust. The logic behind it resides in the theory that whereas Jews who saved their brethren Jews only fulfilled their obligation, non-Jews had no such responsibility toward their Jewish neighbors; hence, those that braved the risks to themselves by extending help to Jews merit a special distinction. This thinking has recently come under criticism by many people. Marion Pritchard, a much celebrated non-Jewish Dutch rescuer of Jews, residing in the USA, and a Righteous title honoree, stated: "Not recognizing the moral courage, the heroism of the Jewish rescuers, who if caught were at much higher risk of the most punitive measures than the gentiles, is a distortion of history. It also contributes to the widespread fallacious impression that the Jews were cowards, who allowed themselves to be led like 'lambs to slaughter.' Nothing is farther from the truth."[1] True to her belief, on her many public appearances in the United States, she urges her audience to promote the cause of Jewish rescuers and give them recognition in keeping with that bestowed upon non-Jewish rescuers.

In this section we have in mind not Jewish rescuers who may have saved one or several of their colleagues, but persons who, acting alone or in unison with others, created rescue networks, and saved dozens and hundreds of Jews. An honoree list of such major Jewish rescuers will include, in the Netherlands, Joachim Simon (known as "Shushu") who operated side-by-side with the legendary Joop Westerweel, and was killed by the Nazis; as well as Max ("Nico") Leons, who masqueraded as a seminarian, and in partnership with Arnold Douwes organized a large-scale rescue of Jews in the off-the-beaten-track village of Nieuwlande. In Amsterdam, the German-Jewish refugee Walter Süskind was instrumental in saving hundreds of Jews under the eyes of the Nazis.

To the south, in Belgium, this special Jewish honoree lists will comprise Fela Perlman and Yvonne Jospa, creators of the Jewish Defense Committee, a clandestine Jewish organization which helped Jews pass as non-Jews and find hiding places for them, especially children. Ida Sterno, one of the organization's Jewish couriers, traveled widely through the Belgian countryside in search of suitable homes for Jewish children on the run. In France, the picture is much larger; there, the multifaceted panorama of Jewish networks is largely to be credited for the tremendous Jewish survival rate in that country — over 200,000. To mention the most prominent networks, one would have to include the OSE children organization and its many operatives, especially Georges Loinger, Jacques Salon, Elisabeth Hirsch, Vivette Samuel,

Nicole Weil-Salon, Huguette Wahl (the last two were arrested in Nice and sent to Auschwitz, where they were gassed upon arrival), Andrée Salomon and Dr. Joseph Weill—all of whom were active in the rescue of, all combined, thousands of Jewish children. Not to be left out are Marianne Cohn and Mila Racine, who escorted many Jewish youth to the Swiss border and across it. Both these brave women paid with their lives; Mila Racine died in Mauthausen, whereas Marianne Cohn was brutally murdered by the pro-Nazi French Milice on the eve of France's liberation. Others meriting mention are Georges Garel, who created his own rescue network (with the support of Bishop Jules-Géraud Saliège, of Toulouse) and played a leading role in spiriting out a large group of children from Venissieux camp, near Lyon. Also, Emmanuel Racine (the brother of Mila), Robert Gamzon (known as "Castor"), head of the Jewish Scout Movement, David Rapoport, who fabricated false papers, and had his base in Paris on Rue Amelot, and the Jewish-born Abbé Alexandre Glasberg, who converted to Catholicism before the war, and during the war was very active in initiating rescue operations of his Jewish brethren. Last but not least for France, Joseph Bass, Denise Siekierski, and Moussa and Odette Abadi saved well over a thousand Jewish adults and children, in separate rescue operations.

In Poland, Avraham Berman was active in helping Jewish children inside the Warsaw Ghetto; then on the Aryan side, he represented the Jewish underground in Zegota, the sole Polish organization committed to the rescue of Jews. Further north, in Belarus, Tuvia Bielski organized a family camp in the forest vicinity of Novgrodek, which included a synagogue, school, dispensary and workshop, as well as a fighting unit. Jews of all ages were admitted in this forest-community. In Slovakia, Gisi Fleischman and Dov Weissmandel unsuccessfully negotiated with SS chief Dieter Wisliceny to save the remainder of the country's Jews, under a project known as the Europe Plan. Fleischmann wound up in Auschwitz, where she perished. In Hungary, Bela Elek, an affiliate of Raoul Wallenberg's network, rescued hundreds of Jews during the infamous Death March to the Austrian border, in November 1944. He was later murdered by the pro-Nazi Arrow Cross militia. Jewish Zionist organizations also planned large rescue operations in that country. Finally, in Switzerland Georges Mantello and the Sternbuch couple (Recha and Isaac) worked frantically, through various channels to save as many Jews as possible, enlisting the aid of whatever source—the pro-Fascist former president of the Swiss confederation Jean-Marie Musy, in the case of the Sternbuchs—the El Salvador government and its Geneva diplomatic representative, José Castellanos, in the case of Mantello. With the exception of the Jewish rescuers operating in Switzerland—all others were in double jeopardy and faced grave dangers to their lives on two counts: as Jews they were on the Nazi death list; as organizers and members in clandestine rescuer organizations, they faced the death penalty for underground activity.

Space, and the book's principal theme, do not allow us to expand on major Jewish rescuers. For this a special study is required. Here, we will mention only several such rescuers; Jewish men and women who were engaged in Herculean efforts to save their brethren, in conjunction with non-Jewish rescuers (who were honored with the Righteous title), and are still unknown to the Jewish public at large. Hopefully, these brave persons will merit recognition, so that they too occupy a dignified place in the annals of humanitarian deeds, and serve as role models for the education of Jewish youth.

Walter Süskind

Saved Children and Adults in the Lion's Den

Upon the occupation of the Netherlands, in May 1940, the Germans gradually moved to rid the country of all Jews, and thereby prepare the conquered nation, considered a lost Germanic tribe, for its incorporation into an enlarged German Reich. The first year of the occupation passed with relatively few measures to arouse concern on the ultimate murderous plan the Nazis reserved for the Jews. Other than the forced registration of all Jews, and their dismissal from the civil service and positions of influence in the life of the country, the Jewish population of 140,000 was left in relative peace. The following year, however, decrees against Jews intensified. In September 1941, the Germans began to segregate the Jews from the non-Jewish population through measures which barred them from schools, parks, zoos, tramways — even the sunny side of the streets. In April 1942 came the imposition of the Yellow Star band on their outer clothes, for easier identification and harassment. Two months later, large scale deportations began to the death camps in Poland. To facilitate the concentration of the doomed victims, the Germans converted a theater in the heart of Amsterdam known as *Hollandse Schouwburg* (Dutch Theater), to serve as a makeshift prison for at least 50,000 Jews, who gradually moved through its doors, on their way to the large Westerbork concentration camp, in the northeastern part of the country, where trains left at regular intervals for the charnel houses in Poland.[2] Lisette Lamon, one of the Theater's internees, recalls seeing people spending days and nights crowded in the auditorium, where no daylight penetrated. Children were screaming, crying, vomiting and soiling everywhere. Hygienic conditions were practically nonexistent. As further told in her sad recollection:

> *When first captured, most prisoners' thoughts were centered around loved ones: 'Will my husband know I am imprisoned? Will I ever see my child again? Who will take care of my mother who is old and gravely ill?... How do I survive today? How can I rid myself of lice?'... Transports were usually at 3 a.m. during curfew hours for the general Dutch population. City tramways waited to take the prisoners to the central train station where they boarded trains for Westerbork.*[3]

Inside the Theater, the SS team in charge refused to deal directly with their victims, whom they considered as the lowest on their scale of "inferior" races, but preferred to pass on orders through Nazi-appointed Jewish intermediaries. The Jewish Council (*Joodse Raad*) was created by the Germans for this purpose as a go-between the Nazi overlords and the Jewish masses. The council's representatives at the Theater were Slutzker and his aide, Walter Süskind who, in practice, was the man who dealt directly with the Germans, and who used his position to smuggle out hundreds (some say close to a thousand) of Jews before their deportation to the camps. Who was this unusual person?

Born in 1906, in Ludenscheid, Germany, one of three sons, the youthful Walter Süskind took a liking to acting and specialized in humorous sketches at a local theater, occasionally filling in the part of a drunk or a singing bum. He also loved the opera, and was especially fond of Verdi's arias. Three years after his marriage to Hanna Natt in 1935, the Süskind family left Nazi Germany for Holland, including Walter's and his wife's mothers. In Holland, he worked for the Unilever company, which had an affiliate in Cambridge, Massachusetts, manufacturing soap, and Süskind looked forward to moving there, and to a job with his company's affiliate. In the meantime, in March 1938, his wife Hanna gave birth to a girl, whom they named Yvonne. After much bureaucratic hassle, he was informed, in June 1941 (Germany and the U.S. were not yet at war), that the immigration papers were in order. Süskind's joy, however, was short-lived. The following month, the Germans clamped down on all Jewish emigration from Holland. The Nazis had something more devilish in store for them.

Thanks to his language and organizational skills, Süskind was appointed by the Jewish Council to be one of its representatives before the Germans at the Dutch Theater. From the start, he decided to use his good rapport with the SS guards and their commander, SS officer Ferdinand Aus der Fünten, to judiciously pull the wool over their eyes, and save as many imprisoned Jews as possible. Non-Jewish Piet Meerburg, whose self-created clandestine student organization spirited many Jews out of the city, in collusion, in many instances, with Süskind, remains convinced that "Walter viewed his mission from the beginning as being just one thing: to sabotage the transports. For this, he put on an extraordinary act," in many ways, one of which consisted of doctoring the list of internees, which carried Aus der Fünten's signature, behind the back of the unsuspecting SS guards — changing and deleting the names of those that Süskind and his aides (such as his right hand man Felix Halverstadt) had arranged to escape and go into hiding.[4] To this day, one is not exactly sure how he managed this. Some speculate that the list was based on individual cards, kept in a file cabinet, and that Süskind simply threw away the cards of those whom he arranged their escape. Those fortunate enough to be chosen by Süskind were generally spirited out of the theater's windows or back entrance, at times in connivance with one or several SS guards, such as the previously mentioned Alfons Zündler.[5] As the man responsible for the administrative side of the operation, Süskind made sure that the paperwork was kept in a disorderly — some prefer to use the term "chaotic" — condition, the better to be able to tamper with the names when the time seemed ripe. In the words of Dutch World War Two historian Johannes ten Cate, Süskind "was clever and secretive. He knew how to bend the rules in his favor." While his immediate and formal supervisor Slutzker did everything by the book, Süskind handled the illegal side — bribing the Germans and corrupting them. One witness describes him as a terrific organizer with a big mouth, who as a German born, knew exactly how to deal with his German overlords.[6]

One of Süskind's antics involved the release of persons already sitting on trains, ready to be taken to Westerbork. This happened after his network had discovered that the keys of the lockers in an Amsterdam bathhouse fit the locks of some transport rail cars, which had been impressed for use in deporting Jews. Sam de Hond, one of Süskind's secret operatives, remembers many Jews being freed with the help of these keys, after Süskind made sure that their names had been removed from the official register.[7] Another antic was to distribute yellow armbands, worn by himself and Jewish council officials, to prisoners driven on trolleys to the train station, and persuading the conductor to release them, on the excuse that this category of persons had been mistakenly arrested and were in truth temporarily exempt from deportation.

As told, Süskind had a special way of dealing with his dangerous SS bosses and knew how to manage them. He found that Aus der Fünten, who was in charge of SS operations in the Theater, had a weakness for spirits, which Süskind exploited to the fullest. According to an unconfirmed report, the two knew each other from their school years in Germany. At any rate, he supplied Aus der Fünten and the SS guards with choice liquors. "It worked well on many occasions," Mrs. Halverstad-Kesner, the widow of Süskind's principal aide, Felix Halverstad, recalls. Süskind would be seen sitting with the fearful Aus der Fünten, together gulping gin and telling salacious jokes, as others sneaked children out of the *Creche*, the prewar Children's Day Care Center, located across the street from the Theater. Süskind's personality also lent itself easily to this type of phony camaraderie. He was, after all, an affable man, with a permanent smile on his cherubic face. Naturally, the people passing through the Theater did not know that, insofar as Süskind was concerned, it was a staged performance to keep the mind of the SS preoccupied (Süskind was not beyond fetching prostitutes to cavort with SS guards) while people were spirited out of the Theater. Undoubtedly, some who saw him frolicking with the Germans, drinking whiskey and smoking cigars with them, or bantering with Aus der Fünten about "the good old days," probably hated him. Few, however, were aware how, at risk to his life, he tampered with files, removing the index cards of those whose escape had been arranged by his accomplices.

Süskind's greatest effort was expended in saving the children who had been separated from their parents and taken across the street to the *Creche*, where they were kept and cared by Jewish nurses, until they were rejoined to their parents upon departure to the concentration camps. The Center's Jewish head, Mrs. Henriette Henriques Pimentel (who was eventually deported and perished) worked closely with Süskind and Halverstad to find escape routes for some of the children. Whenever parents could supply a safe address for their child, Süskind's accomplices on the outside would verify if the people were indeed ready to conceal a Jewish child. Schoontje Kattenburg (today Sieny Cohen) was one of the three nurses who had permission from the Germans to enter the Theater to fetch the arriving children. She worked in the *Creche* for two and half years, and witnessed Süskind's machinations in his concern for the children. When a rescuer family had been located for a child, Sieny's task was to inform the parents. "I was then 19 years old. When I approached the parents, I could not guarantee them anything. If they asked: how and where, I had no answer. I did not know where the children would be taken; this was my supervisor's worry; it was not our business." After the parents' consent, Sieny gave them a small blanket wrapped around a doll, and dressed with rags. "The parents were frightened when I placed this package in their arms, for it weighed almost nothing." When lined up for deportation, the parents held these bundles close to their chest, pretending to rock their sleeping child.

When a child without parents was imprisoned, a frantic search would be started for a family that would shelter the child. In Lamon's words:

> *Walter – the heart and soul of Operation Kidnap – would only allow a child to be smuggled out if it had a verified home. Children were smuggled out of the nursery in rucksacks, laundry bags, crates, bread baskets, burlap bags, or held under a coat. One infant passed through a cordon of SS men in a cake box. Occasionally they were given tranquilizers or sleeping pills to minimize their chance of detection.*[8]

Süskind's nephew remembers one day his uncle appeared sweating profusely. He had smuggled a child from the Creche rolled up in a blanket on the back of his bicycle, when Aus der Fünten stopped him for a chat. Luckily for Süskind, no suspicion crossed the SS officer's mind on the bundle on Süskind's bike.[9] Those who could not be saved – the majority – were awakened in the evening, and hurriedly dressed while still half-asleep, in order to be able to join their parents in the Theater, for the 10 p.m. departure time, three times per week. Their fate was sealed immediately upon arrival at the death camps – the gas chambers. The lowest estimate of children saved through Süskind's operation is 600. Some place it as high as 1000.[10] In light of the estimated total 4,500 Jewish children saved in the Netherlands, Süskind's achievement is quite amazing. The rescue of these children was, in the words of eyewitness Lisette Lamon, "all masterminded by Walter, like an intricate battle plan carefully organized; nothing was done haphazardly. Each step was well thought out and prepared."

Many of the persons on the outside who coalesced with Süskind in this extensive child rescue operation earned the Righteous title by Yad Vashem. Dr. Johan van Hulst headed a teachers' training school, which was separated from the nursery by a backyard fence. Many of his students enlisted in fetching the children and speeding them off to rendezvous with Süskind's rescue co-conspirators on the outside. It would take too long to list all of these brave persons; just a few will suffice to give an idea of the scope of this operation. Dick Groenewegen van Wijk, Gerard Musch and Joop Woortman (a former taxi driver) created their own network, known as the NV Group (the acronym in Dutch for Anonymous or Limited Incorporated). They managed to move over 200 children, mostly to the southern province of Limburg. Some of their associates included Hester van Lennep (she first took the children to a skin treatment institute which she headed), Gesina van der Molen, Piet Vermeer, and Anne-Marie van Verschuer. Former student Piet Meerburg created his own network for the rescue of children and adults.[11] Hetty Voute and Gisela Söhnlein were two of many students committed to this charitable work. Betrayed to the Gestapo, they were deported to Ravensbrück women's concentration camp, which they miraculously survived. These and other rescuers were honored as Righteous by Yad Vashem.[12]

Transports from the Theater ended in September 1943, with the clearing of the last Jews in Amsterdam. Süskind's own safety, as those of the moribund Jewish council, was no longer assured. Eventually, his wife and daughter, as well as his mother and mother-in-law, were arrested and taken to Westerbork. Walter was able to persuade the camp commander, Gemmeker, to allow him to return to Amsterdam so as to settle his affairs. His main effort was now to sabotage deportations from Westerbork, but this effort was frustrated by the camp's Jewish leadership, who feared German retribution. From distant Amsterdam, Süskind nevertheless managed to have some persons freed from Westerbork. No one knows for sure how he achieved this. When, in September 1944, Walter learned that his family was about to be deported to Theresienstadt, he decided to voluntarily join them. His associate Piet Meerburg stated that he and others "tried with all our might to convince Süskind not to go. . . but he went—to his wife in Westerbork. Over there, he wanted to do what he did in the Theater: to play around with the index card, and allow people to escape. However, those in charge there did not dare. . . Süskind had the right approach: If you are a member of the Jewish Council, it is only in order to rescue as many as possible." The following month, the Dutch contingent was deported from Theresienstadt to Auschwitz. His wife, daughter, mother and his wife's mother died there. As for Walter, one witness crossed his path on the Death March of January

1945, when the camp was evacuated, and the remaining inmates taken on a forced march westward in subzero weather. It is believed that he died on that deadly trek.

Boston Globe columnist David Arnold summed up Süskind's role as follows: "He was a master performer. Amsterdam was Süskind's stage: the Nazis were his actors. The script he wrote saved perhaps thousands of lives, although it couldn't save him or his family." Historian Bert Flim, who made a major study of the NV network, confirmed that all the people he interviewed who worked closely with Süskind's network spoke very favorably about him. Lisette Lamon, one of his associates and a courier in the Dutch resistance who was herself eventually deported to Bergen-Belsen but survived, stated that Süskind never asked for or accepted any reward. While he was unable to save himself nor his family, "well over a thousand are living today because of him and those who were his accomplices." He is truly one of the great legendary Jewish rescuers of Jewish lives, a feat magnified by the fact that he was able to accomplish it while being himself a captive of the Germans.

Walter Süskind
Credit: Boston Globe

Moussa and Odette Abadi

Saved over 500 Children

In the testimonies of survivors in southern France, especially in the Nice region, two Jewish names come up frequently — the Syrian-born Jew Moussa Abadi and his companion Odette Rosenstock (the two were married after the war). They headed a private clandestine network in the Nice region, specifically dedicated to finding hiding places for Jewish children whose parents had been snatched by French and German police units, and deported. In one such story, the two Engel brothers were aided by the Abadis after they had been left stranded, following their parents' arrest in a Nazi raid. The two brothers were moved to a children's home, headed by Alban and Germaine Fort, both of whom were awarded the Righteous title. Abadi's name came up again in the cases of Monsignor Paul Rémond, the Catholic bishop of Nice, and several clergy of the Don Bosco Order in Nice, who were also awarded the Righteous title for sheltering Jewish children turned over to them by the Abadi network.[13]

Who was this strange Jewish rescuer?

Born in Damascus, Syria in 1910, Moussa Abadi studied at the local French-speaking Jewish Alliance school, where he earned a scholarship for further academic studies in France. At the Sorbonne, he took a liking to the theater, and appeared in several university-sponsored plays. He joined several students in forming a theatrical troupe, *Compagnie des Quatre Saisons*. The war, however, disrupted his acting career. With the French defeat in 1940, Abadi fled to Nice, in the Vichy non-occupied zone, where he met Odette Rosenstock, a pediatrician and medical school inspector, who was forced to give up her job due to the newly promulgated anti-Jewish discriminatory laws by the Vichy regime.

In Nice, Abadi also met Monsignor Paul Rémond, at a cultural soirée, who, upon learning of Abadi's theatrical record and language skill, hired him to teach grammar and diction to seminarians who needed to brush up on the French language. In the meantime, the situation for the Jews in the "free" zone of France worsened, with the start of forcible roundups in the summer of 1942, such as the raid in Nice on August 26, 1942, in which netted 560 foreign-born Jews were captured and dispatched to Auschwitz via the Drancy transit camp, outside Paris.

On November 11, 1942, the German army took over direct control of the Vichy zone. Thousands of Jews fled to the Nice and Cannes regions, in the southeastern corner of France, which the Germans assigned to their Italians ally; there, the Jews experienced a temporary respite from persecution under the benevolent and non-antisemitic Italian administration. According to one

account, Abadi at first wished to forego all other activity in favor of underground action against the Germans. Two traumatic events caused him to
change his mind. In Nice, he witnessed a French Milice man manhandle a
woman victim. As spectators watched in shock, the man threw her to the
ground, and started stomping on her blood-covered head. Nearby a woman
was holding a child who screamed: "Mama, mama." At that, in Abadi's
words, "I started shouting. . . to God. Why have you abandoned her? Why
at this critical moment?"

At about the same time, Abadi learned that a military chaplain with the
Italian army wished to relate to someone the frightful things he had witnessed while with the Italian army in the Russian sector. "What I am about
to tell," the bearded priest, dressed in a white robe, told the inquisitive Abadi,
"you will not believe. But I have to speak out before I die, so that others may
know." He then related the atrocities committed by the SS against Jewish
children. When he finished, Abadi told him he found it hard to believe the
horrid details. "Even barbarism has its limits," Abadi protested. The priest
held up his crucifix and exclaimed: "I swear by this crucifix that what I told
you is the truth." As they parted, the priest wept. At that, Abadi decided to
forswear armed action against the enemy and instead dedicate himself to
fight the Nazis by saving lives — Jewish children, in particular — and as many
as possible. But how was he, without any practical experience in clandestine
work, to go about it?

Abadi asked for an audience with Monsignor Rémond, the bishop of
Nice, and was warmly received. Facing the bishop, Abadi spoke out: "I am
Jewish, and I come from one of the oldest ghettos in the world. Try to live
up according to your Gospels as I try according to my Bible. You may take
me to the door and throw me out. But without your help, I cannot save
children." Rémond responded that he needed time to think. "As he accompanied me to the door, he stopped and said, 'You have convinced me. You have
converted me.'" Abadi was assigned a room at the Diocese for use in planning the rescue of as many children as possible, should the occasion suddenly
arise. It was still the idyllic period of the Italian occupation.

The situation altered drastically when, upon the Italian capitulation in
September 1943, the Nazis swept into Nice and Cannes, and began hunting
Jews, in homes and hotels and on the streets, headed by the notorious SS
commander Alois Brunner (now hiding in Syria). With the help of local
informers (who were promised 300 to 500 Francs for every Jew betrayed),
the Germans succeeded in rounding up some 1,850 Jews during an initial
three-month period. At this point, Moussa Abadi and Odette Rosenstock
moved into action, picking up Jewish children abandoned after their parents
had been suddenly arrested, or were themselves in hiding, and finding for
them secure hiding places. In the room that Bishop Rémond had placed at
the disposal of Abadi, false credentials were manufactured, such as new

identity cards, baptismal certificates, and ration cards. Rémond also handed Abadi a personal letter of introduction, which opened to him many doors of Catholic institutions.

To cover their tracks, Moussa and Odette assumed new identities, and now appeared as Monsieur Marcel and Sylvie Delatre — respectively, ostensibly educational aides and medical assistants for the Catholic diocese of Nice. Abadi also enlisted the cooperation of Protestant pastors, such as Edmond Evrard, while at the same time coordinating his activities with other clandestine Jewish networks operating in the area, such as the *Service André*, headed by Joseph Bass, and Georges Garel, of the OSE (Jewish children welfare organization). Basically, however, it was a two-person operation: Abadi and Rosenstock. Odette helped by making house calls at homes of prospective host families, paying for the upkeep of the children, and taking note of the children's health and good treatment. Financial aid came through the U.S.-based Joint, the OSE and the Quakers. During the one-year rescue period — September 1943 to August 1944 (when France was liberated) — the Abadi network, known under the code-word *Marcel,* secured safe places for over 500 hundred Jewish children in various children and private homes in the Cannes — Nice region.

To keep track of all children under their care, the Abadis established three separate card indexes: one for the Red Cross, to be stored in Geneva for safekeeping; another for day-to-day work; and a third to serve as a reserve index, in case the other two were misplaced. On the cards appeared vital information, including the child's photo, date of birth, and data on the child's immediate relations. Children were first collected and brought to a secret place, where they were "deprogrammed" of their previous identity. This "depersonalization" included training the children to forget their born names and personal biographies for new ones — before being escorted to their hiding destinations, armed with new false credentials. French-sounding names were substituted for too-conspicuously-sounding Jewish ones, such as Arthieu instead of Artsztein; Bernie — Bernstein; Barot — Borenstein; Raisier — Freiheitier; Calmans — Kalmanovitch; Montel — Mandel; Morini — Morgenstern; and Rameau — Szteinsznaider. To make sure the children had fully absorbed their new identities, one method used was to suddenly call a child by his, or her, previous name. If he responded, it meant that the training was not yet complete for that child. Children were hidden in various religious institutions of the Nice diocese: convents, orphanages, religious schools, and vacation camps, while some were turned over to private homes.

In the meantime, the chase after Jews, estimated to number some 30,000 in 1943, in the Nice — Cannes region, intensified. Four of Abadi's hidden children were discovered and deported. "It was not a time of courage, but of fear," Abadi recalls. "Every morning we asked ourselves whether we will still be here by the evening." Odette Rosenstock was herself arrested in April

1944, by none other than the French Milice, and turned over to the Germans. She was moved to Drancy, after undergoing a brutal interrogation, during which she held her own, and did not divulge information on the scope of the rescue operation. A month later, she was deported to Auschwitz, then to Bergen-Belsen, which she luckily survived.[14]

Back in Nice, with terror stalking the streets of the city, Monsignor Rémond suggested to Abadi that he go into hiding until the police search for him had slackened, an idea which Abadi turned down since it would imply abandoning the hidden children. "Rémond then accompanied me to the door, and said: 'I am left with nothing but to pray for you.' He placed his hand on my head, similar to my grandfather, when he blessed me upon my departure from Damascus to France." During the immediate period after Odette's arrest, with the police frantically looking for him, he stayed hidden by passing nights in a school classroom, which he had to vacate early each following morning. Then, for the next three hours, he attended masses, one after the other, in the city's Catholic churches and chapels. "No practicing Catholic attended so many masses in such a short time as I did," Abadi facetiously recalls. With danger his constant companion, Abadi continued his rescue operation almost single-handedly until Nice's liberation in August 1944. Immediately after the war, he turned over the children's list to Jewish organizations, including information on the current whereabouts of the 527 children, so they could be fetched and reunited with their families and loved ones. After marrying Odette, upon her miraculous survival, he returned to his old interest, the theater, this time as a dramatic art critic on French radio, where he hosted a special program for 22 years.

Abadi's spectacular rescue operation was all but forgotten until recent years, when as earlier alluded, his name cropped up in stories of French rescuers awarded the Yad Vashem Righteous title. The Abadis believed that their rescue of over 500 children did not merit them any honors, for they had simply carried out an elementary humanitarian duty. As stated by Abadi in 1995, two years before his death, during a gathering with a group of his former wards: "There is no need for you to thank us, for you owe us nothing. It is us who are in debt to you," for having naively believed that an event such as the Holocaust could not happen, and therefore neglecting to take preventive measures in time. On that occasion, the first and last such public exposure by the self-effacing Abadi couple, Moussa borrowed an expression from the French author Antoine de St. Exupéry, that one must try to outdo oneself and go to the limit of oneself; that "one must always try to cross over the clouds." Myself and Odette, Moussa humbly stated, we "tried to pass through the clouds." He then added: "We were simply there at the right time and the right place." His parting words were a call not to forget the children of Ruanda, Somalia, and Sarajevo. As he spoke, he riveted his attentive audience with the words: "Do not accept that in this world one kills. Be on guard; be arousers; talk to your children and grandchildren. Talk, yell and scream."

Not able to bear the loss of her beloved Moussa, two years after his passing in 1997, Odette wrote farewell letters to her close friends, and took her life.[15] While still alive, Moussa and Odette Abadi, whose single-handed operation saved the lives of over 500 children, were eventually recognized by their own wards — but, sadly, overlooked by the Jewish community.

Moussa and Odette Abadi

Denise Siekierski and Joseph Bass

The Vast Network of Mr. André

I first met Denise Siekierski in 1984, when she came to Yad Vashem to give
testimony for two women, Emilie Guth and Hermine Orsi, who had helped
Jews avoid deportation, and with whom she recently had renewed contact
in Marseilles. She asked that these two persons be awarded the Righteous
title. At the time, Denise did not divulge her own involvement in a large-
scale rescue operation that lasted over two years. This operation became
more apparent in subsequent years, as she wrote about her war experience,
and after the information she provided was corroborated by documentation
already on hand in Yad Vashem archives. Denise Siekierski turned out to
be an important link in a Jewish clandestine rescue network who contributed,
more than one originally suspected of this self-effacing person, to the rescue
of hundreds of Jews in southern France.

She was born in Marseilles, in 1924, the daughter of Jacques and Andrée
Caraco. Her father had moved to France from Turkey, where he was born,
and opened a women's lingerie shop in Marseilles. He married Andrée
Benchimol, who had come to France from Palestine, where she was born in
the new pioneering settlement of Zichron Yaakov.[16] The marriage between
Jacques and Andrée did not go well, and when Denise was born, the two
had already separated; Denise was partly raised by her mother, who never
remarried, but more so by her grandparents and uncle. At home, her mother
and the rest of the family did not follow the rituals of the Jewish faith and,
as a young girl, Denise even joined the *Unionistes*, a Protestant scout movement. The ambiance at home was strongly French patriotic. Denise's uncle,
Emile Benchimol, had fought for France in World War One, and lost an arm.

When the war broke out in 1939, Denise was 15 years of age, and not
particularly conscious of her Jewish attachment. The war, with its anti-Jewish
persecutions, sensitized her to her Jewish identity which evolved into a
commitment to helping her brethren avoid deportation to the camps. Events
in Marseilles for Jews, however, at first moved at a slower pace than in other
regions of the defeated country, and many French-born and naturalized Jews
were oblivious of the dangers facing them. When all Jews (citizens and non-
naturalized) were ordered by the Vichy regime to register, her family
dutifully obeyed, since "this was the law." In the meantime, Denise
graduated from high school and dreamed of a journalistic career in the
French colonies. But the anti-Jewish laws of the government excluded her
acceptance into the university. Instead, she decided to become active in
Jewish affairs. In September 1941, she was inspired by Robert Gamzon

(known as *Castor*), who headed the Jewish scout movement, to better her Jewish commitment by joining his movement.[17] The encounter with Gamzon was for many an edifying experience which led to a transformation and reawakening of their Jewish identity. Denise describes him as a person dedicated to Jewish causes, who "influenced me and my friends for the rest of our life. He was thin, with shining eyes, smiling, and authoritative."

In the meantime, in August 1942, the French police in Marseilles launched its first massive roundup of Jews, who were imprisoned in the Des Milles camp—a former brick manufacturing firm. At the time, Denise was not in Marseilles but in Lautrec, in the Toulouse region, one of the farm schools headed by Gamzon's scout movement, where students deepened their knowledge of Judaism, while tilling the soil and doing various farm and household chores. The Sabbath was set aside for prayer and togetherness. In August 1942, Denise was asked to escort four foreign-born Jewish girls, speaking poor French, and in danger of arrest, to a rabbi in Limoges who was to take them to a secret place. While in Limoges, Denise attended a leadership course by the Jewish Scouts at Chateau Montintin. There, as part of the seminar, Denise and others were sent to scour the countryside, so as to find possible sheltering places for foreign-born teenagers (including refugees from Germany), who had entered the country after 1936, and were in danger of arrest and internment. These persons had to be spirited away from their homes before and during anticipated raids by the French police, of which they were forewarned by a friendly official in the Vichy government in charge of foreign workers.[18] Denise relates: "we stopped accidentally at whatever farm, and asked, 'you know that there are Jewish children at Chateau Montin-tin. . . It seems that the Germans are going to arrest the children as well. Are you willing to admit one in your home'?" The responses were mixed.

When Denise returned to Marseilles, in mid-September 1942, she learned of the arrest of foreign-born Jews, the previous month, and their internment at the nearby Camp des Milles. In Marseilles, she joined a clandestine Jewish group, who acted surreptitiously to help Jews, who had entered the country after 1936 (who numbered in the thousands) to avoid their arrest and deportation by the Vichy authorities. Included in this voluntary aid group were civic and religious leaders, such as Theo Klein, Rabbi Sammy Klein, professor Adrien Benveniste, Jules Isaac, the future historian Holocaust historian Léon Poliakov, and Joseph Bass (of whom more will be told later), as well as OSE-children organization social workers (including the non-Jewish nurse Emilie Guth).[19] This informal group worked clandestinely to help camp internees find hiding places, either with Jewish French citizens, who at the time were not in immediate danger of deportation, or in non-Jewish homes and institution.[20] Noteworthy among the non-Jewish helpers were Father de Parceval, of the Dominican order, and Father Marie-Benoit, of the Capuchin order. People at Camp des Milles willing to plunge into an illegal type of existence, naturally outside the camp's perimeter, were instructed to ask for a pass to ostensibly visit the OSE dispensary in Marseilles, since medical facilities were lacking in the camp. They had to leave their credentials behind before receiving the one-day *laissez-passer* permit. Once at the OSE dispensary, they were told to return in the evening, after the offices had formally closed, when they would be helped to flee and be sheltered elsewhere. This worked well for a time, since the OSE was at the time still recognized by the Vichy government, and was assisted by a group of non-Jewish religious figures.

The illegal methods used by Denise and her colleagues consisted mainly of fabricating false identities, especially from inside a "laboratory" set up in Benveniste's home. "We did not actually fabricate but 'washed' them," Denise recalls. That is, during the initial period, the original letters on the certificates were removed or changed to suit the new and false ones — new code-names or altogether false names. Already, during her 1935 Scout period, Denise's 'totem' name was *Colibri* — hummingbird — the name friends affectionately still call her to this day. Against her objection, her mother had her registered as Jewish, in obeisance of the law, not suspecting that this would later be used against them. When Denise later learned, through her contacts, that all Jews would have a bold '*Juif*,' in red, stamped on their identity cards, she decided on a gambit. She presented herself at the local police and concocted a story that she had misplaced and probably lost her handbag, which contained her identity card. Told to return in 48 hours, in the hope the handbag would turn up, the friendly police commissioner then issued her a new identity card, in her true name — Denise Caraco — on the basis of her birth certificate and two photos. She now possessed two identical i.d. cards. When, in December 1942, a new edict officially enforced the '*Juif*' marking on Jewish-held identification cards, Denise had it done on her new card, and her compliance was dutifully noted. She then fetched her previous card, the one she claimed she had lost, and which did not carry the "incriminating" *Juif* marking, and carried it with her when traveling and outside her home, without fearing that she would be identified as Jewish if stopped by the police. Her non-Jewish sounding name served as added protection.

With the German occupation of Marseilles, and the whole Vichy zone, in November 1942, this large metropolis too became unsafe for hiding purposes. It was necessary to find alternate shelters in outlying and off-the-beaten-track localities, as well as to smuggle people across the Swiss border. Denise's work, still as part of the Jewish scout organization (known as the "sixth"), now comprised the following activities:

1) Finding refuge homes in various places. Denise recalls a wintry evening, walking from a certain railway station in the dark (her flashlight battery had gone out) in the snow, for a distance of 8 kilometers to a certain priest's home with a letter from Father Benoit asking for his colleague's help in finding a hiding place for Jews.[21]

2) Fabrication of false documents with the help of persons who had become so good at this expertise, that the French underground sought their service as well.

3) Guiding persons to hiding places or to the Swiss and Spanish borders. Once, Denise accompanied a group of people on a train ride to Annemasse, on the Swiss border. Armed with false credentials, with French sounding names, they were told to stay in separate compartments, and not utter a word in Yiddish, these people's mother tongue. After a light nap, Denise decided to check on her group. She frantically looked for them in their prearranged compartments but found them missing — finally locating them in one area, and terrified to hear them speaking loudly among themselves in Yiddish, minutes before a police inspection team was to board the train. She angrily told them to hurry back to their separate compartments and refrain from speaking Yiddish. The group successfully passed the inspection.

4) Social work, such as monthly visits to persons in their hiding places to make sure they were well treated, and distributing money and ration card.

5) Liaison work, including traveling to various places (Marseilles, Nice, Lyon, Grenoble and the Haute Loire region), carrying many documents, such as false credentials and ration cards. Denise's ploy was to stuff these incriminating items in her knapsack, and cover it with spoiled food. The unpalatable smell emitting from the suddenly-opened baggage was enough to discourage the inspectors from proceeding further. Of course, this was always fraught with danger. In her case, the gamble always paid off.

Joseph Bass, one of the members of the informal Jewish clandestine group in Marseilles, was known under different names, but usually as *Monsieur André*. He eventually created his own rescue network, which he named *Action Group Against Deportation*. Taking advantage of his good contacts with various clergymen, he enlisted them in a major rescue operation for persons sought by the Germans and the French police, mostly Jews but not necessarily so, by either finding hiding places in France, such as in the Protestant enclave of Le Chambon, or spiriting them across the border into Spain or most usually, Switzerland. Bass was not an easy person to work for nor contend with. He was known for his authoritarian style and temper, his large blue eyes, and deep voice. "One could either love or detest him," Denise admits; "but one could not help being impressed by him." The future historian Léon Poliakov, who for a time was also part of Bass's team, described him in the following somewhat doubtful flattering terms:

> *André (as he preferred to be called) was unquestionably what the English term 'conspicuous.' Tall and heavy, he appeared larger and bigger than life. He possessed the ability to dominate by his presence the place where he happened to be. It was impossible not to take note of him. This is hard to explain. Those who knew André will understand me – he was cordial and noisy; he thrust himself [on others].*[22]

Another eyewitness described him as a "bon vivant, who loved all the good things in life. . . classical music, books, exchange of ideas, action, risks, humor." He was "open minded, with a total lack of prejudices. . . A Jew conscious of his roots, but without any superiority or inferiority complexes . . . who deeply felt as a brother to all men." At the same time, he was also known for his mercurial temper, which sometimes cast a cloud over his better qualities.[23]

Born in Grodno, Belarus, in 1908, he arrived in Paris alone, at the age of 16. He supported himself by working as a stevedore at the Halles open-air market, while studying for his *baccalaureat* (equivalent to an advanced high school degree); then, while working in a factory, he simultaneously continued his studies in engineering and law. He then dealt as a legal counsel in cases arising out of industrial holdings. On the eve of the war, in 1939, he prudently had his business office registered under the name of his non-Jewish partner, Madeleine Rocca. Interned by the Vichy authorities as still officially a Soviet citizen, he made his escape and arrived in Marseilles, where he earned a living working as a teacher in industrial drawing in a Jewish religious school. After the massive roundup of Jews by the French police, in August 1942, he decided to dedicate himself to the rescue of persons threatened by deportation. After a short spell of affiliation with the Theo Klein group, mentioned earlier, he created his own network, the *Action Group Against Deportation*, but better known as *Service André*. The main financial support for his activity came from Maurice Brener, the American Joint representative, but also from the income of his Paris office, presently operated by his non-Jewish partner Madeleine Rocca (known as "Mickey"), who intermittently visited him in Marseilles.

In the meantime, after occupying the Vichy zone, the Germans had allocated several provinces on the Franco-Italian border to their Italian ally, and this newly-created zone (including Nice), which lasted from December 1942 to September 1943, proved a haven for Jews, with many of them flocking there. Bass was in principle opposed to the concentration of so many Jews in any one place, and instead favored their dispersion in as many localities as possible, as a better insurance for their safety. The Protestant pastors Leenhardt and Heuzé referred him to their colleague André Trocmé, in Le Chambon-sur-Lignon, who agreed to open his Protestant enclave, in the hilly region of Haute-Loire, as a refuge for hundreds and thousands of Jews. It was one of the poorest areas in that region, and inhabited by a Protestant community that took the Bible literally; considered the Jewish people God's own chosen, and to be protected from the Nazis. They lived an austere existence, and were suspicious of all authority, obeying only their conscience and their religious leaders. With the help of his Protestant colleagues, including Jean Severin Lemaire, in Marseilles, Bass now led and directed hundreds of people to the Le Chambon area where they were housed and cared for, with monthly allowances disbursed to the sheltering families. In Le Chambon, the usual meeting place was the Hotel May, where Jean and Eugénie May, the hotel's proprietors, opened their doors for short stays to arriving refugees, until arrangements had been made for their admittance with a host family. Denise often stayed at the hotel during her trips to the village, in 1943, on her rescue mission to arrange hiding places for Jews fleeing from the Marseilles and Nice regions. One of her local contacts was Simone Mairesse, who resided in nearby Mazet-Saint Voy, and who is credited with placing hundreds of people in sheltering homes, as well as providing them with false credentials and ration cards. In Chambon, as well, Denise met Hermine Orsi, a refugee from Mussolini's Italy, who for a while served as a cook and housekeeper at *Les Grillons,* one of the children's homes in Le Chambon, under the guidance of Daniel Trocmé (André Trocmé's distant cousin), where many Jewish children were sheltered. When Daniel Trocmé was arrested by the Germans, Hermine quickly dispersed the 45 Jewish children in surrounding farms. She then became the main escort of Jewish children from Marseilles to Le Chambon, and occasionally hid Jews in her home for brief spells of time.[24]

In Marseilles, in January 1943, Denise continued her clandestine work with the unofficial group of Jewish activists (while officially appearing as a Scout leader). That month, the Germans with the help of the French police suddenly staged a large-scale raid in the Old Port section of the city, netting many Jews who were deported. The city was infested with thousands of German and French police units, with controls at many road intersections. As a precautionary measure, Denise slept in a different place every night.[25] Jewish welfare and aid organizations, still tolerated by the Vichy regime, decided to cease their operations in Marseilles, due to the increasing danger there, and move elsewhere, with the exception of a small office, adjacent to the great synagogue. There, Denise met people during certain hours, to help them with ration cards and nominal money allotments. In this capacity, special attention was paid to persons who sought assistance in finding hiding places and acquiring false credentials. After their story had been checked several times over by Denise and appeared credible, they were directed to a certain address, where they would receive further instructions the following Sunday afternoon. The prearranged place was a large hall used as a Protestant temple, which was served by Pastor Jean Severin Lemaire, whose name was not disclosed to the people referred to this address. Since 1941, when he met Joseph Bass, Lemaire had become committed to help persons fleeing the Germans, including securing for them hiding places, in collaboration with other clergy, such as the Protestant Heuzé, the Dominican De Parceval, the Jesuit Bremond and the Capuchin monk Marie-Benoit, as well as the Jewish rabbis Israel Salzer and Hirschler and the banker Angelo Donati. Lemaire's religious service usually began at three in the afternoon, and was over well before five. Those sent there by Denise were told to mingle with the worshippers, but stay on after the service was over, and the Christian worshippers had left. Then, Lemaire and Denise (appearing as Mademoiselle Bertrand) would distribute false credentials, discuss their future flight into illegality and arrange hiding places for the Jewish persons who had stayed behind.

One had to be wary of the possibility of a Gestapo-planted agent among the stream of help-seekers. A Jew whose family was being held hostage by the Gestapo might collaborate, turning in Jews in hiding and those supporting them, in exchange for the safe release of his family. As a precautionary measure, Denise asked some help-seekers to return twice or three times for a further evaluation of their story. Over time, she developed a knack for this type of work and the people who approached her. Sure enough, as originally feared, one Gestapo agent was able to infiltrate this network and cause great havoc to its operations. In March 1943, a certain Dr. Siegfrid Levy (it was his real name), who claimed to be a Jewish refugee from Belgium, asked for assistance to continue his flight from the Gestapo, who were looking for him. He too was directed to that Protestant meeting place. Soon thereafter, Denise was informed by Joseph Bass, that his contacts in the French police had warned him that Dr. Levy was a Gestapo agent, and would surely lead the Germans to that address the following Sunday afternoon. Bass told Denise to immediately leave Marseilles to avoid arrest, since Dr. Levy had certainly given her description to the Gestapo, in spite of the fact that she had presented herself as Bertrand. Through a special exit from the Terminus hotel, which was filled with German officers, and which led directly inside the train station, Denise boarded a train which headed out of town. Alighting in Grenoble, she joined Theo Klein, as she had previously been instructed to do in case of danger.

That same day, Joseph Bass hurriedly met Pastor Lemaire who had just returned from an out of town conference, and warned him not to show up at his prayer place, as the Gestapo would surely be waiting for him. However, Bass's pleading was to no avail, for Lemaire had in the meantime learned that two young men were wrongly arrested, as co-conspirators of the pastor. Lemaire's improvised temple was located in the back side of a building, which one accessed through a long corridor leading from the street sidewalk, which was adjacent to a bar. Gestapo agents, in ambush for the pastor to show up noticed two young men waiting for the bar to open in the afternoon hours. They mistook the men as the pastor's affiliates and promptly arrested them. The two men denied any complicity in whatever clandestine operation, but the Gestapo, suspecting otherwise, had them imprisoned. The bar owner, who had just arrived on the scene to open his place and witnessed the two men's arrest, hurried to alert Lemaire, who decided to turn himself in so as to have the two innocent men released. He told Bass, when they met in a restaurant, that it was a question of principle for him. To prevent Lemaire's self-sacrifice, the proud and conceited Bass went down on his knees and begged the pastor to save his neck and flee, but to no avail. "It was for me a moral duty to nevertheless be there;" Lemaire wrote in his testimony, "and, if necessary, allow myself to be arrested so that the two persons, not known to me, should be freed." So, on the following Sunday afternoon services, on March 14, 1943, Lemaire showed up at his prayer hall; within moments, the Gestapo had the street cordoned off with armored vehicles and fully-armed men, and Lemaire was apprehended and taken away. Despite a grilling investigation, accompanied with bludgeon beatings and cursing by four Gestapo agents, the pastor held his own and refused to divulge information on his Jewish rescue co-conspirators. Finally, he was told he would be moved to a cell with Jewish occupants: "Since you love the Jews so much, we will place you with them," the Gestapo officer sarcastically remarked. He was thrown in a cell of some twenty imprisoned Jews, of all ages, including a four-year-old girl, who was ill with smallpox, and a 18-month-old baby. There, for two months, he shared the pains and miseries of the others. Lemaire successfully convinced the Germans it was in their own interest to free the sick child, to avoid being contaminated with her disease.[26] As for the baby, he pleaded that she be given milk. He had to watch as one Jewish woman who suffered from diabetes, and who was refused the insulin which she needed, died with great suffering, and in full view of her husband and her children. After one year's imprisonment in this and other jails, in March 1944, Lemaire was sent to Dachau, then to Mauthausen camp, where he stayed until liberation day, in May 1945.[27] Of the 2,800 persons on that convoy, only 52 survived. Weighing only 49 kilos, as against the 84 kilos at the start of his Dolorosa, he returned to France in poor health; sick, tired, "and asking nothing from no one and receiving nothing from no one; only seeking rest, tranquillity and peace."[28] Reminiscing on the agony sustained at the hands of the Germans, he reemphasized: "I do not regret what has happened, nor the decision taken by me. As a Christian and a pastor, I had to be a witness without worrying about the consequences."[29]

In the meantime, arriving in Grenoble, for a time Denise continued her work as a liaison person for the *Sixth*. Returning to Marseilles, in June 1943, she checked on her family, who were for the time safely ensconced in a different locality, and not exactly knowing what to do next, she took a stroll on the Canebière, the city's main promenade boulevard — and ran straight into Joseph Bass. "Isn't it Colibri?" he accosted her; "What, may I ask you're doing here?" Denise told of her visit to relatives in Vaucluse, as well as her grandmother in a Marseilles clinic. "This is not what I had in mind," he quickly retorted, hinting that he had alluded to her clandestine work. "Nothing, Mr. André; I've resigned from the *Sixth*." "So you're doing nothing?" André pounded back; "and for how long?" "Just three days." "This is three days too much," Bass replied. "Since you're doing nothing, you're going to work for me." "Doing what?" Bass assumed an angry tone. "I beg of you, don't act the choir girl. You know exactly what I am involved in." "I need to think it over." "Fine, let's have a drink." After a short stop in a coffee shop, André again confronted her: "It's been half an hour that we've been here. Have you thought about it?" Denise wanted to say that she needed more time to reflect, but heard herself saying: "Well, it's yes." "Good," André quickly responded. "Meet me tomorrow morning, 8 a.m., under the staircase of the train station. We're leaving for Nice." "This is how I joined the *Service André*," Denise later wrote in her testimony. "I was the only young one [in this network] — I was 19 years old."

Life with Mr. André was anything but safe and peaceful; it was, on the contrary, exciting, difficult and dangerous. Gifted with a fabulous memory, and contenting himself with only four hours of sleep, he was a beehive of activity. To add to the risks involved in working with a man of his caliber and idiosyncrasy, on his many trips to plan additional rescue operations, he always traveled first-class, and chose the most flamboyant and expensive restaurants for his gargantuan meals — both usually visited by German officers or underworld mobsters. These measures, he explained to the rather surprised Denise, were for reasons of "prudence." That is, that coupled with his large and heavy physique, his leather coat, the deep voice, the furtive look in his eyes and the prominent leather-case (which was filled with forgeries) — his ventures into the lion's den were to fool passersby and onlookers into believing he was either a Gestapo agent, a top French collaborator with the Germans, or a criminal boss of the notorious Marseilles underworld, and thus remain safe from arrest by the various German and French police security agencies. Denise, who rented a room in a small hotel, occasionally traveled with him, and served as his constant administrative companion.

After the Germans swept into Nice, in September 1943, the dangers increased for Bass's operations. In addition, a non-Jewish nurse named Anne-Marie Quilici, of Corsican origin, who was affiliated with André's network, turned out to be a double agent and occasionally betrayed to the Gestapo persons linked with André's operation. Denise herself luckily escaped arrest on September 23, 1943, minutes before a scheduled appointment with one of her underground coworkers. Finally, toward the end of 1943, André decided to move his base of operations further north, near St. Etienne, to a small hotel owned by Oswaldo Bardone, a former comrade-in-arms of Poliakov whom the latter met while the two were in a prisoner-of-war camp. Earlier, when Poliakov was in danger of arrest in Marseilles, Bardone came to fetch him and arranged for him a job in St. Etienne under a false name. Poliakov now persuaded his friend to allow the André network to install its operations from his restaurant, in La Ricamarie, near St. Etienne. Bardone's restaurant (code-named *Inn of the Musicians*) now served as the group's operation center.[30]

In addition to his vast-scale rescue operation, Bass felt that Jews should not content themselves with hiding from the Germans but also contribute to the military struggle against their enemy. As was his style, he immediately translated this thought into action when he arrived in the Le Chambon area. Assembling a small contingent of Jewish partisans, men and women who sneaked out of their hiding places at night, he saw to it that they receive proper military training, and appropriate weapons from other partisans units. Here too, Denise lent an active hand, carrying weapons, such as pistols and rifles, from one location to another. In addition, Bass mingled with soldiers of the German army, formerly Russian prisoners-of-war and Tartar volunteers from the steppes of Russia, who had enlisted in the German army, and urged them to desert and join the French underground. He distributed among them news in the form of leaflets, reporting the real situation on the various fronts, rather than German propaganda, which showed the Germans steadily withdrawing and losing the war. During the liberation of France, following the Normandy invasion by the Allies, in June 1944, Bass's Jewish partisans fought German troops on their way to relieve their fighting comrades, which resulted in close to a thousand of them surrendering to a battalion commanded by Bass—by now, an officer in the French resistance (known as FFI).[31]

In the meantime, the situation in Marseilles remained dangerous for André's affiliates. On a working visit to Marseilles, in March 1944, Denise narrowly escaped arrest for the second time, while André managed to fight his way out of an actual arrest. On her way to Emilie Guth to deliver money and false credentials for people in hiding, she was warned by the hotel proprietor where she was staying that the Gestapo was looking for her. Her meeting with Guth was to take place at 4 p.m., in the insurance company office of Max Castelli, who was active in the French underground. This time, what saved her was her late arrival, as she learned that Castelli and Guth had been picked up by the Gestapo minutes before. She immediately left Marseilles and returned to Le Puy, in the Le Chambon region. Guth, not Jewish, nor carrying incriminating documents on her, was released after several weeks of imprisonment.[32] Castelli, on the other hand, was deported to a concentration camp, where he died. As for Joseph Bass, he was arrested in a restaurant and hand-cuffed. Before being taken to Gestapo headquarters, he asked for permission to pick up something at his apartment. While there, he offered his captor several glasses of wine, then knocked him unconscious with his handcuffs, snatched the key from the floored police agent and released himself; he handcuffed his captor, and fled the city.

After the war, Denise married, bore two children, left for Israel, and joined a newly-established kibbutz. Family obligations forced Denise and her husband to return to France; thence, for a long stay in Brazil, and finally returning to Israel in 1978, where she now lives in Jerusalem, doing various voluntary organizational work. For a final estimation of Denise Siekierski's work, perhaps it is best to listen to historian Léon Poliakov. In his words:

> Colibri, the 19 year old scout – always on the move; her blue eyes seeming to look at the world with wonder. However, make no mistake, this young maiden meant business. Colibri slept in trains, took her meals in train stations and breakfast in post offices; her coworkers numbered in the dozens, spread over the whole of southeast France – maintaining contact with various leaders, being scowled by André. . . Colibri acted as a fish in water. She began her clandestine work straight out of her high-school bench. . . Small Colibri was André's principal assistant. Everything passed through her hands; nothing was done without her [knowledge].[33]

Her guiding life-philosophy has been and remains the following motto: "That everyone, in his time and generation, and within his possibilities and behavior, should try to do something for the Jewish people." Persons like Joseph Bass and Denise Siekierski, and the others in their league, certainly deserve a marked place of honor in the annals of Jewish heroism during the Holocaust. Under the most difficult circumstances imaginable, they braved dangers to themselves (and some paid with their lives) to save their Jewish brethren from the Nazi inferno. In France, these clandestine networks are credited with the rescue of up to 10,000 children—an achievement of no mean consequence. Certainly, a way can be found for such deeds to be applauded, and their authors accorded a dignified recognition.

Denise Siekierski   One of Siekierski's false papers

Josef Bass ("André"), center, with members of his fighting team in the Chambon area.

Andrée Geulen— Godmother to 300 children

As this book was about to go to press, a recent conference on the Holocaust which took place in Oxford, England afforded me the privilege of renewing my acquaintance with one of the legendary, and thankfully still living, giant rescuers of Jewish children in Belgium. During a break in the conference, I sat down with the 79-year-old Andrée Geulen, under a July sun, in one of the university's spacious and well-tended lawns, to listen to her recollections of the days when being a Jewish child meant being condemned to death, and her undertaking to save them from the Nazis.

Born in 1921 in Brussels into a well-to-do middle class, non-practicing Catholic family, Andrée was oblivious to the presence of Jews at the school which she attended. "Between us," she recalls, "we did not talk about the differences between Jews and non-Jews." To press her point, she mentioned that only during the war did she find out the family's doctor was Jewish. When she asked why the doctor stopped coming, she was told that her father was hiding him somewhere. "Hiding his doctor! I was surprised." In her bourgeois neighborhood, one made no distinction between Jew and non-Jew, as they did in the immigrant neighborhood.

The young Andrée was rebellious by nature, opposing the established order. She had taken an interest in the fate of refugees from the Spanish Civil War, and was also involved with the Red Cross in placing Jewish children arriving from Vienna under the *Kindertransport* program. Then, in May 1940, came the German invasion and occupation of Belgium.

That year Andrée decided to study Latin. However, when the Germans fired the Jewish lecturers at the Brussels university, the school reacted by closing its doors. Andrée enrolled instead in a teachers seminary, and in 1941 received her certificate and began teaching. One day, several of her Jewish students came to class wearing the compulsory Yellow Star. "It was the first time," Andrée recalls, "I came face to face with the persecution of Jews in Belgium. Until then I was not conscious of the anti-Jewish measures in Belgium." She then ordered all her pupils to wear an apron to school, so that the five Jewish children would not have to display their special insignia. "One day I did not see them again; they were picked up in a Nazi raid and deported."

At the time, Andrée also taught at the *Gaty de Gamont* boarding school, headed by Odile Ovart, where she discovered about a dozen Jewish pupils in hiding—brought there by Ida Sterno, a Jewish operative for the clandestine Jewish Defense Committee (CDJ). Ida needed a non-Jewish assistant, to accompany children on the streets and on trolley rides, on the way to their new hiding places. Andrée immediately volunteered. "I wanted to do something. I was impatient; something had to be done, and here came the opportunity." At the time she did not know Ida was Jewish. She was given a new code-name—Claude Fournier—and a false address, and was told from now on not stay with her parents, but move to the boarding school, where she was assigned her own quarters. It was the start of her clandestine work to save Jewish children. Ida Sterno, originally from Romania, headed the children placement section at the CDJ, under the direct supervision of Maurice Heiber and the overall leadership of Yvonne Jospa, both Jewish operatives.

In May 1943, tragedy struck the boarding school. The Gestapo raided the compound in the middle of the night, armed with large flashlights, shouting for everyone to get up. Someone had betrayed them. Since it was the Pentecost holiday, all non-Jewish children had been sent home and only the Jewish ones remained. "I suspect that a parent of one of the non-Jewish children had reported us to the Germans." The Gestapo lined up all the children, and ordered: "every Jew, to the right; every non-Jew, to the left." The Gestapo, nevertheless, took all 12 children, as well as 11 adults who were also hiding there, away for deportation. The Gestapo also interrogated Mrs. Ovart, asking her why she did it. She responded: "I am Belgian, not German, and I don't check one's credentials." She was struck on the face. Andrée's turn came next: "What are your doing here?" I said: "I give lessons." The Gestapo man continued: "Aren't you ashamed to teach Jews?" I responded: "Aren't you ashamed to make war on Jewish children?" The Gestapo man responded: "If one doesn't want to suffer from bugs, one must squash them when they're small."

Andrée luckily escaped arrest. Not so for Odile Ovart, the school's head-mistress, and her husband Remy, who were respectively deported to the Ravensbrück and Buchenwald concentration camps, where both perished. The couple's daughter, named Andrée, spent six months in prison." As for me—they told me to get out and not come back to this place." She then alerted other Jewish children, already on their way to the school, to stay away, and visited others in their homes, imparting the terrible news. She also reported to Ida, who was hiding at a convent. It was then, noticing the Yellow Star on Ida's clothes, that she learned she was Jewish. For Ida's safety, Andrée leased an apartment under her new name, where both stayed as they continued to expand their rescue work.[1]

Jewish persons in Belgium needing help first turned to various organizations to which they belonged. The organizations contacted the CDJ, which, in turn, contacted Ida and Andrée via a few post office boxes, one of which was located in an antiques shop, the other—at the JOC, the Catholic youth organization. Each time the two women went on a mission, they committed names and places to memory, as they did not dare to circulate with written information. The addresses of the children were kept in a secret notebook hidden at home. The notebook also listed other vital information, such as illnesses, and other data the host families needed to know about the children in their care. An additional copy was kept hidden with an CDJ associate. The effort made to keep a faithful record of the child's whereabouts also stemmed from the need to have the child reclaimed after the war, and returned to its own natural family. Another set of notebooks, five in all, listed the most vital information. On the first was the child's real name with a number; such as #10 — Appelbaum Annette. On the second — the number 10 plus the child parents' address; such as *Rue des Vierges*, Bruxelles. On the third — the number plus the child's new name — Appelmans. On the fourth — the various institutions with their code number; i.e., #400 for *Institut Réligieuse*, at Heverlée. Finally, on the fifth, the child's code number alongside that of the placement number. All these notebooks were kept at one address, on *Rue de la Brasserie*, in closets in separate rooms of an empty rented apartment.

Careful preparations were made before venturing out with the children. At first, the parents were visited to discuss the placement of their children, and whether they could share in some of the cost. The children were then taken under an assumed name to a few dispensaries, such as the one headed by Dr. Christine Hendrickx. Then, the parents were alerted for a possible date when the child would be picked up; this, after the child's new name, false credentials and ration cards, and a proper location had been arranged. Much effort was expended to find a suitable place, taking in consideration the child's background, knowledge of the language and looks, so as to mix better in the new surrounding. In one unusual case, a boy in hiding came down with scabies. Andrée took him to a hospital, where he was pronounced dead. Then, under a different name, Andrée placed him with a farmer's family.

Recalling those days, filled with fear of arrest and hope for the children's welfare, Andrée reminisced:

> *Ida and myself would go to pick up the children of the parents who turned to us for help. We told the parents to prepare a suitcase, and we would return in a day or two. I was afraid I might get arrested when I walked with a child next to me. I still weep when I think of the times when I had to snatch children from their parents, especially children 2-3 years of age, without being able to tell the parents where I was taking the children. Surprisingly, the children willingly accompanied us. In some cases, the children told their parents not to weep. We told the children that due to the shortages of food in the city and the threat of air raids, we were taking them to the countryside to enjoy fresh air, food and a good life. So they went willingly. I estimate I accompanied about 300 chldren this way by myself.*

There were, of course, more escorts, such as Brigitte Moens, who was in charge of contacts with Catholic institutions, and of placement in the countryside. "I am not a believer," Andrée freely admits; "however, I will concede that the low-ranking clergy (such as Joseph André, in Namur, and Bruno Reynders, in Louvain) helped us greatly, and without their assistance, we would not have achieved much. Most of the boarding schools were, in fact, under Catholic supervision." Pierre Capart, in charge of the Catholic youth movement, made sure that none of the children under his supervision would be exposed to any overt and subtle attempt to convert them. In general, children over seven years of age were placed in institutions (such as the Leopold III homes, and the earlier-mentioned children home at Jamoigne-sur-Semois, in the Ardennes region), while younger children were placed in private homes.

Once in their new homes, the children began to miss their parents, who were forbidden to visit them, to avoid entrapment. Understandably, many experienced severe mental torment, as they tried to grapple with their new and old identities, as in the following story: A five-year-old boy, placed with a host family, stole and hid a decorative religious artifact, depicting the Virgin and Child in their Bethlehem manger, which the family's eight-year-old girl had received as a gift for Christmas. Questioned on this, after a long silence, the boy timidly admitted: "Little Jesus and the Holy Virgin are Jews; so I hid them. The Gestapo will not have them." Overcome with emotion, he then burst out in tears.

Andrée and her coworkers were constantly on the go, while at the same time trying to outwit the Gestapo and its planted collaborators, to avoid arrest and losing the children.[2] Of the 12 persons who worked under Heiber's supervision on behalf of the children, many were arrested (including Heiber), Jews and non-Jews alike; some were deported, and some did not survive. Ida Sterno's arrest came on May 29, 1944, while conferring with an associate (who was temporarily exempt from deportation), in a Brussels restaurant. Before being led away, she managed to slip some incriminating papers under the table on one of the adjoining chairs, which was hidden from view by an oversized table-cloth. Under questioning, Ida explained her not wearing the obligatory Yellow Star in public on the grounds of being married to a non-Jewish spouse. She was then imprisoned in Malines/Mechelen camp (the main transit camp in Belgium, for Jews on their way to the concentration camps in Poland), where she was assigned to undo pullovers of executed prisoners, in order to recycle the wool for the German war effort. She was fortunate not to be deported, and lived to see the liberation, in September 1944. Luckily for Andrée, she was on her way home on foot (the tramways had stopped running due to an air bombardment alert). Arriving home, she noticed the locks on her ground-floor apartment door.

A neighbor told her to leave immediately, for only seconds before the Gestapo had raided the house. She then hid in various places, continuing Ida's work by herself until the country's liberation. Not forgetting her friend and coworker, Andrée visited Ida at Malines – of course, under a different name. In her words: "When one is filled with self-confidence, when one is on a mission, one does not think about the dangers."

Upon liberation, the work continued, but in reverse direction – to locate the close to 3,000 children and return those who had survived to their parents. Here too, while the war was still on, care had to be taken to either leave the children for the time being with their host families or institutions, until their parents (many of whom were still incarcerated in various German-controlled camps) or other relatives came to reclaim them. In many instances, persons returning from the camps were not yet fit to resume a normal life, and the children had to be cared for a while by various Jewish agencies. Andrée continued her charitable work, dealing with persons returning from the camps. "My job consisted in reuniting family members." Parents who were not in a position to care for their children, were supplied with necessary basic provisions, such as beds and mattresses, as a first step for their return to a normal life. This went on until 1948. She then worked for 30 years at the Social Security office. In 1948, Andrée was married. "My parents did not object when I presented them with my Jewish husband-to-be, Charles Herscovici, whose parents perished in the camps." The couple raised two daughters and are grandparents to five grandchildren. "My husband is a well-known attorney. My youngest daughter is an attorney; her husband as well. My other daughter is a sociologist and a member in the *Green* movement. My daughters consider themselves Jewish, although they're non-believers."

During the post-war years, Andrée never stopped seeing the children she saved. One of her great satisfactions is stopping a former child on the way to work or back home to his or her family. As for herself,

I deserve nothing for what I did. I am not a hero. It is true, that when the war ended I felt satisfaction for what I did. At the same time, I did not seek recognition or medals. I had the privilege of being a teacher and to see things that others did not see and know. Those who refused to help – I do not condemn them. There is fear. I do not say that what I did was the normal thing to do; perhaps it also has to do with my character – of fighting injustice. . . Back in the 1930's I was politically involved, during the Spanish Civil War. At the same time, my truly greatest satisfaction in life was meeting the man with whom I live over 50 years.

During her underground work she told all sorts of stories to her parents, to explain her long absences. After the war, when her family learned of her wartime activities, they all took pride in her. "My father said: 'I always suspected you were doing something forbidden.'"

Before taking leave of this extraordinary person, I asked her what was the event that triggered her decision to take part in such a vast and highly risky undertaking. After some reflection, she responded that once, during the period when she worked as a teacher, at the *Gaty de Gamont* boarding school, she went to tuck the Jewish children who were hidden there into their bunks. "As I kissed one of the boys, he said he wished to tell me a secret, but not to tell anyone. 'I am in fact, Jewish, and my real name is so and so.' I then said to myself, 'What kind of a world are we living when a child must hide his true name? It is a world turned upside down!' To arrest a child was something of a shock for many Belgians who, at first, did not think to help. But, to harm children! It was then that many decided to take in a child." It was then that Andrée also became fully committed to her rescue work.

At the Oxford conclave, the conferees presented learned papers on various aspects of the Holocaust. For myself, the most impressive event was meeting Andrée Geulen-Herscovici, the diminutive person with a giant heart of gold (awarded the Righteous title in 1989), whose presence remained unknown to most of the delegates—a person who holds the record of preserving the life of 300 children; and with her brave companions, Jews and non-Jews alike, a total of 3,000 children.[3]

Above: Andrée Geulen's wartime secret notebook. Right: Andrée Geulen today.

Appendix C

The Unknown Righteous

The over 17,000 rescuers so far honored with the Righteous title by Yad Vashem represent only a fraction of the thousands of others rescuers, throughout Nazi-dominated Europe, whose names remain unknown to us. In some cases, survivors recall with great precision the circumstances of their rescue but not the name of their rescuer, and this causes them much anguish when they wish to nominate their rescuers for the Yad Vashem Hall of Fame. As in the following letter, from an Israeli woman, received in 1989:

Dear Sir,

I saw the TV program "This is your life" on Efrayim Kishon (a noted Israeli satirist; the program dealt with the man's rescuer in Hungary), and I said to myself that this Gentile was lucky; for he lived to be acknowledged for his deeds. I too have a Gentile, but his fate is not known. And that is why my conscience gives me no rest. Here's the story.

On the first day of the war between Germany and Russia, my eldest uncle gathered his widowed sister with her 35-year old son, his second sister with her husband (who were approximately 60 years of age), his brother, wife and her paralyzed mother with their 12-year-old daughter. . . We proceeded on our journey in a carriage drawn by two horses and arrived at a village where we found lodging at a farmer's family in return for payment. There we naively waited for the war to end.

After one or two nights, very late at night, the farmer awakened us with shouting and insisted we leave his house with all our belongings, for the Germans were 15 kilometers from the village, and he was told that they were killing anyone who was sheltering Jews or their property. . . We fled for our lives towards the east, in the direction of the Dniester river, in order to cross it into Russia proper. My parents and myself went on foot. From all our belongings we took only those items which served as seat supports for the elderly ones. We only stopped at night, for the competition between our horses and the German tanks was "a bit unfair". . . On the third night, totally exhausted (our horses as well), we stopped off at a farmer's home, in a large village. We had barely helped the older persons off the carriage and entered the house, when we saw facing us 3 or 4 tall and heavily-built men. They stood next to the door, examining us with "murder in their eyes," and asking concerning our belongings and our money. They then left.

The men in our group interpreted this visit as a rehearsal for robbery and murder and it was immediately decided to leave and continue on our way. We stepped out, only to discover the whole village assembled in front of the house. We asked them gently to help us move eastwards but they refused; this, upon the instigation of the "head group," the ones that had inspected us when we arrived. Whenever someone suggested a willingness to help in return for a price, the heavily-built men made their voices heard and silenced the inquirer. They evidently expected the soon-to-be robbery to bring in more.

Our pleadings intensified, but no one moved. They all stood as a wall, in total silence and no movement. Suddenly, a youngish-looking man (about 20-30 years old) stood out from the group to the right and said: "I will take you." A stir arose around him with people murmuring that he renounce his intention. They also pointed out what awaited him afterwards. But he stood his ground. They continued insisting that he change his mind, when he suddenly shouted at them: "You wish to kill them, I will not allow it!". . . They screamed back at him: "The Germans will kill you if you help them escape." But he remained adamant.

A woman with a baby in her arms came running up to him from the left and implored: "If you do not have pity on me, if you don't care about yourself, protect the child; don't leave us by ourselves. They will kill them, and we have no bread to eat. If they tell the Germans, they will kill you. Why do you care about the Jews?"

Without responding to his wife, and without embracing the infant, the man loaded our family and our belongings on two carriages, and we left. I remember that night as if it were yesterday: A full moon, clear skies, a warm and beautiful night. The man took us on side roads, between fields with corn as high as a horse with rider. . . He took us out of the danger zone, bid us farewell and left. When my uncle and father wished to pay this honest and dear man, he categorically refused any payment. I remember when sitting in his carriage, my father asked him what he planned to do when he returned to the village, with the farmers so hostile toward him. He responded: "If they kill, let them kill. I have discharged my duty. I could not be a party to murder."

Perhaps there is a possibility of immortalizing the deed of this anonymous great man? You will probably ask, why I wasn't compelled earlier to tell about him? Well, my father died in 1954, and my mother did not remember the name of the village. My other relatives who were present during that episode, and were even older than us, remained in the Soviet Union. In their stereotyped letters, they did not respond to any of our inquiries, and now when correspondence is possible, they are no longer alive. That's it. I would be prepared to travel in order to search for the village, but I have no knowledge of the place, and Bessarabia is too large . . . I should be happy if something could be done."

While little, if anything, could be done to try to identify the name of that courageous man, a special monument has been erected at Yad Vashem to commemorate the Unknown Righteous of the Holocaust. As shown on the picture, the monument is sculptured of reddish granite stone. As it rises from the ground, it appears in the form of flames — the flames of the Holocaust. Then the faces of two persons appear. The one to the right covers his face — he does not wish to get involved. He represents the many bystanders during that period. To his left is the other — the Unknown Righteous who gazes straightforward, and below him is the image of a Jewish woman and her child, whom this person is sheltering. This monument is a token reminder of the debt owed by many to the untold thousands of knights of the spirit of that tragic period.

Monument to the Unknown Righteous at Yad Vashem.

Appendix D

Righteous Among the Nations — per Country and Ethnic Origin*

Yad Vashem — Dept. for the Righteous Among the Nations,
January 1, 2000

Poland	5,373
Netherlands	4,289
France	1,913
Ukraine	1,403
Belgium	1,172
Hungary	503
Lithuania	440
Belarus	389
Slovakia	354
Germany	336
Italy	266
Greece	231
Yugoslavia (all nations)[1]	213
Austria	83
Latvia	90
Czech Republic	80
Romania	55
Albania	56
Russia	45
Switzerland	27
Moldova	33
Denmark[2]	14
Bulgaria	13
Great Britain (incl. Scotland)	13

* These figures reflect information made available to Yad Vashem (Dept. For the Righteous) and should not be construed as indicative of the number of Jews saved in each country.

---

[1] Includes: Serbia — 105, Croatia — 65, Bosnia — 31, Macedonia — 9, Slovenia—3

[2] The Danish Underground requested that all its members who participated in the rescue of the Jewish community not be listed individually but as one group.

Norway	16
Sweden	7
Armenia	6
Spain	3
Estonia	2
China[3]	2
Brazil	1
Japan	1
Luxembourg	1
Portugal	1
Turkey	1
USA	1
Total:	**17,433**

---

[3] Rescue operation took place in Ukraine.

NOTES

Chapter 1 — *Setting the Stage*

[1] On the origins of the term "Holocaust," see Uriel Tal, "Holocaust," in Israel Gutman, ed., *Encyclopedia of the Holocaust* (New York: Macmillan, 1990), Vol. 2, p. 681.

[2] Statements by Hitler are taken from: Adolf Hitler, *Mein Kampf* (Munich: F. Eher, 1934), pp. 6, 63f., 70, 91, 169, 193, 253, 305; Joachim Fest, *Hitler* (New York: Harcourt, Brace Jovanovich, 1973), p. 212; Adolf Hitler, *Secret Conversations*. Introduction by H.R. Trevor-Roper (New York: Octagon Books, 1976) p. 269; Allan Bullock, *Hitler: a Study in Tyranny* (New York, 1964), p. 40; Max Domarus, *Hitler, Reden und Proklamationen* (Neustadt a.d. Aische: Schmidt, 1962-63), p. 2005; Phelps Reginald, "Hitlers 'Grundlegende' Rede über des Antisemitismus," in *Vierteljahrhefte für Zeitgeschichte 16* (1968); pp. 406, 415.

[3] Fest, p. 212; Domarus, pp. 1058; and Jeremy Noakes & Geoffrey Pridham eds, *Documents on Nazism: 1919-1945* (New York: Viking, 1975), p. 680.

[4] For more on Nazi anti-Jewish laws in Germany, see Raul Hilberg, *The Destruction of the European Jews* (New York: Harper & Row, 1979), pp. 5ff., and throughout book.

[5] There are various estimates of the actual number of Jews in hiding in Berlin. Some place it as high as several thousand. The exact figure is complicated due to the presence among the runaway Jews, those qualified by the Nazis as half- and quarter-Jews (based on racial definitions), and of baptized Jews, considered by the Nazis as "full-Jews." For more on Berlin Jews in hiding, see Leonard Gross, *The Last Jews in Berlin* (New York: Simon & Schuster, 1982).

[6] Hilberg, pp. 32ff.

[7] Other notoriously known camps and killing sites, include Janowska, Plaszow, Gross-Rosen, Maidanek, Stutthof in Poland; Fort 9 and Ponar in Lithuania; Rubola in Latvia; Jasonevac in Croatia; Sachsenhausen, Dachau, Bergen-Belsen, Ravensbrück, Neuengamme and Buchenwald in Germany; and Mauthausen in Austria. In France, Drancy camp served as the main conduit for the Jewish deportees, on their way to the concentration camps. Similarly for Malines/Mechelen, in Belgium, and Westerbork in the Netherlands.

[8] This, indeed, is the title chosen for her book, by the Holocaust historian Lucy Dawidowicz, *The War Against the Jews: 1933-1945* (New York: Holt, Rinehart & Winston, 1975).

[9] For more in-depth study of the Holocaust, the reader is referred to the

books by Hilberg and Dawidowicz (notes 4 and 8), as well as: Nora Levin, *The Holocaust: the Destruction of European Jewry* (New York: Schocken Books, 1973), and Y. Arad, I. Gutman , & A. Margaliot, eds., *Documents on the Holocaust* (Jerusalem: Yad Vashem, 1981).

[10] All stories mentioned in this study, unless otherwise indicated, are based on files at the Department for the Righteous, Yad Vashem, prefixed by code M31. Victor Kugler and Miep Gies, file 706; Malgorzata Wolski, file 4252; Jan Zabinski, file 170; Jonas Paulavicius, file 2472; Manko Szwierczszak, file 2644.

[11] Berthold Beitz, file 299; Julius Madritsch, file 21; Alfred Rossner, file 6239; Hermann Graebe, file 116; Oskar Schindler, file 20.

[12] Raoul Wallenberg, file 31; Giorgio Perlasca, file 3911; Carl Lutz, file 46; Angelo Rotta, file 7690.

[13] Tadeusz Soroka, file 2695; Arrigo Beccari, file 35; Beniamino Schivo, file 3362; Joop Westerweel, file 32; Aristides de Sousa Mendes, file 264; Jan Zwartendijk, file 7793; Chiune Sempo Sugihara, file 2861; Paul Gruninger, file 680. See also my article: "Radical Altruism: Three Case Studies," in *Midstream*, Vol. 33/4, April 1987, pp. 35-39.

[14] Yvonne Nevejean, file 99; NV Group (headed by Jaap Musch and Joop Woortman), file 2083; Rita Breton, file 2290; Denise Bergon, file 1807; Rolande Birgy, file 2613; Helga Holbek and Alice Synnestvedt, file 2142; Irene Sendler, file 153; Matylda Getter, file 3097.

[15] Malgorzata Wolski, file 4252; Jan and Stanislaw Kurdziel, file 5134; Zofia and Jakob Gargasz, file 1622; Heinrich List, file 5525; Ilse Totzke, file 6335; Giovanni Palatucci, file 4338; Henry Thomsen, file 471; Father Jacques (Lucien Bunel), file 3099; Suzanne Spaak, file 62; Joop Westerweel, file 32; Jaap Musch and Joop Woortman, file 2083; Albertus Zefat, file 731; Adelaide Hautval, file 100.

[16] For a discussion of the "risk to life" clause, see my article: "To the Righteous Among the Nations Who Risked their Lives to Rescue Jews," in *Yad Vashem Studies 19* (Jerusalem: Yad Vashem, 1988), pp. 403-425.

Chapter 2 – *Protest and Alarm Sounding*

[1] Even a philosopher of the caliber of Martin Heidegger, fell sway to Nazi propaganda and, as rector of his university, signed the order dismissing Jewish teachers.

[2] Otto Krayer, file 5531. See Avram Goldstein, "Otto Krayer: 1899-1982." Reprinted from: *Biographical Memoirs*, Vol. 57 (Washington, DC: The National Academy Press, 1987).

[3] In 1895, Alfred Dreyfus, a Jewish captain in the French army was

condemned to long-term imprisonment on false charges of having spied for Germany. In his open letter to the French government, the noted writer Emile Zola accused antisemitic elements in the government and the army of the distortion of justice. Zola was forced to flee the country, but his protest created a public outcry and eventually led to Dreyfus's vindication, and he was restored with full honors.

⁴ Armin T. Wegner, file 306. See also, Sybil Milton, "Armin T. Wegner: Polemicist for Armenian and Jewish Human Rights," in *Armenian Review* 42 (Winter 1989) 4:168.

⁵ Jan Karski, *Story of a Secret State* (Boston: Houghton Mifflin), p. 322, as well as several other passages quoted from this book.

⁶ His research into modern Polish history led to the publication, in 1985, of *The Great Powers and Poland, 1919-45* (From Versailles to Yalta).

⁷ Jan Karski, file 934.

⁸ One finds it hard to believe that many church enthusiasts felt that with the rise of Hitler, a new and better spiritual era had dawned upon Germany. In April 1933, the Evangelical Church celebrated the Nazi rise to power with the following declaration: "A vast and growing reform of the Reich is manifesting itself in the German nation. We extent a grateful welcome to this turning point in history. It was given to us by God." Similar statements of rejoice were voiced by Wilhelm Niemöller, the future celebrated anti-Nazi, and Superintendant Dibelius. See Saul Friedländer, *Counterfeit Nazi: the Ambiguity of Good* (London: Weidenfeld & Nicolson, 1969), pp. 18-19, 22. Further references and quotes in the Gerstein story are taken from this book, as well as: Pierre Joffroy, *A Spy for God: the Ordeal of Kurt Gerstein* (New York: Harcourt Brace Jovanovich, 1969), and documentation in the Kurt Gerstein file, at Yad Vashem, number 7984.

⁹ Friedländer, p. 80; and Joffroy, p. 88.

¹⁰ Joffroy, p. 132.

¹¹ Friedländer, p. 103.

¹² Auschwitz was to become the chief killing site at a later date.

¹³ Joffroy, p. 173f. This incident with the Nuncio also served as backdrop for the celebrated play by Rolf Hochhut, "The Deputy," in which he took the Vatican to task for its failure to publicly denounce the Final Solution, and call upon all Catholics to have no part in this murder but rather help the Jews to avoid arrest and deportation to the camps.

¹⁴ One Degesch employee, named Peters, recounted a conversation with Gerstein in June 1943, during which the latter procured an order of 1,200 or 1,500 kilograms of prussic acid known as Zyklon B. During this conversation, Gerstein asked whether a liquid form of Zykion B could be produced, so as to mitigate the suffering of those fated to die by the inhalation of this gas. Gerstein admitted to Peters that the poison was needed to do away with a

certain number of criminals, incurable mental cases, and other undesirable elements – this, by order of SS chief Himmler. He only wished to reduce the suffering of the condemned persons, by making the poison work faster, and by removing an irritant substance in the solid poisonous pellets. Gerstein then described the quantities required by the Auschwitz and Oranienburg concentration camps. This was ten months after his traumatic experience at the Belzec killing site.

¹⁵ Friedländer, p. 199.

¹⁶ In addition to the Gerstein Kurt file at Yad Vashem (# 7984), and the Friedländer and Joffroy books (note 8), see also: Léon Poliakov, "Le Dossier Kurt Gerstein," *Le Monde Juif* (Paris), January/March 1964.

Chapter 3 — *Escape and Visas*

¹ His rank came from the military, when he served as an officer in the British army during World War One.

² Similarly for Ernest Ruppel's father, who was released from Buchenwald camp, after his non-Jewish wife received from Foley a visa, and on the basis of this, a boat ticket. An SS officer had previously stated that he would be released if shown a boat ticket leaving Germany.

³ "My Life with the Pimpernel: Katharine Foley, in an interview with Anthony Hancox." *Sunday Mercury* (England), 7 May 1961. The question of Frank Foley's diplomatic immunity has not been satisfactorily resolved. In his book, *Foley: the Spy Who Saved 10,000 Jews* (London: Hodder & Stoughton, 1999), British author Michael Smith claims that Foley did not enjoy such immunity. This has been supported by Gill Bennett, Chief Historian, Foreign & Commonwealth Offices, in a letter to Yad Vashem. However, some persons familiar with the diplomatic status of persons in a high position such as enjoyed by Foley, question this assertion.

⁴ Foley was particularly concerned about his epileptic daughter Ursula. In his 1945 letter to Dr. Senator, he expressed the hope that "as I helped so many doctors, fate would arrange for me to meet *the* doctor who would cure her. We [i.e., he and his wife] feel that some such man exists." Tragically for Ursula, she was not cured, and she died in 1982, after an epileptic fit.

⁵ In another part of his deposition, Pollack states that to many people who came to thank him for arranging their departure from Germany, he responded: "Go instead to Tiergartenstrasse 17, and thank Captain Foley. Thank him for your visa – not me!" Hubert Pollack, "Captain Foley & Other Persons." *Yad Vashem Archives*: 02/340, p. 5.

⁶ Francis Foley, file 8378, from which most of the previous information was gathered.

[7] Mary Jane Gold, *Crossroads Marseilles 1940* (Garden City, N.Y.: 1980), pp. xii-xiv.

[8] Gold, xvi. Fry Varian, *Surrender on Demand* (New York: Random House, 1945), pp. x-xi.

[9] Henry and Elizabeth Urrows, "Varian Fry: the Civilian as War Hero." *Harvard Magazine*, March-April 1990, pp. 43-4; Lisa Fittko, *Escape through the Pyrenees* (Evanston, Ill.: Northwestern Uni., 1991), pp. 117f; Fry, pp. 10, 12; Gold, p. 150; Gabriele Tergit, "A Hero of Our Time: In Memory of Varian Fry," *AJR Information*, July 1968; p. 6. In 1941, as its activities expanded, the *Centre Amé rican de Secours* moved to ever larger facilities, finally settling in Villa Air Bel, an 18-room out-of-town location. There, Fry hosted some well-known artists for informal gatherings: such as the surrealist André Breton, painters Max Ernst (just out of an internment camp), Wifredo Lam (a student of Picasso); novelist Victor Serge, and others. See, Urrows, p. 46.

[10] Fry, p. 97.

[11] Fry, pp. 15, 31, 37, 164, 170.

[12] Fry, pp. 28, 80.

[13] Fry, pp. 188-9. According to Mary Jayne Gold, the ERC handled some 2,000 cases, representing over 4,000 persons. Of these, more than 1,000 were sent out of France by legal or illegal means. See also Gold, p. 398.

[14] For Fry's letter to his wife, see Varian Fry, file 5525. For Lion Feuchtwanger's flight, see Gold, p. 188. It took some talking to persuade Marc Chagall to abandon the pastoral setting of his home and flee the country. Oscar Goldberg used the Martinique route, where no transit visa was required. To help Arthur Wolff, a Berlin criminal lawyer, wanted by the Nazis, he was first taken for his safety to Villa Air Bel. Then, via connection with a gangster organization, he was smuggled over to Spain, from whence he proceeded to Cuba. See, Fry, pp. 130, 183, 187, 192; and Gold, pp. 327, 399f.

[15] Fry, p. 224.

[16] Fry, p. 229.

[17] Fry, p. 219; Urrows, p. 45.

[18] Urrows, p. 45.

[19] All quotes in the Fry story, also appear in his file at Yad Vashem (Dept. for the Righteous), number 5525.

[20] On Sugihara, see: Mordecai Paldiel, *The Path of the Righteous* (Hoboken, N.J.: Ktav, 1993), pp. 252-5; and by same author, *Sheltering the Jews* (Minneapolis, Minn.: Fortress, 1996), p. 141.

[21] After Zwartendijk's departure from Lithuania, the Swedish consul-general in Stockholm, de Jong, continued to issue Curaçao-style visas by mail, to persons in Lithuania requesting it.

[22] Hillel Levine, *In Search of Sugihara* (New York: Free Press, 1996), p.

240.

[23] In fact, none of the Curaçao visa people ever reached the island for a variety of reasons. Evidently, had they arrived there, as foreigners they would have been refused entry in a place where crude oil was being refined for war purpose. Besides, the Curaçao visa was merely a plot, with which to get as far as possible from the Nazis. Once out of reach of them, the refugees moved to various temporary and permanent locations: Japan (Kobe), China (Shanghai), Canada, the USA, and Israel.

The information on the Zwartendijk story is mainly based on material in the Jan Zwartendijk file (#7793). See also, Isaac Lewin, *Remember the Days of Old*, 1994; and Zerach Warhaftig, *Refugee and Survivor* (Jerusalem: Yad Vashem, 1988), especially Chapter 14. See also, Sempo Sugihara, file 2861.

Chapter 4 — *Sheltering and Hiding*

[1] Felix Zandman (with David Chanoff), *Never the Last Journey* (New York: Schocken Books, 1995), p. 86.

[2] Zandman, p. 84

[3] Zandman, p. 89. Also Puchalski Jan & Anna, file 3466.

[4] Zandman, p. 107.

[5] Zandman, p. 229.

[6] Zandman, p. 396.

[7] Zandman, pp. xv and 295.

[8] Shmuel Spector (ed.), *Lost Jewish Worlds: the Communities of Grodno, Lida, Olkienki, Vishay* (Jerusalem:Yad Vashem, 1996).

[9] Zandman, p. 420-1.

[10] Jonas Paulavicius, file 2472.

[11] Helena Pawlikowska, file 7809.

[12] Boguslaw Howil, file 5780.

[13] Joseph Jaksy, file 4893.

[14] Elisabeth Wust, file 6097. See also: Erica Fischer, *Aimée und Jaguar: Eine Frauenliebe, Berlin 1943*. Köln: Kiepenheueur & Witsch, 1994.

[15] Refik Veseli , file 3768.

[16] This recalls, and is in some respect similar, to the touching responsive words by Ruth, the Moabite, to her mother-in-law, Naomi. Book of Ruth 2:16.

[17] Mustafa and Zejneba Hardaga-Susic, file 2811.

Chapter 5 — *Subterfuge Methods*

[1] Jacob Presser, *Ashes in the Wind: the Destruction of Dutch Jewry* (London: Souvenir Press, 1965), p. 297.

[2] Gerhard Wander , file 925.

[3] Stokvis' full statement, and other eyewitness accounts are to be found in the Gerhard Wander file, number 925. Also Presser, p. 304.

[4] Presser, p. 301. Also Calmeyer file at Yad Vashem (#4997).

[5] Presser, pp. 308-310.

[6] Jaap van Proosdij, file 7763; Cornelis Teutscher, file 2478.

[7] Presser, pp. 298-299.

[8] Hans-Georg Calmeyer , file 4997.

[9] Recently, the Dutch historian Conrad Stuldreher has questioned this decision, arguing that had Calmeyer been morally upright, he should have resigned from a post which was based on Nazi racial theories. Another historian, Gerhard Hirschfeld, is currently assembling all the relevant data, in preparation for a renewed evaluation of this case. This author, as most students and historians familiar with the Calmeyer story, is still convinced of the justified attribution of the Righteous title to this man.

[10] In Yiddish: "*Yidden, seit nisht ka nerunem! Geht nisht, when m'rift eich!*" Alfred Rossner, file 6239.

[11] In June 1944, Cesia Rubinstein was deported to Annaberg; thence, to Auschwitz, Ravensbrück and Bendorf, and liberated on May 4, 1945. Had she been deported earlier, as during the August 1943 action, her chances of survival would probably have been less fortuitous. In her words: "I essentially owe my survival to the above-mentioned Herr Rossner." Likewise for Edward Retman, who was rescued during this action by one of Rossner's German aides, named Pajza, who led him through the streets of Bedzin to Rossner's factory. "He pressed the bell and when the door opened — pushed me in. Later I found out that his Fabrickstrasse shop was already full of people, and that it had been Rossner's order to take as many Jews out of the waiting transports as possible!" See, Rossner file 6239.

[12] Philip Friedman, *Road to Extinction: Essays on the Holocaust* (New York & Philadelphia: Jewish Publication Society, 1980), p. 362. On one occasion, Merin stated: "I will not be afraid to sacrifice 50,000 of our community in order to save the other 50,000." On another — "I feel like a captain whose ship was about to sink and who succeeded in bring it safe to port by casting overboard a great part of his precious cargo." Also, Raul Hilberg, The *Destruction of European Jews* (New York: Harper & Row, 1961), p. 316. Merin, of course, miscalculated the intentions of his overlords. When he had helped them deport all the Jews in his region and was no longer needed, he was sent off to Auschwitz and killed.

[13] Alfred Rossner , file 6239.

[14] Kalman Horvath, file 5012.

[15] Eugene Levai, *Black Book on the Martyrdom of Hungarian Jewry* (Zurich: 1948), pp. 358-9, 387-8. Randolph L. Braham, *The Politics of Genocide: the Holocaust in Hungary*, Volume 2 (New York: 198 1), pp. 1092-3. Also: Enrico Deaglio, *The Banality of Goodness: the Story of Giorgio Perlasca*, Translated from the Italian by G. Conti (London: University of Notre Dame, 1998), p. 20.

[16] In this regard, see especially the testimony of Avraham Ronai, in Giorgio Perlasca, file 3911.

[17] As told to journalist Michael Ryan, and printed in *Parade Magazine*, August 19, 1990.

[18] Deaglio, p. 87.

[19] See the Rotta story in Chapter 8.

[20] Deaglio, p. 103.

[21] Deaglio, pp. 5, 142.

[22] Deaglio, p. 133. Also by Michael Ryan, in *Parade Magazine*, August 19, 1990.

[23] See document in Giorgio Perlasca, file 3911.

[24] Perlasca's name and photo also appear on a special stamp issued by Israel's postal service, in honor of diplomats who rescued Jews from the Nazis.

[25] Selahattin Ülkümen, file 4128. Maurice Soriano, postwar head of the dwindling Jewish community in Rhodes, together with his family, were among those saved by Ülkümen.

Chapter 6 — *Rescuers Who Were Punished for Showing Compassion*

[1] Both the Portuguese and Swiss governments recanted, after many decades of stubborn opposition to annul the judicial measures against these two public servants, and restored them, alas posthumously, their status and rights. See Mordecai Paldiel, *The Path of the Righteous*, pp. 59-62; and *Sheltering the Jews*, pp. 68-9, 49-59, 136-7.

[2] Heinrich List, file 5525.

[3] Robert Gellately, *The Gestapo and German Society: Enforcing Racial Policy 1933-1945* (Oxford, England: Clarendon, 1991), pp. 180 ff.

[4] *"Ich trage mich schon seit längerer Zeit mit dem Gedanken aus Deutschland zu flüchten , da ich mich unter der Regierung Adolf Hitlers nicht wohl fühle. Vor allem habe ich das Nürnbergergesetz unbegreiflich gefunden, aus diesem Grunde habe ich auch die Beziehungen zu den mir bekannte Juden aufrecht erhalten."*

[5] *"Ich möchte nochmals erwöhnen, dass ich aus Deutschland flüchten wollte, weil ich den Nationalsozialismus ablehne. Vor allem kann ich die Nürnbergergesetze nicht gutheissen. Ich hatte die Absicht, mich in der Schweiz internieren zu lassen. In Deutschland möchte ich unter keinen Umständen weiterleben."*

⁶ Ilse Sonja Totzke , file 6335.

⁷ Adelaïde Hautval , file 100. See also, Mavis Hill & Williams L. Norman, *Auschwitz in London: a Record of Libel Action* (London: Macgibbon & Kee, 1965), Adelaïde Hautval and Hallam Tennyson, "Who Shall Live, Who Shall Die?" in *Intellectual Digest*. March 1972, Vol 2/7, New York, pp. 52-54; and "Auschwitz in an English Court: the Dossier on Dr. Dering," in *World Jewry: Review of the World Jewish Congress*. May/June 1964, Volume 7/3.

⁸ Stefan Sawa, file 5093.

Chapter 7—*Saving the Children*

¹ Hein Korpershoek and Wibo Florissen, , file 3651.

² In the original French: *"Oh! Chère madame Taquet / Je l'avoue, ce n'est pas vous qui m'avait elevée / Quand j'étais a peine née. / Mais maintenant, quand j'ai besoin du secours / C'est vous avec votre grand amour / Qui me nourit alors, qui me prend / Pour me soigner comme son enfant / Et depuis alors elle m'a soigné tout le temps. / Oui, tout cela, madame Taquet / Pour moi vous avez fait / A l'occasion de la fête du mère / Je me permets, de faire ces quelques vers / Et, les meilleurs voeux de bonheur / Je vous souhaite de tout mon coeur."*

³ Marie Taquet-Mertens, file 3773. For Andrée Geulen, see file 4323.

⁴ Franciscus and Hillegonda Snel, file 2622.

⁵ Hajrija Imeri-Mihaljic , file 4939.

⁶ Joseph and Yvonne Smeesters , file 6173.

⁷ Franciszek and Stanislawa Kaczmarek, file 7435; Charlotte Rebhun, file 7809.

⁸ Piotr and Emilia Waszkinel, file 6564. Also Roger Cohen, "For a Priest and for Poland, a Tangled Identity." *The New York Times*, Sunday, October 10, 1999, pp. 1, 6.

⁹ Genowefa Pajak, file 2379. Also: Tamar Dror, *A Green Parrot: the Unearthed Memories of a Jewish Child Living under Nazi Occupation* (Glebe, Australia: Book House at Wild & Woolley, 1999).

Chapter 8—*Clergy in Various Robes*

¹ For some of the literature on the attitude of the churches, the reader is referred to: Guenter Lewy, *The Catholic Church and Nazi Germany* (New York: McGraw-Hill, 1964); Richard Gutteridge, *Open Thy Mouth for the Dumb: the German Evangelical Church and the Jews* (Oxford, Basil Blackwell, 1976);

Otto Kulka and Paul Mendes-Flohr (eds.), *Judaism and Christianity Under the Impact of National Socialism (1919-45)* (Jerusalem: The Historical Society of Israel & Zalman Shazar Center for Jewish History, 1987); John F. Morley, *Vatican Diplomacy and the Jews During the Holocaust 1933-43* (New York: Ktav, 1980); John Cornwell, *Hitler's Pope: the Secret History of Piux XII* (Viking, New York, 1999).

[2] Simon Gallay, file 4363; Albert Simond, file 4363a; Pierre Mopty, file 4245;Albert Gross , file 4096; Pierre Chaillet , file 1770. Jean-Joseph Rosay was another priest who was associated with Gallay's rescue efforts and helped Jews escape to Switzerland. He suffered martyrdom at the hands of the Germans (dying in a concentration camp)—file 3580. Other lay rescuers linked to this rescue operation, who were awarded the Righteous title, include Jeannette Brousse (who as secretary in the Annecy municipality helped fabricate false credentials) and Rolande Birgy; files 804 and 2613.

[3] Wladyslaw Bartoszewski and Zofia Lewin, The *Righteous Among the Nations* (London: Earls Court, 1969), p. 515.

[4] Bartoszewski, p. 514, 516.

[5] Anna Borkowska , file 2862; also Israeli daily journal *Maariv*, August 3, 1984.

[6] Translated from the Russian, in T. Stratton-Smith, *The Rebel Nun* (London: Pan Books, 1967), p. 162.

[7] Stratton-Smith, p. 114.

[8] Stratton-Smith, p. 204, Philip Friedman , *Their Brothers' Keepers* (New York: Holocaust Library, 1978), p. 31.

[9] Skobtzova and Klepinin file at Yad Vashem, number 3078.

[10] Mark Vishnyak, in *Yiddisher Kempfer*, New York, October 12, 1945.

[11] In a lighter moment, during the ceremony, Klepinin's daughter, Helena Arjakovsky, told of Leon Trotzky, who Mother Maria, in her earlier revolutionary days as Elizabeth Skobtzova, thought of assassinating, and who was now also a fleeing refugee (from Stalin' vindictiveness), and met Mother Maria, when passing through Paris. He asked her what he could do to compensate the help she was receiving from him. To which she replied, that she would be satisfied if he were to pay his laundry bill.

[12] Stratton-Smith, p. 127.

[13] Jeno Levai, *Hungarian Jewry and the Papacy* (Dublin, 1968), p. 63.

[14] The Portuguese diplomat was Carlos de Liz-Texeira Branquino; the Swiss—Antoine J. Kilchmann.

[15] In a communication to the Vatican, on November 27, 1944, Rotta informed that he had issued 13,000 protective letters to many Jews and baptized Jews, thus postponing their deportation.

[16] The Hungarian government of Horthy, nominally an ally of Germany, and whose troops participated in the Russian campaign, pursued an

antisemitic policy (moderate by comparison with Nazi Germany), gradually restricting the privileges of Jews in the economic and social spheres, but stopping short of killing them, as the Germans continually insisted. This situation lasted until the takeover of Hungary by the German army.

[17] Jozsef Lowi, today in Bnei Berak, Israel, told this author that in summer 1944, the rumor had spread among the men in his Labor Company (101/343) that persons who converted would not be deported, and that 22 men had indicated their readiness to take this step. This information was passed on to the Nunciature in Budapest. Soon thereafter, a priest came and handed the commander Vatican protective letters for all the 220 men in his unit. As for the willing 24 men, it took the priest only 1.5 hours to carry through the conversion process! It is clear from this that the intent was to save, not to convert.

[18] J. Levai, p. 63. On the many letters of protest by Rotta to the Hungarian government, and his messages to the Vatican, see *Actes et Documents du Saint Siège Relatifs à la Seconde Guerre Mondiale*. Volume 10. *Le Saint Siège et Les Victimes de la Guerre*; Janvier 1944-Juillet 1945 (Libreria Editrice Vaticana, 1980); especially the entries for May 15, August 21, November 17, and December 23, 1944. See also Rotta's dispatches to Maglione for May 23, May 24, June 18, July 14, December 11. Also to Tardini, on November 27–all in 1944.

[19] Sister Margit Slachta reports on the rescue of a group of Jewish children in a monastery, with the personal participation of Rotta, who came especially from Buda to Pest to oversee the rescue, including a standoff with the Arrow Cross militia. See Margit Slachta, file 495.

[20] One Commission member likened Rotta to Bishop John of Speyer, Germany, who in 1096 protected the local Jewish community from a ravaging mob of Crusaders, by sending his militia to protect the Jews and punish those who had killed Jews during the riot. As an added precaution, he hid some of the Jews in surrounding villages. The Jews of Speyer hailed him as "a Righteous Among the Nations, and God merited him with being a rescuer, for the Lord filled his heart to maintain their lives without bribery." *Encyclopedia Judaica*, Vol 15, 263a.

[21] Sandor Ujváry, file 3110. Also, Levai, p. 44. Rotta also handed Ujváry a power-of-attorney, which read in part as follows: "Budapest, November 19, 1944. The Apostolic Nuncio in Budapest confirms that the Nunciature has entrusted Mr. Sandor G. Ujváry, the representative of the International Red Cross, with the task of inquiring after all persons of Jewish origin under the protection of the Apostolic Nunciature, who have been removed from Budapest contrary to the agreements legally concluded between the Apostolic Nunciature and the Hungarian Government and are on the way to the west, and to bring them home from the camps. Mr. Sandor Gyorgy Ujváry

has also been empowered to intervene where necessary with the authorities in the name of the Nunciature."

²² See statements by Orit Mozes and Hedvig Szekeres, as well as Tibor Baranszki's own account, in the Tibor Baranszki, file 1548. Asked for his thoughts on the Holocaust, Baranszki said: "God gives us a free will. A free will is a knife. You can make beautiful carvings. Or you can kill."

²³ Angelo Rotta, file 7690.

Chapter 9 — *Death Marches*

¹ Erwin and Gertruda Moldrzyk, file 4023.

² Konrad and Regina Zimon , file 4530.

³ British POWs honored with the Righteous title include: Stan Wells, George Hammond, Tommy Noble, Alan Edwards, and Roger Lechford; file 4042.

Chapter 10 — *Those Who Did Not Qualify*

¹ In this respect, see Yehuda Bauer, *Jews for Sale?* (New Haven & London: Yale University, 1994).

² This is known as the Joel Brand mission, further to his meeting with SS Colonel Adolf Eichmann who, in May 1944, was in charge of the deportation of Hungarian Jews to Auschwitz.

³ Hecht's more immediate task was to organize illegal immigration of Jews into British-controlled Palestine.

⁴ For more on Musy's political thinking and action, see Daniel Sebastini, "Jean-Marie Musy dans l'orbite du Reich d'Adolf Hitler," in J.C. Favez, H.U. Jost, and E. Phython, *Les Relations Internationales et la Suisse* (Lausanne: Switzerland, 1998), pp. 231-264.

⁵ For more on this and the Musy initiative, see: Alain Dieckhoff, *Rescapés du Génocide: I'Action Musy* (Basel & Frankfurt/Main: Helbing & Lichtenhahn, 1995).

⁶ The debate erupted during the Kasztner trial in Israel, in 1954, with Reuben Hecht repeating his version of the Musy initiative.

⁷ Hecht also asked the Righteous title for Musy's son, Benoit Musy, who joined his father on his many trips into war-torn Germany, and in Hecht's words, was instrumental in exacting from the SS more favorable conditions for concentration camp inmates, including the cessation of "death marches."

⁸ Jean-Marie Musy, file 3841.

⁹ See, for instance, the statements of Louis van Coevorden, Jacques van

der Kar, Lex van Weren, Anna Groenteman-Wertheim, Mrs. B. Hollander, Marianne-Henriette Dwinger, Sam de Hond, and Mrs. Swaab; in Alfons Zündler, file 5831.

[10] Especially Ralph Polack, who argued strongly against the man's recognition by Yad Vashem.

[11] See in this regard the testimony of Marianne-Henriette Dwinger.

[12] He is reported, in one incident, to have referred to Süskind as his "boss." See the testimony of Mr. and Mrs. De Haan-Cardozo. Another witness, Carla Kaplan-Gobitz also reports Zündler stating to her that he worked closely with Süskind. Walter Süskind is to be credited with the saving of hundreds of Jews. See chapter on Jewish rescuers for more on this remarkable man and his tragic fate.

[13] As per the testimony of Mrs. Swaab.

[14] Some sources speculate that it may have been in another camp, located in the Danzig region. See Dr. Johannes ten Cate's extensive report on Alfons Zündler, in the Zündler file.

[15] The SS unit to which Zündler was assigned, the Dirlewanger Brigade, had a notorious record of treatment of conquered civilian populations.

[16] The Commission could not fail to notice that even those whose testified in Zündler's favor, mentioned and emphasized Zündler's womanizing with Jewish women in the Theater.

[17] Alfons Zündler, file 5831.

[18] The man's name has appears under various spellings, such as: Szeptycki, Szeptyckyi, Scheptycki, Scheptytzkyi, Scheptytzkyj, Scheptickyj, Sheptyckyi, Sheptytzky, Sheptyts'kyi and the one chosen by us, Sheptitzky. Similarly for his first name: Andrew, Andreas, Andrei, Andrii and Andrej.

[19] The city, now in Ukraine, is today known as Lviv. In a recent book, Kurt Lewin has vividly described his wartime experiences, in hiding in several monasteries, under the assumed name of a Uniate monk. Kurt I. Lewin, A *Journey Through illusions* (Santa Barbara, Cal.: Fithian, 1994), especially chapter 2.

[20] It consisted of a church (St. George Cathedral), the residence of the Metropolitan, and administrative offices.

[21] See, for instance, the testimony of Edward Harvitt, formerly Adolf Horowitz, in the Sheptitzky file (#421).

[22] Ivan Hirnyj, a former chauffeur for the Uniate church, testified to his moving Jews (mostly children) from one Uniate religious home location to another, on orders of Abbot Klement, Andrei Sheptizky's brother, who was responsible for the church's monks. This included placing eight Jews in a shoe-factory, in Lwow, operated by the monks. Michael Kuzyk, known as Brother Laurentij, confirms meeting Jews in the shoe factory, where he too was employed.

²³ Rabbi Kahana's testimony was taken down in the early 1970's, when he petitioned Yad Vashem for Sheptitzky's recognition.

²⁴ Brother Theodosi was especially attentive to the rabbi's needs and commiserated greatly with the tragedy befalling the Jewish people. He kept Kahana informed of the ongoing killings of Jews in the streets of Lwow.

²⁵ Shimon Redlich, "Metropolitan Andrii Sheptyts'kyi and the Complexities of Ukrainian-Jewish Relations," in, Zvi Gitelman, ed., *Bitter Legacy: Confronting the Holocaust in the USSR* (Bloomington & Indianapolis: Indiana Univ. Press, 1997), pp. 61-76; p. 68.

²⁶ This initial phase of Nazi terror also cost the life of the first German-appointed head of the ghetto, Dr. Parnas, who was shot dead for refusing to increase the contingent of Jewish forced labor, which he rightly suspected was slated for murder.

²⁷ Following is a recapitulations of these killing raids: "Jail Action" of June 30-July 3, 1941: 7,000 victims; "Petlura Days" — July 25-28, 1941: 2,000 victims; Action Against Soviet Sympathizers—July 1941: 2,000; Hostage Action—August 1941: 1,000; "Bridge Actions"—November 15 to mid-December 1941: 10,000; Expulsion Action—March 1942: 15,000; "Blitz Action"—June 1942: 6-8,000; Major Action—August 1942: 60,000; Special Action—November/December 1942: 15,000; Random Action—January 5-7, 1943: 10,000; "Reprisal Action"—March 17, 1943: 1,000; isolated actions during March 1943: 3,000; "Liquidation Action"—April to June 16, 1943: 20,000. See doctoral dissertation by Eliyahu Yones, *Lwow Jews During World War Two and the Holocaust* (Hebrew, unpublished), Jerusalem, 1993, p. 159. Much of the information on the condition of Jews in Lwow under the Nazis is taken from this masterly study.

²⁸ For one frightening reportage of "life" in this camp, see Leon Wells, *The Janowska Road* (New York: Macmillan, 1963).

²⁹ Redlich, p. 65.

³⁰ Redlich, pp. 64-5.

³¹ Redlich, p. 72.

³² Redlich, p. 72. Also, David Kahana, *Lwow Ghetto Diary* (Hebrew, Jerusalem: Yad Vashem, 1978), p. 158. In a conversation with the French pro-German collaborator, Dr. Frederic, he reports that Sheptitzky agreed with him that Judaism represented a mortal danger to Christianity, but insisted that the extermination of the Jews was not permissible. See also, Hansjakob Stehle, 'Sheptyts'kyi and the German Regime," in Paul Magocsi, ed., *Morality and Reality: the Life and Times of Andrei Sheptyts'kyi* (Edmonton: University of Alberta, 1989), pp. 125-144.

³³ No copy exists of this letter, but Rabbi Kahana claims that Sheptitzky showed it to him during one of his visits to Sheptitzky's study. It is believed that he handed the letter to Johannes Peters, a German ordained by

Sheptitzky in 1937, who became his private secretary, and often traveled to Berlin, where he claims to have posted the letter. Stehle, pp. 131-2. Two months earlier, in a meeting with SS officer Losacker and district governor Karl Lasch (to discuss the possibility of an independent Ukraine) in end 1941, Sheptitzky protested the shootings and executions which he was hearing even next to his residence.

[34] Stehle, p. 134; and Redlich, p. 69.

[35] Stehle, p. 138.

[36] Stehle, p. 136.

[37] Kurt Lewin, *Aliti Mi-Spezia*. In Andrei Sheptitzky, file 42 1.

[38] Redlich 62.

[39] Stehle, p. 126.

[40] Redlich, p. 67.

[41] Stehle, pp. 128-131; and Redlich, p. 67. Already earlier, on July 22, 194 1, Sheptitzky, in a telegram to Berlin, referred to the "New Order" which would be jeopardized by the cancellation of plans for an independent Ukraine. Stehle, p. 128.

[42] Redlich, pp. 72-3.

[43] Redlich, in a private written communication to this author. Sheptitzky's immense popularity (and perhaps "untoucheability" from harm) may be gauged by the fact that at his funeral, in November 1944, even a top communist leader (representing a movement and philosophy which Sheptitzky deeply abhorred and feared), such as Nikita Khrushchev (the future head of the Soviet Union), were among the hundreds of priests and religious figures who attended.

[44] Stehle, p. 138.

[45] Most of the data in this case is taken, unless otherwise indicated, from the Yad Vashem (Dept. for the Righteous) file of Andrei Sheptitzky (#421). While denying the title to Sheptitzky, the Commission voted to award the Righteous title to several of Sheptitzky's aides, such as Abbess Josefa Witer, and Brothers Klementyi, Nikanor, Lazars and Marko Stek.

[46] Willi Friedrichs, file 502.

[47] During the court hearings, it was disclosed that Rolf, as a *Mischling*, that is, a half-Jew, due to his mother's non-Jewish origins, did not have to fear deportation in 1943. In fact, he was doing labor in the Todt organization, a major govemment-controlled industrial complex.

[48] Mathias Niessen , file 1841.

[49] The Labor Battalions were special units within the Hungarian army, where able-bodied Jews were forced to do various military-related physical work.

[50] In the outlying provinces, over 400,000 had already been deported to the death camps by the SS, with the acquiescence of the Hungarian

government.

[51] For more on the "protective homes," see the stories of Perlasca and Rotta, in Chapters 6 and 9.

[52] Oskar Ebers, file 2549.

Concluding Thoughts

[1] For more by Levinas, see Emmanuel Levinas, *Total and Infinity* (Pittsburgh: Duquesne Univ., 1969); also: *Alterity and Transcendence* (London: Athlone, and New York: Columbia Uni., 1999).

[2] This proposition was succinctly restated by Jan Karski: "We have an infinite capacity to choose between evil and good, and God gave us free will. What I did not realize is that only individuals have souls; government, nations, society, have no souls." In: Gay Block and Malka Drucker, Rescuers: *Portraits of Moral Courage in the Holocaust* (New York: Holmes & Meier, 1992), p. 172.

[3] Block and Drucker, p. 81. See also Aart and Johtje Vos, file 2435.

[4] Block and Drucker, p. 185. See also Stefania Burzminski-Podgorza, file 1524.

[5] Lorenzo Perrone, file at Yad Vashem (# 8157). Quotes also appear in the books by Primo Levi , *Moments of Reprieve* (New York: Summit Books, 1986), and *If This Is a Man* (London: Orion Press, 1959).

Appendix A

[1] In a private communication with the author, as well as words spoken at public gatherings.

[2] It is estimated that close to 100,000 passed through its gates on their way to the death camps. Trains left every Tuesday, with up to 3,000 people on board.

[3] Testimony of Lisette Lamon, in file of Walter Süskind, Department for the Righteous.

[4] A duplicate of the registration list at the Theater was taken to the Jewish Council offices, 15 blocks away, and was then forwarded to Westerbork camp together with the transport of the people on that list. Felix Halverstad's background was in graphic design, which he utilized in redrafting the registration lists, deleting the names of the missing, and forging the signature of Aus der Fünten.

[5] Persons brought into the Theater, after being flushed out of hiding

places, had a big S sign stamped on their card. This meant that once he, or she, reached Westerbork he was to be immediately deported to the death camps. Süskind paid special attention to facilitate the escape of some of these persons.

[6] Johann ten Cate, as well as Bert Jan Flim (who made a study of the rescue of Jewish children), in private communications to the author.

[7] See David Arnold, "Quiet Hero of the Holocaust," *The Boston Globe*, October 21, 1990, magazine section, pp. 20-38.

[8] Lamon testimony, op. cit. Especially touching is the story of the child Remi. When he was brought in, he could hardly stand. With time, he stood up in the crib. The SS, who occasionally dropped in to visit, were especially fond of him. No one knew from where he came, and whether he was Jewish. He was named Remi after the hero from a popular book *Without a family*. The Germans settled the issue after checking the size of his skull and his ear lobes – the child was definitely Jewish. The fact that they knew him and visited him, sealed his fate, and he could not be stolen out. He left with the last transport, in September 1943, with a big teddy bear clutched to his arm – a gift from Wolf, one of the SS guards. See, Anita van Ommeren and Ageeth Scherphuis, "De Creche, 1942-1943," in *Vrij Nederland*, January 18, 1986, pp. 9-10.

[9] Arnold, op. cit.

[10] Van Ommeren and Scherphuis, p. 2.

[11] Van Verschuer recalls the frightening nights when the Germans and Dutch police raided Jewish homes. "After 8, there was total silence in the city. Then one heard the trucks, and the cries of people, and the shouts and the howling of dogs. These sounds, which I heard with my head buried under the blankets, are deeply ingrained in my mind." Van Hulst also recalls watching from the window as people "were thrown into vans with terrible beatings," including the Jewish patients of a blind institute, who were forced to jump on trucks, while the guards laughed at them. Van Ommeren and Scherphuis, pp. 7-8.

[12] Woortman's wife, Semmy Glasoog-Woortman, was also an operative of the NV group. Gerard Musch and Joop Woortman (also known as Theo de Bruin) were eventually arrested by the Germans, and assassinated on Dutch soil. On both, as well as Dick Groenewegen and Semmy Glasoog, see file 2083; Willem Witjens, file 2221; Jan Westbroek, file 973; and Menno Goudberg, file 564. These are some of the persons who admitted into their homes Jews saved by Süskind's network, and were subsequently honored by Yad Vashem as Righteous. Also honored was the Dutch policeman Anton Japin, who forewarned Süskind's associates of anticipated raids (file 564). Hetty Voute and Gisela Wieberdink-Söhnlein, both, file 3853; Nico Dohmen, file 2878; Hannah van der Voort; file 966; Pieter Meerburg, file 862; Gesina

van der Molen, file 8228; Hester Lennep and Piet Vermeer, file 2018; and Jan van der Hulst, file 580. See also, Jan Bosch, file 2150; and Arie van Mansum, file 494.

[13] Alban and Germaine Fort, file 2150; Paul Rémond, file 5061. Persons associated with the Don Bosco operation who were awarded the Righteous title, include Vincent Simeoni, Michel Blain, and Josephine Chopin, file 7836.

[14] The harrowing story of her oppressive mistreatment at the hands of the Nazis appears in a book which she published after the war, under the title: Odette Abadi-Rosenstock, *Terre de Détresse: Birkenau — Bergen-Belsen.*

[15] Yad Vashem archives (Department for the Righteous), Moussa Abadi file.

[16] Denise's maternal grandfather, Yaakov Benchimol, came from Spanish Morocco to France to study in the Alliance Israélite school. In 1875, he was sent to Palestine to teach French in the agricultural school in Mikveh Israel; then, to the new settlements of Rishon Letzion and Rosh Pina, which were being supported and administrated by Baron Edmond Rothschild, in Paris. There, he met the beautiful Jenny Bliden, the daughter of a Safed physician, and the two married. The couple bore seven children, including the youngest, Andrée, Denise's mother. In 1890, the couple moved to France.

[17] The Jewish scout movement is sometimes referred as the "Sixth," since in the reorganized and Vichy-supervised umbrella Jewish federation (known by its acronym as UGIF), the sixth division dealt with Jewish youth. When the UGIF was later disbanded, the "sixth" continued its activities but as an independent clandestine organization. Denise Siekierski had originally joined the Jewish Scouts in 193 5, but was not particularly active during this early period of her life.

[18] This man, Gilbert Lesage, was recognized by Yad Vashem as a Righteous. See file 3012. At first, persons who had entered the country since 1936 faced internment. In 1942, the Vichy government upped the arrest list to foreigners who had entered France as early as 1927.

[19] After the war, Theo Klein headed for many years CRIF — the main umbrella Jewish organization in France.

[20] Denise recalls placing one Jewish couple in a mental institution, and the terrifying visits to that place from time to time to verify that this couple, who were quite healthy in their minds, and for whom the clandestine Jewish network contributed for their upkeep, were well taken care. "I had nightmares from these visits," Denise recalls, "for to get to them, I had to pass a hall where various types of seriously deranged persons were held in chains. I was afraid."

[21] Father Marie-Benoit (born Pierre Péteul) was awarded the Righteous title by Yad Vashem. File 201.

[22] Léon Poliakov, *L'Auberge des Musiciens* (Paris; Mazarine, 1981), p. 93.

[23] See the testimony of Denise Siekierski in this regard, in her private collection.

[24] Jean and Eugenie May, and their two elder children, Roger and Germaine, as well as Simone Mairesse and Hermine Orsi were recognized as Righteous by Yad Vashem — on the basis of evidence on their behalf submitted by Denise Siekierski. See files 3899, 4012 and 3211.

[25] During these tense days, Denise desperately sought to save her family in Marseilles, who had earlier registered as Jews and were hence in danger of arrest and deportation. She enlisted the aid of a former schoolmate, Annie Chartron, who in turn asked her father, Paul Chartron, to help save Denise's family. The Chartrons lived outside the city and owned a car, registered under the metallurgical firm which Paul Chartron operated. He drove into the police-infested city, and collected Denise's mother, uncle, and grandmother, hid them in his car, and crisscrossing police-controlled streets and intersections, made his way to his home. There they stayed for a week, while thousands of Jews were being rounded up in Marseilles. Chartron then commissioned a Red Cross ambulance (Denise: "I don't know by what miracle!") and took the three far away from the city and its outskirts. Paul Chartron and his wife Marie-Gabrielle were awarded by Yad Vashem the Righteous title. File 4881.

[26] The little girl, Francine Abravanel-Weil, later testified in favor of Lemaire, whom she then mistook for a rabbi because of his beard, who helped them celebrate the Sabbath and tried to lift their morale.

[27] As for the informer, Dr. Levy, he too wound up in the same prison as Lemaire. The pastor had to fend for him to avoid his assassination by the enraged Jewish inmates. Fate swiftly caught up with this betrayer of his own people. Upon his arrival at Auschwitz, he was killed by persons who recognized him as the one who had betrayed them to the Gestapo.

[28] During Lemaire's imprisonment, Joseph Bass had taken care to provide Mrs. Lemaire and her children, who had fled to a village, with necessary funds to support themselves.

[29] On the theme of forgiveness, Lemaire had this to say. "Man may forgive for himself, man's laws cannot, however, always forgive; political authorities cannot grant amnesty to everyone; only God can forgive everything. He has, however, not given men, with their passions, the authority to invoke His pardon, for they do not obey His voice." Lemaire was awarded the Righteous title; file 1039.

[30] The name Inn of the Musicians, in French L'Auberge des Musiciens, served as a title for Léon Poliakov's war memoirs, published in 1981. Oswaldo Bardone undertook several dangerous missions for André, which led to his arrest by the Gestapo. Luckily for him, the suspicions against him could not be corroborated and he was released. He, and his wife Lea, were

awarded by Yad Vashem the Righteous title. File 579.

[31] Léon Poliakov parted ways with Bass on this point, feeling that Bass did not have the necessary qualifications to create and lead a military-type fighting organization. Bass's unwillingness to abide by the traditional Jewish non-combative role came to light during a religious seminar for his co-workers, when he heard the lecturer expound that the Jewish people resembled olives: "for something good to be extracted, one needs to squeeze them, to crush them." At this André, fuming with rage, screamed: "No! I refuse to be a squeezed olive."

[32] Emilie (also known as Helene) Guth was awarded the Righteous title by Yad Vashem; file 3210.

[33] Léon Poliakov, pp. 126, 148-9.

Appendix B

[1] It is interesting that Andrée, at first, did not suspect that Yvonne Jospa, one of the leaders of the CDJ, was indeed Jewish. Andrée freely admits: "I did not know how to distinguish between a Jew and a non-Jew." Yvonne used beauty and feminine charm to solicit hiding places for CDJ's wards.

[2] In one instance, 13 Jewish children were discovered hiding in a Catholic institution in the Brussels region. The Mother Superior pleaded with the Gestapo for time to prepare the children for their departure to an unknown destination. Immediately after the Germans had left, promising they would return later that evening, she alerted the underground, who hurriedly came to fetch the children and take them to a safe location. To protect the nuns from retribution, they were gagged and locked up in the building's cellars. The telephone line was also cut. Neighbors then heard muffled noises from the institution pleading for help. When the Gestapo returned, they were told by screaming and angry nuns that a group of persons, whom the nuns mistook for German plainclothmen, suddenly appeared, and after locking them up, snatched the children. Fuming with rage at being outwitted, the Gestapo left without harming the nuns.

[3] Andrée Geulen, file 4323; Odile and Remy Ovard, file 6279; Christine Hendrickx, file 1840c. Also Yad Vashem Archives files 02/961, 029/20, and 02/571, for files on Andrée Geulen, Maurice Heiber, and Ida Sterno.

SUGGESTED SHORT BIBLIOGRAPHY

Anger, P., *With Raoul Wallenberg in Budapest: Memories of the War Years in Hungary* (New York: Holocaust Library, 1981).

Arad, Y., Gutman I., A. Margaliot, eds., *Documents on the Holocaust* (Jerusalem: Yad Vashem, 1981).

Bauer, Y. , *Jews for Sale?* (New Haven, Conn.: Yale University Press, 1996).

Braham, R.I., *The Politics of Genocide: The Holocaust in Hungary, 2 volumes* (New York: Columbia University, 1981).

Cargas, H. J., *Voices from the Holocaust* (Lexington, Ky: University Press of Kentucky, 1993).

Dawidowicz, L. S., *The War Against the Jews 1933-1945* (New York: Holt, Rinehart & Winston, 1975).

Eckardt, A. L., *Burning Memory: Times of Testing & Reckoning* (New York: Pergamon, 1993).

Fleischner, E., *Auschwitz: Beginning of a New Era?* (Hoboken, N.J.: Ktav, 1977).

Fogelman, E., *Conscience and Courage: Rescuers of Jews During the Holocaust* (New York: Doubleday, 1994).

Friedman, A. J. , *Their Brothers' Keepers* (New York: Holocaust Library, 1978).

Fry, V., *Surrender on Demand* (Boulder, Col.: Johnson Books, 1997).

Gerlach, W., *And the Witnesses Were Silent: The Confessing Church & the Persecution of the Jews* (Lincoln, Nebraska: University of Nebraska, 2000).

Gilbert, M., *The Holocaust: The Jewish Tragedy* (London: Fontana, 1986).

– *The Macmillan Atlas of the Holocaust* (New York: Macmillan, 1982).

– *Never Again: A History of the Holocaust* (London: HarperCollins, 2000).

Gross, L., *The Last Jews in Berlin* (New York: Simon & Schuster, 1982).

Gut-Opdyke, I., *In My Hands: Memories of a Holocaust Rescuer* (New York: Alfred A.Knopf, 1999).

Gutman, I., ed., *Encyclopedia of the Holocaust, 4 volumes* (New York: Macmillan, 1990).

Gutman, I. and Zuroff, E., eds., *Rescue Attempts During the Holocaust* (New York: Ktav, 1978).

Hackel, *Pearl of Great Price: The Life of Mother Maria Skotsova 1891-1945* (London: Darton, Longman & Todd, 1981).

Hallie, T., *Lest Innocent Blood Be Shed: The Story of Le Chambon and How Goodness Happened There* (New York: Harper & Row, 1979).

Hellman, P., *When Courage Was Stronger Than Fear* (New York: Marlowe, 1999).

Hilberg, R., *The Destruction of the European Jews, 3 volumes* (New York: Holmes & Meier, 1985).

Huneke, D., *The Moses of Rovno* (New York: Dodd, Mead & Co., 1985).

Kubar, Z., *Double Identity: A Memoir* (New York: Hill & Wang, 1989).

Lazare, L., *Rescue & Resistance: How Jewish Organizations Fought the Holocaust in France* (New York: Columbia University Press, 1996).

Levi, P., *If This Is a Man* (London: Orion Press, 1959).

Littell, F. H., *The Crucifixion of the Jews: the Failure of Christian to Understand the Jewish Experience* (Macon, Ga.: Mercer University Press, 1996).

Marino, A., *American Pimpernel: the Man who Saved the Artists on Hitler's Death List* (London: Hutchinson, 1999).

Marrus, M.R. and Paxton, R.O., *Vichy France and the Jews* (New York: Schocken Books, 1981).

Michman, D., ed., *Belgium & and the Holocaust* (Yad Vashem: Jerusalem, 1998).

Morley, J. F., *Vatican Diplomacy and the Jews during the Holocaust 1933-1943* (New York: Ktav, 1980).

Morse, A. D., *While Six Million Died: A Chronicle of American Apathy* (New York: Random House, 1967).

Oliner, S.P. & P.M., *The Altruistic Personality: Rescuers of Jews in Nazi Europe* (New York: Free Press, 1988).

Paldiel, M., *The Path of the Righteous: Gentile Rescuers of Jews during the Holocaust* (Hoboken, N.J.: Ktav, 1995).
— *Sheltering the Jews: Stories of Holocaust Rescuers* (Minneapolis, Minn: Fortress, 1996).

Presser, J., *The Destruction of the Dutch Jews* (New York: E.P. Dutton, 1969).

Rittner, K. and Meyers, S., eds., *The Courage to Care* (New York: New York University Press, 1986).

Silver, L., *The Book of the Just* (London: Weidenfeld & Nicolson, 1992).

Tec, N., *When Light Pierced the Darkness: Christian Rescue of Jews in Nazi-Occupied Poland* (New York: Oxford University Press, 1986).

Ten Boom, C., *The Hiding Place* (London: Hodder & Stoughton, 1971).

Wells, L., *The Janowska Road* (New York: Macmillan, 1963).

Wiesel, E., *Night* (New York: Hill & Wang, 1960).

Yahil, F., *The Rescue of Danish Jewry: Test of a Democracy* (Philadelphia: JPS, 1969).

Zandman, F., *Never the Last Journey* (New York: Schocken Books, 1995).

Zuccotti, S., *The Holocaust, the French & the Jews* (New York: Basic Boooks, 1993).
— *The Italians and the Holocaust: Persecution, Rescue, & Survival* (New York: Basic Books, 1987).

INDEX